THE TOUCH OF AN
ANGEL

JEWISH LIVES IN POLAND

POLIN Museum of the History of Polish Jews is the first and only museum dedicated to restoring the memory of the civilization created by Polish Jews in the course of a millennium. As an educational and cultural institution, the museum is dedicated to stimulating dialogue in the spirit of mutual understanding and respect.

The KARTA Center is an independent nongovernmental organization that documents and popularizes the recent history of Poland and Eastern Europe, including the history of Polish Jews. KARTA's main areas of activity are publishing, documentation, and education.

We would like to express our appreciation to the Conference on Jewish Material Claims Against Germany (Claims Conference) for supporting this publication. Through recovering the assets of the victims of the Holocaust, the Claims Conference enables organizations around the world to provide education about the Shoah and to preserve the memory of those who perished.

The Tadzio Kolski Fund supports academic research and publications about prewar life of Polish Jews and the history of the Holocaust. The fund was created by Tadzio Kolski's cousins to commemorate the death of this fifteen-year-old boy shot by the Nazis in Warsaw July 20, 1944 (on the day of the assassination of Hitler).

THE TOUCH OF AN ANGEL

—ɯ—

HENRYK SCHÖNKER

Translated from Polish by Scotia Gilroy

INDIANA UNIVERSITY PRESS

Published in association with the KARTA Center Foundation and
POLIN Museum of the History of Polish Jews

This book is a publication of

Indiana University Press
Office of Scholarly Publishing
Herman B Wells Library 350
1320 East 10th Street
Bloomington, Indiana 47405 USA

iupress.org

© 2020 by Indiana University Press
First published in Polish by KARTA Center Foundation
(2005). Original title: *Dotknięcie anioła*

All rights reserved

No part of this book may be reproduced or utilized in any form or by any means, electronic or mechanical, including photocopying and recording, or by any information storage and retrieval system, without permission in writing from the publisher. The paper used in this publication meets the minimum requirements of the American National Standard for Information Sciences—Permanence of Paper for Printed Library Materials, ANSI Z39.48–1992.

Manufactured in the United States of America

ISBN 978-0-253-05033-5 (cloth)
ISBN 978-0-253-05034-2 (paperback)
ISBN 978-0-253-05035-9 (ebook)

First printing 2021

This book is dedicated to my parents.

CONTENTS

Polish Publisher's Note   ix

Acknowledgments   xi

Prologue   1

Oświęcim   15

Kraków   61

Wieliczka   83

Tarnów   129

Bochnia   199

Bergen-Belsen   217

Tröbitz   251

Return to Oświęcim   299

Appendix   379

Index of Names   389

Index of Place Names   395

Illustrations follow page 166.

POLISH PUBLISHER'S NOTE

IN THE POLISH EDITION, THE Polish Jews series became a collection of canonical depictions of the Holocaust. *The Touch of an Angel* is one of the most vivid memoirs of the series, an extraordinary book that tells a story of endurance—testimony from a time of mass death that speaks of the survival not only of individual people but of humanity itself.

The Holocaust is Henryk Schönker's main realm of experience, even though he was only a child at the time. He emphasizes this period in his memoir, but death and the threat of death don't make up its primary content. In this story, it's extraordinary and wonderful how life can defy destruction, how a person's spirituality can protect his physical existence, and how real the presence of higher powers can turn out to be if one never loses faith in their existence.

Henryk Schönker was eight years old in 1939; with each month of the Holocaust that passed, however, he became an increasingly conscious and attentive observer. The period from late 1939 to early 1940 is of great significance in this memoir. Schönker's description of this period isn't based on his personal experiences, although his childhood memories have confirmed some of the images and atmospheres. It's based on notes and oral accounts by his father, Leon Schönker, who wished to proclaim to the world something to which he, himself, had been a credible witness—that Oświęcim didn't have to become the symbol of the Holocaust and could have become a place where Jews were saved if the world hadn't shown indifference at the beginning of the war.

Henryk Schönker's testimony was written in Israel more than sixty years after the events it describes: the main part of the book was completed in Tel Aviv in 2001, the prologue was written in 2005, and the final chapter ("Return to Oświęcim") was written in 2013. After two editions of the book were published in Poland (in 2005 and 2006), the book's description of the opportunity for mass emigration of Jews from Oświęcim to Palestine at the beginning of World War II was confirmed thanks to research conducted by Dr. Artur Szyndler and documents he found; we present these documents in the appendix. After becoming acquainted with these documents, historians who had previously questioned the veracity of Leon Schönker's testimony, given here by his son, acknowledged that this revelation was accurate.

And so we now face a fundamental question: Could the fate of Jews in Poland under German occupation have been different if the Western world hadn't ignored their desperate pleas for help? If it's true that "the Jews of Poland were alone," as Henryk Schönker states in his memoir, the entire world carries the moral burden of the Holocaust, not only the perpetrators—the genocidal Germans and their European collaborators.

The Touch of an Angel is, above all, a book about survival. It is not only about the incredibly fortunate events thanks to which a Jewish family was able to survive the war but also the aspects of this terrible world that bring salvation, and the realms of human spirituality that overcome human insignificance—and protect the meaning of our existence.

Henryk Schönker is not only an author but also an extremely energetic person. While we were clarifying certain things during the preparation of this book for publication, extraordinary coincidences occurred and surprising discoveries were made. We were certain this would continue, and we were right—it came true in the form of the documents discovered by Dr. Szyndler and the beautiful documentary film based on the book. And this surely isn't the end, for the fate of this book will continue to let us feel its *touch*.

—Zbigniew Gluza, KARTA Center Foundation

ACKNOWLEDGMENTS

I WOULD LIKE TO EXPRESS my sincere gratitude to Halina Zawadzka and her late husband, Joel Sack, from Sarasota (Florida, United States), for showing me, by writing and publishing their memoirs, that even after so many years have passed, it's possible to overcome internal difficulties and describe one's experiences from the nightmarish period of World War II. By sharing their experiences, impressions, and feelings with me before the publication of their books, they awoke in me a desire and need to write my own memoir. Although I've always felt obligated to write a book about my wartime experiences, I was unable to find enough strength to do it for many years. My stimulating conversations with Halina and Joel gave rise to a conviction in me that I, too, was capable of it.

I owe the publication of this book, above all, to my editor, Katarzyna Madoń-Mitzner, who invested in it a great deal of tireless work and energy. Her sensitivity and understanding of me, from the very first moment we met, filled me with conviction that this book needed to be written. I thank her with all my heart.

I would also like to thank Dr. Karl Liedke and Dr. Thomas Rahe from the Bergen-Belsen Memorial—for sending me materials from Bergen-Belsen and the Politisches Archiv des Auswärtigen Amts in Bonn. They revealed to me—after I'd already written my memoir—important matters concerning the people I had described.

I'm also grateful to Stefan Essle from Tyresö, Sweden, for allowing me to include a letter in my book written by his grandfather, the actor John Gottowt. My deepest gratitude also goes to the film historian Olaf Brill from Bremen, Germany, for helping me establish the identity of John Gottowt. I would like to thank Deutsches Filminstitut in Frankfurt am Main for permitting me to publish a photograph of Gottowt from its archives.

I would also like to thank my wife, Helena, for her advice and careful reading of my first draft and for the deep understanding she gave me during the entire period of time when I was writing my book.

I'm grateful to the editor in chief of KARTA Center's publishing house, Zbigniew Gluza, as well as the director of the History Meeting House in Warsaw, Piotr Jakubowski, and the deputy director, Katarzyna Madoń-Mitzner. They spared no efforts in helping my book be published. I would also like to sincerely thank Dr. Artur Szyndler, a historian from the Auschwitz Jewish Center. His research and several years of exploring in archives led to the discovery of documents that not only confirm but also expand upon what I've written in this book about the failed attempt of Jews to emigrate from Silesia in 1939 after the outbreak of World War II, which my father, Leon Schönker, strove to realize. I would also like to thank him for writing an appendix for my book about this matter and including historical footnotes.

I would like to express special thanks to Professor Tomasz Szarota who, ever since the first edition of this book was published, has publicly supported the claims expressed in it concerning the failed emigration of Jews.

I would like to thank the editor of the Polish Jews series at KARTA, Hanna Antos, for her constant contact with me and her supervision of the entire process of publishing this book. I'm also grateful to another editor at KARTA, Maria Krawczyk, for her thorough and highly intuitive editing of the final chapter, which was not an easy task since it contains the most important themes from the manuscript of my new book, *W pogoni za początkiem życia* (In Pursuit of the Beginning of Life).

I sincerely thank all the employees of KARTA and the Jewish Historical Institute who helped this book come into being.

—Henryk Schönker

THE TOUCH OF AN
ANGEL

PROLOGUE

I'VE OFTEN WONDERED HOW MY parents, my sister, and I managed to survive the war. Luck was certainly on our side, and completely unbelievable events often happened to us. I'm sure all Jewish people who survived the war in Poland can say the same about themselves. Now, however, after writing my memoir, it seems to me that our salvation was largely thanks to the initiative of my father, Leon (Eliezer) Schönker (1903–1965), who always tried to find a way out of seemingly hopeless situations.[1]

My father never waited passively for catastrophic events to develop. He was blessed with an extraordinary instinct and was always ready to escape, to take a huge leap, even straight into the unknown, if he felt it might change a situation that would certainly have led to our doom if he had remained passive. We weren't aware of it at the time, but my father's instinct always found the right path for us to take so that we could be saved.

Now, while thinking about my family's history, I realize that my father's active searching for a way out of every situation was one of his main character traits. It was evident long before the war. Thanks to his presence of mind and readiness to act, my father prevented various family misfortunes several times and sometimes even managed to protect us from severe oppression.

Above all, however, his instinct, originality, accurate assessment of situations, and swift orientation aided him in his own life. I think he most likely inherited these traits from his mother, Fanny (Feiga) Schönker, née Hollender, who is said to have been a very energetic and determined woman.

My grandfather, Józef (Josef) Schönker (1872–1945), was one of the most well-respected citizens of Oświęcim and owned a factory there called Agrochemia, which produced artificial fertilizers. He was socially active and served many times as a member of the town council; he was a consultant at the City Savings Bank and also actively participated in the life of Oświęcim's Jewish community. He possessed vast Talmudic knowledge, which he'd learned from his father, Izaak Aron, in his youth.

He and his wife, Fanny, had four children: Sarah (Sala), my father, Liba, and Emanuel (Mendel). Fanny, my grandmother, was from Rzeszów, and she was the sister of my other grandmother, Fryderyka (Friedl)—my mother's mother. We called her Frydzia. My father and my mother, Mina (Dwora Mindla, 1905–1976), were cousins. My other grandfather, Markus (Mordechai) Münz, nicknamed Motele, lived in Rzeszów and was from a wealthy family that owned vast estates and a brick factory.

During World War I, both of my grandfathers escaped to Vienna with their families. My mother was nine years old, and my father was eleven years old. There, in Vienna, they fell in love with each other. My mother told me that my father bought dolls for her. Love distracted them from the harsh reality around them. Despite the war, they managed to take beautiful trips together to Tyrol and other places. Both of them always recalled this period in Vienna as one of the most pleasant times in their lives. They attended school there together, too, and became perfectly fluent in Viennese German.

My father was very talented artistically and spent all his free time drawing landscapes and portraits. In 1916, Józef Schönker asked Professor Kohn, a famous professor at the Academy of Fine Arts in Vienna, if he could visit him with his son for a consultation. Professor Kohn examined my father by asking him to draw a vase. After this exam, Professor Kohn convinced my grandfather that my father should attend the art academy, and he took him under his guidance as an exceptional student.

After the war, both my mother's and father's parents returned to Poland. My father, however, went to Amsterdam to study painting at the Academy of Fine Arts there. Then he continued his studies in Paris. In 1922 he received a telegram that his mother was on her deathbed, so he rushed back to Oświęcim, where he managed to bid her farewell in the final moments of her life. My father's home sank into a state of mourning.

A year later, my father, at the age of twenty, decided to ask for my mother's hand in marriage. This wasn't a simple matter because her father was a very pious man—a Hassid who followed a rabbi whose name I can't recall, but whom people called the Bluzhover Rebbe.[2] He viewed my father with suspicion since he'd just returned from Paris, which was considered a sinful city. Furthermore, my father didn't have sidelocks and wore flamboyant, striped velvet clothes and a large, black silk bow tie, which were completely unacceptable.

In her love letters, my mother constantly asked my father not to come yet with his marriage proposal, for there was the risk of him being rejected. My father, however, grew tired of constantly delaying the engagement and decided to act. He'd heard from my mother that her father never made any decisions without first consulting with his rabbi. My father understood that the key to concluding the whole matter in a positive way lay in Bluzhover Rebbe's hands.

One Friday he told his father he was going to visit his aunt and uncle in Rzeszów and that he intended to ask Uncle Motele for his daughter's hand. Grandpa Józef advised my father to wait a little while longer, since Motele might eventually forget that my father had just returned from Paris, and then he could make a better impression on him. Grandpa Józef was afraid my father wouldn't be considered a suitable candidate for the son-in-law of such a devout Hassid, due to his art studies.

Grandpa Józef was very wise, but he obviously underestimated my father's inherent capabilities. My father timed his journey on a Saturday so that on the way to Rzeszów, shortly before the beginning of the Sabbath, he reached the village where Bluzhover Rebbe lived and stopped to visit him. He told him that he was on his way to his uncle Motele Münz's house, but that he'd heard so much about Bluzhover Rebbe that he wished to meet him in person. He'd also heard the rabbi collected pipes, so he was taking the liberty of giving him a rare jubilee-edition Bruyère pipe as a present.

Bluzhover Rebbe was delighted by the pipe. He invited my father to stay as his guest during the Sabbath, since it was too late for him to reach Rzeszów before nightfall. My father agreed and went with the rabbi to pray in the synagogue, which he always did every Sabbath in Oświęcim. The following day they continued to pray, and the rabbi gave a sermon. They went for a stroll after dinner and discussed various worldly matters. In the evening they went to the synagogue again for the ceremonial farewell to the Sabbath.

The next day my father said goodbye to Bluzhover Rebbe and his wife. Both had been very charmed by him. After arriving in Rzeszów, my father immediately asked Motele for his daughter's hand in marriage. It was a difficult decision. Uncle Motele held Józef Schönker's family in high esteem, but his son was a rather strange person, for what normal Jew travels to Paris to learn to paint pictures? Who knew what else Leon had learned there? He decided not to answer too hastily and promised my father he would inform him of his decision a few days later.

I know the rest of this story from my mother. Two days later, Motele made an appointment to meet with Bluzhover Rebbe to discuss an urgent matter. When he arrived, he told the rabbi that he was faced with a difficult dilemma—his daughter's cousin, Leon Schönker from Oświęcim, had asked him for her hand in marriage. It was true that the two youngsters loved each other, and he would be happy to see his daughter join Józef Schönker's family. But how could he possibly entrust his daughter to someone who had recently returned from Paris and had decided to occupy himself with such frivolous matters as painting pictures? Who needed these pictures? And who really knew what kind of person this Leon Schönker was? The fact that he had come to him in a velvet hat with a wide brim didn't testify to his character, did it?

A huge surprise was awaiting Grandfather Motele. Bluzhover Rebbe declared that he knew Leon Schönker very well and considered him to be an exceptional person. He told Grandfather Motele that he'd held long conversations with Leon on various subjects. "Motele," he said, "you have nothing to fear. Your daughter will have a good life with him." A great weight was lifted from my grandfather's heart. He didn't dare ask the rabbi any further questions since he knew that a common person was incapable of seeing the truth that a rabbi sees. The following day my father received a positive reply, and the wedding took place soon afterward.

Grandpa Józef owned a plot of land opposite his villa, and that's where my father's villa was built. My grandfather lived at 36 Jagiellońska Street, and the young couple lived at number 41. My mother grew accustomed to Oświęcim very quickly because, after all, Grandpa Józef was not only her father-in-law but also her uncle.

Grandpa Józef convinced my father that after starting a family, he would have to take up a serious occupation of some kind, apart from painting. Times were hard, and it was impossible to make a living as a painter. At first my father wanted to move to Kraków, where there was a vibrant artistic community, but in the end he yielded to his father's wishes and remained in Oświęcim.

The town was undergoing electrification at that time, and my father, with my grandfather's financial support, opened a lamp shop. There was a huge demand for lamps, and many of Oświęcim's residents became my father's customers. He imported a great number of lamps. My grandfather generously provided capital, for he was pleased his son was finally running a business and had begun a normal life.

And so while his friends were beginning their painting careers in Paris, my father was selling lamps in Oświęcim.

My grandfather constantly invested money in this business, even though the shop seemed to be prospering. After a while he sent a bookkeeper from his factory to check how the shop was doing. The results of this inspection were disastrous. It turned out that my father was mainly selling lamps on credit. He'd kept records at the beginning, but the business was growing so fast that he had eventually stopped writing anything down and simply trusted people. After all, most of the residents of Oświęcim were his friends. Nobody had been doing any bookkeeping, and there was a terrible mess. Nobody knew who owed money or how much they owed.

My grandfather wrung his hands; he realized that not only had he lost a huge amount of money but that his beloved son was useless at running a shop. He had no choice but to agree to my father moving to Kraków to continue his artistic career.

It was said that most of the town's inhabitants had obtained lamps in my father's shop for free. My father became a local hero. To this day I suspect that he planned the whole affair himself.

In Kraków, my father soon became a renowned portrait painter. He also painted landscapes and still lifes. He received a very illustrious commission to paint the interior of the historic Wolf Popper Synagogue in Kraków, and the Jewish community was extremely pleased with his work. His works were presented in many individual and group exhibitions. One of his paintings was bought by the Hermitage in Leningrad, and another by the museum of the Bezalel Academy of Arts in Jerusalem. He regularly wrote articles about art for *Nowy Dziennik*. In the 1930s he was the president of the Association of Jewish Painters and Sculptors in Kraków.

We were born in this city: my brother, Musiu, and I, and later my sister, Lusia. Our apartment at 2 Szczepański Square became a meeting place for actors and artists of various kinds. Many of them became very dear friends of ours.

Things went well for my father in Kraków, and Grandpa Józef always helped him when he had financial problems. Grandpa Józef was the head of the family and the director of the family business—the Agrochemia factory. Unfortunately, everything did not always go well there. It started out as a joint-stock company, and in addition to my grandfather, who had founded the factory with his brother Eber in 1905, several banks held shares in it. Later, my grandfather bought all the shares and became the sole owner.

Superphosphates were manufactured at my grandfather's factory. Sulfuric acid was needed in the production of superphosphates. Large superphosphate factories in Poland had their own sulfuric acid factories, which was a huge investment. We didn't have such a factory, and Agrochemia depended on deliveries of this acid, primarily from steelworks. But because the production capabilities of superphosphate factories in Poland were much greater than the market's demand, a cartel was established that focused on large factories. The cartel decided how much each factory could produce and tried to suppress small factories, which were depriving it of consumer markets. The cartel accomplished this most frequently by exerting pressure on steelworks and other enterprises to decrease supplies of sulfuric acid to factories that weren't members of the cartel. This caused difficulties for Agrochemia many times.

One day, while walking down a street in Kraków, my father noticed a beautiful living room set from the era of Louis XVI in an antique shop owned by a friend of his named Stieglitz. The living room set was genuine, not a copy, and was being sold by an aristocratic family. My father had a passion for antiques, and so, after negotiating a price, he immediately gave Stieglitz a down payment for the living room set. He signed a contract and was expected to pay the rest of the money by the end of the week. Various people owed him money, and he hoped he wouldn't have any trouble obtaining the remaining amount.

It was a large sum, however, and my father soon discovered he was unable to obtain it. Having no alternative and fearing he would lose the down payment, my father went to Grandpa Józef to borrow some money. But he was greatly disappointed to discover that the Agrochemia factory was once again facing difficulties because the steelworks in Katowice refused to supply it with sulfuric acid. My grandfather told my father that the factory would be able to continue production for only two more weeks, and then he would have to shut it down. He was in despair. Under these circumstances there was no way he could lend my father any money.

The following day, my father visited Stieglitz's shop to cancel the transaction. Stieglitz wasn't there, so he decided to wait for him. The living room set was no longer in the shop, and my father assumed it had been put in the storeroom. Stieglitz appeared about fifteen minutes later. When he saw my father waiting for him, he grew pale and started stammering. He begged him not to be angry, but something unfortunate had happened—he'd sold the living room set to someone else. Two days after my father had been in the shop, Michał Grażyński, the provincial governor from Katowice, had seen the living room set and had, quite simply, forced Stieglitz to sell it to him. Stieglitz had tried to explain to him that it was no longer for sale. The governor had refused to yield. He'd said he would settle the matter with Schönker and would take full responsibility for the situation. Right there, on the spot, he had paid the full price and had taken the living room set.

Stieglitz told my father that of course he would return his down payment, and he apologized profusely for this unpleasant incident. He asked my father if they could cancel the transaction and told him he was willing to offer my father something from the shop as compensation. My father pretended to be very upset. He declared that there could be no talk of cancellation and left the shop.

Stieglitz ran into the street after him, trying to appease him, but my father was implacable.

That very day he went to Warsaw and visited a well-known lawyer named Zygmunt Hofmokl-Ostrowski. He presented the situation, and the lawyer was delighted. He enjoyed cases that caused scandals.

"Mr. Schönker," he said, "if you let me handle this case, I'll take it on for free. We'll cause a scandal throughout Poland."

My father said he wasn't interested in a scandal; he wanted to settle the matter amicably.

"In that case, I'll write a letter, and you can be sure it'll affect him greatly," said the lawyer.

Two days later my father received a phone call from the governor, who was clearly outraged. "Mr. Schönker, why did you send Hofmokl-Ostrowski after me? We can reach an understanding between ourselves. There's no need to create such a huge fuss."

My father made an appointment with Grażyński and went to Katowice. The two men came to an agreement there. In my father's presence, the governor arranged over the telephone that the steelworks in Katowice would supply Agrochemia with sulfuric acid for the entire season. And he also promised to make an exact copy of the living room set and send it to my father as a present.

Unfortunately, a year later, in 1937, Agrochemia's troubles with sulfuric acid supplies resumed. The cartel was trying to stifle our factory again. My grandfather was told that the deliveries would be terminated. He faced rejection everywhere he turned. My father called the governor, but this time Grażyński told my father that he wasn't responsible for Agrochemia. It seemed the factory's fate was now sealed, and it would have to be shut down. This would mean bankruptcy, since the factory owed a lot of money for raw materials. And it would mean the ruin of our entire family.

By this point my grandfather had become completely despondent, but my father refused to give up. He remembered that the president of Poland, Ignacy Mościcki, had been on Agrochemia's board of supervisors in the 1920s when it had been a joint-stock company. In those days, the board had met several times a year, and Mościcki had come to the meetings from Lwów,[3] where he was, at that time, a chemistry professor at the polytechnic institute. Every time he had come to Oświęcim for a board meeting, he had stayed for a while at my grandfather's house. He liked my father very much, and after the meetings he used to have long conversations with him. Later, after he had become the president of Poland, he visited my grandfather several times while passing through Oświęcim and even signed his guestbook.

My father decided to make use of this old friendship and went to Warsaw. He reported to the president's office in the castle and asked to meet with the president. He was given a form to fill in and was told that he would receive a reply, but that it might take several months. My father answered that he would like to see the president that very day. The astonished secretary asked my father if he had an appointment.

"No, I don't have an appointment, but the president will know who I am," he answered, handing her his business card.

Soon he was informed that the president was waiting for him. My father was led into a large, very elegant office. President Mościcki approached him, smiling, and shook his hand. He asked how my grandfather was doing, whether he was healthy, and if everything was going well for us. Then he sat down behind his desk, and my father sat across from him.

"What has brought you here to see me?" Mościcki asked.

My father told him that Agrochemia was on the verge of catastrophe because the cartel had interrupted its supplies of sulfuric acid in an attempt to stifle the factory's production. The cartel's actions would cause Agrochemia to go bankrupt. Several hundred families in Oświęcim would lose their jobs.

"But that's sabotage!" exclaimed Mościcki. "Sławoj, did you hear this?"

Only now did my father notice that someone in a uniform was standing by the window with his back to them.

"I heard," answered the officer. Then he turned around. My father immediately recognized him—it was General Felicjan Sławoj Składkowski, Poland's premier and minister of internal affairs.

"This is a scandal!" said the president. "Please take care of this matter."

"The matter will be taken care of immediately," said Sławoj Składkowski, and he smiled at my father.

The meeting came to an end. My father left the castle in an excellent mood and decided to visit a friend. They went out for dinner together, and my father returned to his hotel very late in the evening. The hotel's manager was waiting for him at the reception desk, highly agitated.

When he saw my father, he shouted, "For the love of God, Mr. Schönker, where have you been? We've been looking for you everywhere for several hours!"

"What happened?"

"I've been receiving urgent phone calls for you all day. They ordered me to find you, at any cost."

"What is it about?"

"I don't know exactly, but they told me Sławoj Składkowski wants to send several directors of some cartel to the Bereza Kartuska prison. Everyone is extremely agitated, and they want to speak with you. Here's the phone number," he said, handing him a piece of paper. "They want you to call them as soon as possible."

My father dialed the phone number he'd been given and gave his surname. Someone began to explain something to him in an irate voice, but my father couldn't understand what he was saying. He asked the man to speak more calmly. It turned out that he was speaking with the director of the artificial fertilizer cartel.

He informed my father that the cartel agreed to accept Agrochemia into their group and there wouldn't be any further problems with sulfuric acid supplies. The factory would also receive a larger trade quota. He begged my father to agree and to immediately inform the premier and the minister of internal affairs that the matter had been settled in a satisfactory manner for the Schönker family. My father replied that first he needed to discuss it with the owner of Agrochemia.

"Quickly! Quickly! Please hurry, because police officers are waiting downstairs here, at my villa."

My father phoned my grandfather and explained to him what had happened and that Agrochemia was going to be accepted into the cartel. My father had to repeat the news several times because my grandfather thought he was drunk.

My father called the cartel's director again and told him that Józef Schönker agreed in principle, but that the trade quota was too small and had to be increased. The director of the cartel immediately agreed and invited my father and grandfather to a ceremonial acceptance of Agrochemia into Poland's artificial fertilizer cartel.

My grandfather asked my father to return to Oświęcim to help him run the factory. He offered him 25 percent of the ownership and the position of vice director. After discussing it with my mother, my father agreed and they moved back to Oświęcim.

Agrochemia could have saved our entire family from the Holocaust, but fate decreed that things would happen differently. In 1938, while taking a train from Katowice to a cartel meeting in Warsaw, my father shared a sleeping car with a young American named Harriman. He was traveling to the same meeting. His father, Averell Harriman, a railway tycoon, had sent him to Poland several times to familiarize himself with the heavy industry in Upper Silesia. He had large shares in the coal mines and steelworks there, as well as in artificial fertilizer factories, within a huge syndicate called SACO (the Silesia-American Corporation).

Harriman described to my father his very pessimistic view of the situation of Jews in Poland and throughout Europe. He believed we should leave Poland.

He proposed that we sell Agrochemia to his father; he was ready to pay $100,000 in gold for it. The payment would be made in New York or London—wherever our family decided to go. This was a very large amount of money in those times. My father told him he would inform his father of this offer.

After returning to Oświęcim, he told my grandfather about it. My grandfather met with Harriman in Katowice. It was a serious offer, and my grandfather needed to make a decision. My entire family met at my grandfather's house to discuss the matter. In the end, however, they decided not to accept the offer because my grandfather's second wife, Regina Grossfeld, née Schwartz, didn't want to part with her son and his family who lived in Kraków.

Toward the end of the 1930s, Agrochemia became extremely prosperous. My parents were very content with their lives in Oświęcim. They lived in a lovely villa with a beautiful garden, took part in the town's social life, had many friends, and were well-respected citizens of the town. My father improved many things at the factory, and everything he did was successful. Grandpa Józef was very satisfied with my father and consulted with him on all important matters.

However, despite my father's vitality, originality, and resourcefulness, my mother was the true backbone of our home. She gave stability to our life. She devoted herself entirely to the family. She always had an optimistic outlook and never lost hope, even in the most difficult situations. She always stood by my father's side and was his greatest support. My father appreciated this, and they loved each other very much. Bluzhover Rebbe had been right—it was a truly wonderful marriage.

My parents experienced the entire war together and supported each other with every bit of their strength. They managed to save themselves and their children. It's true that it was my father who always took the initiative. But it's also true that in moments of great danger and suffering, often on the very threshold of death, we were always saved by some kind of extremely fortuitous event.

I've always felt—and still feel today—that we were saved by the touch of an angel.

I was supposed to die before I was born. I owe my life to my mother not being aware she was pregnant. Knowing of her new state, she undoubtedly would have ended my life. She once told me this herself. Nevertheless, she was the most perfect and loving mother I could ever imagine. She was also the most wonderful person I've ever met in my life. I've often asked myself how she, such a wise and intelligent person, could not have realized she was pregnant. For many years

I was unable to understand this. Today I believe that even then, while in the womb, a greater power of some kind already had me under its care.

My mother's intention has never surprised me. She was afraid her next child would be like Musiu—her first son, who was five years older than me. As an infant he became paralyzed and almost completely lost the use of both legs. My parents went to great efforts to improve his state, even just partially. For many years, professors, doctors, and physiotherapists worked hard to cure him. A great success was when Musiu was able to walk very slowly by himself, leaning on two canes with both legs supported by braces.

Despite his serious disability, Musiu was a happy child. His joyful laughter still rings in my ears today. He accepted the life he'd been given. Led by a remarkable instinct, he made use of each day to the fullest. He was able to enjoy everything—every little thing that for other children was meaningless. His joy was contagious to others; it was pleasant to be in his company. My parents and I loved him deeply.

Other people who were much less seriously crippled than Musiu and suffered less than him locked themselves up in their own worlds and isolated themselves from their surroundings. Musiu was different. He was interested in everyone and treated people equally. He didn't divide people into categories and respected everybody. He was very intelligent and talented; at the age of five, he was already reading books. In school he was good at math, and children often came to our house to ask him for help with their homework. My mother wasn't pleased about this at first, since it took up a lot of Musiu's time. But she agreed to the visits after seeing how happy they made him. Musiu felt happiest when he could help people and express love toward them.

All his classmates were very fond of him. However, children in other classes often bullied him. But he never felt insulted and tried to ignore their taunts. He explained to me that people are never as bad as they seem; their further behavior toward us depends on how we react to their negative words. I didn't really understand what he was saying at the time, but I felt there was something important in it.

When I was six years old, Musiu fell ill with encephalitis, lost consciousness, and died a few days later. I remember my father painting a portrait of him while he lay on his deathbed. His death plunged our home into deep pain and mourning. It was a pain that remained with us forever. It was the first time I experienced the death of a very close and beloved person.

I didn't understand how Musiu, who had become an important part of my childhood world, could suddenly leave us. I cried at night, secretly, for a long time. Throughout all my later years, I've lived with vivid memories of Musiu. I've asked myself why such a good and innocent person, so deeply loved by us, who had never done anything bad to anyone (who, on the contrary, had done so much good) had to die. Why did he have to suffer so much? Why was he burdened with a physical disability?

Later, other questions haunted me. How was it possible that Musiu, despite his serious disability, was so happy during his short life? What source did he draw so much joy from—despite so many sacrifices and even humiliation—that everyone near him also felt blessed with it? Unable to find any answers to these questions, I started doubting whether life makes any sense at all.

A year after Musiu's death, my sister was born. Nobody had prepared me for her arrival, and nobody had talked about it in my presence. On the night of the birth, Musiu appeared to me in a dream and told me that I had a sister. In the morning, my father woke me to tell me the joyous news. Before he managed to say anything, however, I asked him where my little sister was, whom Musiu had sent from heaven. My father was speechless with amazement.

That same year, we moved from Kraków to Oświęcim, where my father's family lived. This move distracted me from thinking about Musiu and slightly dispelled my sadness. Suddenly I had uncles, aunts, and cousins near me. Everyone was very kind to me, and I was passed from lap to lap. I was caressed constantly, as if I were a small child. All of this attention embarrassed me, but I tried to be kind to everyone, for that's how I thought Musiu would have acted.

I deeply loved my uncle Emanuel, whom we called Mendek. He was the only one who talked to me as if I were an adult. He bought me a small dog right after we arrived in Oświęcim, and he often gave me money to go to the cinema. He was an exceptionally pleasant person, always smiling and cracking jokes. A lightness of being and unshakeable optimism radiated from him. He had a four-year-old son named Izaczek and a daughter who was born just before the war. His wife, Rózia, often invited me to their house for delicious cake. I also started going to school at this time, and I began to feel that the world was smiling on me once again.

Shortly before the Germans attacked Poland, our entire family fled to Kazimierz Dolny because it was believed that the Germans wouldn't reach this town very quickly. Everyone was influenced by Polish propaganda and thought that Poland would be able to defend itself. In the worst scenario, people expected trench warfare similar to World War I.

Before fleeing to Kazimierz Dolny, I took five złoty to school because there was a collection for the Antiaircraft Defense Fund. I was sure my contribution, which I'd requested from my father, would help stop the Germans because five złoty was a huge fortune for me. A person could go to the cinema ten times with this much money—admittedly only in the first row, but who sat in any other row at my age?

Everywhere I looked, I saw the slogan "We won't give a single inch of land." But my favorite poster was the one that read "We won't give a single button." I was sure there was nothing to fear and that no enemy would be able to capture Poland. After all, these posters couldn't lie.

My father remained in Oświęcim and tried to dispatch the fertilizer from the factory that had been manufactured for the fall season. But he soon found this to be impossible. All trains were now occupied by the army, and there was chaos, confusion, and general destruction everywhere. This was extremely ominous, but I was too young to understand it.

NOTES

1. Jewish people in Poland usually had two first names—a Hebrew name and a Polish equivalent. For example: Mojżesz (Moses)—Maurycy; Eliezer—Leon.
2. Tzvi Elimelech Spira (Polish: Cwi Elimelech Szapiro) (1841–1924): a *tzaddik* from Bluzhov (Polish: Błażowa). He was known as the Bluzhover Rebbe.
3. Translator's note: Now Lviv, Ukraine.

OŚWIĘCIM

I WAS SUPPOSED TO BEGIN my second year of primary school in Oświęcim on September 1, 1939, but instead I found myself in a forest near the town of Kazimierz Dolny with a large crowd of frightened and anxious people who were staring up at the sky in terror. German planes were circling above us. And then I heard, for the first time in my life, the whistle of falling bombs, followed by explosions. Everyone in the forest fell to the ground, but I remained standing, astonished. Someone pushed me roughly to the ground, and only then did I understand that it was a serious situation. One of my uncles shook his finger at me, and I stuck my tongue out at him.

It was already clear in the first days of the war that there was a power imbalance. The German army advanced swiftly. The Polish government and many high-ranking dignitaries escaped to Romania through Zaleszczyki. Later, my father told us they had passed through Oświęcim in cars loaded with suitcases. Some of them stopped at our villa to stock up on water, and some even stayed overnight. The inhabitants of Oświęcim stood next to the road, glaring contemptuously at the men who had promised them so much but were now the first to flee.

The Germans were conquering more and more of Poland. One morning we woke up to find that the Germans had also taken over the town near Lublin to which we had fled from Kazimierz Dolny. We decided to return to Oświęcim.

The roads were filled with German soldiers, Polish prisoners, and masses of refugees who were either returning to their homes or leaving them. In many cases these were groups of emaciated, starving people—women, children, and elderly people who, completely disoriented and pulling their possessions on carts and wagons, were looking for shelter of some kind, even just for one day or night. Some were heading east, others west. There were traffic jams on the roads stretching dozens of kilometers. Columns of German soldiers cleared the way by shoving people into roadside ditches.

I rode in a peasant wagon with my mother; my little sister, Lusia; my grandfather; and my grandfather's wife. The rest of the family had become separated from us. We experienced a horrible ordeal, often traveling without food or water. We changed wagons several times, and sometimes we covered many kilometers on foot. My two-year-old sister cried the entire time because her body was covered in festering sores. A doctor we encountered on the road said it was because she had a vitamin deficiency. We were afraid Lusia wouldn't survive our journey.

Wishing to avoid the long traffic jams on the highways, we rode and walked along narrow village roads that often led us in the wrong direction; then we had to retrace our steps and look for a different road. We slept in roadside huts and were often given food and shelter for free, since our money had almost completely run out. I still feel grateful to a boy who gave me a slice of bread with butter on it and patted my head. The peasants who helped us were very poor, but they shared with us what they could. They didn't say much, but we could sense they sympathized with us and considered the Nazi attack our shared misfortune. Others, however, shut their doors when we approached.

Finally, after wandering for several weeks, completely exhausted, we reached Kraków, where we stayed with my mother's sister. We sent a message to my father in Oświęcim that we had arrived and were waiting for him to come to Kraków to take us home.

At that time, I thought the torment we had just experienced was the worst thing that would happen to me during the war. I had witnessed so much human suffering, pain, sadness, and hopelessness during this journey that it was difficult for me to imagine anything more terrible. However, I was only eight years old and still very naive.

On September 1, 1939, the Germans bombed many Polish towns, including Oświęcim. Bombs struck two buildings in Church Square and destroyed them completely. The inhabitants of these buildings had left earlier, joining the flood of refugees, and this saved their lives. My father ran to his factory because he was afraid a fire might break out in it. Only the custodian and his wife (Władysław and Maria Goslar) were in the factory, since they lived there. The warehouses were full of artificial fertilizer that was ready to be shipped out for the fall season.

My father was standing with Goslar and his wife in front of the office building. With great astonishment they saw a formation of German airplanes in the sky that, without any hindrance from Polish antiaircraft defense forces, were flying right over their heads. Suddenly some of these planes dove, and there was a crackle of machine guns, a loud whizzing sound, and then an explosion of bombs, which once again struck the town. My father and the Goslars threw themselves to the ground.

A moment later, my father lifted his head and was terrified to see a burning plane flying right toward them. Thankfully it didn't hit the factory and only exploded in a nearby field. Then a small cloud appeared in the sky with a black dot beneath it. The cloud quickly transformed into a white parachute, and the black dot into a person. The parachute fell close to the factory's fence.

My father and Goslar ran over to it and saw a pilot in a German officer's uniform sitting on the ground with his face contorted in pain. It was clear he was wounded, since he was clutching his arm. My father was faced with a difficult decision. The law required him to inform the authorities immediately and turn the pilot over to them. On the other hand, he thought about what would happen if the Germans took over Oświęcim and found out that he, a Jew, had handed a German officer over to the Polish authorities. Although Goslar had German ancestry, he was utterly devoted to my father and would go along with whatever decision he made.

My father also realized there wasn't really anyone to inform. The town was in a state of extreme chaos, and the bureaucratic offices were no longer functioning. The nation's entire system was collapsing. Even the police chief had escaped with his family in a fire engine that the town had recently bought. My father considered himself a loyal Polish citizen, and it was difficult for him to break the law in such a serious way, especially since Goslar could denounce him in this case. Poles might still manage to regain control, and if someone found out that my father hadn't fulfilled his obligations, he would be forced to face the military court and possibly a death penalty.

There was clearly no good option. It occurred to my father that even if he informed the authorities as the law required, and someone could be found who would take care of the matter, they would simply place the pilot against a wall and shoot him, out of pure vengeance. He might meet an even worse death. The pilot should be taken to a prisoner-of-war camp, but there was no way to do so in the midst of all the chaos. If my father did what the law required, it would lead to the murder of a defenseless person. He looked around. The factory was surrounded by fields, but the peasants who worked in them had fled in panic from the bombing planes. The fields were empty.

He told Goslar to bring a stretcher and a first aid kit with bandages and medicine. He examined the pilot and discovered that his collarbone was broken and perhaps also one arm. My father and Goslar immobilized the bones and bandaged them. Then they gave the pilot some painkillers and carefully laid him on the stretcher. They threw the parachute into the airplane, which was still burning. In the factory there was a section where glue was produced. It contained tunnels for drying the glue, and this is where my father hid the wounded pilot.

That very day, seeing the growing panic and mass exodus of Oświęcim's residents, my father also decided to leave the town. After a long march among refugees, he was able to board an overcrowded cargo train and reached Kraków the next day. There was general panic there, too, and people were fleeing eastward in droves, toward Lwów.

On Wednesday, September 6, the Germans entered Kraków. My father, who was staying at the home of his friend, a sculptor named Henryk Hochman, ran out of the building to see what was happening.[1] The street was empty. The cobblestones were strewn with belongings left behind by people who had fled. The only living creature was a dog that was tearing apart a rag doll with its teeth. My father told me later that there was a strange silence, like right before a storm. Suddenly a piano sounded loudly from a window somewhere. Someone was playing Chopin's "Funeral March" with intense feeling. Then my father heard some quiet sobs. Hochman was standing next to him, crying. He was over the age of fifty and looked like a prophet with long gray hair.

"I have the feeling that something very dear to us has died," my father said.

"Yes, what has died is our past, and for many—the future," answered Hochman.

That day, my father decided to return to Oświęcim. The roads were full of chaos. Crowds of terrified, disoriented refugees were hurrying aimlessly in various directions, as if flight itself would save them. Every now and then people were pushed into roadside ditches by columns of German vehicles, which were swarming over the roads like locusts.

My father finally managed to reach Oświęcim and entered the town from the side where the factory was situated. He found out from Goslar that the Germans hadn't yet entered the town because the engineering division was repairing a bridge over the Vistula River that had been blown up by the Polish army. My father told the German pilot that the Germans were expected to enter the town at any moment. He assured the pilot he would immediately inform the Germans that he was in the factory. The pilot was very happy and shook my father's hand in gratitude. He said his name was Tezner. He was from Linz, Austria, and was the commander of an aerial squadron. He also told my father he would repay him. My father wasn't yet aware of who the Germans were in Hitler's time or what their plans were, so he didn't attach any special importance to the pilot's words.

A few hours later, the German army entered Oświęcim. It was the same military engineer squad that had repaired the bridge. The Germans had precise maps of the entire town. Even houses that could be of special importance to them were marked. German military headquarters had been in my grandfather's villa during World War I. A military unit now, once again, immediately took over the villa.

My father was summoned to a German officer, Oberleutnant Kleinbühl, who declared that his staff was taking over the villa and my father was no longer allowed to enter it.

"Do you understand?" asked the German.

"I understand," answered my father in perfect German. Then he informed the officer that a wounded German pilot was hiding in his factory. Astonishment and incredulity were visible on the officer's face. But he didn't say anything; he just passed the information on to another officer, clearly of a higher rank, who was busy right at that moment looking at my grandfather's books. This officer ordered my father to go to the factory with a soldier and show him where the pilot was.

After reaching the factory by motorcycle, they approached the opening of the tunnel, but the pilot had disappeared. The soldier called out loudly: *"Kamerad, komm heraus! Kamerad, komm heraus!"* (Comrade, come out!) It was quite a while before the pilot's head appeared in the opening of the tunnel. It turned out he'd been afraid my father had led Poles to him and that my father had told him the Germans were about to invade only so that he would let his guard down.

It was decided that my father would remain with the wounded pilot, and the soldier would return to the town to get help. With tears in his eyes, the pilot once again thanked my father for having saved his life. Soon a military ambulance arrived and took him to the hospital. My father went home, convinced this was the end of the whole adventure. However, a few hours later the same ambulance brought the pilot to our villa, for he wished to remain under my father's care until he was well again. He preferred to stay in a private apartment rather than at the hospital. Many officers started visiting our home, and they treated my father as if he were an exotic animal.

Meanwhile, more and more Jews were returning to Oświęcim, bringing with them frightening news of the Germans' antisemitic actions and the burning of synagogues in nearby villages. These reports triggered fear and misery among Jewish people, but we all reassured ourselves that perhaps it would be different in Oświęcim. Then came news that thirty-two Jews had been shot in Wieliczka, and now an even greater fear overwhelmed the Jewish residents of Oświęcim.[2]

My father, in his naiveté, reported to the leader of Oberleutnant Kleinbühl's team and, informing him of the execution in Wieliczka, demanded an immediate explanation from competent military authorities. Kleinbühl was astonished by my father's complaint. It was clear he was unsure what to do. Finally, he answered that this execution hadn't been carried out by Wehrmacht divisions and that it had been in retaliation for the killing of Germans in Bydgoszcz and Poznań.

As he left my grandfather's villa, my father realized for the first time that Jewish lives were worthless to the Germans.

Life in Oświęcim became increasingly difficult. Wehrmacht soldiers began to amuse themselves by catching Jews and cutting off their beards and sidelocks. Men and women were rounded up for various kinds of work. Homes were searched, and possessions were confiscated. It was necessary to intervene constantly with the military authorities to lessen these persecutions, at least to a small extent. The military commander of the town refused to speak to anyone except the chairman of the Jewish community council. Nobody, however, was willing to fill this role, for everyone was terrified.

My father was asked to perform this function. He stubbornly refused, explaining that he'd never taken part in the Jewish community council's administration and had no experience in how it operated. His categorical refusal wasn't accepted, and a few days later, a delegation visited him and very forcefully renewed the request. My father's subsequent refusal had no effect, nor did the objections he put forward. They explained to him that there was the danger that the Germans themselves might appoint a leader of the Jewish community who would cooperate with them and follow all their orders, even orders that would harm Jews.

They also touched on a sensitive issue for him—namely, that as the grandson of Izaak Aron Schönker and the son of Józef Schönker, he had no right to refuse a request from the Jewish community when it found itself in danger. These words had an effect on my father; he felt that a further refusal would truly constitute disloyalty to Oświęcim's Jewish society.

My father realized that taking on this role would mean flirting with death. He told the delegation that they were forcing him to live in constant danger. He couldn't be expected to submit to all the demands of the Jewish community or the German authorities. He would accept the position, but only on condition that the members of the delegation who were asking him to take on the role of leader and would be working with him in the future agreed that there was a limit to the execution of German orders, even under threat of death.

My father repeated these words at the first meeting of the Jewish community council. Everyone told him they would never agree to becoming a tool in the Germans' hands. When my mother, sister, and I returned to Oświęcim, my father was already the official leader of the Jewish community.

We returned to Oświęcim easily, thanks to the German pilot living in our house. An officer he knew was heading to Kraków in a military vehicle, and my father asked if he could go with him. Chełmek and Libiąż—small villages near Oświęcim—had burned to the ground, and the driver found it difficult to steer the car along the road through the ruins and ashes. In Trzebinia they drove past a burned-out synagogue where several Jews were praying, leaning against the charred wall.

When the car arrived at Augustiańska Street in Kraków, where we were living with my mother's sister, we were all frightened by the sight of a stranger, and I hid under the bed. The stranger turned out to be my father, whom we didn't recognize because he had shaved off his beard. He had to knock on the door for a long time and then even started pounding on it before we opened it. After we recognized my father, we embraced him joyfully. We quickly packed a small suitcase and got in the car, which took us to Oświęcim without encountering any trouble.

The German commander of Oświęcim often visited the pilot, and my father managed to communicate with him very well in German. He complied with various requests my father had as the leader of the Jewish community, and this made the lives of Jews in Oświęcim, during the time that this officer was the commander, easier than in other places. The town's authorities permitted Jewish New Year to be celebrated; my father also managed to arrange exemptions from forced labor for many people. He was even promised that searches in Jewish apartments, confiscation of property, and persecution of Jews would be stopped. For a while, things were truly peaceful.

However, it wasn't long before the Germans closed all the Jewish shops in Oświęcim. My father once again went to the town's commander to complain. The commander showed him the order he'd received from Katowice to install Aryan supervisors in all Jewish shops. The supervisors had to be, if possible, Germans or *Volksdeutsche*. The commander wanted to receive a list of such supervisors from him a few hours later. Since there weren't enough Germans in the town, the list could contain Poles, and my father agreed to be responsible for adding them. A few hours later, the list was sent to the commander, who then gave an order for the shops to be reopened. Each of the Polish supervisors, most of whom were senior citizens, received 300 złoty per month.

In the end, my father rescuing the German pilot had a positive impact on the entire Jewish community of Oświęcim. The pilot asked the town's commander, with whom he'd become friends, to act favorably toward my father to whatever extent possible. Thanks to the pilot's efforts, there was a relatively peaceful atmosphere in the town at the beginning of the German occupation, and some lives were spared.

One morning, Stasia, our Polish housekeeper, who still lived with us and didn't want to leave, woke my father. She told him that the abbess of a Catholic convent in Oświęcim wanted to talk with him about a very urgent matter.

My father managed, with great difficulty, to calm the sobbing, hysterical abbess enough to understand what the matter was. She told my father that during a search of the school run by the Salesian monastery, the Germans had found guns hidden beneath a staircase. These guns were useless and were used only for military training exercises. Regulations in prewar Poland had required every educational institution to carry out such exercises.

Immediately after invading Oświęcim, the Germans had issued an order for all weapons to be handed over to them; those who didn't comply would face the death penalty. After the guns had been found, twelve of the priests were arrested and were about to be shot. The nun said that everything depended on the German chief of staff. She asked if my father could intercede for the priests, just as he had often interceded for Jewish people.

My father immediately went to my grandfather's villa. Kleinbühl was working in his office and let my father in, surprised to see him at such an early hour. My father explained that the guns weren't real but just harmless pieces of wood used in exercises and that in no way could they be considered weapons. It hadn't occurred to anyone that these pieces of wood should be turned in, for in that case it would be necessary to hand over all "guns" made by children out of sticks while playing war games.

Kleinbühl stared with increasing amazement at this Jewish man who was fighting so passionately to defend Catholic priests. My father's words moved him, and he told a soldier to bring several of the guns that had been found at the monastery. While they were waiting, my father noticed some stamp albums on Kleinbühl's desk. Some were open, and a magnifying glass was lying on one of them. The officer began to look at them and casually told my father that he'd be grateful if my father could find some interesting stamps for him.

The guns were brought in, and it turned out that one of them was missing its lock, another lacked a muzzle, and another didn't have a trigger. None of them worked. Kleinbühl started laughing and agreed that these childish toys couldn't be considered weapons. He phoned the prison and ordered the priests to be sent back to the monastery. My father thanked him and hurried home to give the joyful news to the abbess, who was waiting for him there. Despite my father's protests, she started kissing his hands, and she would have thrown herself at his feet if he and Stasia hadn't stopped her.

News of my father's intercession and the release of the Salesian priests, who were highly respected and loved throughout the town, spread with lightning speed. People said that a miracle had happened at the monastery. My father, meanwhile, spent the entire day gathering stamps from stamp collectors he knew. Some people, when they heard where the stamps were going, offered their collections to my father themselves. That same evening, my father went to Oberleutnant Kleinbühl and gave him three albums full of stamps. Kleinbühl looked through them and was clearly pleased.

After several peaceful days, the army closed off all the streets, and searches began in all Jewish homes throughout the town. Objects made of silver were confiscated (all jewelry and objects made of gold had already been handed over immediately after the Germans entered the town). And once again my father's interventions were effective—the Germans agreed to give back objects that had been confiscated from poor people. These were primarily silver menorahs, in which candles were lit on Friday and Saturday evenings. These menorahs had been passed down from generation to generation. Several months later there were more searches, and the objects that had been returned were then confiscated permanently. But there's no doubt that these months of relative peace were a great gift to the Jewish residents of Oświęcim.

I spent entire days at home, where my mother tried to teach me, because Jewish children were no longer allowed to go to school. I often went to the Soła River to play with other children. Sometimes, in the evening, my former first grade teacher, Ms. Dyczkowska, would visit us secretly to give me lessons. She never wanted to be paid for this and said that God would one day reward her for it. She was a very pious person and went to church every day.

And so I had two teachers, and I was very busy because they gave me a lot of homework. I hadn't yet become aware of the danger surrounding us. At home the atmosphere was always tense—my father would return home tired and despondent, and my mother was always sad—but we all hoped God wouldn't abandon us.

Not far from us lived a fourteen-year-old Polish boy named Tadek who felt animosity toward me, even before the outbreak of the war. When he saw me on the street, he always blocked my path and sneered: "Hey, Jew! Get to the other side of the street!" If I didn't obey him immediately, he would hit me. At first I tried to stand up to him, but I always came out of it with a bloody nose or a black eye. Finally, I acknowledged that he was stronger than I was, and there was no sense in fighting him. When I saw him, I always crossed to the other side of the street right away.

One day I was heading home along the bank of the Soła River, lost in thought. When I was close to our house, I saw Tadek using a large rock to smash the spokes of a bicycle that was lying in front of him in the road. Unable to believe what I was seeing, I went closer; I couldn't suppress my curiosity. I thought perhaps I was wrong and it wasn't a bicycle, for how could a person destroy such a valuable object? A bicycle was a precious treasure. But it turned out that it was, in fact, a bicycle, seemingly a brand-new one since the paint was shiny. On its frame there was a red square with a black swastika inside a white circle.

I stood there, stupefied. Suddenly I heard a warning whistle from one of Tadek's friends who had clearly noticed someone approaching. Tadek tossed the rock, climbed the nearest brick wall like a cat, and disappeared over the other side. A second later he stuck his head above the wall and, seeing me standing next to the bicycle, shouted: "Henryk, for the love of God, run! Run or that German will kill you!"

I immediately started running, but then I heard a German shout loudly behind me: *"Halt! Halt!"* I kept running with the German following me. I looked around. He was roughly twenty meters behind me, wearing a light-brown uniform and a red armband with a swastika on it. He was holding a revolver with its barrel pointed upward. He shouted again: *"Halt! Halt!"* Then he fired his revolver, seemingly into the air since I wasn't struck. I was terrified and about to stop running, but at that moment, I saw a horse-drawn wagon coming around a corner; instinctively I felt there was a chance it would block the German who was chasing me, since the road was very narrow.

Suddenly I felt as if somebody pushed me very forcefully; a shot rang out, and I fell to the ground. This time the revolver had been aimed at me, but it went over my head and hit the wall in front of me. Splinters from the wall struck my forehead; I felt a sharp pain, and above me I heard the whinnying of the horses, which, frightened by the loud noise of the gun, had broken into a wild gallop and knocked the German down. I jumped to my feet, with my face covered in blood and my knee hurting, and ran away.

When I reached our house, Stasia became so frightened when she saw my blood-covered face and shirt that she nearly fainted. She started wringing her hands and wailed: "Oh Lord! Mother of God!" Thankfully my mother soon arrived. They laid me down on the sofa and carefully wiped my face. The wound on my forehead turned out to be very shallow, and it was enough to disinfect it with iodine and bandage my head.

When I told my mother and Stasia the whole story, they decided I shouldn't leave home for several days, at least while I still had the bandage on my head, for the Germans might be looking for me. Afraid that someone might be able to see me through our windows, I hid in the attic for a while. Right after this event, we lived fearfully because we worried there might have been people looking out their windows while I had been running away, and they might turn me in to the Germans. It would be very difficult to explain my innocence since nobody had seen Tadek smashing the bicycle. But the following days passed peacefully. The bandage was taken off my head, and I went out into the street again.

The most interesting part of this story was that—as we found out later—many residents of Oświęcim had seen me running away from the German, and everyone was sure I had destroyed the bicycle. Not only did nobody turn me in, but I also became a hero of the town. The destruction of the German bicycle was regarded as the first brave act in retaliation against the occupiers. Tadek stopped beating me up. When he saw me, he winked conspiratorially and smiled at me with visible kindness.

Some time passed. Just like every year before Christmas, children walked from house to house carrying nativity scenes and singing carols. I happened to be in the street when a group of children between the ages of eight and twelve came toward me with a large nativity scene. One of the boys, seeing me, stepped forward and started singing, right behind my back: "Hey, Jew, hey, Jew, death is pursuing you." He repeated this verse several times to the delight of the other children. I didn't know what to do—whether to run away or keep standing there. I was afraid they would start hitting me, and there were a lot of them. I became very scared.

All of a sudden, someone poked me in the side. I saw Tadek walking next to me. I became even more frightened, but to my amazement, Tadek said to me, loudly, "Don't listen to what he's saying because he's an idiot." I looked at him in disbelief. Then he turned to follow the boy.

I couldn't hold myself back and said to him, "But you used to be like that, too."

Tadek replied, "And I was an idiot, too." He grabbed my shoulder and said, "I'm sorry." Then he leaned over, because he was much taller than I was, and kissed me on the cheek. I stood there, completely bewildered. After a while I realized I was alone in the street.

One morning a soldier came to my father and ordered him to go with him immediately to the commander of the town, who was waiting to discuss an urgent matter. My father understood that something very important must have happened, since he had never been summoned before at such an early hour.

The commander himself opened the door of his office and invited my father in. My father tried to conceal his anxiety. There was no way of knowing what kind of new order had just come from the gestapo's headquarters in Katowice, which controlled all Jewish affairs in the territories annexed by Germany.

The commander sat down in the armchair behind his desk and gestured to my father to sit down as well. Seeing his anxiety, he said, with a jovial smile, "You have nothing to fear, for this time I have some good news. I've received an order for an emigration office to be opened in Oświęcim to enable Jews to emigrate to Palestine.[3] I'll entrust the opening of this to you. Emigration is optional. The German leaders would like the largest possible number of people to sign up, and we hope emigration will begin soon. Due to various technical and organizational limitations, this emigration will happen gradually, but if everything goes well and the initial difficulties are overcome, it will be a massive emigration, and everyone will be able to leave."

Then he told my father to begin immediate preparations for opening the emigration office and to hang posters throughout the town informing people about the registration of Jews wishing to leave for Palestine. That very day, my father opened the emigration office in a restaurant owned by his best friend, Shmuel Schnitzer, in the Haberfeld house in the center of town, near a bridge over the Soła River. Józef Manheimer was appointed as manager of the office.[4]

The posters made a huge impression on all the residents of Oświęcim. Jewish people were happy that the Germans had set a limit to their brutal behavior. A similar emigration office had previously existed in Kraków and had closed shortly after opening. Something obviously must have changed if there was a command for it to be opened again, this time in Oświęcim. Our town was clearly intended to become a gathering point for the emigration of Jews from Silesia. People thought that eventually emigration would expand to include Jews from the *Generalgouvernement*.

Fresh hope sprung up among the Jewish residents of Oświęcim. Registration began in the town and it was treated very seriously; some people even considered learning Hebrew.

Meanwhile, several people from the HIAS camp in Slovakia secretly visited my father.[5] Their aim was to smuggle a group of young people along the Danube River, all the way to the Varna, Constanta, and Sulina ports on the Black Sea. From there, they would travel to Palestine by ship, also in secret, this time hiding from the English.

These messengers told my father that the refugee camp was completely overcrowded and the conditions there were extremely difficult. It was impossible to wait any longer; the whole operation needed to begin immediately. They asked my father to help organize the escape route for the young Polish Jews. It was necessary to create smuggling points—to find people who would provide the refugees with supplies and places where they could be sheltered until the next phase of their trip. My father devoted a great deal of effort to this and helped them organize everything.

And so, while everyone was beginning to hope for a mass emigration, an underground effort to smuggle young people to Eretz Israel began. Unfortunately, this effort didn't last long; the English soon found out about it and, unwilling to allow Jews to emigrate to Palestine, closed off the Varna, Constanta, and Sulina ports with their battleships. Ships were unable to leave these ports without a thorough inspection.

In November 1939, my father was summoned again to the town's commander, who told him to go to Bielsko, together with another member of the Jewish community council, and report to an officer named Rüdiger; he gave my father the office's address. Bielsko was the main city in the county to which Oświęcim belonged.

At the same time, Zyleg Königsberg was arrested in Oświęcim along with another Jew whose name I can't remember, but who was the son-in-law of our friend Feniger. Königsberg was arrested after being denounced by a janitor in the Kuźnicki factory where he worked. The janitor, a *volksdeutsch*, informed German authorities that Zyleg Königsberg had hidden canisters of gasoline in the factory by burying them in the ground. Feniger's son-in-law was arrested as well, after a similar denunciation.

Standing in front of the town's commander, my father asked him to set free the two arrested men. The commander interrupted him to say he was unable to do anything about it because they had already been sent to the gestapo in Bielsko, and he advised my father to talk with Rüdiger about the matter. In this way, my father found out that the man to whom he was meant to report was a gestapo officer. Until then he hadn't had any dealings with the gestapo, since Oświęcim was under the control of military authorities.

The commander handed my father a letter in a sealed envelope and asked him to give it to Rüdiger. My father traveled to Bielsko with Józef Manheimer. They arrived a bit early and first went to the leader of the local Jewish community council, Józef Roter, to gain some information about Rüdiger. It turned out that Roter, an old, weak Jew, had also been summoned to appear before this officer at the same time.

Roter described Rüdiger as a wild animal, claiming that never in his life had he met anyone as brutal or ruthless as this gestapo officer. He advised my father and Manheimer to be restrained in their conversation with him and to watch their words carefully if they wished to leave this meeting alive. If Rüdiger was upset even slightly, it could lead to the death of all of them.

My father also heard from Roter about new, terrifying events that showed how much effort the Germans were making to get rid of the Jews. Roter told them that transports of Jews had been leaving Bielsko in sealed freight cars, the kind usually used to transport cattle—eastward, toward the town of Przemyśl near the Soviet border. The freight cars were unloaded there, and the people tried to cross the river into Soviet territory. Unfortunately, the Soviets didn't want them to enter; while crossing the river, Soviet soldiers shot at them. A transport was leaving that day with people from two seniors' homes and some of the Jewish intelligentsia that still remained in Bielsko. Roter believed that most of the people from the seniors' homes wouldn't even survive the trip and would die in the freight cars.[6]

My father and Manheimer were shocked by this news. Only now did my father understand the meaning of reports he'd heard of trains passing through Trzebinia with sealed cattle cars and thirsty Jews begging for water through small, grated windows.

On the way to see Rüdiger, my father and Manheimer recalled the vow they'd made earlier—that in no case, even at the cost of their own lives, would they agree to help the Germans send people to their deaths. Both now felt convinced they'd been summoned by Rüdiger to discuss the organization of such transports from Oświęcim. As he walked through the gate of the gestapo building, my father bade farewell in his mind to his family, for he was sure he would never see us again.

The gestapo's headquarters were located in Bielsko on the grounds of a former Jewish-owned textiles factory near the railway station. One of the guards reported their presence by telephone and led them upstairs to Rüdiger's office. Behind the desk stood a young, slender man with a pale, severe face and piercing blue eyes. My father handed him the letter from the commander in Oświęcim. They stood motionless, and Rüdiger sat down behind the desk and began to read the letter. Eventually he stopped reading and ordered my father to sit down. Manheimer and Roter remained standing.

Rüdiger finished reading, stood up, put a cigarette in his mouth, and nervously searched for a lighter in his pockets. Roter obligingly handed him a lit match. Rüdiger shoved his hand away and uttered such a string of abusive insults and curses that all three of them were speechless. It was evident to my father that they were dealing with a professional murderer for whom there was no concept of human dignity at all, and that the decision concerning a person's life or death depended merely on his whim.

The minutes dragged on, endlessly. The tension was overwhelming. At last Rüdiger lit his cigarette, sat down again behind the desk, and looked at my father. My father didn't look away. He had the impression that his fate was in the balance. Very calmly, Rüdiger asked him if he had any requests. My father replied that he would like to request the release of two unjustly arrested Jews from Oświęcim, and he said their names. Rüdiger picked up his phone and gave an order to release the two prisoners and put them on a bus heading to Oświęcim.

Then my father asked for the people in the two seniors' homes in Bielsko to be taken to Oświęcim and for the transports of Jews to the eastern border to be halted until the Russians agreed to accept them. Rüdiger agreed, but only on condition that my father accept in Oświęcim the remaining Jews from Bielsko, Katowice, and Cieszyn. After reflecting for a moment, he added that in this case he would be prepared to halt the transports of Jews. My father immediately agreed to accept them and to take responsibility for their accommodation, and Manheimer pledged to register them immediately with the emigration office. Then he handed Rüdiger a report on the progress of registration at the office.

Rüdiger said that his assignment was to rid the entire region of Silesia of Jews. Then he stated that my father had to travel to Berlin with representatives of Oświęcim's Jewish community council and other Jewish communities in Silesia, as a delegation, in order to receive orders concerning the emigration of Jews from the central German authorities in charge of Jewish affairs.[7]

Rüdiger ordered my father to give him a list as soon as possible of the Jewish representatives who would take part in this delegation so that he could arrange travel documents for them. It was agreed that the list would contain representatives of the Jewish communities in Oświęcim, Bielsko, Katowice, and Cieszyn.

After returning to Oświęcim, my father received an order via telephone to appear before the town's commander to give him a report on the conversation with Rüdiger. That very day, Jews began to arrive from Bielsko and move into apartments in Oświęcim. The next day, people from the seniors' homes in Bielsko started arriving. The Jewish community council hurriedly arranged a new seniors' home in the Talmud Torah school. Construction work also began in a building called the Schönkerówka (since it was owned by our family) to turn it into a hospital. This gave many Jews a chance to avoid forced labor for the Germans.

The day soon came when my father had to depart for Berlin. Hofman, Manheimer, and my father left Oświęcim. Hofman lived in Kraków and had been the director of the emigration office there before it closed down, but my father supplied him with documents stating he was a member of the Jewish community council in Oświęcim. He did this at the request of the directors of the Zionist

Council of Kraków, Dr. Chaim Hilfstein and Leon Salpeter, with whom he was in constant contact and from whom he had earlier received approval to open the emigration office in Oświęcim.[8] My father had been friends with Salpeter, a pharmacist in Kraków, for a very long time.

News of the Jewish delegation's departure to Berlin spread quickly through Oświęcim and the nearby towns. Local Jews were utterly confused. On the one hand, although the repressions here had been much lighter than in other towns, the Jews of Oświęcim lived in constant fear that a wave of persecutions could soon reach them, too. On the other hand, the Jewish delegation's trip to Berlin to receive instructions concerning the emigration that was supposed to take place indicated that the Germans had a plan for the Jews, and there was hope that this would save them.

On the day of the departure, a group of sobbing, distraught women descended on my father and other members of the delegation at the Oświęcim train station and, wailing, asked them to intercede for their arrested husbands. A few days earlier, a dozen or so Jews had been arrested in Chrzanów, a small town thirty kilometers from Oświęcim, under a vague pretext and were now facing execution.

The delegates traveled at night, in darkened train cars, passing through various checkpoints on the way. After arriving in Berlin, they went to the emigration office, which had been located on Meinecke Street for a long time. Hofman had known the director of this office, Dr. Pick, since before the war.[9] This made it easier for them to talk, since German Jews were very cautious when dealing with foreigners. Dr. Pick immediately informed Professor Leo Baeck of the Polish delegation's arrival. Professor Baeck was a great Jewish celebrity and social activist. At that time, he was the director of the Association of Jews in Germany—or, rather, of the remnants of the Jewish communities that still existed there.[10]

On the first day, the delegation stayed in rooms at the Carlton Hotel that had been reserved for them. It was clear this was a result of special permission given by the Germans. The following day they were taken to a private apartment. On the day they arrived, the delegation was invited to one of Berlin's theaters in the evening for a *Kulturbund* gala—a charity event to aid Jews during the winter. To the great astonishment of the visitors from Poland, the male guests arrived in tuxedos, and the ladies were wearing elegant dresses, although without jewelry.

Everyone already knew of the arrival of delegates from Poland and anxiously waited for the official segment of the gala to end so they could speak with them. Very disturbing news had been reaching Berlin from the territories annexed by the Germans. Many of the people attending the gala had relatives who had been transported to Poland via Zbąszyń in 1938; now they were very concerned about their fate.[11]

The members of the delegation, including my father, didn't withhold any information and told the whole truth, even though they'd been warned earlier to be careful, since among the guests attending this gala there could be people who collaborated with the gestapo. The words spoken by the delegation from Poland made a deep impression on the listeners.

The next day, before noon, there was a special meeting of the Alliance of Jews in Germany, led by Professor Baeck. At this meeting, my father presented a report on the situation of Jews in Silesia and asked for swift aid in the matter of emigration as well as financial support for the Jewish communities there.

The members of the alliance promised to satisfy these requests to whatever extent possible. They said they had large funds blocked in banks. They could, in fact, use these funds, but only after receiving permission from the Reichssicherheitshauptamt (the Reich Main Security Office), the director of which was a high-ranking SS officer named Eichmann.[12] They promised to submit a request promptly for some funds. The delegation was also told that this office granted permission for Jews to leave Germany, as long as there were no objections against them.

My father told the gathered people about the order to open an emigration office and the transport of Silesian Jews to Oświęcim, where they were supposed to await emigration. He also said he was in contact with the HIAS organization, which was attempting through various means to smuggle Jews to Palestine. The members of the alliance told my father that in two days a delegation of Jews was scheduled to arrive from Istanbul, and this matter would be discussed with them.

During this meeting, my father learned that there were already over twenty thousand Jews in camps established in Varna and Sulina, and not a single country was willing to open its borders to them. Huge efforts had already been made, but nobody would accept them. Nor was it possible to find ships that were willing to disregard England's ban and transport Jews to Palestine.

It was hoped, however, that due to the drastic deterioration of the situation for Jews in Poland and the danger threatening them, the English would give permission to the representatives of the Alliance of Jews in Istanbul to transport a certain number of Jews to Palestine. Members of the delegation found out that the Germans wouldn't oppose this, for their aim was to get rid of all Jews at any cost. Unfortunately, Jewish people did not receive any help from anyone in the world. All doors were closed to them.

After this meeting, Professor Baeck invited my father to have dinner with him, and the other members of the delegation went sightseeing in the city. A well-known Jewish activist in Poland named Dr. Tohn, an acquaintance of my father's, turned out to be a close friend of Professor Baeck's. My father had painted several portraits of Dr. Tohn, and while painting him they had come to know each other very well. This connection clearly had a strong influence on Professor Baeck, for he had a very friendly attitude toward my father.

First he asked my father if he knew anyone from Sosnowiec by the name of Moniek Merin.[13] Sosnowiec was close to Oświęcim, but my father didn't know the name. Professor Baeck warned him about this person because reports had been reaching Jewish communities that he was a trusted confidant of Himmler and Eichmann. He also apparently had a letter from them stating that all German authorities had to follow his orders. A Jew possessing such a document had great power over other Jews. Merin's office was situated in the gestapo headquarters in Katowice, which was, in the case of a Jew, completely extraordinary. Apparently, the Germans were involving Merin in some significant plans. My father said he would watch out for this man.

Then Professor Baeck told my father about the situation of Jews in Germany. They no longer worked in their professions, nor did they conduct any business. There were still a few petty merchants, but the rest were people in seniors' homes or hospitals who had already, long ago, lost hope of returning to their normal lives. There were hardly any young people left. Everyone was waiting for certificates and visas so they could emigrate from Germany. Professor Baeck believed that those who wouldn't be able to emigrate would die in concentration camps or from starvation. The Germans called this "a natural solution to the Jewish problem."

Then he began to blame Jews and their leaders throughout the world—for the fact that they weren't doing anything to aid their brothers and sisters under Hitler's rule. The Association of Jews in Germany had sent desperate appeals many times to various Jewish leaders, through Rabbi Ehrenpreis in Stockholm, but no answer had come from anywhere.[14] There was a conspiracy of silence. Nobody did anything, and nobody wanted to know anything. Western countries had closed off all escape routes—they had no intention of helping.

Considering the merciless behavior of the Germans, it was obvious that a physical annihilation was awaiting the Jews. Professor Baeck believed that the United States could save Jews by opening its borders to them and also by exerting pressure not only on the Germans to allow Jews to emigrate but, above all, on Western nations to accept them.

The professor stated that the visit from the Polish delegation was of great importance because it would allow them to provide the delegation from Istanbul with a factual picture of the situation of Jews in Poland, and perhaps they would now be able to convince the English to change their stance. At the same time, he expressed concern that it would soon be winter and the Danube River would freeze over, which meant that the last escape route would be closed off.

Professor Baeck concluded with these words: "If the West doesn't help us, the Jews will have all that is left in us squeezed out, like a lemon, and will be deprived of all means of life, and then will be tossed away and burned like a used-up lemon peel."

There were times later when, remembering these prophetic words spoken by Professor Baeck, my father bowed his head to him in admiration of his wisdom and his awareness of what was awaiting the Jews.

Next, my father traveled to Pal-Amt.[15] This building's cellar held the camouflaged headquarters of an underground Jewish organization called Irgun Zvai Leumi that arranged illegal emigration to Palestine.[16] He found out there that it was possible to obtain citizenship of various South American countries, but only through ownership of land. There was a travel agency in Berlin through which it was possible to buy parcels of land in South America, and they would also arrange passports. This opportunity required, however, large sums of money, and was thus impossible for most Polish Jews, who didn't possess such funds.

It was very difficult for Jewish people to obtain normal entrance visas to Western states. Embassies required a "certificate of morality" to be attached to visa applications. The German authorities, however, were willing to issue such certificates only when an entrance visa to a specific country had already been granted and the visa was attached to the application for the certificate. The embassies of Western countries and the German authorities were conducting a bureaucratic game, playing with Jews whose lives meant nothing to anyone. The cynicism in these proceedings was an integral element of the crime that was being committed against the Jews.

While the delegation visited Pal-Amt, they learned that the sole emigration possibility remaining for Polish Jews was the route through Varna and Sulina. The following day an order came for the delegation from Poland to appear immediately in the Reich Main Security Office and report to the director of the Bureau of Jewish Affairs, Adolf Eichmann. After waiting half an hour in the lobby, they were led into an elegant office where an officer in an SS uniform with a pale face and his mouth set in a slight grimace sat behind a desk. In a soft, quiet voice he asked each of the visitors to present himself, after which he ordered them to sit down and declared that all matters concerning Jews were controlled by the Reich Main Security Office. Then he ordered them to give a report on the organization and operations of the emigration office in Oświęcim, which was supposed to be facilitating the emigration of Jews from Silesia.

My father and one of the other members of the delegation presented him with a report that showed that Silesian Jews were ready to emigrate. Eichmann listened attentively and didn't ask any questions. After this brief report, he stood up, and all the members of the delegation stood up, as well.

My father, who was standing directly in front of Eichmann, said, "I have a request."

"What request?" asked Eichmann.

"We ask for your benevolence and request the release of the Jews who were arrested in Chrzanów, near Oświęcim."

Eichmann made a note of this and said, "The request will be considered."

The meeting came to an end.

The following day, the representative of Berlin's Jewish community council led the delegation around the Jewish districts of Berlin. They visited an enormous, excellently equipped hospital and a pleasant seniors' home in which the residents had private rooms furnished with belongings brought from their own apartments. There were enormous libraries and modern dining rooms. The old people living in this home behaved normally without showing any fear or anxiety. It was quiet throughout the building and very peaceful. Sitting in comfortable armchairs, people were reading books or playing chess. It was clear they were living in an illusory world, not realizing it had been created by German propaganda.

Not far from this seniors' home was a huge building that housed the offices of the Jewish community council of Berlin. Entering the building, one had the impression it was the administrative center of a city with millions of inhabitants. Dozens of office workers were hurrying down long corridors with folders and documents in their hands. Everyone had serious, focused expressions on their faces and seemed to be very busy. Seeing that the delegation members were surprised by this, it was explained to them that creating an impression of extreme activity was necessary in order to ensure work for Jews here, for it was their only way to make a living.

In a large, very tidy office, the members of the delegation were welcomed by Dr. Stahl, the chairman of the Jewish community council in Berlin.[17] He was visibly pleased by the positive impressions the Jewish community's institutions had made on the delegation from Poland, and he pledged to supply medical equipment and medicine as soon as he received permission to do so.

In the evening, after they'd returned to the apartment where they were staying, the members of the delegation were informed that the German authorities refused to release funds or to transfer medical equipment and medicine. The delegation was ordered to return immediately to Poland, so they left that very night.

Jewish people had only one way of ensuring safety for themselves—emigration. The delegates still held hope that perhaps the people who were coming from Istanbul, after receiving a report on the situation of Jews in Poland, would smuggle the report to the West and that it would influence public opinion. My father submitted such a report, containing a precise description of the Germans' treatment of Jews, to the Alliance of Jews in Berlin. There was a delusional belief that our brothers in other countries would force their governments to open their borders to us.

At the Katowice train station, while waiting for a train to Oświęcim, members of the delegation met a Jew who told them some horrible news: the Great Synagogue in Oświęcim had been burned to the ground. This terrible deed had been carried out by a special division of the gestapo that had appeared in the town, closed off the streets around the synagogue so nobody would be able to put out the fire, and then, after pouring gasoline on it, set this beautiful building on fire.

The town became overwhelmed by profound mourning and fear. Jews were shocked and heartbroken. Everyone felt they had lost something very special and precious to them, something that had been the core of their lives up until that time. This was the reality to which the delegation returned, with my father leading them as the head of Oświęcim's Jewish community. After arriving at the spot where the synagogue had been, they discovered the Jewish cemetery had also been devastated by the Germans—many tombstones had been smashed or knocked down. One of Oświęcim's rabbis stated at that time, "It's clear to me that with this act, the Nazis have sealed their fate."

A few days later, the synagogue's shamas (the rabbi's assistant in liturgical and organizational matters) died. His heart hadn't been able to bear the loss of the synagogue. During his funeral, homage was paid to the dead man as well as to the Great Synagogue. People felt as if they were attending their own funerals and gazing into their own graves. Jachcel, a gabbai (caretaker) of the Great Synagogue, gave a speech at the grave. He tried to comfort everyone and lift their spirits. He said they would build a new synagogue that would be even lovelier than the one the Germans had burned. If not us, then our sons would build it. If not in Oświęcim, then in Jerusalem. We would build more beautiful synagogues there and beautiful people would serve in them as shamas, like the man who had just left us. He had completed his duty and God had called him.

The cemetery was completely silent; not even any sobbing could be heard. The words of the last caretaker of the Great Synagogue, Jachcel, went straight to heaven. They were prophetic words from a person who, facing the majesty of death, could see the future.

My father felt so devastated by the burning of the Great Synagogue that it was difficult for him to sit in his office and concentrate on his work. His despondent state worsened; he felt himself growing weaker and decided to submit his resignation since he felt he was no longer capable of fulfilling his role. He confided in Jachcel, who was also a member of the Jewish community council. Jachcel was angry at my father and told him his resignation was out of the question. He convinced him that now was precisely the time when he should demonstrate strength of spirit. It was no time for weakness; a great deal depended on my father's actions.

That day, several women came to the Jewish community council from Chrzanów and joyfully informed my father that their arrested husbands had been released from prison on the same day that the delegation had returned from Berlin. This good news reassured my father. He began to work intensively again. An increasing number of people were becoming dependent on help from the Jewish community council in Oświęcim.

At a special meeting of the council, my father gave a precise and very sad report on the delegation's visit to Berlin. During his speech, my father's deputy, Abraham Gross, fainted. Everyone understood that the only hope was for someone far away, in a foreign country, to take pity on them.

Soon afterward, my father was summoned by the town's mayor, who informed him that he'd received an order from the gestapo in Bielsko to fill the empty barracks in Zasole, on the other side of the Soła River, with Jewish people. It was from these barracks that the world's greatest nightmare would arise: the Auschwitz concentration camp.[18]

The mayor of Oświęcim at that time was German—a former baker from Silesia. My father suspected he wanted to create a ghetto in our town, and he stubbornly opposed it. The mayor began to shout and threaten him, but my father told him he wouldn't carry out this order. He was aware of the danger to which he was exposing himself, but he hoped the mayor's command had resulted from his own initiative. Up until that time, all orders from the gestapo concerning Jewish matters were sent to the town's commander. For this reason, my father went directly to him.

He presented the town's commander with the mayor's demand and declared that if the mayor continued to expect him to carry out this order, he would resign as the president of the Jewish community council. The commander immediately phoned the mayor and told him severely that as a member of the party he should obey the party's commands, and not get mixed up in Jewish matters.

That day my father decided to disobey the German order concerning forced labor and told people to stay home. Groups of Jews went to work every day, primarily cleaning the town. There was also a group that helped the Polish police in various types of physical and organizational work. This group didn't go to work that day, either. When the police asked why these people hadn't shown up for work, my father answered that the Nuremberg Laws prohibited Jews from working alongside pure Aryans. The astonished chief of police summoned my father to him and demanded an explanation. Instead, my father informed him that if he continued to demand that Jews work for him, he would send a complaint to the gestapo. And the police chief withdrew his demand!

The next step taken by the Germans against the Jews was an order to wear the Star of David on our arms. My father didn't hurry to carry out this order, either. Some members of the Jewish community council thought he was attempting to commit suicide with this behavior. Others approved of what he was doing because it was important for the Germans to know they could encounter resistance from Jewish people. At the next meeting of the Jewish community council, all members unanimously supported my father, even the skeptical ones. Everyone was prepared for the worst, however.

Not long afterward, my father received a phone call from Rüdiger. He asked my father why the Jewish community council had stopped sending people to work. My father answered that he needed these people to build a seniors' home and hospital. If he had to send people to carry out other work, the transports of people from Silesia to Oświęcim would have to be halted. Hearing this, Rüdiger told my father to make people work wherever the Jewish community council needed them the most. Thus, Jews stopped doing forced labor for a short time; they worked where the Jewish community council told them to work.

It was clear to everyone that this state couldn't last long. They knew that if emigration didn't begin soon, and if they couldn't find a country that agreed to accept Jewish people, they would be faced with catastrophe. Hardly anyone was aware of how serious the threat was, however. An increasing number of Jewish people were coming to Oświęcim, and it was becoming more difficult to find accommodation for them. Everyone was waiting for help.

Major von Greif, the highest-ranking German officer in Oświęcim at that time, lived in the villa of Dr. Druks, a Jewish lawyer. One day my father was summoned to him. Von Greif received him in his office. He sat behind his desk and invited my father to sit across from him. Then he paused for a moment and looked him straight in the eyes. My father felt he was about to hear something very important. Major von Greif stated that he and his unit were leaving the town and that someone else would be taking his place. Then he took a small piece of paper with something typewritten on it from a drawer in his desk and handed it to my father.

"You need to keep this document with you at all times," he said.

The document stated that my father had saved a German officer—the pilot. There was a stamp on it and Greif's signature. Then this proud German officer stood up and shook my father's hand, thanking him for saving the pilot. They left the room together, and Major von Greif led my astonished father to the door of the villa and then even farther, all the way to the garden gate. This gesture of kindness was something very rare at that time.

Opening the garden gate, von Greif remembered something and asked my father to return to his office with him. There, in a quiet voice, he told him to be wary of a certain Moniek Merin from Sosnowiec and his superior, a lieutenant named Dreier from the gestapo in Katowice. Von Greif stressed that he was telling my father this in the greatest secrecy and trust. This was the second time my father had received a warning about this person. He decided to find out who Moniek Merin was.

Nobody in the Jewish community council knew this name, which wasn't unusual since there wasn't any contact between the Oświęcim and Sosnowiec Jewish communities. Jews were unable to move freely from town to town; it was necessary to have special permits. Several days later, a Jewish man came to my father from Katowice. He told him who Moniek Merin was.

Right after the invasion of Sosnowiec, the Germans began to catch young Jews for forced labor. They turned one of them, Moniek Merin, into a *Gruppenführer* (a brigadier). He was a married man from a good family, but a careerist. At the beginning of the German occupation, there was still a normally functioning Jewish community council in Sosnowiec consisting of important and respectable citizens. Merin was willing to gratify German officers' and soldiers' needs of all kinds. It wasn't surprising that he quickly gained their trust.

Merin informed the Jewish community council of the Germans' constant demands. The Jewish community council tried to satisfy the demands, but they were becoming increasingly difficult and were eventually impossible to carry out. At that point Merin started inciting the Germans against the Jewish community. In contrast to Oświęcim, which had been under the direct authority of the Wehrmacht until that time, the Jews of Sosnowiec, since the very beginning of the German occupation, had found themselves under the authority of the gestapo in Katowice, which was increasing its antisemitic persecutions. The gestapo agents were very dangerous.

Merin, taking advantage of the situation and scheming on all sides, strengthened his power with the Germans' active support. Lieutenant Dreier from the gestapo in Katowice soon appeared in Sosnowiec, terminated the town's Jewish community council, and appointed Moniek Merin as *Judenältester*.[19] In this role, he was expected to select, at his own discretion, what was called in German a *Judenrat* (a Jewish council) and to serve as its leader.

For the *Judenrat*, Merin selected some simpletons from the town who would be completely submissive to him, and he put members of the intelligentsia to work for him as clerks. Everyone quickly became aware of who Merin was. At the gestapo's orders, he also organized *Judenrats* in Zawiercie and other towns near Sosnowiec. All the original Jewish community councils in these towns, consisting of members that had been selected by the Jewish residents, were dissolved.

After being granted absolute power in Sosnowiec, Merin ruled with an iron fist. A taxation system that he created, in the form of what he called "contributions," functioned very effectively. Merin himself established how much each person was obligated to pay; he demanded astronomical sums from the rich and well-known Jews of the town. There were cases when people refused to pay. They were taken to a camp close to the town and thrown into dark, cramped cells. They were beaten and tortured by the gestapo every few hours, and after a short time they agreed to hand over all their property.

It was clear to my father that Merin would soon visit Oświęcim and transform the Jewish community council into a *Judenrat*. He knew he would then face mortal danger, and he decided to prepare himself for the worst. He told my mother that if he was arrested, she should try to go to Kraków with us and stay with my grandfather Józef.

Meanwhile, an increasing number of Jews were coming to Oświęcim from surrounding towns. They had nowhere to live and nothing to eat. It was extremely difficult for the Jewish community council to find lodgings for them. Public kitchens were established, where everyone donated what they could, but poverty was rampant. They wrote requests, distributed petitions, and begged for help, but no help came. The Jews of Oświęcim, like all the Jews of Poland, were utterly alone and abandoned to their fate.

There's no doubt the Germans were anticipating an opportunity for Jewish people to emigrate, since otherwise they wouldn't have ordered the establishment of the emigration office in Oświęcim. Nor would they have ordered my father and the delegation to travel to Berlin. After they returned from Berlin, hope was renewed that the United States and England, along with other nations, would change their stance toward the Jews and would open their borders to us.

Jews have always lived with hope in their hearts, and perhaps this is what has enabled them to survive for centuries. Even when finding themselves at the edge of an abyss, they've always kept hope alive. This time, however, despite prayers, cries, and entreaties to the entire world for help—their hope failed them. This is why, with a weeping heart, I'll repeat this terrible sentence: *the Jews of Poland were alone.*

The living should still be reminded of this hope, on behalf of those who died. Their hope, however, eventually became an accusation.

—⁂—

The situation in Oświęcim continued to worsen. After von Greif's unit left the town, the German pilot who had lived with us soon bade farewell to us, as well; he went to Linz on holiday, and we never saw him again. Another German officer took his place in our villa. He allowed us to live in my father's painting studio, which was on the second floor and had a separate entrance.

A German *Arbeitsamt* (employment office) was set up in my grandfather's villa. It sent young Polish men, mostly farmers from surrounding villages, to Germany to perform forced labor. Those who refused to go were beaten until they signed the agreement. I often woke up in the middle of the night because the loud, animalistic screams of beaten and tortured people could be heard in our villa. My mother calmed me; I still remember the touch of her hand on my forehead.

Changes were also made in the Jewish community council. Some of its members insisted on operating independently because the matter of emigration had come to a standstill. HIAS envoys from Slovakia tried to convince them to at least send the children of people who had signed up for illegal emigration to Slovakia, from where it would be possible to smuggle them down the Danube River. They would travel to Cieszyn and then walk across the border at night.

My father heard about the German army's movements on the Slovakian border and hesitated to make a decision. He felt it was too dangerous, especially when it concerned children. Nevertheless, without his consent but with the consent of the children's parents, such a transport was organized and several dozen children left under the care of HIAS envoys. Unfortunately, the entire group was caught on the border by the Germans and sent back to Oświęcim with a military escort. The children's parents were arrested in Oświęcim.

The interrogations lasted for many days and nights. In this group there were boys between the ages of fourteen and sixteen years old, employed by the Jewish community council, who testified that my father hadn't known anything about the transport. These testimonies saved my father, who was intervening everywhere and attempting to convince the Germans that it had just been a childish prank. Finally, the children and their parents were set free.

A few weeks earlier, Biberstein, the chairman of the *Judenrat* in Kraków, phoned my father to tell him that a famous rabbi from Góra Kalwaria, Gerer Rebbe, would be traveling through Oświęcim by train in one hour with his family—on the way to Palestine.[20] Biberstein asked my father to provide them with food and warm drinks at the train station.

Rabbi Abraham Mordechai Alter, known as Gerer Rebbe, was considered by many Hassids to be a miracle worker. He had been bought from the Germans by rich foreign Jews. Hearing that he was going to travel through Kraków, hundreds of people gathered at the train station so they could see him and touch his hands. But the Germans didn't allow anyone to approach the train cars.

My father hurriedly gathered several members of the Jewish community council—Aron Silbiger, Abraham Jachcel, Michael Sander, Abraham Gross, and Itzhak Huterer—and they all headed to the train station with bread and thermoses of hot tea. Soon the train pulled up to the platform. The rabbi was in a separate second-class train car with his family and a doctor. The car was guarded by gestapo agents who allowed my father and his colleagues to get close enough to hand the food through the window.

Because the train's stop was very short, everything happened quickly. Gerer Rebbe was seventy-three years old at that time. He was a small, thin man with gray hair and a very keen, intense gaze. He stood at the window with his hand raised and bade farewell to the Jews. Then he looked at my father and signaled to him to come closer. With visible effort he leaned out the window and took my father's hands in both of his. For a moment he held them motionlessly; then he said, as if he were blessing my father: "I wish for you, your wife, and your children to live long lives and to survive this war."

The train started moving, and for a while the rabbi's hand was still visible, waving out the window. All members of the Jewish community council watched longingly as the train carried Gerer Rebbe to freedom.

On the way home, Abraham Gross expressed surprise that the rabbi had bade farewell to everyone but hadn't blessed anyone except my father. My father also wondered why the rabbi had said "I wish for you, your wife, and your children to live long lives" and not "for you and your family to live long lives," which would have been more natural.

Everyone who bade farewell to Gerer Rebbe at the station died in the Holocaust except my father. Nearly all of my father's large family perished, except for his wife and children. Furthermore, during this terrible war, despite what was happening all around us, never did the certainty leave us that we would survive. Throughout the entire war, I had the feeling that some higher power was interested in my survival and was guiding everything. My father was convinced that with this blessing, Gerer Rebbe interceded with God to save us.

Not long after this, something strange and amazing happened to me. I went to the Soła River every day and became friends with a mentally disabled boy who was slightly older than I was. He was about eleven years old, and his name was Aleks, but everyone called him "Aleks the Stork." He had acquired this nickname because whenever he was given a small coin and told to do "the stork," he would stand on one leg, bend his arms as if they were wings, stick his lips out as if he had a beak, and emit a squawk, like the sound of a stork.

Everyone laughed, including Aleks the Stork, although his smile seemed to me more like a sad grimace. When he was given a larger sum of money, he would dance in that position. He made me feel very sad, for his mental disability reminded me of the physical disability of my dead brother, Musiu.

Aleks would sit on the bank of the Soła River for hours, and even sometimes for days on end. He would gaze at the sky and watch the birds. This was his main activity. He rarely spoke, and when he did, it was only disjointed, incomprehensible words or sentences.

Our friendship was based on me bringing him two pieces of buttered bread every morning. He let me sit next to him, and he would put his arm around me. I felt that he was my only true friend. I didn't have any other friends, and I desperately needed some. Aleks was always hungry, so sometimes I also brought him dinner, though we didn't have much to spare.

I would sit with Aleks on the bank of the Soła and watch the birds for hours. I knew it wasn't possible to talk with him, so I kept silent, like him.

One day Aleks suddenly turned to me, pointed at the other side of the river, and said, in a completely normal voice, "There, in Zasole, the Germans are going to build chimneys and burn all the children of Abraham."

I jumped up and stared at him in fear and amazement. I didn't understand what his prophecy meant, but I felt it was something very important. He pulled me closer to him and said, "You have nothing to fear."

"How do you know?" I asked anxiously.

"The birds ... the birds told me about it," was his answer. He put his arm around me even more tightly, as if he wished to protect me from some invisible danger.

We sat silently together for a while, and then Aleks added, while looking at the sky, "They told me there'll be a terrible stench here, and they'll have to leave me."

His voice and face were full of sadness. I wanted to ask him more about this, but his eyes once again clouded over, and he lost contact with the world. We sat in silence for a while longer, and I felt he was embracing me with even more tenderness.

This conversation took place in the winter of 1939–1940. Aleks predicted what would happen several years later and pointed precisely to the spot where it would happen.

The order to build the Auschwitz camp was given by Himmler on April 27, 1940. The construction of the camp began soon afterward, when we were no longer in Oświęcim. The camp was built in an area called Zasole. The first prisoners arrived there in June 1940. They were Polish people—political prisoners. In March 1941, construction began on the second part of the camp, called Birkenau, which was much larger. We called this place Brzezinka; it was also situated in Zasole. This was the precise spot to which Aleks had pointed. It became the main location of the annihilation of the Jewish population.

Oświęcim, my hometown, became famous not for being where the emigration of Jews began, but because it's where a new kind of evil was created: the murder of people on an industrial scale. At the end of January 1940, what my father had feared so deeply finally happened: a Volkswagen stopped in front of the Jewish community council's building and a short, thin, elegantly dressed thirty-year-old man stepped out of it, accompanied by a young, blonde woman. It was Moniek Merin and his secretary. The pair marched into the building, and Merin asked to be led to my father's office. After a brief greeting and introduction, he asked my father to tell him about his visit to the offices of the Association of German Jews and Pal-Amt in Berlin. My father gave him several casual answers without going into detail.

Then Merin showed great interest in how the Jewish community council in Oświęcim supported itself and how it had managed to protect Jewish shops from the mandatory seizures. My father immediately had the sensation that he was speaking with a person who was very unkind, cunning, and insincere—and also dangerous. He could tell that Merin was couching reprehensible intentions in pleasant words.

After this conversation, Merin asked my father to go with him to Sosnowiec because he wanted to show him how he had organized the Central Office of the

Jewish Councils of Elders in Upper Silesia. The official German name of this office was Zentrale der Jüdischen Ältestenräte in Oberschlesien.[21]

On the way to Sosnowiec, Merin took a document out of his wallet—the same document Professor Leo Baeck had told my father about in Berlin—and showed it to my father proudly. The document stated: "Israel Moniek Merin is acting on my behalf. All representatives of German authority must obey his orders as if they were expressed by me personally. In matters requiring clarification, it is necessary to contact me directly.—Heinrich Himmler." This document contained a photograph of Merin. It was undoubtedly one of the strangest German documents issued during World War II.

Merin, obviously relishing my father's amazement and wishing to increase it, told him that his office was located in the gestapo building in Katowice, and his superior was Eichmann in Berlin.

After arriving in Sosnowiec, my father noticed that Merin had a massive number of unsavory assistants of various kinds who, judging by their appearance and behavior, belonged to the lowest strata of the local Jewish community. His bodyguards were utterly devoted to him and ready to obey every order he gave. Merin also had a newly organized Jewish police force at his disposal. They wore dark-blue caps with red bands. Each had a tin Star of David on his chest and an armband with *Ordnungsdienst* (Jewish police force) written on it. Merin told my father that soon they would receive uniforms. Merin himself wore a decorative label on his clothes that said *Judenältester*.

Merin led my father around various offices, explaining their functions to him. He didn't attempt to hide his pride at his high-ranking position. He explained how the central office worked. All Jews had to pay the taxes he imposed on them. My father asked if people were paying the amounts he demanded. Merin answered that it was becoming more difficult to collect the taxes, especially since all Jewish shops, along with their goods, had been confiscated by the Germans. People clearly had no more money. For this reason, Merin and his people were now imposing a so-called contribution on all Jewish communities that were under his authority—in other words, a collective payment from the entire community. My father asked what happened when a Jewish community was unable to pay the contribution demanded from it, and Merin answered that in such a case everyone would be arrested and sent to a labor camp.

My father's questions were becoming increasingly unpleasant for Merin, and finally he stopped talking about financial matters. He led my father into a large room and introduced him to a delegation of youths from a labor camp in Środula, one of the districts of Sosnowiec. They were young people who, before the war, had planned to emigrate to Palestine and had gathered at a preparatory camp called a *Hakhshara*.[22] The outbreak of the war had shattered their plans. Now, hearing that my father was in Sosnowiec, they sent a delegation to meet with him to find out if it was still possible to emigrate to Palestine.

The news of the opening of the emigration office in Oświęcim, and of my father's trip to Berlin concerning the matter of emigration, had spread widely, and now these young people viewed my father as their last hope.

My father told them that, for the time being, legal emigration was impossible, but he was waiting for further news in this matter. Then he told them there existed a possibility to emigrate illegally. Hearing this, Merin became increasingly uneasy. My father could sense that the boys wished to talk with him privately. One requested this of Merin, but he stubbornly refused, took my father's arm, and led him out of the room, telling him they needed to hurry to dinner.

Merin and his people had a special, private restaurant in which delicious Jewish dishes were served. All the meals were huge and exquisitely prepared, served by elegantly dressed waiters. During this feast, which took place in the evening, several agitated people entered the room. They approached Merin and whispered something in his ear. Merin and several other members of the Jewish council quickly stood up and left the room.

My father followed them out because he was curious about what was happening. On the street he saw an incredible sight. German soldiers in black SS uniforms were standing on both sides of the street, forming a double row. Each was holding a flaming torch. Other soldiers were walking between them, leading a group of heavily beaten and bloodied people. The whole scene looked as if it were taking place in medieval times.

Merin called two soldiers over to him and started talking to them. My father found out that Merin's central office had levied a contribution of 30,000 German marks on the Jewish community council in Zawiercie, and since it was unable to pay that much money, all its members had been arrested. These were the beaten and abused people my father saw in the street—including elderly men who were barely able to move and were being carried by some of the others.

Merin began haggling with these people, and after a while he finally agreed to accept a lower sum after they promised that the community in Zawiercie would do everything possible to eventually pay the missing amount. Merin displayed no human feeling at the sight of his victims. His indifference to suffering had something bestial in it. My father was under the impression that Merin had no awareness at all that he was dealing with living people.

Merin then indicated to the German SS commander to approach him. This officer briskly pushed his way through his soldiers and the people gathered in the street and stood at attention in front of Merin. Merin ordered him to release the beaten people. The soldiers extinguished the torches and retreated. My father wanted to help the wounded people, but Merin insisted that he return to the restaurant. Seeing my father continue to stand in one spot, he once again took him by the arm and forcefully pulled him inside. Despite the shock my father had experienced and the repugnance he felt toward Merin, he managed to get a grip on himself and agreed to take his place again in the restaurant, since he realized it could be dangerous for him to refuse.

He looked around, not believing his eyes. There was a joyful atmosphere in the room as if a great victory had been won. Waiters brought increasingly lavish meals, including various kinds of meat that most Jews hadn't seen for many months. My father didn't touch the food, and after a short time told Merin he had to go home. Merin summoned his chauffeur and told him to drive my father to Oświęcim.

Several weeks later, my father received a letter from Merin's central office in Sosnowiec. It informed him that following an order from Lieutenant Dreier of the gestapo in Katowice, he must call a meeting in Oświęcim of representatives of Jewish communities in order to consult with them on the emigration of Jews and organizational problems connected to it. The following day, my father received a similar letter from Rüdiger of the gestapo in Bielsko.

My father sent out invitations to many Jewish community councils in Poland, including in Warsaw and Łódź. Representatives of Jewish communities in Silesia were the only ones who came to the meeting. The others didn't receive permission for the trip from the local German authorities.

Merin appeared at this meeting and presented a letter from the gestapo in Katowice, which declared that he had now been appointed leader of all *Judenrats* in Silesia. All Jewish community councils, including the one in Oświęcim, had to become *Judenrats* and would be subordinate to Merin's central office in Sosnowiec. A great commotion broke out in the room because this meant the communities would lose their independence and become impassive tools in the hands of Merin and his men.

Wishing to gain control over the situation, my father immediately called a meeting in a different room, without Merin, so he could consult with the representatives of the Jewish community councils on how they should proceed. After this consultation, my father and the other men declared to Merin that they refused to obey his order to submit to the central office in Sosnowiec since they weren't representatives of *Judenrats* but of religious communities. Merin was shocked that the delegates dared to oppose such clear orders from the gestapo. Unable to control his outrage, he left the room.

It was clear the Germans would now dissolve all the Jewish community councils and form *Judenrats* in their place, which would be led by people recommended by Merin. The Jewish community council representatives took into account that they might face personal repressions. None who were present at the meeting were willing, however, to submit to Merin, for this would mean direct or indirect collaboration with the Germans.

On this note the meeting ended, the aim of which was supposed to have been the further discussion of emigration possibilities. From the very beginning it had been clear, however, that emigration would be impossible without help from abroad and willingness to accept Jewish people. No country offered such help, however, and so the community councils' delegates were powerless.

My father sometimes wondered what the Germans' aim had been in calling this meeting. After all, they were aware that no countries had agreed to accept Jews, and that every possible means were being employed to make escape attempts more difficult. The Germans must have had a plan of some kind. Did they perhaps want to gather the community council delegates under the pretext of emigration so that Merin could give them the order to form *Judenrats*? This was doubtful, since Merin could have much more easily, and with a more definite result, summoned the communities' representatives individually to his gestapo office in Katowice and given them the order there. Then he certainly wouldn't have encountered such resistance.

Furthermore, the order to call this meeting, which my father received from the gestapo in Katowice and a day later from the gestapo in Bielsko, must have been issued somewhere else—in Berlin, to which both institutions were subordinate. It was clear that something important was at stake, and Merin's order to create *Judenrats* was simply a case of him making use of the opportunity rather than the main aim of the gathering.

In any case, my father knew that from then onward, his days as leader of the Jewish community council of Oświęcim were numbered. He decided to endure for as long as possible, however, and not abandon the post of his own volition.

Everyone waited anxiously for events to develop further. A few days later, despite the Jewish community council in Oświęcim not being officially subordinate to Merin, my father received a letter from him that a "contribution" of 30,000 marks was being levied on the Oświęcim Jewish community. Merin demanded that it be paid immediately. A meeting was called, and it was decided to pay the money. Over the next few days, the entire amount was collected and placed in the council's safe.

At the same time, my father sent a telegram and letter to the Berlin office of the Association of Jews in Germany with a request for directions on how he should proceed. And a strange thing happened. Two days later, my father received a telegram from the gestapo in Katowice stating that the contribution had been nullified. Another meeting of the council was called to decide what to do with the money that had been collected. Despite objection from several of the council's members, my father decided to return the money, which was immediately done.

Two weeks later, a person from Dąbrowa named Bernstein appeared at the office of the Jewish community council. He gave my father a letter from the gestapo in Katowice in which Bernstein was named the national chairman of the Jewish community. From the moment the letter was delivered, he was supposed to take over the leadership and begin his duties.

My father immediately called a meeting of the Jewish community council, the minutes of which were recorded; he said there was nothing left for him to do but go home. Along with my father, other members of the council also resigned: Itzhak Huterer, Abraham Jachcel, Baruch Grinbaum, and Abraham Gross. These people knew they were exposing themselves to great danger, but they didn't want to become tools in Merin's hands.

However, the matter didn't end there. Two weeks later my father was summoned to the community council office. Merin was already there as well as several gestapo officers, including Lieutenant Dreier from Katowice and Rüdiger from Bielsko. Dreier approached my father and, in a threatening voice, asked him if he knew what a concentration camp was. My father answered that he did.

Dreier came even closer to my father and shouted in his face: "That's where you belong!"

My father remained silent. Dreier took several nervous steps around the room, after which he asked him, "Since you know what it is, will you retract your earlier decision and agree to serve as the leader of the Oświęcim *Judenrat*?"

My father, who had already prepared himself for the worst, answered, "I don't agree."

The Germans were astonished. Merin's face became flushed, and he nervously wiped the sweat from his forehead. Lieutenant Dreier turned to the window and stood for a moment in silence, as if considering the situation. Then he ordered one of the gestapo officers to arrest my father and take him to the prison in the town hall.

My father found himself alone in a prison cell and—as he told me later—began preparing himself spiritually to leave this world. He didn't have much time for reflection, however, because the cell's door soon opened, and other arrested men were led in: Abraham Jachcel, Itzhak Huterer, Abraham Gross, and Baruch Grinbaum.

A *Judenrat* was established in Oświęcim. Józef Gross was named the *Judenältester*, and his brother-in-law, Lerhaft—who later became the commander of the *Ordnungsdienst* in Sosnowiec—also joined the *Judenrat*.

Two weeks later, all the arrested men, including my father, were released from prison. The day before, my mother had been coming down the stairs in our house with my sister and me when we noticed a slender man in an elegant navy-blue suit and tie entering the front hall. I remember he had dark, smooth hair that was shiny with pomade and combed toward the back of his head. It was Merin, who had come to talk with my mother.

I remember that I was standing on the stairs, and my mother was holding Lusia in her arms. I was nine years old at the time, but I understood every word of this conversation and was very clearly aware that my father was in grave danger—and that we were, too. Every morning I recited the Shema Yisrael prayer. I asked God for nothing bad to happen to my father and for him to be set free from prison. I instinctively felt at that moment that a great deal depended on this person standing in the entrance hall.

Merin told my mother that her husband was a terribly stubborn man who didn't understand that it was necessary to be flexible. Under the conditions that existed then, her husband would normally be dead already. He didn't want, however, anything bad to happen to him, and for this reason he was willing to consider releasing him from prison—but only if my mother promised that my father would leave Oświęcim immediately after his release. My mother entreated him to free my father, pointing to me and Lusia. Merin made a face as if he cared about us somewhat, and even smiled at me. My mother told him that my father would leave Oświęcim, and then the conversation came to an end.

My father returned home, and people visited him all day long to greet him and congratulate him on his release. In the afternoon, my mother was summoned to the *Judenrat*. Merin was waiting there for her. He told her that he knew my father was accepting people into our home. He warned my mother once again that if my father was still in Oświęcim the next day, something very bad would happen to him.

The following day, my father went out through the back gate of our garden and headed through fields and along rural paths to the nearest village. A railway worker he knew put him in an empty freight car of a train heading to Trzebinia, which was located on the border of the *Generalgouvernement*. In Trzebinia there was an agency—founded by my father and people from HIAS—that issued fake travel documents to smuggled people. The next day, with fake German documents, my father crossed the border, got on a *Nur für Deutsche* bus, and went to Kraków. He read a copy of *Das Reich* newspaper the entire trip.[23]

Two days later, my mother, carrying Lusia in her arms, and I left home in the morning and went to a spot where a peasant wagon was waiting for us that had been arranged by Stasia, our former housekeeper. We had decided to travel to Trzebinia separately from my father, since there were frequent inspections on the trains. It was about thirty-five kilometers to Trzebinia, and my mother expected us to arrive there at noon.

Before leaving home, my mother told me several times to behave calmly and not attract attention to myself, even if something unexpected happened, because this could be dangerous for us. When I left the house, I solemnly swore to myself that I would be indifferent to everything. How surprised I was, however, when I saw my friends Aleks the Stork and Tadek waiting for me in front of my house. I stood there, stunned, not knowing what to do. There was no time to think about it, however, for my mother pulled me after her and urged me to hurry.

Aleks the Stork and Tadek stood off to the side and smiled at me. Unable to resist the temptation, I tore myself away from my mother and ran up to them. Aleks threw himself around my neck and embraced me tightly. I could feel that he was crying.

Tadek came up to me and said, "Aleks told me yesterday that you're leaving. I decided to say goodbye. Don't worry about Aleks. I'm going to bring him food now. May God watch over you, and don't forget about us." Tadek was crying, and tears started running down my cheeks, too. My mother stood to the side, surprised, and let me say goodbye to them.

The previous day, when I'd brought Aleks breakfast, I'd told him I wouldn't be able to see him anymore because we were leaving Oświęcim. Aleks had looked at me and nodded his head sadly several times to signal that he understood. Now, walking away with my mother and wiping my tears with the sleeve of my coat, I felt that this was my farewell to the entire town of Oświęcim. I turned around. Aleks the Stork and Tadek were still standing in the same spot and waving goodbye to me. And then Aleks, as if he didn't want me to forget him, struck his stork pose.

The wagon was waiting for us in the previously arranged spot. The driver let me sit next to him and hold the whip, which made me very happy. The blanket wrapped around me smelled like horses. As we traveled, we were covered in blankets and kerchiefs like villagers, and the driver talked to the horse the whole time. I remember that I had an extra pacifier for Lusia in each pocket; without one she cried, and it was impossible to calm her. I was so afraid of losing them that I kept one in my hand at all times.

We switched to a second wagon in a village and soon arrived in Trzebinia. My mother had a real German document stating that she and her children lived in Kraków; she'd received it immediately after we'd returned to Kraków in September 1939. It was clear that with such a document it was possible to cross the border. Standing in a long line in front of the border guards' booth where inspections were carried out, my mother discovered that proof of residence wasn't enough, since several days before there had been a change in the rules. Now it was necessary to have a special pass—it was written in large letters on a board.

I noticed that at some point, my mother became very agitated. I thought it was because the line was moving very slowly and it was difficult for her. She was holding Lusia and had a bag slung over her shoulder. I was carrying my schoolbag, full of things for Lusia. There were still a dozen or so meters between us and the booth where a German soldier, after checking documents, was stamping them and allowing people to cross to the other side. A second German, an officer, was standing in front of the booth, watching people. From time to time, he ordered someone to open a bag or suitcase.

It was primarily Polish people standing in the line—old women and peasants from villages. They were clearly traveling to the city to buy or sell something. Wagons were waiting for them on the other side of the border.

Suddenly my mother, as if she'd lost control of herself, started shouting in German, with a perfect Viennese accent, in the direction of the officer who was standing in front of the booth.

"I'm supposed to stand here in line with all these Poles?"

The German officer, astonished, looked in our direction. My heart froze with fear. The German came closer to my mother and bowed.

"You've made a mistake, madam," he said. Then he smiled and added, "There's a different crossing for us."

He led us to the other side of the street, ordered a barrier to be opened and allowed us to cross. My mother smiled at him and said, "*Danke*," which was probably a mistake, since the German officer, who perhaps was from Austria, became even more obedient and led us to the same *Nur für Deutsche* bus in which, the day before, my father had traveled. My mother didn't have fake identity documents, so it was very dangerous to travel in such a bus. But we boarded it.

The officer approached the bus driver, whom he probably knew. He told him that my mother was from Vienna and asked him to help her if she needed anything. Then he stood at attention and saluted my mother, and she smiled at him again; she prodded me, so I also smiled and waved my hand. I regretted that my friends couldn't see me then.

Later my mother told me she didn't know where her courage had come from. Words had simply escaped from her mouth without any thought. Her own boldness had startled her.

There were several civilians and two soldiers in the bus. The driver started up the engine, and I sighed with relief. But before the bus left, a German gendarme with a tin badge on his chest approached it. He stood in the bus's doorway, on the step near the driver, and glanced inside.

"The same as usual?" he asked the driver.

"The same," answered the driver.

They seemed to know each other, since they smiled at each other and shook hands.

"And who's that woman?" asked the gendarme, pointing at my mother.

"She's from Vienna, Hans's friend," and he motioned with his head toward the officer by the border guards' booth.

"Ah, he's got friends everywhere," the gendarme said with a smile. Then he saluted my mother.

The bus started moving, and my mother began to powder her face, holding her powder puff in front of her. I was impressed she was able to do this while holding a sleeping child in her arms. But I noticed that her hands were shaking.

Less than an hour later, we reached Kraków without any trouble along the way. My mother hired a horse-drawn cab, and we went to her sister's house on Augustiańska Street. My father was waiting for us there.

Thus ended the first period of my life in Oświęcim. And then began a period of increasing danger and struggle for survival.

I must briefly describe the final days of the Jews of Oświęcim. Instead of becoming the first Jewish emigrants from this weary, enslaved country, they became some of the first to be murdered in the concentration camp that was built in their hometown.

My father was the last freely elected leader of the Jewish community council in Oświęcim. After the *Judenrat* was established, the situation of Oświęcim's Jews began to worsen. At first it seemed that everything would remain as it had been before. Shops were even prospering because their Polish superintendents placed signs on them stating that they were owned by German citizens. For this reason, German soldiers didn't dare pillage these shops, nor did they ever leave them without paying for goods.

This didn't last long, however. After a while, all the shops, along with their merchandise, were confiscated and given to German people who were brought from the Reich for this purpose. The Polish superintendents of these shops were fired.

The oppression of Jews increased in frequency and brutality. Young Jews were sent to labor camps in Germany, where they worked in munitions factories in inhumane conditions, were tormented by illness and starvation, and died of exhaustion or were beaten to death. In Oświęcim, people were sentenced to death for any reason at all, no matter how insignificant. The dream of receiving help from abroad had come to an end. Instead of hope, hunger was rampant everywhere, and diseases, particularly typhus and tuberculosis, were spreading rapidly.

The Jews of Oświęcim were in agony.

The Germans decided to prolong this agony. Under Merin's command, the expulsion of Oświęcim's Jews began in April 1941. First they were sent to the ghetto in Chrzanów, and then, after the liquidation of the Chrzanów ghetto, the remaining Jews from Oświęcim were transferred to the ghetto in Sosnowiec.

In January 1943, the Germans began a mass concentration of Jews in the Środula camp in Sosnowiec, which was a sign that they were about to be sent to their deaths. All such mass concentrations of Jewish people ended with them being sent to death camps.

On August 1, 1943, the final liquidation of Jews began in Silesia, including the Jews in Sosnowiec. The camp in Środula was surrounded by SS and SA divisions supported by SS units of Lithuanians and Ukrainians. The nationalities of these murderers were very symbolic—the East and the West had come to an agreement: the Jews needed to be annihilated.[24]

The liquidation of the camp in Środula didn't go easily for them, however. Despite extremely harsh conditions, constant inspections, terror, and beatings, a Jewish combat organization was active on the camp's grounds, the members of which decided to sell their lives at a high cost.[25] They fiercely defended themselves in several buildings that they'd previously fortified. The Germans and their minions suffered losses of both human life and equipment. The Jewish fighters fought to their very last breaths and last rounds of ammunition. Nearly all of them were killed in this imbalanced battle. Some of the last Jewish inhabitants of Oświęcim were among them.

The rest of Oświęcim's Jews were sent to the gas chambers in Auschwitz, in their hometown. The smoke from their burned bodies joined the smoke from their brothers and sisters who had been murdered there earlier.

While I write these words, I feel like I'm standing over a huge, open grave that will never be covered.

I would also like to describe what happened to Merin. After creating the *Judenrat* in Oświęcim, Merin subjugated an increasing number of Jewish communities in Silesia. His central office in Sosnowiec continued to expand, and in the years 1940–1943, it had forty-five Jewish community councils under it that had been transformed into *Judenrats*. These communities numbered, in total, over one hundred thousand people.

Merin ruled with an iron fist. Whoever disagreed with him or presented even the slightest resistance to his orders met a tragic end. Merin was generally detested by Jews, but he was always surrounded by his guards, and it was impossible to do anything to him. Despite this, the Jewish combat organization that was active in Sosnowiec issued a death sentence on him and tried to kill him. The assassination attempt failed. It was followed by repressions, and many people were arrested.

Merin also established an emigration office in Sosnowiec, which took care of distributing certificates and passports that relatives in foreign countries sent to their family members who were trapped in the ghettos of Silesia. Some people in Palestine who had the necessary connections and money pretended to have received permission from English authorities for their Polish relatives to travel to Palestine. A certificate or affidavit (a document guaranteeing the right to travel) was sent to Poland through a neutral country, usually Switzerland. These documents came to Merin's emigration office and, in most cases, after the photograph had been changed, were given to someone else in exchange for a huge sum of money.

From time to time, the Germans registered people possessing such documents and sent them to special camps. They used them as merchandise waiting to be sold, because they were the only people whom someone from abroad was interested in. Those who sent such documents had no contact with the addressee and didn't know what was happening to him or her. The Germans then expected payments for them, but no Western country was interested in buying this merchandise. Why should they pay for something that could previously be obtained for free?

The passports that came to Merin's emigration office in Sosnowiec were either real or false and were bought in Switzerland. They were passports from various South American countries and were sold at a high price.

Merin's star began to fade when the final liquidation of Silesian Jews, planned for August 1, 1943, turned him into a useless, worn-out tool that could be discarded by the Nazis.

At that time, a certificate arrived at Merin's office for a young woman. In his usual way, Merin changed the photograph and sold this certificate to someone else, and the woman was sent to a work camp in the Sudeten Mountains. The woman somehow found out that someone else had received her certificate and managed to inform her relatives living outside Poland.

In the second half of June 1943, a commission from the passport office in Berlin came to the gestapo in Katowice and caused a huge uproar. Merin was summoned to the gestapo. He drove there with his secretary, not expecting anything unpleasant. After arriving at the gestapo's headquarters, he was immediately arrested and escorted by the SS in his own car to the Auschwitz concentration camp.

It was already evening, and news of detested Merin's arrival spread from block to block at lightning speed. One of the groups of men returning from work recognized Merin and attacked him. There was a huge commotion. The German escort started shooting into the air. There was no way for Merin to escape. He was lynched and nearly torn to pieces by the prisoners.

That same day, Merin's closest collaborators and guards were thrown into the camp.

This is apparently how Merin, the "king of the Jews" in Sosnowiec, traitor to the Jewish people, met his end.[26]

NOTES

1. Henryk Hochman (1879–1943) was a member of both the Association of Jewish Painters and Sculptors and the Association of Polish Artists and Designers. He studied at the Academy of Fine Arts in Kraków and in Paris, under the guidance of Auguste Rodin. His sculptures were exhibited in Kraków, Lwów (Lviv), Munich, Vienna, Budapest, and Venice.

2. The German army entered Wieliczka on September 7, 1939, and the first executions took place on September 12. Thirty-two men from wealthy Jewish families were forced to gather in Wieliczka's main square. They were transported from the town and murdered in a forest near the village of Taszyce. The men were buried the following day in the Jewish cemetery in Siercza.

3. See appendix.

4. Józef Manheimer (1891–1943) was a Zionist who was active for many years in his hometown of Oświęcim. He was the founder and leader of the local branch of Poale Zion ("Workers of Zion"—a movement of Marxist-Zionist Jewish workers) in the years 1920–1921, and later he created and led the Hitachdut Zionist Workers' Party (1929, 1932). In September 1939 he joined the Jewish community council. In the years 1940–1941, together with Pinkus Bronner, he ran the department of work and career training, and was responsible for organizing career training courses run by the Jewish community council in Oświęcim. In April 1941, he was forcibly resettled in Sosnowiec along with all the remaining Jews of Oświęcim. In 1943 he was forced into the Sosnowiec ghetto, together with his wife, Janina, and his children: Mela, Dorota, Chaim, and Leon. During the liquidation of the ghettoes in the Zagłębie Dąbrowskie Region they were most likely sent to Auschwitz and killed there.

5. HIAS (Hebrew Immigrant Aid Society) was an international organization that aimed to provide support for Jewish immigrants. It was established in New York in 1909, and branches were opened in Central and Eastern Europe after World War I. During the German occupation in World War II, HIAS operated illegally.

6. Most likely this concerned a group of Jews from Bielsko, Chorzów, Katowice, Lipin, and Świętochłowice (about one thousand people) who were rounded up in Katowice on October 20, 1939, and sent to the town of Nisko, where they were forced, at gunpoint, to cross the border into the USSR. A second group, equally large, was forced to gather soon afterward, on the night of October 27, and were transported to the same spot. A third transport from Sosnowiec (fifteen hundred people) was planned but never carried out.

7. See appendix.

8. Dr. Chaim Hilfstein (1876–1950) was an internist and political activist involved in the Zionist movement. He was the founder and leader of many Jewish organizations and committees (during the interwar period he was a member of the administration committee of the Zionist Organization of Western Małopolska and Silesia and the director of Kraków's emigration office). During the war, he was active in Jewish mutual aid societies in Kraków. In 1944 he was added to the famous list known as "Schindler's List" and ended up in the Gross-Rosen camp in the town of Brněnec, Czech Republic.

Leon (Lejb) Salpeter was a Zionist activist from Kraków. In the 1930s, he was a member of the administration committee of the Zionist Organization of Western Małopolska and Silesia. In 1944 he was also added to the famous list known as "Schindler's List" and ended up in the Gross-Rosen camp in the town of Brněnec, Czech Republic.

9. Dr. Rudolf Pick was the director of the emigration office in Berlin (Palästina-Amt), which was located then at 10 Meineckestrasse.

10. Leo Baeck (1873–1956) was a rabbi, philosopher, and spiritual leader of German Jews under Nazi rule. From autumn 1933 to 1943 he was the chairman of the Association of Jews in Germany, to which all German Jews were forced to belong, according to the Nuremberg Laws, regardless of religion or faith. The association was subordinate to the Reich's Ministry of Homeland Security, and then (from the end of 1939 onward) to the Office of Jewish Affairs at the Reich Main Security Office, which was run by Adolf Eichmann. Baeck was deported to the Theresienstadt concentration camp in 1943, where he survived the war.

11. In the years 1938–1939, there was a transit camp for Jews in the town of Zbąszyń, near the Polish-German border. It was created after the Polish government, witnessing the worsening situation of Jews living in Germany who were Polish citizens, decided to deprive them of their Polish citizenship. This decision was motivated by the fear that these Jewish people might return to Poland. The Polish government issued a decree in September 1938 that obligated Polish citizens with permanent residence outside of its borders to confirm their citizenship. A failure to react to this decree resulted in the loss of Polish citizenship as of November 1, 1938. In turn, the Germans, fearing the consequences of these legal regulations, began the Polenaktion (Polish Action) and deported about seventeen thousand Polish Jews to Poland, six thousand of which were imprisoned in the camp in Zbąszyń. The living conditions in the camp were very poor. The matter

became an international scandal. At the beginning of 1939, the German-Polish negotiations concerning this situation came to an end. The German government allowed some of the deported people to return to Germany, and the Polish authorities agreed to accept some of the people, only if they were able to provide proof that they had family members in Poland who were able to accept them as refugees. The last of the prisoners left the camp before September 1, 1939.

12. In August 1938, Adolf Eichmann organized the Zentralstelle für jüdische Auswanderung (Central Agency for Jewish Emigration) in Vienna, the only bureaucratic office authorized to issue travel permits to Jews from Austria and Czechoslovakia. Because of the experience he gained at that office, from October 1939 onward he led the Reichszentrale für jüdische Auswanderung (Reich Central Office for Jewish Emigration) in Berlin, and in December 1939 he became the director of the Office of Jewish Affairs in the Reich Main Security Office. At first the Office of Jewish Affairs was concerned with emigration, but in later years it became the primary headquarters for realization of the plan known as the Final Solution of the Jewish Question.

13. Mojżesz (Moniek) Merin (1906–1943) was the controversial director of the Central Office of the Jewish Councils of Elders in Upper Silesia. Before the outbreak of World War II, he was involved in the Zionist movement. At the beginning of September 1939, he became the leader of the Jewish community council in Sosnowiec. Over time—due to the zealous manner in which he carried out German orders and his organizational talents—Merin obtained an increasing number of favors from the German authorities. In December 1939, Hans Dreier, the director of the Katowice gestapo's Office for Jewish Affairs, made Merin responsible for carrying out all actions concerning the Jewish population in the Katowice district. He was known for his cruelty and fierceness, particularly toward insubordinate Jewish communities and Jewish activists in the region under his control.

14. Markus (Mordechai) Ehrenpreis (1869–1951) was a literary critic, essayist, philosopher, rabbi, and Zionist. In Lwów (Lviv), where he was born, he attended courses organized by the Mikra Kodesh Association (1883), which was considered the first Zionist association in Galicia. Later he studied in Berlin and at other universities in Germany. During the first Zionist Congress and the congresses that followed, he was one of Theodor Herzl's main advisors. He eventually left the Zionist movement. He served in Dakovo, Croatia, as a rabbi (1896–1900), in Sofia as Chief Rabbi of Bulgaria (1900–1914), and then as Chief Rabbi of Stockholm (1914–1951).

15. Pal-Amt (German: Palästinaamt)—also known as the Palestine Office or the Jewish Agency for Palestine—was a Zionist institution that provided support for Jews emigrating to Palestine. Pal-Amt offices were run and financially supported by Jews living abroad, who also provided information about living conditions in Palestine and distributed certificates issued by British Mandate authorities. Pal-Amt offices operated in most capital cities of Europe. In Poland

they were present in Warsaw and several other cities. After the outbreak of World War II, the Pal-Amt offices in Vienna, Geneva, Munich, and Marseille attempted to evacuate Jews from Europe.

16. Irgun Zvai Leumi (Hebrew for "National Military Organization") was a secret Jewish organization active in Palestine in the years 1937–1948, established by Zionist revisionists who had left another military organization—Haganah ("Defense"). Both organizations were supported by the Polish government in the 1930s and provided with aid that included military training, weapons, and arrangement of illegal emigration to Palestine. In the spring of 1939, the Polish government also organized a secret military training camp in the Carpathian Mountains for twenty-five Irgun Zvai Leumi commanders from Palestine. They organized campaigns that included military and terrorist attacks against the British and Arab populations in Palestine.

17. Heinrich Stahl (1886–1942) was the head of the Jewish community in Berlin in the years 1933–1942. He was deported to the Theresienstadt concentration camp, where he died in November 1942.

18. The decision to create a concentration camp in Oświęcim was issued on April 27, 1940, by Reichsführer-SS Heinrich Himmler, based on a plan presented by Rudolf Höss. The task of establishing the camp was given to Richard Glücks, the concentration camps inspector. The camp was built on the grounds of former artillery barracks on the outskirts of the town. At the beginning of May 1940, at the request of Rudolf Höss, the future commander of the camp, the German mayor of Oświęcim ordered the Jewish community council to supply 250–300 men per day for the construction work on the grounds of the former barracks. The first transport of Polish political prisoners arrived in Auschwitz on June 14, 1940.

19. Translator's note: A *Judenältester* (Elder of the Jews) is a German term for a Jewish man who was appointed by the Nazis as the chairman of a *Judenrat* (a Jewish council created by the Nazis to enforce their policy on a local level).

20. Professor Marek Biberstein, a teacher and social activist, was the first chairman of the *Judenrat* in Kraków after it was created in September 1939. In 1944 he was murdered in the work camp in Płaszów. Abraham Mordechai Alter (1866–1948), Gerer Rebbe, was the fourth *tzaddik* of the Ger dynasty (in Góra Kalwaria). He was one of the founders of the Agudath Israel Orthodox Jewish Party and one of the most influential figures in Jewish life in Europe before the Holocaust. At the beginning of the war, he managed to flee occupied Poland with his family. In 1940, he reached Palestine via Italy.

21. The Central Office of the Jewish Councils of Elders in Upper Silesia (Zentrale der Jüdischen Ältestenräte in Oberschlesien), with headquarters in Sosnowiec, was established in January 1940. Its founder and leader was Mojżesz (Moniek) Merin. The central office was shut down when the ghettoes in Będzin and Sosnowiec were liquidated on August 1, 1943.

22. *Hakhshara* (Hebrew: "building resilience") were training camps of the Zionist movement that prepared young people to leave Poland and settle as pioneers in Palestine and later Israel.

23. The first part of this book is partially based on Leon Schönker's text in *Sefer Oshpitsin: Oświęcim–Auschwitz Memorial Book*, published by Irgun Yotzey Oświęcim (The Association of Former Residents of Oświęcim) in Jerusalem, 1977.

24. At the beginning of October 1942, Jews from Będzin and Sosnowiec began to be resettled in sealed-off areas outside the town centers—Środula, Stary Sosnowiec, Kamionka, and Mała Środula. Środula and Stary Sosnowiec were sealed off on March 15, 1943, and only ten days later, the decision was made to liquidate the ghetto in Stary Sosnowiec and resettle some of the Jews living in it to Środula. In May, the resettlement of Jews from Będzin to Kamionka and Mała Środula was completed. In this way, two huge ghettoes were created right next to each other, where tens of thousands of Jewish people were crowded together. The liquidation of both ghettoes began during the night of July 31, 1943. The liquidation lasted until August 7, during which roughly thirty thousand people were sent to concentration camps, primarily Auschwitz.

25. This was a youth group affiliated with the Zagłębie Jewish combat organization. It fought against the Germans by shelling them from three bunkers that had been prepared in advance. The uprising was defeated, and nearly all the Jews who took part died during the battles. They were primarily members of the Jewish resistance movement recruited from Zionist youth organizations. The organizers of this uprising included the brothers Józef and Bolesław Kożuch from HaNoar HaTzioni (Zionist Youth), Frumka Płotnicka (a Jewish combat organization emissary from the Warsaw ghetto), and Tzvi Brandes, an activist from HaShomer HaTzair (Young Guard) and one of the leaders of the Jewish combat organization in Będzin. A certain number of fighters managed to survive the liquidation of the ghettoes in the bunkers. Some of them—with help from Jews who were already on the "Aryan" side and several Polish families—managed to reach Hungary, Slovakia, and Palestine through an illegal route.

26. Details concerning the final days of Moniek Merin's rule are not completely clear or well documented. It's known that on June 19, 1943, a message arrived at the central office in Sosnowiec that about a dozen members of the HaNoar HaTzioni Zionist youth organization had obtained documents giving them the status of foreigners and allowing them to travel abroad. The trip never happened, however. That same day, the members of the Zionist youth organization and the directors of the central office (including Merin) were summoned to the police headquarters in Sosnowiec, and from there they were all unexpectedly transported to Auschwitz.

KRAKÓW

I HAD LEFT KRAKÓW SEVERAL years earlier, and it seemed to me like the most beautiful city in the world, inhabited solely by good-hearted people with kind intentions. I remember strangers often patting me on the head and saying nice things to me.

Ewcia, our governess who took care of Musiu, lost me twice in the Planty while I was playing hide-and-seek with other children, and each time I was led home by strangers. I would receive a reprimand from my mother, and we would go to find Ewcia, who was looking for me, terrified, throughout the entire Planty while Musiu sat alone on a bench, waiting for this tragedy to end. As soon as Ewcia saw me, she would raise her hands to the sky and exclaim joyfully, "Thank God! Where were you, you little scamp?" Strangers would laugh with us. My mother would buy ice cream for all of us, and we would return home merrily.

Now it seemed like a completely different city to me. People slipped past, pressed right up to the walls of buildings, leaving the center of sidewalks free for Germans and policemen. The long-ago lighthearted, joyful atmosphere of this city had changed into a constant feeling of danger. It seemed to me that people had stopped laughing completely. Everything was gloomy. I still felt threatened. It was an impression that was passed to me by my parents.

Most Jews lived in Kazimierz, the Jewish quarter. My mother's sister also lived there. She warned us to be careful and to go out on the street as seldom as possible because Jews were constantly being rounded up and beaten. My father was afraid that after escaping from Oświęcim, the gestapo might be looking for him. He didn't want to stay in Kazimierz, and a few days later, he managed to find a room in a Jewish woman's house on Dietla Street, in a different, much better neighborhood.

She rented out her second room to a young man named Birnbaum, who was constantly playing his violin. Right on the first day, my mother asked our landlady if she could ask the violinist to take a break in his playing because Lusia couldn't sleep. The landlord said this was impossible because Mr. Birnbaum needed to practice. He was a well-known violinist in Kraków's symphony orchestra who had lost his job, like all Jews in institutions, schools, and offices; but someday this war would end, and Mr. Birnbaum would play in the orchestra again. This was precisely the atmosphere among Jews at that time—someday this whole nightmare of the German occupation would end, and everything would return to normal—everyone just needed to survive until then.

And so we sat in our room for entire days on end, listening to Mr. Birnbaum's music—whether we wanted to or not. At first it seemed to me that my ears were hurting from the music, but later I grew accustomed to it, and certain melodies even started to make me happy. Lusia also got used to it and slept well while he played. Perhaps this was because my father asked Mr. Birnbaum if he could play more soothing melodies during her naps. Then the violin would emit melancholy, plaintive tones that also lulled me to sleep.

From my parents' conversations, I gleaned that we were in a difficult financial situation. My mother still had the diamond from her wedding ring, but they decided to wait to sell it. My grandpa Józef was also living in Kraków and promised my father some money as soon as he sold his expensive gold watch, which had been manufactured by the Swiss firm Patek Philippe. This turned out to be difficult, however, since nobody was willing to pay much money for it. My grandfather was attached to his expensive watch and didn't want to sell it for a pittance.

Our money soon began to run out. It was particularly hard for us because my father didn't register us in the *Judenrat*, since he was afraid of the gestapo. We thus didn't receive any food cards and had to buy food on the black market at extremely inflated prices. Food was cheaper in the center of the city, in the main square, but Jews weren't allowed to go there. Inspections and roundups were carried out there frequently by the Polish police.

I remember the day when our money ran out, and my mother ripped open a seam in her winter coat and took out our last treasure—the diamond from her wedding ring. My father was going to take it to an acquaintance who would serve as a middleman. Suddenly Grandpa Józef jubilantly entered the room, told us the watch had been sold, and proudly handed my father a wad of banknotes.

My grandfather had finally entrusted this sale to a distant relative of ours from Oświęcim, Mansfeld, who was now also living in Kraków. He'd managed to make a profitable transaction because, as my grandfather pointed out, "he must have found someone who was able to appreciate the true value of my precious watch."

We found out only later that Mansfeld had sold this watch for a lower sum and had added some of his own money out of respect for my grandfather.

That same day, despite my mother's protests, my father went to the main square and returned with a large bag of food. My father possessed forged German identification documents, but if the Germans had found out, he would certainly have been executed. Despite this, he went to the main square two more times to buy food. He said there were no longer any inspections and the roundups had ended because Jews no longer dared to go to the center of town.

One of my father's friends also had forged German identification documents, but he was recognized in the city center by a Pole and denounced to the Germans. He was immediately arrested and shot several days later in the Montelupich Prison in Kraków. Then my father burned his fake documents. If my father's friend had been caught without documents, he would have spent a few days in prison and might have been beaten, but they would have released him eventually. At that time Jews were not yet being killed for such violations.

In the neighborhood where we were staying, it was also dangerous in the streets. Jews who hid their beards in their coats and their sidelocks under their hats were caught, and German soldiers, together with Polish policemen, cut off their beards and sidelocks to the great delight of the Polish people who stood and watched. A photograph was usually taken as a souvenir while it was being done. It was then that I realized for the first time that so many Poles—residents of Kraków who had lived harmoniously with Jews up until this time—disliked us so much. I began to fear people. I felt that I was worth less than others.

For hours on end I listened to Mr. Birnbaum's music, which reached us from the other room. A young, blond, very pretty woman often visited him, and she also had a violin. They would play together, and our landlady would sit in the corridor, in front of Mr. Birnbaum's room, listening to their music with her eyes closed and a dreamy expression on her face. She told my mother that this woman was his fiancée.

I was very curious about how it would sound when they played together, and one time, seeing that the door to Mr. Birnbaum's room was slightly ajar, I gathered some courage and stuck my head in. They were standing in front of music stands, playing from sheet music. Seeing my curious face, the pretty lady stopped playing and looked at me, smiling. Then she took me by the hand and led me to a sofa against the wall, facing their music stands. Mr. Birnbaum also smiled at me but didn't stop playing. His fiancée began to accompany him, and I sat in front of them, listening.

After a while, I felt as if the sounds of their violins were speaking to me in an indecipherable language of some kind; they were telling me something very important, something that couldn't be expressed in normal speech. Their music had a strange effect on my feelings. I felt deeply comforted, as if someone were embracing me. Sometimes the sounds of their violins were so quiet and delicate that I felt just like when I was very small and Ewcia sang me to sleep with her quiet, silvery voice. Sometimes they were intense again, aggressive, perhaps even angry, and then I felt as if I were in the midst of a huge quarrel in which people were presenting their arguments and shouting at each other. There were also sounds that were like such deep laments that it seemed impossible for any words to express so much pain and sorrow. I connected it to our personal situation, and tears welled up in my eyes. They flowed down my cheeks, but I didn't realize it because I had closed my eyes.

I don't know how long I sat absorbed by this music, but after a while, I realized the room had grown silent. I opened my eyes and saw Mr. Birnbaum standing with his violin lowered in front of his music stand, looking at me. The woman was doing the same, but there was a smile on her face while Mr. Birnbaum looked serious and focused.

I was slightly perplexed; I felt that I'd experienced something new and wanted to share it with Mr. Birnbaum and his fiancée, but I had no idea how to express it. To my surprise, Mr. Birnbaum bowed to me solemnly and said, "Thanks to you, I now know how I'm supposed to play this." I didn't really know what he was talking about, but when I saw his fiancée's smiling face, I understood that I hadn't done anything wrong.

I wanted to leave the room, but at that moment they started playing again, this time with an amazing momentum. I felt a heavenly rapture as if someone powerful and good were comforting me and whispering to me not to worry or cry, because everything would be fine. It seemed to me that this music wasn't flowing from the violins but from their bodies, from inside them. I sat there, fascinated, and felt that I was experiencing something great, though I wasn't aware of what it was.

Then it came to my mind that there was music in every person, and it was possible to hear it and bring it out, even without an instrument. You just had to learn to listen to yourself.

When they finished playing, I stood up and started clapping for them, like I'd once seen in the cinema. Mr. Birnbaum put his violin down, and then his fiancée did, too, and they both began to clap. I had no idea why they were doing this, and I was even slightly embarrassed by it, but I felt that if Mr. Birnbaum was doing so, it was part of the ceremony and that was how it should be.

From then on, I was a frequent guest in Mr. Birnbaum's room, and every time I left, I felt deeply comforted and in a better mood.

My father often visited his friend, the sculptor Henryk Hochman, to paint and sculpt with him, since there wasn't enough space in our small room. Hochman lived and worked in his art studio, which was in a single-story wooden shed. Before the war he'd lived there with his life companion, a painter from Paris. Her name was Henryka Kernerówna. She had sixteen Siamese cats that she cared for as if they were her children.

When we escaped from Oświęcim to Kraków, Kernerówna was already gone. She'd returned to Paris right at the beginning of the war. But she'd left the cats with Hochman. Now they wandered all over the studio and ate everything they could find. They also rummaged in the neighborhood's rubbish bins. They'd grown slightly thinner, but they were all still alive and always returned to the studio. I often went there with my father and played with the cats.

One time, Hochman was sculpting and my father painting when a military car stopped in front of the studio. We all ran to the window. A German officer got out of the car and, opening the door, stood at attention in front of an elderly man wearing the uniform of a high-ranking officer who was getting out of the car. I noticed he was limping heavily and supporting himself with a cane. The adjutant opened the studio's door for him and followed him inside. They both immediately took out handkerchiefs and held them to their noses. They looked around the studio. My father and Hochman stood at attention, and, seeing this, I tried to copy them. Everyone knew at that time that when Germans entered a room it was necessary to stand at attention. If people didn't do this, they were immediately beaten.

"What is that stench?" asked the officer in German.

"It's from the cats," answered my father.

Only then did we realize we'd become so accustomed to the stench that we were no longer aware of it at all.

The officer remarked, grimacing, *"So eine Schweinerei"* (How disgusting). Then he asked his adjutant to introduce him.

The adjutant stood at attention once again and shouted, "General von Smelke!" Or perhaps his name was Melke, or something similar to this. My father's uncle's last name was Smelke, and it seemed to me that the surname must be different, since it was impossible for a German officer to be related to us. At that time, I thought that if people had the same surname it meant they were related to each other.

I remember that I wasn't afraid at all and felt fascinated by the wonderful striped trousers the general was wearing. The cats also sat motionless, watching him. The general gave a signal, and the adjutant said they'd heard there were painters here, and the general wished to see their paintings.

"I know you're Jews, but if you're good painters, perhaps we can do some business," interjected the general.

Hochman answered that he was a sculptor, and his friend—he pointed at my father—was a painter.

The general stood in front of a painting my father was working on and looked at it carefully.

"Do you paint portraits as well?" he asked.

"I mostly paint portraits. I'm a portraitist," answered my father.

"I'd like to see a portrait you've done."

Hochman took down from the wall a portrait of himself that my father had recently painted and showed it to the general. The general stated that the following day at ten o'clock in the morning, a car would come for my father and take him to his headquarters, where my father would paint his portrait.

"Should I bring a canvas with me?" asked my father.

"No. A canvas, paints, paintbrushes, and everything else you need will be there," answered the general. Then his voice became less commanding, even a bit gentle. "I'd like to pay you," he continued. "How much do you charge for a portrait?"

"I wouldn't dare ask for a payment from you, sir."

"I don't confiscate artistic talent, nor do I accept presents," answered the general with a smile.

He took a banknote from his pocket and handed it to my father.

"Take it, and then I'll be certain we've made a deal."

My father took the banknote. It seemed like he wasn't going to say anything, but then on seeing the general's questioning look, he finally said, "Thank you."

"Don't forget. Wait in front of this building tomorrow," said the general, and then he turned and limped toward the door, leaning on his cane.

When he was on the threshold, he turned to us again and asked, "Do all artists in Kraków live in such filth?"

"Not all of them," answered my father. "Only those who don't have the heart to kick cats out of their homes."

The general looked severely at my father, nodded his head, and said, *"So, so,"* which meant "I see." And then he left.

This entire situation was completely surreal. No German in Kraków ever bought anything from Jews, and the only times they approached them were when they wanted to cause them harm or ridicule them. A meeting between a Jew and a German general who spoke to him in a civil manner was completely unimaginable. My father and Hochman stared at each other in disbelief. I noticed that all the cats were still sitting motionless.

Hochman was the first to break the silence. "It seems, Leon, that we're human beings after all."

"We'll see. At the moment I don't feel like it," answered my father, and he handed the banknote to Hochman. "Take it; you're more in need of money right now."

"I'll take it only because I have a large family," said Hochman, and he looked at the cats. He said to them, "From now on, you'll no longer rummage in garbage cans because the German general is looking after you."

The following day, my father was taken to a castle near Kraków, where the general lived. It turned out he was a Wehrmacht general who had been injured recently in a car accident and had come here for a holiday with his wife and children. He was going to be there for three more weeks. During that time, my father painted two large, life-sized portraits of him standing in a pompous pose. He also painted a portrait of his wife and one of his children.

My father tried several times to strike up a conversation with the general about the persecution of the Jews, but he didn't want to talk about it or listen to any accusations. My father painted intensively from morning to evening, and every time he returned with a large package of food, for he told the general he preferred food to money.

At the end, the general was very pleased. He shook my father's hand and bade him farewell. He said, "It's a pity that we met at such a time and in such circumstances."

"Sir, I wasn't the one who created these circumstances."

"Please don't think all Germans wanted this war. I didn't want it, and I wasn't the only one."

It seemed to my father, then, that the general wished to appease his conscience. On the other hand, he saw in this farewell something like a seed of protest against Hitler's policies.

Thanks to the food packages from the general, which even contained chocolate and cocoa, we lived well for the next few weeks—my family, our landlady, Mr. Birnbaum and his fiancée, Hochman and his cats.

I spent many hours in Mr. Birnbaum's room, listening to the two musicians play. I had the impression that a brighter and better world was being revealed to me. Something in their music spoke to me and never ceased comforting me. It seemed to me that their violins knew what mood I was in and were trying to guide me, explain things to me, and soothe my anxiety. Mr. Birnbaum was clearly happy with me, for he always responded to my applause with a deep bow.

My parents were also pleased, for they preferred me to listen to music than play ball with some local boys I'd met. One time, while crossing the street, I noticed a few boys playing ball in a small park nearby. Unable to restrain myself, I started watching them.

One turned to me and called out, "Come play with us." And so I started playing ball with them. They were Polish children, about my age. They were genuine Krakovian urchins, but frankly speaking, I looked no different from them. After our game they asked me what my name was. I answered, "Henryk." And then each of them also introduced himself. I was blond with blue eyes, wearing tattered sandals and ragged shorts. None of the boys suspected I was Jewish.

"We play ball here every afternoon. You can play with us if you want," said the oldest boy.

And so, from time to time, I went out and played with them. This allowed me to forget about the terrible reality in which we were living. I didn't want to hear the news being passed around not only in our apartment but throughout the entire building. Several times a day, someone came and told us about new persecutions of Jews and what had happened to so-and-so. With each surname that was mentioned, the faces of those who were listening became increasingly worried and sometimes terrified. The reports were brought to us mostly by our landlady's Polish neighbors, with whom she was on friendly terms. There were two other tenants described by our landlady as antisemites, whom she told us to avoid.

Sometimes one of our landlady's neighbors would come to our apartment wringing her hands, saying over and over again, "Oh my God, oh my God." Then she would tell us what had happened. I didn't always understand what was going on, but watching those who were listening, I knew that something very bad had happened.

I wanted to escape from this terrible atmosphere, from worries, fear, and distressing news. I only had two places where I could forget about it all—Mr. Birnbaum's room and the little park where I played ball with the boys. Sometimes I envied my sister for being so young and not understanding anything. My mother often went with her to visit a neighbor who was renting two rooms with her father in a Polish woman's apartment above ours. They preferred living here than in their apartment in Kazimierz, where most of the Jewish people were. All the Germans' attacks against Jews—roundups for forced labor, searches of apartments, and confiscations of valuable objects—happened mainly in Kazimierz.

The neighbor's name was Mela, and she was the same age as my mother but much fatter. Mela was always very kind to me. When I visited her, looking for my mother, she would give me a glass of hot milk and say, "Drink, drink, it's very healthy. If you drink milk, you'll grow fast." Mela didn't know that her words didn't encourage me to drink milk, for I didn't want to grow quickly at all.

Quite the contrary—I thanked God that I was small, since I didn't have to worry, like my mother and father did, about what was happening all around us and what would become of us. I didn't feel responsible for anything and, apart from Lusia, whom I sometimes took care of, I didn't have to look after anyone in those difficult times. I left all worries to my parents. I believed in them and knew they'd do everything they could to keep bad things from happening to us.

My mother and Mela were very close friends, and despite our sad reality, they often told each other stories from their lives and laughed loudly. I didn't always understand what they were laughing about, but I was infected by this laughter and laughed, too. I remember Mela once telling my mother, "Your Henryk is extremely mature if he can laugh about such things." And my mother patted me on the head proudly.

I witnessed this many times during the war—Jews trying to live a normal life even in the most difficult conditions. This was also true for Mela's father, Abraham. He was about seventy years old and had a long, gray beard and curly sidelocks that hung down from his temples, which he was always stroking with his fingers. I wondered why his sidelocks weren't completely gray, too, like his beard, but rather reddish-brown. He sat in his room all day long, studying the Talmud. Sometimes, when Mela was busy with something, my mother would serve him tea and exchange a few words with him.

He was always in a good mood and told my mother that everything happening at that time in Kraków was written in the Talmud.

"The end will be good," he assured her.

"But will we live to see the end?" asked my mother.

"We are unimportant," he answered. "What's important is the Jewish nation, and it will always emerge stronger from all of its crises."

My mother said, "From your lips to God's ear."

Abraham immersed himself in his huge book again, and my mother left his room, strengthened in spirit.

I remember my mother telling Mela a few times that it was very dangerous to have a beard and sidelocks because the Germans had issued an order for them to be cut off. Mela said her father absolutely refused to cut them off, despite her pleas, because without them he'd feel like a cripple. This was why he never left home. In the Polish woman's apartment and in this neighborhood, there was no fear of Germans conducting a search.

One day I was heading home with my friend Staszek after playing ball. Staszek, who was a bit older than me, said we should go to Starowiślna Street because his older brother walked around there, selling Penguin ice cream from a wooden box; maybe we'd be lucky and he'd give us some. Starowiślna Street was one of the main streets of Kraków and connected Dietla Street, where we lived, with the Jewish district of Kazimierz. It was a long street always full of people, with lots of elegant shops on both sides. Jews weren't allowed to walk down this street.

Staszek was a cheerful boy, and it was very fun to spend time with him. He always had something funny to say. Laughing and joking, we walked along Starowiślna Street, and Staszek looked for his brother. Suddenly the expression on his face became very serious, and he pointed straight ahead. About twenty meters in front of us, I saw a group of people watching something that must have been very funny, because everyone was laughing. More people were running from the other side of the street to see it, too. A small crowd was forming.

I didn't know why Staszek was standing there looking so solemn. I asked him what was happening.

He answered, "It looks like they've caught another Jew."

I stood there feeling terrified and didn't know what to do. But I didn't have time to think about it because Staszek took my hand and made me run with him to see what was happening.

I noticed there were also many people who rushed past the crowd or turned away. I saw a woman cover a child's eyes with her hand and try to get away from the scene. We reached the spot slightly out of breath and started squeezing between people so we could see better. The people standing there let us through. Everyone was in a jolly mood—laughing, talking, and pointing at something. A young man turned around and, seeing Staszek and me pushing our way through the crowd, helped us stand in front of him.

There were three Germans several steps ahead of us, cutting the beard and sidelocks off an old Jewish man. They were doing it very slowly as if they were enjoying it. They posed for a photograph at the same time, taken by another German. A Polish policeman in a navy-blue uniform was keeping order and not allowing anyone to get too close. After each photograph, the Germans burst into laughter, and the amused onlookers chimed in with giggles, jeers, and various derogatory remarks about this tired old Jew.

Nearly his entire beard had been cut off, and only part of his sidelocks remained. He was standing calmly, wide-eyed and with his head raised, as the Germans had commanded him to do. He seemed completely detached from his surroundings. His eyes were huge with fear. At a certain moment he looked at me, and I saw his eyes grow even wider. Only then did I recognize him: it was Abraham, Mela's father. I was petrified by fear.

"What's wrong?" asked Staszek. "You're so pale."

I didn't answer, but at that moment I remembered my brother Musiu's eyes when he fell once from a bench in the Planty and couldn't get up, and I was unable to help him because I was too small. They were the eyes of a helpless, desperate, vulnerable, and suffering human being. I felt my heart dying inside me. I was very upset. I felt as if I'd received an electric shock. My vision grew dark, and I lost consciousness.

I don't know how long I fainted for; I opened my eyes when someone sprinkled water on me and slapped my cheeks. I saw faces bent over me. They were all serious and concerned, and Staszek's face was among them. Now he looked very pale and was biting his lips.

Someone said, "He must have epilepsy." Someone helped me to my feet. I felt better, and I looked at Mela's father. He was still standing there. Without his beard and sidelocks he looked like a frightened bird whose feathers had been plucked. He was unrecognizable, but I knew it was him. He smiled at me when I stood up and seemed relieved that nothing had happened to me. The Germans were gone.

The policeman in the blue uniform approached me and handed me the scissors. "Go over to him," he said, pointing at Abraham, "and pretend you're cutting his hair off. We'll take a photo of you as a souvenir, to make you feel better after that unpleasant experience."

I looked helplessly at Mela's father. He nodded his head as if signaling for me to do it. It seemed like he expected this to be the end of the whole ceremony and that they would then let him go home. I tried to take the scissors, but a terrible thing happened. I lost control of my right hand! I couldn't feel it anymore. The policeman tried to help me and put the scissors in my hand, but my hand fell limply, and the scissors dropped to the ground.

"His hand is paralyzed," said the policeman.

Staszek looked at me, frightened, and timidly said to the policeman, "This is my friend Henryk. He has never had a paralyzed hand before."

The policeman tried to move my hand again and repeated, "Paralyzed." Then he said to Staszek, "Go home."

He turned to everyone else and ordered, "Disperse!"

He shook his finger at Mela's father threateningly and said, "Never dare walk down Starowiślna Street again! And when your beard and sidelocks grow back, you have to shave them off because those are the orders!" Then he quickly walked away.

The people started dispersing, but several remained. Suddenly a man approached Abraham and punched him in the face so hard he fell backward.

"Why are you hitting him?" someone asked.

"Didn't you see this Yid put a curse on that boy and paralyze his hand?!"

I saw Abraham struggle to his feet, but someone else ran up to him and kicked him twice. Others followed. Instinctively and completely unaware of what I was doing, I started screaming with all my strength, "Enough! Enough! Stop hitting him!"

Staszek joined in, "Stop it, you bastards!"

But nothing helped. Terrified, screaming, I started jumping from one foot to the other. I seemed to have stepped on the foot of a man standing behind me because he pushed me very hard, causing me to fly straight toward Mela's father. I fell right on top of him. The crowd stopped beating him because I was in the way; I wrapped one of my arms around him, while my other arm hung at my side.

"Get off that scoundrel!" I heard someone say above me. But I didn't move.

Abraham whispered to me in Yiddish, "Get up, or they'll beat you, too."

Just then Staszek also threw himself on top of us. I raised my head and saw the attackers standing around us, undecided. Their faces were twisted in a strange spasm of hatred, and in the eyes of one of them, I saw death. I don't understand how so much hatred and anger could collect in these people, for this old Jew hadn't caused them any harm. Other people were standing and laughing.

Then out of the corner of my eye, I saw a middle-aged woman running toward us from the other side of the street. She ran up to us breathlessly and, turning to those who had been attacking the old man a moment before, started shouting at them in an angry and emotional voice: "What are you doing?! Aren't you ashamed of yourselves?! You blasphemers! You're crucifying Jesus Christ all over again! He wanted to redeem the world with his suffering, and you're killing our Lord again with your wicked actions! Why aren't you ashamed of mistreating an old man this way?! You're a disgrace to us all! Go away and leave him in peace!"

She turned and looked at Mela's father. Then I saw that she was shaking with indignation, and there was disgust in her eyes and deep condemnation of what she had seen. The people surrounding us seemed as if they were waking up from a dream; they had solemn expressions on their faces and withdrew a few steps. Two of them said goodbye to each other. A moment later they were all gone, and we were alone.

The three of us helped Abraham to his feet. He was breathing heavily, and blood was flowing from his nose and mouth. He was in pain, but it was clear he wasn't seriously injured since he was able to walk with our help. Staszek helped him take his coat off so he wouldn't be burdened by it. My right hand was still numb.

Soon afterward, Staszek's brother ran up to us after having noticed us from afar. He was about twenty years old and had a wooden ice cream box hanging from his shoulder. "What happened, Staszek?" he asked his brother in surprise.

"Some bastards beat up this man after the Germans cut off his beard," Staszek answered. His brother looked at the woman questioningly, and she said, "A profanation . . . a profanation of Jesus Christ."

We stepped into the entranceway of a building, and Staszek's brother wiped the blood off Abraham's face with a handkerchief. Then he took some ice cream out of his box and held it to his face.

"The last package," he told Staszek. After a while he managed to stop the flow of blood with this ice cream, and we all started heading toward Dietla Street.

"It's close; I can get there on my own," said Mela's father.

The woman seemed to be thinking about it, and then Staszek's brother said, "We'll take him home."

Turning to Abraham, the woman said, "May God watch over you, sir, and all the rest of your people." She looked straight into his eyes; then she smiled and left.

I saw that Mela's father was crying; perhaps this was why he didn't say anything. I don't know who this woman was, but her kindness, nobility, and courage probably saved his life and perhaps mine, too. Whenever I think of her, I'm grateful and proud that such people exist in this world and brighten our lives with their mercy and compassion. I also recall Staszek with great fondness. This ten-year-old boy was an example of true friendship.

I told Staszek then that I was Jewish and lived in the same building as this beaten Jew. This didn't seem to matter very much to him.

He said, "For me, the most important thing is that you're my friend and you're good at playing ball."

And then his brother extended his hand to me in a sign of respect. I couldn't take it, though, because my right arm was still numb, as if paralyzed. Only then did I realize there must be something seriously wrong with my arm, and I was very scared. Noticing my fear, Abraham reassured me and told me everything would be all right.

"How do you know?" I asked him in a tearful voice.

He stopped walking, patted me on the head, and said, "Because you're a *tzaddik*."

I looked at him in disbelief. "Why am I a *tzaddik*?"

"Because today you passed through the gate that all *tzaddikim* pass through. Whoever passes through this gate is a *tzaddik*."

I hadn't fallen on him deliberately—it had been a lucky accident.

"I don't know how it happened," I said.

"But I know," he answered.

We said goodbye to Staszek and his brother in front of our building. Mela's father thanked them for their help. Standing in the doorway, this old, beaten-up Jew turned to Staszek and said, "You're a *tzaddik*, too."

"What's a *tzaddik*?" asked Staszek.

"The righteous of the world," he answered, and his smile had a hint of pain in it.

My parents were very worried about my arm. Mela knew a doctor, who immediately came to visit her father, and then he visited us. He examined me and said that such things often happen after a shock of some kind or a traumatic experience and that it would probably return to normal soon.

Abraham lay in bed for a week because he had two broken ribs and a broken nose. He recovered quickly, however, and continued to immerse himself in his books all day long. He no longer left the apartment at all. It turned out that on the day he was beaten he had left home to go to a synagogue in Kazimierz, for that day was the anniversary of his father's death, and he wished to recite the Kaddish for the dead. He'd hidden his beard in his coat and his sidelocks under his hat, and thought nobody would notice him. He'd been completely unaware that Jews were no longer allowed to walk on Starowiślna Street.

Our neighbor went to the village where her family lived and brought back some medicinal honey that was believed to have miraculous properties. It was recommended by her brother, who was a folk healer. My mother rubbed this honey on my numb arm twice a day, and then she made a dressing with the honey. I was very happy about this because I would sneakily unwind the bandage and lick the honey off; then I would wind the bandage around my arm again. When my mother unwound the bandage, she comforted me by saying this was clearly a very special kind of honey since it had soaked in very nicely, and I'd surely recover soon.

She was right; a week later I was able to move my arm again. Everyone in the house rejoiced with us. Mela was even kinder to me than usual and often brought me a glass of hot milk and several times even cocoa—I have no idea how she managed to get it. Cocoa was a great rarity that Jewish children had long forgotten about. Poverty was increasing rapidly because Jewish people were deprived of their opportunities to work and earn money.

Now I stayed at home more than before and constantly listened to Mr. Birnbaum's violin. I became increasingly attached to his music; its tones spoke to me more and more. I felt they were meant directly for me. There was a kind of friendly understanding between us. I had the impression that Mr. Birnbaum was expressing to me what someone was telling him to express and that he wasn't the creator of these sounds. The strangest thing was that after such a concert, I always felt certain there was nothing to be afraid of and nothing bad would happen to me. Everyone around me was living in a state of uncertainty and anxiety, but I was growing calmer despite my awareness that life was getting harder.

One day someone came to us and said that Hochman was ill and asking for my father to visit him. My father quickly gathered a bit of food and went out, and I followed him because I liked Hochman very much. On the way, we noticed that the streets were almost empty. It was a beautiful, sunny morning. The streets were usually full of people at this hour. But now we were walking completely alone. There was only a disabled person hobbling along with a cane on the other side of the street.

"Something must have happened," my father said anxiously, and he decided to take side streets rather than the main street that we usually took. There were more people on these streets, but a strange excitement was in the air. People were running and disappearing through doorways of buildings.

Suddenly we saw a military vehicle parked sideways at the end of a street and German soldiers jumping out of it. Someone opened a window and shouted, "A roundup! A roundup! Run!" Then he shut the window quickly. We started running in the opposite direction. But Germans drove up from that side, as well, and then the street was completely blocked off. We stood there uncertainly, looking around for an open doorway to hide in. But they were all closed.

Someone shouted right behind us: "Mr. Schönker! Mr. Schönker! Come here! Quickly! Quickly!" We turned and saw a woman waving desperately at us from an open doorway. We ran to her, and she immediately locked the door behind us.

"Don't you recognize me?" she asked my father.

It was quite dark in the entrance hall, so my father went very close to the woman to see her better.

"Oh! Małgorzata! What are you doing here?" he exclaimed.

"I'm the caretaker of this building. I saw you through the window. Come with me. There's no way of knowing what's going to happen here today," she said in an agitated voice.

The door to her apartment was right next to the building's main entrance. She led us into a room that clearly also served as her bedroom, since there was a large bed on the left-hand side, next to the wall. The entire room was wallpapered in a floral pattern, and a large painting of a Catholic saint hung above the bed. Across from the door there was a chest of drawers with a crucifix and two large candles on it.

"How's Franek?" asked my father.

"He's completely healthy," she said. To my surprise, she placed a chair on the bed. Then she added, "Thanks to you."

I saw joy on my father's face, but I was focusing all my attention on the woman who was now standing on the chair. I didn't understand what she was doing. She tilted the painting, and it turned out to be hanging over a small, secret door. She opened it, and we saw a dark hole in the wall.

"Go inside," she said, "because we don't know what the Germans will do to us today."

"What happened?" asked my father.

She looked at him in surprise. "Don't you know anything? Two German officers were killed not far from here. Everyone knows about it except you. Quickly, hide, because they might search people's homes. Quickly! Quickly!"

We climbed onto the chair and crawled into the hiding place, and then the woman closed the door behind us. The hiding place was about one meter by two meters, and it was possible to sit in it. It wasn't completely dark because a bit of light was coming from somewhere up above. We hadn't even managed to get settled in very well yet when we heard gunshots in the street. After a while, Germans started banging on the building's entrance door with their rifle butts, shouting, *"Los, los, öffnen! Öffnen!"* (Open up!) We froze, and I hugged my father and began to recite the Shema Yisrael prayer silently, in my mind.

Małgorzata opened the building's front door, and we heard Germans running into the entrance hall. Several of them rushed into her apartment and shouted at her: *"Männer, Männer, sind hier?"* (Are there any men here?) Małgorzata obviously didn't speak German, for she only managed to stammer: *"Nix Mener, nix Mener."*

We waited inside the wall for three hours. Then Małgorzata called out to us, "You can come out now; the roundup is over."

My father opened the little door, and we saw Małgorzata standing at the window, leaning out and observing the street. She shouted, "Go back in! Go back in; hide yourselves and close the door! I'm about to have a visitor!" We quickly closed the secret door from inside.

Only now did I notice a small hole in the wall, covered with pink glass, through which it was possible to observe the entire room. Someone rang the doorbell, and Małgorzata went to open the entrance door. A moment later she came back into the room accompanied by a Polish policeman. He had a truncheon at his side and was carrying a large paper bag, which he put on the table.

"Sugar from the police chief," he said, sitting down at the table.

"Please thank him," said Małgorzata.

I couldn't see very well, but it seemed to me that she had a strange expression on her face.

"Any news?" asked the policeman.

"No news," she said in an indifferent tone of voice.

She set a glass of vodka in front of him as well as a small plate of sausage and a slice of bread. The policeman drank the vodka, then handed the glass to Małgorzata.

"Another," he said.

Małgorzata brought him another glass of vodka. He knocked it back and asked, "Do you know what happened today?"

"I know. Everyone knows," she replied, shrugging.

The policeman looked at her and began to speak in a monotonous voice: "You still need to watch what's happening in this building. We want to know if a new tenant moves in. Every suspicious thing must be immediately reported. There's a trend now among Jews to rent rooms and apartments under false names. They also have forged documents. Sometimes it's hard to tell the difference. We want to know what's going on. You've got to report everything. One more glass wouldn't hurt."

Małgorzata brought him another glass of vodka. After drinking it, he stood up, walked over to the window, leaned out, and, greatly pleased, remarked, "You have a good view of the whole street. You must keep watching. I'll come again in a few days."

He turned to her, waved goodbye, and left the room.

We waited for Małgorzata to tell us we could come out of the hiding place, but to my astonishment she took the crucifix and both candles off the chest of drawers and put them on the table. She took matches out of a drawer and, crossing herself in front of the crucifix, lit the candles. Then she folded her hands together, knelt down, and started praying fervently. When she was finished, she crossed herself again, blew out the candles, and put them and the crucifix back in their places. She went to the window and looked through it again, after which she turned to us and said, "You can come out now."

We emerged into the room, and I squinted in the bright light.

"Where's the bathroom?" asked my father.

I also desperately needed to use it.

"Follow me," Małgorzata said, and she took from the table the paper bag the policeman had brought her.

The bathroom was in a small corridor that connected this room with the kitchen.

"Right here," she said, pointing to a door. She opened it and went in first.

All three of us found ourselves in the bathroom together. My father looked at her in surprise. Without saying anything, she opened the paper bag and started pouring its contents into the toilet bowl. It was pure white sugar.

"What are you doing?" shouted my father. "That's precious! Who throws away sugar?!"

But she continued to pour the sugar out, very slowly as if she were relishing this act. My father and I watched in consternation. It was about two and a half kilograms of sugar.

After pouring out the bag's entire contents, she turned to my father and shouted in a loud, angry, agitated tone of voice, "This isn't sugar; it's disgrace—disgrace that men such as this policeman wish to bring upon our country! They think I'll spy for them! I'd sooner be crucified!"

I stood with my father in silence, not knowing what to say. When Małgorzata noticed I was putting one leg in front of the other, she added with a smile, "I'll leave you two alone now. It's good that it's Jews who'll piss on this sugar, since it's not worth more than that." And she left the bathroom, closing the door behind her.

When we returned to the room, she told us this policeman was trying to catch Jews who were hiding as Poles and was forcing other people to cooperate with him. "A son of the devil," she added. "He brings us sugar for it. My toilet is the sweetest toilet in Kraków. I've already cleaned it a few times with this policeman's sugar." She grew solemn and said, almost to herself, "I pray that disgrace and divine punishment will fall only on people like him, and not on all of us." Then she turned to my father. "Believe me, there are many others like me, but they're afraid."

Then she told my father about Franek. I found out that he was her sister's son who, after various physiotherapy sessions in a hospital, had recovered completely from his paralysis and could now walk again. My father was clearly happy to hear this and listened to her with great interest.

Małgorzata wanted us to stay with her for a while, but my father explained that we were in a hurry to see a sick friend. At her request, he promised he would return to her for help if it turned out to be necessary.

"Because I still haven't fully paid my debt to you," she said in conclusion.

My father went up to her and kissed her on the cheek, then whispered, "You've already paid it."

She led us to the building's entrance. She went into the street, looked around in all directions, then told us we could come out.

Hochman turned out to be bedridden with a serious case of influenza. His cats had completely taken over the studio and had knocked everything over while searching for food. My father gave Hochman something to eat and made him some tea. We tidied up the studio and fed the cats. Then my father told Hochman what had happened to us.

Hochman listened in disbelief and kept repeating, "Incredible! Unbelievable!" From what my father said, I learned that Franek lived with his parents in a village and was the same age as Musiu. He had also been afflicted by paralysis, but at a later age than Musiu. His mother came to Kraków with him for hospital treatment and stayed with her sister, Małgorzata, who at that time was the caretaker in our apartment building. Franek was released from the hospital in Kraków with a paralyzed leg. Doctors recommended physiotherapy, but it was expensive, and Franek's parents couldn't afford it.

At that time, Musiu was having physiotherapy sessions in a special, very expensive clinic in Warsaw. It was known as the best clinic of this kind in Poland. My father took Franek there with his mother and paid in advance for several series of physiotherapy sessions. He also found a room for his mother in Warsaw and even gave her some money to live on. My father wasn't doing very well financially at that time, but he borrowed this money from my grandfather. We left Kraków soon afterward, moved to Oświęcim, and lost contact with them. Now it turned out that the physiotherapy had helped Franek.

Hochman told us that shortly before we came, a friend had visited him and told him about the attack on the two German officers and the Germans' retaliation. Apparently many people had been arrested, and several had been shot in the street.

We didn't know what would have happened to us if they'd caught us. But we felt certain Małgorzata had saved us.

"What do you make of this?" my father asked Hochman.

"If I believed in miracles, I would say this was a miracle," Hochman answered solemnly.

"So what was it, if not a miracle?"

"Let's say it was something bordering on a miracle." Hochman spread his arms helplessly, as if he himself couldn't believe that he'd said it.

My father looked at him, surprised.

"I see you've made a huge compromise, because until now you've refused to believe that something bordering on a miracle could exist."

They both laughed, but I didn't know what it meant for something to "border on a miracle." There was no time for questions, however; we had to hurry home because the curfew hour was approaching.

Some time later, Jews started being displaced from Kraków to smaller towns close by. My parents wondered whether we ought to leave instead of waiting for the Germans to expel us. I saw that they couldn't make up their minds. Grandpa Józef was in Kraków, as well as all of my father's friends. Among them, I most vividly remember the painter Abraham Neumann and the composer Mordechai Gebirtig.

Neumann was much older than my father and said he didn't want to leave Kraków because he loved the city. He'd recently returned to Kraków after living in the United States for two years. He was a great painter and—according to my parents, who were his closest friends—a wonderful person with a gentle heart.

In 1942, he was shot by the Germans in the Kraków ghetto. Gebirtig was killed then, too.[1] One of his songs, "Es brent" ("It's Burning"), which he composed shortly before the war, was a prophetic vision. In the song he described a time when the whole city would go up in flames, and people would stand idly, silently, doing nothing, watching the city burn. Gebirtig addresses them in the song, asking, "Why are you standing there doing nothing?" Later, this song became a symbol of the Holocaust.

Nobody had yet become aware of the nightmare that was awaiting us, but we were aware that every decision we made could have a profound impact on our lives. So I understood why my father was hesitating. I assumed he didn't want to be as lonely as I was, and therefore it was hard for him to leave Kraków. Apart from my friends who played ball with me, I didn't know anyone my age. I could find ball-playing friends anywhere, but each change was difficult for me. I thought it must be even harder for my father, since he didn't play ball.

One day Mr. Birnbaum came home beaten up and covered in blood. Someone had attacked him in the street. He lay in bed all day, and his fiancée made compresses for him. The next day, hearing music, I slipped timidly into his room and sat down in my usual spot on the sofa. His head was bandaged, and he was playing with his eyes closed, with more emotion than ever before. In his music I heard deep sorrow and lamentation.

I closed my eyes, too, and began to cry. I asked myself how a person could play this way. Never in my life had anyone communicated to me in words what this music expressed to me. I had a heavenly sensation of lightness and felt like I was flying in the air like a bird, toward a greater brightness. I also felt like I was becoming part of the music and belonged to it.

Mr. Birnbaum stopped playing. I opened my eyes and realized we were both crying.

That evening my parents decided to leave Kraków the following day and go to Wieliczka. This decision probably saved our lives—nearly all of Kraków's Jews later died in the ghetto.

NOTE

1. Abraham Neumann (1873 or 1875–1942) was a painter and graphic artist. He studied at the Academy of Fine Arts in Kraków under the guidance of Leon Wyczółkowski and Jacek Malczewski, as well as in Paris. He was a lecturer at the famous Bezalel Academy of Arts and Design in Jerusalem; he was a member of the Association of Polish Artists and Designers as well as the Association of Jewish Painters and Sculptors in Kraków. His works were featured in many European and Polish exhibitions. He was shot, along with his friend, the famous poet and composer Mordechai Gebirtig (born in 1877), on June 4, 1942, during the liquidation of the Kraków ghetto.

WIELICZKA

WIELICZKA WAS ONLY TWENTY KILOMETERS from Kraków, but on the way there, I felt like we were leaving a familiar world and heading toward something completely new. This caused anxiety in me, and even fear.

It was the autumn of 1940. We traveled to Wieliczka by train, and Lusia cried the entire time; it was impossible to comfort her. The train crawled slowly through Kraków, and I kept looking around to see if any danger was close by. I remember my father saying to my mother, as we passed through the Borek Fałęcki station, "Not much farther now."

A woman sitting near us answered, "Thank God, because my ears are aching from that crying."

In our compartment there was also an older gentleman and two women. Everyone started laughing, which made the woman who had complained also laugh.

Now in a slightly better mood, she asked my mother, "Are you coming from far?"

"From Kraków," answered my mother.

With slight hesitation and curiosity in her voice, the woman asked, "You're not Jews, are you?"

My mother answered in an irate voice, "Why on earth would you think such a thing?"

"I'm very sorry," she answered, embarrassed. "I didn't want to offend you, but these days many Jews are escaping from Kraków."

"Are you aware, madam, with whom you are speaking?" asked my mother severely, and then she shouted at Lusia in German: *"Bleib schon still!"* (Be quiet now!) Amazingly, Lusia fell silent.

The woman had a frightened look on her face and said to my parents in a conciliatory tone of voice, "Once again, I'm very sorry. It was simply a mistake. I didn't mean to insult anyone."

The other passengers fell silent. I learned in that moment that in the eyes of some people, it's shameful to be Jewish. I also found out that if you wrongly suspect someone of being Jewish, you should apologize.

At the train station in Wieliczka, we took a horse-drawn cab and went to the home of my father's uncle. His name was Chaim Schenker (this branch of the family spelled their last name differently). He owned a tannery and was very wealthy. The German supervisor, a so-called *kommissarischer Verwalter*, allowed Chaim to help him in the tannery because he had no idea how to manage such a factory. After a while, Chaim came to an agreement with him and then actually ran the entire business.

Chaim and his wife welcomed us very warmly. We spent several days with them. They still lived in their own home on the second floor of a pretty, modest house. They had two children: a son named Lulek, who was over twenty years old, and a daughter named Muszka—a very pretty, sweet, modest, brown-haired girl who was about seventeen years old.

There were hardly any Germans in this area. Chaim's tannery was located in the neighborhood of Klasno, quite far from the center of town. It had once been a village to the south of Wieliczka that over time had become incorporated into the town. Poor people lived in Klasno, mostly Jews.

The very next day my father found a boarded-up building that, until recently, had served as a warehouse. It was very dilapidated, but the upper floor was very spacious. With Chaim's help, my father rented the upper floor and decided to create an apartment there for us. Chaim sent workers who, in just a few days, built wooden stairs on the side of the building and renovated the upper floor. A new floor was constructed from wooden boards that was about one meter above the ceiling of the warehouse on the ground floor, in order to decrease the height of the rooms. A living room and kitchen were created. We were happy to have a home of our own once again.

Chaim also brought some leather from his tannery so I could have new shoes, and he paid a shoemaker to make them. Winter was approaching, and I was still walking around in worn-out sandals or barefoot. My father went to the shoemaker with me and asked him to make the shoes slightly too large so they would last a long time. The shoemaker was too enthusiastic when following my father's request, and the shoes came out several sizes too big. They were attractive shoes of light-brown leather with thick soles that were so stiff they almost didn't bend at all. They made a loud slapping sound when I walked in them. Other children called after me: "A stork! Here comes a stork!" This didn't bother me at all because it seemed to me that my friend Aleks the Stork from Oświęcim was sending me greetings this way.

Soon I made friends with several Jewish boys who were slightly older than me, and nobody dared call me "stork" anymore. I remember three of them particularly well because they became my close friends. One was named Jankiel and lived with his family near the synagogue. He was very pious but discreet about it. His parents had cut off his sidelocks so he wouldn't draw attention to himself; instead of wearing a black yarmulke, he wore a cap. Most of us walked around without head coverings.

Jankiel acted as a judge in our group. When arguments broke out, he would arbitrate them, and everyone always agreed with his verdict. We considered him the wisest of us all. He never argued with anyone, nor did he try to force anyone to agree with his point of view. When someone didn't see eye to eye with him, he would just smile kindly and say, "Everyone is free to have his own opinion."

I once asked him why he didn't try harder to convince others of his point of view. He answered that when someone is very certain of his own opinion, there's no point in trying to convince him otherwise, and his opinion should be respected even if you don't share it.

"Why?" I asked.

"Because a person's opinion is part of who he is, and every person should be respected as long as he's not doing anything immoral." Jankiel was eleven or twelve years old at that time.

My other dear friend was Adam. He was only eleven years old, but his hands were already as rough from work as the hands of an adult.

He described to me many times the macabre scene when the Germans, immediately after invading Wieliczka, murdered his father. Adam was living with his father and grandmother in a small farmhouse in the field behind our new home in the warehouse. His father was a farmer, and his mother had died before the war. His grandmother was ill and partially paralyzed, and spent most of her time in bed.

One day the Germans came and dragged Adam's father out of their house. He resisted and refused to go with them. They shot him in front of the house. Adam showed me what had happened to his father after each shot, how he leaned to one side, then the other, and how long it lasted before his knees gave way beneath him and he fell to the ground. Lying in a pool of blood, he struggled to get up and only died when the last bullet hit him in the head. Adam was very proud of how strong his father had been and that it had been necessary for the Germans to shoot at him for such a long time before he died.

I often spent entire days with Jankiel and Adam. They visited us frequently, and Adam ate dinner with me. Then my mother would give him food for his grandmother. Adam didn't observe the Jewish religion or its rituals, even though he was a Jew and considered himself to be one. Jankiel, on the other hand, only ate at his own house. It was interesting to observe how they tolerated and liked each other. They respected each other's customs.

There was also a boy named Zylek, who was much older than us. He was about fifteen years old. He smoked a lot of cigarettes but never had any money to buy them. So we walked around the streets and collected cigarette butts for him, which we called "thumbs." My mother sometimes gave me money for candy, and we spent it on cigarette paper so we could roll cigarettes for Zylek. He showed his gratitude for this by defending us against other boys, and so everyone was happy. At the age of nine, I made my first attempts at smoking. A year later I smoked regularly—hiding it from my parents, of course.

After a while, Hochman also moved to Wieliczka. He gave all the cats away and let a friend have the studio. He was no longer able to sculpt—it was impossible in his new apartment, and he suffered greatly because of this. He wandered the streets aimlessly and sat motionless for hours on end, immersed in his own thoughts. My father tried to cheer him up, but Hochman's mental state was constantly deteriorating.

One day he came to us in a joyful mood and announced, in a voice overcome with emotion, "Peter has come."

My parents and I shouted simultaneously, "Who is Peter?"

"My beloved cat," said Hochman, with tears in his eyes.

It turned out this cat had run away from the people to whom Hochman had given it. The cat had walked all the way to Wieliczka, covered in mud and starving, and had found its master here. We all went to the room Hochman was renting and saw the cat sleeping on his bed. We looked at it in disbelief.

"How is this possible?" my father asked.

And then Hochman, who had always laughed at everyone when they talked about miracles, said, deeply moved, "I'll tell you something, Leon; this is a real miracle."

"But you've always said there's no such thing as a miracle," answered my father with a good-natured smile.

Hochman thought about it, then answered as if he were talking to himself: "That's what someone thinks until a miracle occurs. When it happens, a person changes his mind. Nobody believes in miracles when they happen to someone else."

He spread his hands helplessly, and we all laughed. Then he put a finger to his lips and whispered, "Hush, Peter's sleeping."

The cat's return restored Hochman's mental balance and filled him with new energy. He began to paint landscapes and even found a space where he could create small sculptures. My father kept thinking about what had happened with the cat and asked Hochman what he thought about it two more times. The first time he didn't answer, but when several days later my father asked him again, Hochman answered, "Love, true love ... makes anything possible."

Weeks passed quickly, and our lives became normalized to a certain extent. The Germans seemed willing to cooperate with the Jewish community and left us in peace, more or less. There weren't any serious antisemitic attacks or murders. Young people were forced to work, but they weren't treated with brutality. They mostly worked in the construction of roads, sewers, and barracks. Everything was organized by the *Judenrat*, which functioned very efficiently. It was also easy to communicate with the German mayor, Rosing. It was even said that his attitude toward Jews was quite favorable, which was unusual.

News of the relative peace that prevailed in Wieliczka quickly spread to surrounding areas, and an increasing number of Jews began to arrive, especially from Kraków. A month after we moved there, my father's sister, Liba Hofstetter, and her two daughters, Fela and Francis, arrived. Fela was seventeen years old, and Francis was eight. They were both beautiful. My mother always drew my attention to how well-behaved they were and told me to try to act like them.

I often visited them, and Aunt Liba always had a treat for me. She was a tall, slender, very good-looking woman. We lived on the main street of Klasno, and they lived not far from us in a rented farmhouse in the middle of a meadow.

I often walked around this meadow with Francis. She was very lively and always laughing. I enjoyed spending time with her. We also sometimes went to the lake and met Lulek and Muszka there, as well as some other young people. In particular I remember Dorcia, an extremely beautiful girl the same age as Muszka. She was also a distant relative of ours. We spent many pleasant hours with them.

I no longer felt lonely, and it seemed to me that the world had begun to smile on me. I often spent time with Francis in the fields and meadows near her home, or with Jankiel and Adam. We discussed the world's problems in our childlike way, but we didn't manage to solve any of them conclusively enough to be certain that our point of view was valid. Francis said that everything would become clear to us when we got older, because only adults know everything. Jankiel thought that whoever thinks he knows everything actually knows nothing. Adam, in turn, promised he would have a talk with his dog, Rose, and would answer us later, since the best thoughts always came to his mind while talking to Rose.

We laughed a lot in those times, and it seemed that the war had forgotten about us. Our parents had their worries, but we, the children, lived for the present day and didn't think about the future.

Sometimes I helped Francis and Fela make beautiful dolls from colorful rags. I found the rags for them and also brought them sawdust from a carpenter, with which they filled the dolls' bellies. Then they gave these dolls to small children as presents. Soon Francis and Fela became the darlings of the entire neighborhood. Francis put one doll of each kind aside for herself. She had a beautiful collection of them, and I felt that these dolls belonged to some kind of dreamland.

Zylek started working in road construction because he wanted to bring his parents larger food rations. He worked from morning to night and had no time for us. There was no longer anyone to roll cigarettes for, so Adam and I started rolling them for ourselves.

At the end of 1940, something completely unexpected happened to me. It struck me like a bolt of lightning from a clear sky. I fell in love. The object of my affection was the neighbor's daughter. Her name was Nina Armer, and she was about fifteen years old. Her mother, a stout and very kind woman, had several children and ran a grocery shop near our house. They lived above the shop. Nina's father was one of thirty-two Jews whom the Germans had shot in September 1939, right after entering Wieliczka. Nina was the oldest child. She helped in the shop and at home.

For me, she was the embodiment of beauty, delicacy, and kindness. The sight of her filled me with a feeling I'd never known before, and I was drawn to her by some kind of magnetic energy. This energy overpowered me, and I felt completely helpless. I constantly sought opportunities to see her. I tried to remain calm while doing this, but I always felt myself reddening at the sight of her, right up to my ears. She was a bit plump and had a very nicely developed womanly body. She was the personification of everything that a nearly ten-year-old boy like me could ever dream of.

I dreamed of her, especially at night. I often sighed in my sleep, and my mother would come to see what was wrong. She would put her hand on my forehead to check if I had a fever, and she would ask me in the morning if I was in pain. I couldn't tell her how much my heart ached. Meanwhile, Nina didn't pay any attention to me at all. My greatest dream was to kiss her.

One time my mother asked me to return two baking pans to Mrs. Armer that she'd borrowed. I took the pans, ran down the stairs, and rushed into their shop, slightly out of breath. A Polish policeman was standing at the counter, talking to Mrs. Armer, and Nina was standing off to the side. The policeman had a truncheon at his waist.

Oblivious to the fact that I was interrupting their conversation, I said quickly to Mrs. Armer, "My mother would like to give you back the pans and thank you," while setting them on the counter. Before I managed to put them down, however, I felt a very strong blow to my head. Everything went dark in front of my eyes, and my legs buckled under me. With the remnants of my consciousness I could hear, as if from a great distance, the noise of the pans falling to the floor, and then . . . I lost consciousness.

I don't know how long I was unconscious. When I opened my eyes, I didn't know what had happened to me or where I was. I saw Nina's face above me and—amazingly!—her hand was stroking my head. I blinked several times to check if it was a dream, and then, spontaneously, without hesitation, I said to her, "Kiss me." Her face came closer to mine, and her lips touched my lips. I felt her hands under my head and then . . . then . . . Nina kissed me firmly, and I closed my eyes. I felt like I was in heaven, and I nearly fainted again.

It took me a long time to return to my senses. Nina helped me stand up and led me to our apartment. When we got there, she told my mother what had happened. The policeman had felt insulted that I'd interrupted him in midsentence and, without even a moment's hesitation, had hit me in the head very hard with his truncheon. When he realized I'd lost consciousness, he told Mrs. Armer, "Resuscitate him and kick him out." And then he left the shop.

My mother put me to bed and applied pressure to my bruise with a large kitchen knife. She looked at me with surprise because instead of screaming in pain, I was smiling blissfully. I couldn't explain to her how happy I was.

From that day on, I tried even harder to find opportunities to be close to Nina, and one time I asked her if there was anything I could help her with. Seeing my imploring gaze, she suggested I help her make the candies that she and her mother sold in the shop. First she made a paste from honey, sugar, and milk; then she poured a thin layer of this mixture into a baking pan and put it in the oven. After it was baked, Nina used a sharp knife to cut the mixture, which was now solidified, into small rectangles, and I wrapped them in little pieces of paper. This is how *krówki* ("little cows") were made. The name came from the fact that there was a picture of a cow on each wrapper.

One day, after a long period of reflection, hesitation, and inner struggle, I summoned the courage to say to Nina, "My head hurts again . . . Give me another kiss."

Nina gave me a strange look and answered, smiling, "Take a little cow and pretend it's a kiss from me." Then she shook her finger at me and added, "If I'd known you were such a rascal, I would never have kissed you."

At the beginning of 1941, I started visiting a private teacher every day who formed two classes in her apartment for pupils roughly my age. She taught us history and Polish, and one of her family members taught us math and physics. He had previously been a lecturer at the Jagiellonian University in Kraków, but immediately after the Germans invaded, he had been expelled from the university and moved to Wieliczka.

This teacher often forgot he was speaking to children and not to his university students. He told us about something that seemed crazy to us, called "quantum theory." It was his favorite topic. None of us understood anything he said, but this apparently didn't bother him. A bit of it has remained in my memory. For example, he told us that one thing could be in two places at the same time, and when a pupil pointed out to him that this was contrary to logic, the teacher asked, "What logic?" And then he answered the question himself: "It only goes against the logic that man now has at his disposal. Just as we discover new laws of nature, in the same way we must develop our logic so that it keeps up with these discoveries."

Another boy asked, "How can we be sure that something can really be in two places?"

"At the moment this is only a theory, but I predict that by the end of this century, it will have been practically and physically proven."

That day he also told us that a person and his life are merely a form of energy, and for this reason a person can never die. Death exists only in a person's imagination, not in nature. This was extremely interesting for me because of Musiu, and I wanted to hear more about it.

But at that moment, the female teacher entered the room and reproached him by saying, "When will you stop bothering these children with your idiotic ideas?"

I asked Jankiel what he thought of all this. He thought about it; then he said that nothing was impossible for God. And Adam confided in me that sometimes he distinctly felt that his father was with him, so perhaps this crazy teacher was right.

We weren't given any homework because the female teacher didn't want us coming to her with notebooks; someone might notice it and inform the Germans. So we were taught illegally and in secret. My afternoons were free, and I spent them with my friends, my cousin Francis at Aunt Liba's house, or—most importantly—Nina, when she needed me to help her make little cows.

Francis was only eight years old, but she spoke like an adult. She was getting prettier. She had a long braid that flew in the wind when we ran across the field in front of her house. Aunt Liba made sure that Francis was always nicely dressed, and this made the girl stand out from the other children of the neighborhood. She had a winter coat lined with fur, which all the children admired. We liked each other a lot, but I was only in love with Nina.

At the end of January 1941, a very unfortunate thing happened to me that nearly killed me. It all began with a simple toothache. My father took me to a dentist, who said my tooth needed to be pulled out. He gave me two injections of anesthetic and extracted the tooth. A few days later, I had a very high fever and my mouth hurt. A doctor named Edmund Fiszler examined me and said I had a blood infection.

Edmund Fiszler was a gynecologist, but he also knew about various diseases, and my parents trusted him completely. He was the husband of my father's cousin, Lonka. They had also escaped from Kraków to Wieliczka. Dr. Fiszler came every day and injected me with a red liquid, but my state worsened very quickly. I felt something hard growing beneath my chin, as if I had a rock there. Several of my friends kept a constant vigil at my bedside.

Francis brought me a fruitcake that Aunt Liba had baked for me. I liked it a lot, but I couldn't eat it because it was becoming increasingly difficult for me to swallow. Nina brought me some artificial cocoa to drink, which was considered a very special treat at that time. She even tried to feed me with a spoon. Her visits made me happy.

After a while, my neck completely disappeared, and there was a sack of pus beneath my chin, which oppressed me greatly. Not only was it impossible for me to eat, but it was very difficult to breathe. Soon I started losing consciousness for several moments at a time. Then I would fall into a black abyss. Sometimes I looked forward to this because fighting for every breath was exhausting.

I remember it being very calm, pleasant, and quiet there, in that oblivion. Then a miraculous light appeared far off in the darkness, and I drew closer to it, feeling an increasing bliss and joy. I felt this light inviting me to enter it, beckoning to me. I saw myself running toward it with open arms. But then I remembered my parents and friends—Jankiel, Adam, Francis, and Nina—who were waiting for me to return to them. I felt my will playing a decisive role in this.

I hesitated, not knowing what to do. I was standing in front of this light, undecided. I knew I just needed to take one more step to join it forever. Then Nina's face appeared to me, and I saw tears in her eyes. She took me by the hand and led me back. I found myself in darkness once again and—struggling to free myself from it—regained consciousness, completely exhausted spiritually and physically.

Seeing my state, Dr. Fiszler told my father it was absolutely necessary to bring an important professor, an acquaintance of his, from Kraków. After many phone calls and a great deal of pleading, the professor was finally convinced to come by taxi from Kraków.

He appeared the following morning. There was suddenly a large commotion in the room. My parents went out to greet him, and Lusia sat on the floor, crying. After everyone had entered, it seemed like a crowd was surrounding my bed. The professor was wearing a beautiful fur coat, which he unbuttoned. He examined me thoroughly; I was conscious the entire time. He said that my condition was very serious and I needed an operation immediately. I had a sack of pus under my chin that was pressing on my larynx and making it hard for me to breathe, which meant I could suffocate. Perhaps it was already too late to cut it open, and then it would be necessary to remove my jaw. He concluded his diagnosis by saying that if my parents wished me to live, he would have to take me to Kraków immediately and operate on me in his hospital that very day.

After a brief consultation with each other, my parents agreed. The professor ordered the taxi driver to start his car, and everyone began preparing me for the journey. I was semiconscious and having trouble breathing. My arms and legs were starting to go numb. My parents set me on a chair, wrapped me in a blanket, and were about to carry me downstairs to the car when the taxi driver rushed into the room and announced that he couldn't leave because the car had broken down.

"How long will it take you to repair it?" asked the professor.

"It'll take a long time because the radiator exploded."

It was decided that my father would go to the center of town to look for a taxi or some other car. It was a difficult undertaking because there weren't many taxis in Wieliczka at that time, and private cars were also a rarity.

I was put back in the bed. The professor stayed with me all the time and checked my pulse every few minutes. My mother sat by my bed and recited psalms. I saw tears flowing down her cheeks when she leaned her head over the yellowed pages of the prayer book, as if salvation could be found there.

Less than an hour later, my father ran into the room out of breath, exclaiming, "A car is waiting downstairs!" I was placed on the chair again and wrapped up in the blanket. Everyone helped, and the professor held my hand. Then something unexpected happened. I felt an intense pain in my throat; I started choking, and a torrent of yellowish-gray liquid gushed from my mouth and drenched the professor's beautiful fur coat from top to bottom. I saw his astonished face and horror in my mother's eyes, and then . . . I lost consciousness.

Opening my eyes again, I saw my frightened mother wiping the professor's fur coat with a towel. He pushed her away and then, looking at me, said, "Please don't worry about my coat and look at your son." Then he exclaimed, "A miracle has happened here! I've never seen anything like it!"

A few minutes later, when everyone had calmed down, the professor went up to Fiszler and congratulated him: "Your injections saved him. I've been saying for a long time that they're the only chance of a recovery in such a case, but many of my colleagues refuse to accept it."

The professor also said I no longer had to go with him to Kraków and that I'd soon recover. He wrote a prescription and, handing it to my mother, added with a smile, "Madam, your prayers also clearly played a role in this."

My father wanted to pay him, but the professor asked him only to pay for the taxi. In the end, he agreed to accept one of my father's paintings as a gift.

I began to breathe normally again. Never before had I realized that the simple act of breathing could give a person so much joy.

Francis and my friends continued to visit me, and I began to find joy in everything. Nina brought me artificial cocoa. One evening Zylek even visited me and brought me a new ball. It's impossible for me to put into words what it meant at that time to have my own ball, and a brand-new one, moreover—it was a fantastic present.

Two weeks later I was completely healthy again, which surprised even Dr. Fiszler. It was obvious that my joy had helped me recover more quickly. I remember my father going to the synagogue and saying a prayer of gratitude for my miraculous recovery.

After a while, unsettling news of persecution, and even murder, of Jewish people in other cities and towns started reaching us from various sources. Wieliczka had been peaceful in this respect until that time, but these reports made the Jews here very uneasy. Nobody knew what was going to happen to us in the near future. Once I heard my father tell my mother that we should thank God for every peaceful day. My physics teacher in the secret courses told us the same thing, except that he expressed it differently. He stated that a person is always learning.

"A person can do it consciously, as we are now, or unconsciously; in other words, he can learn things through life itself. It's precisely in this way that a person proves he is a cognizant being. Unfortunately, the time we have at our disposal has become so uncertain that you, young adepts of the art of thinking, must very quickly absorb what other people have many years to learn. For there's nothing sadder than leaving this world in a state of ignorance, for then it's as if you had never lived at all. This is why you should rejoice and give thanks for each day in which you can learn, for such a day extends your life by many days."

He paused briefly here and then added, "Life is not made up solely of hours, months, and years of breathing, but it's also the sum of our impressions and the knowledge we've managed to acquire."

It rained a lot in the spring of 1941, and the roof of our house began to leak. It needed to be repaired quickly, but it wasn't possible to get tar paper anywhere. My father remembered that he had a good friend who was the owner of a large tar paper factory in Tarnów and was still running it, even though the Germans had taken it away from him and appointed a German supervisor. My father's friend was named Fessel, and his factory was called Papapol. He helped the German supervisor run the factory, like Chaim Schenker at his tannery in Wieliczka.

Until the autumn of 1941, it was still possible to travel freely to and from Wieliczka. My father decided to visit Fessel and ask him for several rolls of tar paper.

Near the factory, my father encountered a huge German roundup of Jews. Terrified people were running in all directions, not knowing where to go because vehicles were constantly arriving with German soldiers jumping out of them. Screams and gunshots could be heard. In the midst of this tumult, my father saw Heniek Mansfeld, the son of one of our relatives (the one who had sold my grandfather's watch in Kraków), standing helplessly on the street and looking terrified. He was about eighteen years old at the time.

My father ran up to him, grabbed him by the hand, and shouted, "Come with me!"

They ran through a gate, and my father managed to reach Papapol, where they both hid until the evening.

That day in Tarnów, the Germans carried out a roundup of Jews who were living there illegally. At that time there wasn't yet a ghetto in Tarnów, and many Jews hoped that a better fate awaited them there. Everyone who was caught that day was shot. Heniek Mansfeld had escaped from Kraków and was staying in Tarnów illegally. My father saved his life.

In the summer of 1941, we stopped studying because our teacher had been warned that she should end the lessons. I was unhappy because I really enjoyed them. They made me feel that I was a normal person, just like the Polish children who went to school.

My parents asked around to see if there was anyone who would teach Jewish children, but their efforts were in vain. And so I began to spend my mornings wandering the streets with my friends or sitting at Francis's house. Nina stopped making little cows because she no longer had any milk or honey, and so I couldn't visit her. We started rolling cigarettes again and playing ball for them. All my friends now smoked, except for Jankiel.

One morning I heard the bell of a fire truck in our street. I got dressed quickly and went to see what was happening. A wooden shed was on fire. The blaze was put out quickly, so I started heading home again. Suddenly I saw a man in an unfamiliar uniform standing in front of a closed shop. I stopped in my tracks because I wanted to make sure I wasn't in danger.

To my surprise, I saw that the man was inspecting the padlock hanging on the shop's door. If he hadn't been wearing a uniform, I would have thought he was a thief. But he had a wide leather belt and a revolver at his side, and a narrow strap across his chest like a policeman. He was also wearing a cap similar to a policeman's cap, except that it was a lighter color. He stopped examining the padlock and walked up to me.

"I can see you're afraid of me," he said with a smile.

He seemed very friendly, but I could've been mistaken, so I didn't say anything. I was only thinking about how I could escape if necessary.

"You have nothing to be afraid of. I like kids," he added. "What's your name?"

"Henryk," I answered timidly.

"I've known a lot of Henryks, and they're all nice. You look nice, too. Where do you live?"

"Not far from here." I pointed toward our house. Then I summoned all my courage and asked, "Who are you?"

He pointed to the tin badge on his chest and his cap. The word "Inspection" was written on it, but I still didn't understand. He smiled again.

"'Inspection' is a company that protects shops and houses from being robbed. Every morning and evening I check whether there have been any break-ins and if the shops are locked up. Sometimes I check at night, too."

"Were there any break-ins last night?"

"No, but I haven't checked all the shops yet. If you want, you can come with me, and we'll check them together."

"But I'm . . . I'm a Jew," I said, ashamed.

He smiled at me again, and this time his smile was even kinder.

"You should be proud of that," he said in a serious tone. He looked me straight in the eyes and nodded, as if to emphasize his words.

"Why should I be proud of it?" I asked, looking at him in disbelief.

"Because we're in the midst of such times, now, when he who suffers has a reason to be proud."

I didn't really understand what he meant, but I liked what he said. We walked through Klasno together, checking the shops. Then he said goodbye to me and suggested that I accompany him in the evening as well. From then on, I walked with him twice a day and helped him check that the shops were all locked up.

It turned out that he was a junior high school teacher who had lost his job because he'd carelessly said something during a lesson that was forbidden to say. Since then, he hadn't been able to find any other position within the education system. And so he'd found a job as a guard in the inspection company. While we walked around together, he gave me lectures on a different topic every day.

He spoke in a very interesting manner and, most importantly, in language that was comprehensible to me. He wanted me to understand what he was saying, so he often explained the same thing to me in different ways. He even allowed me to wear his strap sometimes, which made me feel very proud. He told me I could call him by his first name, Stanisław, and he called me Henius, the diminutive form of Henryk, which expressed his affection for me. They were the best lessons I've ever had in my life and, moreover, they were completely free.

We grew accustomed to each other and waited for each other every morning and evening at a prearranged spot. My parents allowed me to do this because they found out that Stanisław was a decent person and that he had been a well-loved teacher.

During this time, my father met a Jewish man from Germany and became friends with him. He had been, apparently, a very famous actor in Berlin. The Germans had deported him to Poland—or he had come here of his own volition—and after many difficulties he had ended up in Wieliczka. His name was Gottowt, and he was about sixty years old.[1] He was completely helpless, so my father started taking care of him. It was impossible to find a room for him in Wieliczka because the whole town was overflowing with Jewish refugees. Wieliczka was still regarded as the most peaceful place for Jews.

Gottowt lived with us and slept on a fold-out bed. After a while, my father came up with the idea of renovating an annex of the house where my aunt Liba lived and making a room for Mr. Gottowt there. Chaim Schenker once again sent workers from his tannery, and a few days later there was a large, pretty room ready for Gottowt. The only problem left was the roof, which needed to be covered with tar paper. So my father went to Tarnów again.

This time it turned out that Fessel was being very closely watched and couldn't supply tar paper without permission from the German supervisor. But he promised my father he would try to find a solution and invited him to stay the night. The following day, Fessel went to Papapol, and my father stayed in his apartment. At midday a messenger came from Fessel and took my father to the factory, where he was led to the supervisor's office.

Fessel introduced my father by saying, "This is the famous portrait painter Schönker, whom I told you about."

To my father's astonishment, the supervisor stretched out his hand to him and said, *"Guten Tag."*

Fessel had convinced this German to commission a portrait of himself from my father. My father was driven in a factory vehicle to get some paint and other supplies, and that very day he started painting a portrait of the supervisor. In total, he painted several portraits of him and his wife. The Papapol car came for him every few days, and each time he would bring home a roll of tar paper or a small amount of food, which helped us very much.

Mr. Gottowt's room was completed and more or less furnished. Two of my father's paintings were hung on the wall, and near the entrance stood a small sculpture that Hochman had given him. Mr. Gottowt was so overjoyed that he kissed all of us and assured us that it was the happiest day of his life.

Gottowt was overall a very cheerful person. He seemed eternally happy and often uttered a strange expression: when someone asked him *"Wie geht's?"* ("How are you?"), he always answered, with a smile, *"Alles in Butter,"* which meant that everything was going as smoothly as if it were in butter. My father said this expression showed what a kind and pleasant man Gottowt was.

We all liked him because he was always in a wonderful mood. Aunt Liba also felt safer when someone was living in her house with them. Gottowt helped her do work of various kinds. He was most adored by our trio: Francis, Fela, and me. Gottowt performed for us as if he were on a real stage. We didn't always understand what his performances were about, but watching him act was a wonderful experience.

Tragic news sometimes reached us about Jews being killed and persecuted, but Gottowt wasn't disturbed by it. I once asked him if he was afraid. He said he wasn't because a true actor lives not only his own life but also the lives of those whom he portrays onstage. In this way he had already survived many tragedies; he had died and been reborn many times. Each time there were new joys, new reasons to be happy, and new tragedies. According to Gottowt, the essence of life wasn't eating, sleeping, and toiling away until the day one dies. The essence of life was its continuity and the playing of one's role as well as one can in every single scene—for life is eternal.

"Why should I be afraid, then?" he asked.

"I'm afraid—maybe because I'm not an actor," I said.

Gottowt smiled at me. "You're also an actor. Every person is an actor, though he doesn't know it."

I spent more and more time with him. Right after doing the rounds with Stanisław, I went to visit Gottowt. My friends were slightly unhappy about my new friendship because I spent less time with them, but Gottowt attracted me so strongly that I wasn't willing to leave him for any reason. I also brought him packages of food, like I did for Aunt Liba, because my father had begun to paint portraits of two other German officers in Tarnów and received food from them.

In the summer of 1941, Iziu Grossfeld came to Wieliczka from Kraków with his wife, Madzia, and their twelve-year-old son, Adaś. Iziu was the son of my grandfather's second wife. He ran a book-lending library in Kraków. He was also a renowned philatelist. I became very close friends with Adaś. Mr. Gottowt agreed to let him take part in our plays, too. I had more time now because one day my rounds with Stanisław came to an end. He told me that his manager had been replaced, and the new one forbade him from taking me on his rounds. While saying goodbye to each other, we both had tears in our eyes. Stanisław told me not to worry because he wasn't going to spend his whole life inspecting locks, either.

Seeing how dejected I was, Adaś tried to cheer me up, and when nothing helped, he suggested we go around together checking the shops.

"We don't have to work for the inspection company to do it," he said, as if it were his favorite activity. I agreed, and a few days later my depression passed, and I began to laugh again.

Out of gratitude, I introduced Adaś to my friends, who taught him to play soccer. Up until then Adaś had rarely gone outside, because he spent his entire days either reading books or looking at his stamp albums. He was very intelligent. I remember that he had a book titled *Chemistry Is Conquering the World*, which he almost knew by heart, and he taught me things from it.

But the most profound experience for me at that time was the new world that had opened up before me—the world of stamps. It was unbelievable how much emotion we invested in them and how many diverse and marvelous things I learned thanks to them. So many stories, famous people, and exotic countries spoke to me from the stamps. Adaś could say something about almost every stamp, and when he didn't know, he asked his father.

They lived near the center of Wieliczka. A close friend of theirs, a Polish man, rented his apartment to them and went to live with his mother in the countryside. He was also a philatelist, and Adaś's father paid him rent in stamps. Sometimes I stayed the night with them because I wanted to keep looking at the stamps. I started collecting them, too, and Adaś gave me his duplicates.

Considering the conditions around us, we could thank God that we weren't worse off. My father sold my mother's diamond, and we lived off this money for a while. There wasn't a ghetto in Wieliczka, and Jews lived with the hope that this relative peace would last until the end of the war. After all, the war had to end eventually. The only one who warned us was Gottowt. I heard him once tell my father that it was as if all the people in Wieliczka were hypnotized and had deluded themselves into thinking this peace would last forever.

"After a long silence, a storm comes. I know the Nazis very well, and I know what they're capable of."

"So what are the Jews supposed to do? We don't have any means of escape. With their silence, the nations of the world have condemned us to death," answered my father.

"You know, Leon, death isn't the worst thing a person can experience."

My father looked at him in surprise, and Gottowt added, "Death is only the worst thing if a person isn't prepared for it."

"Preparing oneself for death is like surrendering to it. I want to fight for life, not give in to it."

But Gottowt was insistent. "You say yourself, Leon, that the nations of the world have condemned us to death, so why delude ourselves?"

"We won't all die, and those who survive will describe what happened here and will reveal the shame of those who condemned us with their silence. It will be the duty of those who survive. This is why we must all fight to live."

"Leon, you're quite an optimist if you think the nations of the world are going to care about that accusation at all."

"I know they won't, but they'll be forced to face it by the judgment of history, and I believe the world will no longer be how it was before. I believe it will be better."

Seeing the doubt on Gottowt's face, my father told him, "I advise you, too, not to give up and to fight for your life."

Gottowt smiled and said, "It will depend on the Great Director." And he pointed at the sky. "But you also need to know when it's time to leave the stage."

At the end of 1941, my father started painting again—this time a portrait of a general from Gliwice. The general had been at a party in Tarnów hosted by one of the officers my father had painted and, seeing his portrait, had expressed a desire for my father to paint him, too. This suited my father very well because then he was given a pass allowing him to travel freely. On the way, he always bought food for us in villages, which was much cheaper than in Wieliczka. At that time, it was no longer possible to leave the town without special permission. My father took this opportunity to suggest to the officer in Tarnów that he paint one more portrait of him, to which the officer agreed.

On December 11, SS troops conducted a huge roundup in Tarnów. My father happened, by chance, to be there at that time. Jews were caught in the streets and taken out of their apartments. Goebbels's newspaper, *Das Reich*, later wrote that a Jewish uprising had been suppressed in Tarnów.

My father was also caught and ordered to stand against a wall in a square along with the others. Every tenth Jew was shot. My father wasn't shot, but then he and another Jewish man were ordered by an SS soldier to drag the bodies of the murdered men to a gate. Some green police vehicles were already parked in the square with SS soldiers inside them who were going to take away the arrested Jews. My father saw an evil glint in the eyes of the SS soldier who had given him the command, and he sensed the soldier wanted to shoot him.

When my father had laid the last corpse by the gate, he started running as fast as he could to a police vehicle and jumped into it. The SS soldier couldn't shoot at him because there were other SS soldiers next to him, guarding the arrested men. He ran up to the vehicle and hit my father in the head with the butt of his rifle, wounding him. Thankfully my father was wearing a hat, and this saved his life. My father feared another blow, but the vehicle started moving.

The men were transported to a prison in Tarnów, where they had to hand over all their belongings. My father gave them his wallet, which contained the letter from Major von Greif from Oświęcim stating that he'd saved the German pilot. Then they were crammed into small cells—several dozen people in each. Someone in the cell made a bandage for my father from a shirt and stopped the flow of blood.

It was terribly stuffy in the cell, and people began to faint. They were given nothing to eat or drink. At night, drunk Germans entered the cell and pulled all the men out into the corridor. They were ordered to lower their trousers and underpants and face a wall with their behinds stuck out. The Germans whipped the prisoners and forced them to shout in German, "I'm guilty of the war with America!" (It was precisely on that day, December 11, 1941, that Hitler declared war on the United States.) They repeated this routine every night.

The prisoners were given almost nothing to eat and very little water. Older people lay on top of others, semiconscious. My father later told my mother that he started preparing himself for death because he felt utterly helpless. He understood, then, what Gottowt had meant.

A few days later, he was summoned from his cell. His possessions were given back to him, and he was released from the prison without a single word of explanation. The Germans must have found the letter about saving the pilot. My father seems to have been the only prisoner who was released. All the others were sent to Auschwitz, where they were murdered.

News of the roundup and the murders in Tarnów had reached Wieliczka by this time. Because my father hadn't returned at the agreed time, my mother was very afraid he'd been killed. I clearly remember her fervently reciting psalms while her tears pattered onto the soaked pages of her prayer book. Lusia was standing next to me, very sad as if she understood what was happening, and I was looking out the window at the back of our house. In my mind I recited a prayer that I'd learned in kindergarten. I didn't confine myself solely to its words but also, in my own words, begged God not to take my father away from me.

Then I saw someone off in the distance, slowly walking toward our house. It was a man with something white on his head. Suddenly ... my heart nearly stopped from joy and excitement—I recognized my father. I wanted to tell my mother, but I couldn't control my voice and only managed to stammer a few inarticulate sounds. My mother raised her head from the prayer book, and I pointed out the window.

She ran over and, recognizing my father, shouted, "Thank you, dear Lord!" Then she sat down on a chair as if all her strength had left her. We all ran out of the house to meet him.

On Saturday my father once again said a prayer of gratitude, this time for his survival.

My father's experiences in Tarnów shocked my family and made us aware that the relative peace in Wieliczka could end at any moment. New, terrible rumors of the persecution of Jews in nearby towns started reaching us. Murders were now part of the daily routines there. My mother begged my father to stop traveling, but he thought it might enable him to make contact with someone and find a place where we could switch to Aryan papers. However, despite his searches, he didn't find anyone he could trust.

Many people in Wieliczka were under the illusion that the Germans had other plans for this town because they were allowing the *Judenrat* to organize a soup kitchen for poor Jews, which distributed over twelve hundred meals per day in the first months of 1942. The *Judenrat* also created workshops where uniforms were sewn for the Wehrmacht, and those who worked there hoped this would save them.

My father continued to look for some way to save us, and painted as many portraits as possible. Sometimes by doing this he was able to find out something from the Germans, and he passed these pieces of information to his friends. In Tarnów the roundups and murders of Jews were becoming more frequent, but my father kept going there. He became, however, increasingly pessimistic.

In the first half of June 1942, the Germans sent thirty-five hundred Jews from Tarnów to Bełżec to be killed. Several days later another ten thousand Jews from Tarnów were sent there. The German machinery of death had begun to work at full steam. Immediately after this transport, a ghetto was created in Tarnów.

My father used his pass to go in and out of the Tarnów ghetto, where he was sometimes forced to sleep when he finished painting late in the day. It was a very dangerous place, but he had to do it because the people who were posing for his portraits knew who he was and where he lived. My father was afraid that if he didn't show up when they were expecting him, they might send the gestapo after him. Now every time he left Wieliczka, he said goodbye to us as if we were seeing each other for the last time.

Soon, however, my father's journeys ended. The general left Gliwice, and my father painted the last portrait of the officer in Tarnów. He had to give back his pass, and without it he could no longer leave Wieliczka. His efforts to find us a safe place to hide came to an end.

At the beginning of July 1942, a strange anxiety overcame the Jews of Wieliczka. The entire atmosphere of the town changed, and everyone felt some sort of tension hanging in the air.

An instinct of self-preservation forewarned us and strained our nerves. It spread to children, too—the subject of death appeared in our conversations. Jankiel told me he'd had a dream about "soldiers of death" who were surrounding Wieliczka. They were wearing black uniforms and had glowing coals instead of eyes. Adam said that if the Germans came for him, he would be shot just like his father—and he showed us how it was going to look. He leaned to one side and then the other, shouting, "Bang! Bang!"

Watching this, Zylek told me, "You see, Henryk, there are people for whom death isn't so terrible."

I didn't want to resign myself to it. I couldn't accept this at all, because I wanted to live. I so desperately wanted to live! I looked for someone who could cheer me up. I wanted to hear from someone that there was still hope and that perhaps the worst wasn't awaiting us. But everyone was gripped by fear because right at that time, in July 1942, the Germans demanded a huge sum of money from the Jews, and it wasn't certain whether the *Judenrat* would be able to collect the required amount.

Adaś told me he'd begun to take his stamps out of the albums and put them in small paper bags, which would be easier to take with him if he needed to escape. He suggested that I help him do this. It was necessary to separate the stamps and make sure they were all in the proper bags. Under normal circumstances I would have been pleased to do such a task, but at that time I refused because I felt I didn't have enough patience for it. I was only eleven years old then, but I felt much older. The general despondency of the Jewish people in Wieliczka was affecting me. I felt numb. I hoped to find someone who could pull me out of this torpor.

Even Francis, who had always been in a good mood, became quiet and serious. I often found her in deep reflection, as if detached from everything around her. I asked her if she was scared.

To my surprise, she answered very calmly, "No, I'm not scared . . . not even of death." And then she asked me, "Are you scared?"

"I'm scared of death," I admitted, because I wanted to be honest with her. I couldn't understand how it was possible not to be afraid of it.

"How is it possible not to fear death?" I asked.

Her answer surprised me even more.

"I don't know how you can do it, but I've got reassurance," she said hesitantly, as if wondering whether to tell me this.

"What kind of reassurance?"

To which Francis answered, very seriously and as if in a reverie, "Several times at night an angel has appeared to me and told me that when my time comes, he'll take me to him, and I'll be happy in a new world."

I was stunned by this conversation, but it seemed to me that Francis was making it all up.

"Have you told your mother or Fela about this?"

"No, you're the only one who knows."

I couldn't resist asking her, "And wouldn't you be sad to leave this world? Your mother, Fela, and me?"

"I would be sad, but the saddest thing for me would be to abandon my dolls and leave them all alone."

"Leave them all alone?" I repeated her words. "But your dolls aren't alive."

She looked at me as if she didn't understand what I was saying.

"My dolls live their own lives, connected to mine. If I leave this world, they'll stop living, too."

It was a strange conversation. Later I thought about it many times.

One day I went to visit Francis, but she wasn't home, so I went to see Gottowt, who was cooking something.

"Wie geht's?" I asked him, as usual.

Gottowt turned to me with a radiant smile. *"Alles in Butter,"* he answered, as if he had some happy news to give me.

"What's going as smoothly as butter?" I asked.

At the same time, my heart felt lighter because I'd found someone who was still in a good mood.

Gottowt approached me, looked into my eyes, and gently took hold of my chin.

"All of human life is as smooth as butter."

"I don't feel it."

"Because you don't want to feel it. If you decide to feel this way, you'll feel it. It depends entirely on you, nobody else. Not even on the situation you find yourself in. It's solely your decision."

"But . . . but . . . the Germans might kill us," I answered, my voice filled with terror.

Gottowt sat down and pulled me closer to him.

"The Germans won't kill us; they'll only kill themselves."

"But we're the ones who might leave this world and lose our lives," I said in a mournful voice.

"We can leave this world, but we won't lose our lives, because a human life is eternal and not dependent on the Germans. Live and enjoy every day, because this is the life that you've received. Life is always a great gift from heaven, even when a person is suffering."

We looked at each other, and I felt much better. I felt in control of my life again and certain that my fate was in my own hands.

"Alles in Butter?" asked Gottowt.

I laughed and answered, *"Alles in Butter."* That was the very last time I heard him say this.

The *Judenrat* in Wieliczka finally managed to collect the amount of money demanded by the Germans, and a "contribution" of 150,000 złoty was paid. The atmosphere of fear and anxiety didn't diminish, however, because the Germans were forcing an increasing number of Jews into Wieliczka from the surrounding towns and villages.

It was clear to my father that something terrible was about to befall the Jews of Wieliczka. While traveling around, he had often seen that whenever a large number of Jews were being gathered together, they were transported to death camps soon afterward. There was no way to escape, so he decided to build a bunker for us, where we planned to hide during a roundup operation.

At that time, the concept of *judenrein* ("cleansed of Jews") was still unknown. A roundup operation of this type usually lasted one or two days. A certain number of Jews were sent away, and the rest continued to live where they were until the next deportation. This is how it had been happening in nearby towns so far. If you managed to survive one of these roundups, it was followed by another period of relative peace.

My father decided to build the bunker under the floor of our apartment. Between the floor and the ceiling of the warehouse beneath us there was a large space. Some friends recommended a good, reliable carpenter, a Polish man—someone we could trust not to betray us. He built a trapdoor in the floor that could be opened, and he fitted it so perfectly that it was nearly invisible. Beneath the trapdoor there were several stairs down to the hiding place.

My father told Aunt Liba that we had a large bunker and invited her to hide there with us. But she already had a hiding place in the countryside guaranteed for her by the Polish woman who owned the house where she was currently living (or perhaps one of her relatives).

After finishing the work and painting the floor with red varnish, it was impossible to see the trapdoor to our bunker. They covered it with a small carpet, on which they set a table. My father was satisfied and paid the carpenter the sum he'd asked for. He was a kind man, and it was clear he was trying very hard to help us. After he was paid, he and my father sat together at the table and drank tea. The carpenter told my father he'd done the best he could, but in his opinion such a bunker was not very secure because the Germans could come here with dogs that would immediately detect the scent of people. Furthermore, there was no way to know how long such a roundup operation could last and whether Klasno would continue to be surrounded by Germans for a long time afterward.

"So what can we do?" asked my father.

The carpenter thought for a while, as if considering various options. Then he said, "I'm willing to hide you at my home. I have a large farm near Wieliczka, without any neighbors. You'll be much safer there, and I'll tell you when it's safe for you to return to Wieliczka."

My parents consulted with each other in the bedroom, and after establishing how much the carpenter would be paid for helping us, they agreed. It was decided that if the situation in Wieliczka got worse, we would go to his house. But my father was still happy that he'd made the bunker because if we were taken by surprise, it would give us a chance to survive.

The situation in Wieliczka was unclear. On the one hand, an increasing number of Jews were flowing into the town, which was a sign that a deportation was soon going to take place. But on the other hand, in the middle of August, the Germans ordered the *Judenrat* to organize a Jewish hospital. My father thought this might be merely an attempt to distract people and dull Jewish people's vigilance. He informed Gottowt about our bunker and told him he could use it. Gottowt thanked him but said he had other plans. My father wanted to tell Hochman about it, too, but he'd disappeared from the town.

On August 20, the Germans began to resettle Jews from Niepołomice and Dobczyce to Wieliczka in massive numbers. For my father, this was a sign that something significant was beginning, and the following day he asked our carpenter friend to take us to his house.

The carpenter came in a horse-drawn wagon to pick us up late in the evening. We dressed ourselves in peasant clothes and traveled with him along dirt roads. Lusia slept the whole trip, and I also dozed from time to time. I remember that it was a clear night. Eventually we stopped near a large barn. Our friend helped us get out of the wagon, and then we all went inside. A single light bulb was glowing. In the barn there were several cows and one horse. We entered the second half of the barn, where hay was stored.

The carpenter pushed several bundles of hay to the side and lifted a trapdoor, and then we saw a dark opening. He entered first and helped each of us descend. There was very little space there, but we settled inside somehow. We had a small battery-powered flashlight. The carpenter told us that during the day there was a bit of light from a gap in the wall. The gap wasn't visible because it was covered with thick glass. He gave us water, half a loaf of bread, a bit of butter, and several apples. There was an empty bucket there, too.

"You can stay here for a few days. I'll bring you food. You have nothing to fear; nobody will find you here," he said, to lift our spirits. He also pointed out that the walls and floor of the bunker were lined with tar paper and planks to keep out moisture.

In the bunker there were some straw mattresses, which we lay down on. My mother turned on the flashlight, read a passage from a psalm, and kissed me and Lusia. The Book of Psalms accompanied my mother throughout her entire life, and she was absolutely convinced that they helped her in every situation and brought her everything she asked for.

It turned out we had left Wieliczka at the very last possible moment. On the morning of August 22, 1942, the town was surrounded by German troops, and checkpoints were set up on all roads to the town. Nobody could leave.

Our host brought us some food in the morning and told us what was happening. We were certain the roundup operation had begun and that it would last only a day or two.

There was very little air in the bunker. The carpenter took me and my father to another hiding place in the attic of his house, right beneath the roof. We spent an incredibly difficult day there because the roof tiles were heated by the sun, and it was as hot as a furnace in the hiding place. In the afternoon, when our host brought us some more food, we were nearly fainting. I kept falling asleep, and my father would wake me up. We were lucky to have bottles of water there, and we drank constantly, since otherwise we wouldn't have emerged from that hiding place alive.

My father asked the carpenter to take us back to where my mother and Lusia were hiding. In the evening we returned to the bunker in the barn. Our host fixed something so there would be more air for us.

Another day passed, but there was no news of a roundup operation in Wieliczka. On August 24 we found out that a Jewish hospital had been opened there, which gave us hope that somehow everything would turn out okay. But the very next day, August 25, special units of the *Einsatzkommando* arrived in Wieliczka—professional murderers who specialized in mass killings. It was then that the operation began.

Jankiel's dream became reality.

On August 26, early in the morning, eleven Jews were shot near the German military headquarters, which was situated in a district called Lekarka, and they were buried nearby. At midday, the Germans evacuated over one hundred patients from the Jewish hospital that had just been opened, on their orders, only two days before—they took them away by truck in an unknown direction.

The brutality of this evacuation surpassed all limits of the imagination. The invalids were beaten and thrown into trucks as roughly as sacks of flour. In the evening our host, very frightened, brought us news that these invalids had been taken to a hill called Goat Mountain, in a forest near Niepołomice, where they'd been shot. They were buried there in a mass grave.

The Jewish doctors of this hospital didn't know where their patients had been taken, but they'd witnessed how the Germans had treated them. The scale of this crime was so horrible and inconceivable for a normal person that in the afternoon of that same day, several dozen people—doctors and nurses from the hospital—gathered in the offices of the *Judenrat* to protest the Germans' inhumane treatment of the invalids. Even then, the doctors, as well as the entire hospital staff, didn't realize who they were dealing with.

The relative peace in Wieliczka up until this point had caused Jews to let their guard down. It all ended in a cruel and irreversible manner. Everyone who took part in the protest was beaten severely by the Germans right there, in the *Judenrat* building. Then they were forced into trucks and taken to Goat Mountain—where they were shot and buried next to their patients. We found out about all this much later.

Our host was in a changed mood that day; it was clear there was a struggle going on inside him. He told us that it seemed like this wasn't a normal roundup, and so he could no longer hide us because it would endanger himself and his family. The Germans were walking around the whole area looking for Jews. When a Jew was found, he or she was shot on the spot. Many informers were revealing Jews' hiding spots. We had to leave his barn that very night and find somewhere else to hide. My father reassured him and gave him some money to keep us for a few more days.

At night we heard gunshots in the fields, some very close to us. That night our host came to us twice, and my father gave him money each time. He told us increasingly terrifying news.

That day the Germans had announced that all the remaining Jews in Wieliczka had to gather in the market square at seven o'clock in the evening. In the market square, they were told that the following day, August 27, they had to gather at seven o'clock in the morning in a meadow in Bogucice, by the train tracks, near the Wieliczka train station. The Jews were ordered to take enough food with them for four days and were allowed to take ten kilograms of personal belongings per family.

On August 27, gunshots could be heard all day long. Later we found out that about eight or nine thousand Jewish people had gathered in the meadow in Bogucice. The Germans had made a selection on the spot. Seven hundred old and disabled people were taken in trucks to Goat Mountain and shot there. All the rest were locked up in freight cars and transported to the death camp in Bełżec.

That day, the *Einsatzkommando* began a systematic search throughout Wieliczka. They walked around with dogs, searching for hiding places and bunkers. They were already very specialized in this, and hardly anyone managed to escape them. Individual Jews were killed on the spot. Larger groups of people were led to the cemetery and shot there. The sounds of gunshots reached us, but we couldn't hear people's screams.

On August 28 it was the same. The massacre of Jews continued all day long. Everyone was murdered—children, women, disabled people, young and old alike—in the same way that chickens are slaughtered. For the *Einsatzkommando*, it was simply work that needed to be done.

That day our host became even more uneasy and insisted more strongly that we had to leave. My father reassured him again and asked him to keep us for a few more days, because the massacre would surely end at some point. He promised we would leave immediately after it ended. He gave him some more money, and our host agreed.

All night long, from August 28 to 29, my mother kept her hand on my forehead because I was constantly waking up, terrified. I had a terrible nightmare and was delirious. My mother's hand was the only thing that calmed me. When I woke up in the morning, my heart was racing, and I had a strange foreboding that something very important was going to happen to me that day, something decisive in my life.

That day is extremely memorable for me—August 29, 1942. What happened to me then was terrible, bewildering, and incomprehensible.

Early in the morning, the bunker's trapdoor flew open, and above us we saw an old woman waving her arms and screaming angrily, "Get out of here, Jews! Clear out of here immediately because if you don't, I'll call the Germans! Quickly! Quickly! Go away and never come back to our house!"

It was the carpenter's mother. My parents understood there was nothing we could do, so we climbed out of the bunker one at a time.

The woman was glaring at us as if we were devils and shouted, "The nerve of you to endanger innocent people!"

She turned around, went to the barn door, and stood next to the wall. Waving an arm toward the field in front of the barn, she continued to scream, "That's where you belong, not here!"

We went out into the field in silence. We were shocked and terrified. My father picked Lusia up, and we began to walk straight ahead. The woman shouted after us, "Don't show up here again, you Jews!" Then she closed the barn door.

We walked through the meadow. The grass seemed even greener to me than usual. We had no set direction or aim—we just walked, without thinking. We wanted to get as far away as possible from this house, which was supposed to have served us as a shelter but now turned out to be a very dangerous place. After a while, we noticed bushes in the distance and my father decided to head toward them. Suddenly we saw something lying in the grass several steps ahead of us. We went closer to see what it was—and my mother screamed in horror. She covered her face with her hands and would have fallen to the ground if my father hadn't held her up.

In front of us lay the corpses of two women. My father shouted, "Oh! It's Gizela!" Her body was contorted in a strange spasm. She was barefoot and wearing only a nightgown. I knew her well, too. She was my father's aunt who lived in Wieliczka—Gizela Schenker, a very nice old lady. We'd heard she was also going to hide in someone's house in this area. Next to her lay the body of a young woman, also nearly naked. Her wide-open eyes were staring at the sky. She was also a relative of my father's and Gizela's, but I no longer remember exactly who she was.

We couldn't stay there very long because in this spot we were visible from far off. We reached the bushes, and my father went to check if it was possible to hide in them. The bushes turned out to be not very dense; anyone who came close to them would be able to see us. There was nowhere else for us to go, however, so my father decided we would wait there until evening.

We lay in these bushes for about two hours, hungry and thirsty, and Lusia started crying. My parents discussed whether one of us should go back to the carpenter to ask him for bread and water. They abandoned this idea, however, because it was too dangerous. Instead, my father decided to find out what was around the spot where we were hiding. He soon returned and told us we were very close to a stream. We went to it and drank some water. It turned out we weren't far from a dirt road that led to a village; in the distance we could see several farmhouses. I offered to go to the village to buy some bread.

My father didn't want to let me do this, but I insisted, and finally he agreed. Then I had to convince my mother, who was very worried, but she also finally agreed. I took off my sandals because I wanted to go barefoot. In my short, ragged trousers and with my blond mop of hair I looked like a typical village urchin. My father gave me some money for bread, and I cautiously emerged from the bushes. Trying to memorize the hiding spot and the road, I headed toward the village, where I expected to find a small grocery shop of some kind.

My hopes were dashed because it turned out there wasn't a village—just a few isolated houses. I decided to keep going and find some bread at any cost. My mission seemed so important to me that I believed our survival depended on it. And so I walked straight ahead and realized I was walking in the direction of Wieliczka. I decided that if I saw a policeman on the road, I would turn back. But I hoped I would reach a grocery shop before a policeman came along.

I passed some people on the road, but nobody paid any attention to me. I was afraid to ask them anything, for the question itself could give me away. Some buildings began to appear. On the first house I saw two large posters hanging next to each other. They were bright yellow and stood out very distinctly from the walls of the house. One was in German, and the other in Polish.

I read on the posters that on August 27, 1942, an operation had begun to remove all the Jews from Wieliczka. Then there was a list of all the things that were forbidden for the Polish residents of Wieliczka and the surrounding areas. For hiding Jews the punishment was death; for helping Jews in any other way, the punishment was death . . . All the points of the edict carried the threat of execution. Now I understood why the carpenter's mother had been so terrified.

I hurried onward so as not to draw attention to myself, and several dozen meters farther, I finally spotted what I'd urgently been seeking—a grocery shop. I looked around. Not seeing anything suspicious, I went inside. In the shop there was an old woman talking to the shopkeeper. I waited patiently for them to finish their conversation.

I heard the woman say, "You know, it was impossible to reach your shop all week long. The roads were full of Germans, stopping people. They only took down the checkpoints today."

"They went completely crazy with the Jews," said the shopkeeper.

"Only the Jews? I'm scared they'll do the same with us later," said the old woman.

This didn't make any particular impression on the shopkeeper, and she calmly answered, "You know what our priest said in church last Sunday? 'He who lives by the sword will die by the sword.'"

"I hope he's right. Goodbye."

The shopkeeper looked at me curiously and asked, "What would you like?"

"A loaf of bread," I answered, trying very hard to remain calm, but my heart was pounding inside me.

She brought me bread and put it in a paper bag. "Anything else?" she asked. I looked around the shop. A sausage was hanging there, and at the sight of it my mouth started watering, but I knew I didn't have enough money, so I shook my head.

I noticed that the woman was looking at me rather strangely. I paid for the bread and was about to leave, but she stopped me, cut off a large piece of sausage, and gave it to me, saying, "Here, it's a present from me."

I took this sausage from her slowly, like something extremely precious. I thanked her and left the shop. I desperately wanted to eat a bit of the sausage, but I decided to take it to my parents and Lusia. There was no space in the bag the bread was in, so I put the sausage in my pocket. It stuck out, but it didn't inhibit my walking.

I was going to head back, but it occurred to me that if there were no longer any police checkpoints on the road, perhaps the roundup operation was over. I thought perhaps we'd be able to return to Wieliczka that night and hide there. I decided to find out what was happening. But I promised myself I'd immediately turn back if I saw German soldiers.

And so I continued onward. My heart started pounding harder. All my senses were strained, and I was ready to run away at any moment. I passed more and more people, but nobody looked at me. Suddenly I realized that the area I found myself in was very familiar. Here, behind this house, was the road to the lake, and from there it wasn't far to Francis's house. I decided to go there. Maybe I could find out what had happened to them.

I went to the edge of the lake. A boy my age was standing there, fishing. My heart froze. Off in the distance, I saw four Germans in black uniforms who were laughing and walking toward me. I didn't know what to do. I decided to run away, but fear froze me to the spot. I stood there, petrified.

After a while, completely instinctively, I approached the boy. Pointing at his fishing rod, I said, "Let me hold it for a little while." I said this so calmly that I surprised myself. He looked at me and handed me the rod. I grasped it the way a drowning man grasps a life preserver. "You'll catch something for sure because there's a big worm on the hook," he assured me.

He was about to say something else, but the rod began to jerk.

"Pull it up!" he shouted.

Together we pulled on the rod, and there was a small fish flopping at the end of the line.

I watched the Germans out of the corner of my eye the entire time. They stopped to light a cigarette; then they started walking in our direction again. They came very close to us.

My companion took the fish off the hook and put it in his sack. There were already three fish in it.

"Would you like to put a new worm on the hook?" he asked.

He handed me a small tin can full of worms. They were alive and wriggling like tiny snakes. I took one in my hand, but I couldn't put it on the hook because each time it slipped between my fingers. My hands were shaking, but I also felt sorry for the worms because they were so helpless. Seeing the trouble I was having, the boy put some new bait on the hook himself.

The Germans walked past, not paying any attention to us. I sighed with relief. I decided to wait a bit longer until they were completely gone.

My new friend gestured with his head at the Germans as they walked away and asked me, "What does your father say about what they're doing here?"

"My father doesn't say anything," I answered carefully.

"Mine says it's a wicked crime."

I didn't answer and pretended to focus all my attention on fishing. The Germans were no longer in sight. I waited awhile longer, then said, "I have to go home now. I forgot that they're waiting for me there."

I picked up my bag with the bread in it and said, "So long." I started walking away.

The boy shouted after me, "Come back tomorrow. I'll be here every day, until school starts."

"I'll come as soon as I can," I shouted back and quickened my pace.

Only then did I realize that for normal children, it was summer vacation, and a new school year would begin in a few days. The world seemed very cruel. We were the same age, and we lived in the same town, but our fates were so different. He was catching fish and thinking about school while I was sneaking around as if I had no right to live at all.

I knew this road very well because I'd been here many times with my friends, and sometimes also with Francis. To reach her house, I had to go close to the center of town, but it was also possible to take a longer route through a field behind some houses. Suddenly I realized that if I turned here, I'd be very close to Adaś Grossfeld's apartment.

I stood there, undecided. Adaś was my best friend, and I was very curious about what had happened to him. I thought that perhaps he and his family might still be in their apartment because it was owned by a Polish person. Perhaps the

Germans hadn't checked it. Adaś had also told me his father was trying to obtain Polish identity documents for them.

"Maybe they're still here?" I repeated to myself hopefully. I decided to find out. I turned off the road, crossed a field, took a shortcut through a garden, and then walked out into a street where there were almost no people. There were posters hanging everywhere announcing the expulsion of the Jews.

Unnoticed by anyone, I entered the apartment building where Adaś lived and quickly ran upstairs. I stood in front of the door to his apartment, and all my courage left me.

"Maybe the Germans are still here," I thought. I listened carefully at the door, but the apartment was silent. On the ground floor, someone entered the building's hallway from the street. I couldn't keep standing like this in front of the apartment door. I had to either enter the apartment or leave the building.

I was afraid of ringing the doorbell and thought that if the door was locked, I'd go back. I took a deep breath and, gathering all my courage, turned the door handle gently. Amazingly, the door opened. I tiptoed into the entrance hall and advanced very cautiously. A moment later it became clear to me that the apartment was empty. I went back to the door and closed it.

First I drank some water because I was very thirsty and ate a few pieces of dry bread that I found in the kitchen. The apartment looked as if they'd just left for a vacation. It was extremely tidy. The dishes in the kitchen cupboard were washed, and the garbage can was empty. I suddenly felt very sad and heavyhearted. I sat down on a chair, and their faces appeared to me in my mind. They were happy, kind, and understanding—just as I remembered them.

I was about to leave when I noticed that the desk was covered with a bedspread. It looked strange. I lifted it, and to my astonishment I saw dozens of small paper bags on the desk full of stamps. All the bags had been numbered, and next to them lay a list of which series of stamps were in each of them. There was also a large pile of stamps next to the bags waiting to be sorted. Adaś clearly hadn't managed to finish his work.

I felt sad that I hadn't agreed to help him when he'd asked me to. It would have allowed us to be together longer. I sat down at the desk and sank my hands into the stamps. I knew all of them very well because I'd looked at them many times with Adaś. We'd talked about them, admired them, and loved them as if they were living beings. I'd wanted to have such stamps, too. Now I felt them beneath my fingers, and it seemed to me that each stamp was crying. I sat at the desk and cried with them. I said goodbye to Adaś at that moment. It felt like a part of him was there with me.

I don't know how long I sat there, but at some point a clock on the wall began to strike. I realized I shouldn't stay there too long. I stood up from the desk, kissed the stamps, covered them again with the bedspread, just as someone covers a dead person, and left the apartment, remembering to take my bag of bread with me.

I was so stunned that I forgot about the danger I faced and walked to Francis's house along the street, instead of through the meadow. I was overcome by a feeling that I was protected. I saw Germans going in and out of houses, I saw them on the street, but I was certain that nothing bad was going to happen to me. I even heard gunshots twice, but they didn't disturb me at all.

I was surprised at this and felt something strange happening to me. I'd never been very brave, but now I felt no fear at all. I even started whistling a popular tune and walked down the street completely carefree, as if hypnotized. There were far fewer people on the street than usual.

"Polish people are clearly scared," I thought. "But I'm not scared," I declared jubilantly.

Nobody paid any attention to me. Only one woman cast me a scornful look and called out after me, "I don't know why you're in such a good mood." I didn't answer her and kept whistling.

Finally, I turned onto the small dirt road that led to Francis's house. A few moments later, I was standing in front of her apartment door. It was open. I walked in and saw a huge mess in front of me. Furniture was overturned, drawers were hanging open, and their entire contents were all over the floor. Everything was scattered around: clothes, kitchen pots, underwear. Clearly the place had been searched not only for hiding places but something else. Mattresses had been dragged off the beds and slashed with knives. The same had been done with quilts and pillows. The whole bedroom was full of feathers. I'd never seen an apartment in such a state. Suddenly all my courage left me again, and I looked around me in terror.

Then I saw them . . . Francis's dolls, which she'd loved so much. They were lying against a wall in the corner of the room with their bellies slashed open and sawdust spilling out of them. Someone had been looking for something inside them, too. Now they were truly dead, and even Francis would have agreed, I thought.

"Where is she now?" I wondered. Then I remembered our conversation about death, and my terror increased. I was shaken. "My darling Francis, what have they done to you?" I thought.

A terrible feeling came over me. I clutched my bag of bread to my chest and ran out of the apartment. I felt my legs giving way beneath me and weakness spreading through my body. I took several steps and realized I was standing in front of the door to Gottowt's room.

I pushed the door gently and it opened a crack. I opened it very slowly and cautiously. I tiptoed in, expecting to see the same chaos here as in Francis's apartment. But my mouth fell open in astonishment at what appeared before my eyes.

I saw a large crucifix on the night table by the bed—a black-and-silver cross with Jesus on it—and a Catholic picture above the bed. To the side, by the window, with his back to me, sat a priest in a black cassock, reading.

"Someone has already taken his room," I thought, and I began to slip away quietly.

But the priest must have heard a rustle because he stood up and turned toward me. I looked at him and couldn't believe my eyes! It was Gottowt!

I shouted and raced toward him. I hugged him and we stood with our arms around each other in silence for a long time. Then he sat me down on a chair by his table and looked into my eyes. I saw that he was crying. It was the first and last time I saw him so overcome with emotion. I told him what was happening with us. He gave me something to eat and drink because I didn't want to touch any of my bread or sausage.

Then he told me what had happened. He'd decided not to hide but to dress as a German priest. He'd managed to acquire a cassock, crucifix, and picture of a saint. His German identity document, which he'd brought with him from Germany, had been altered in such a way that the word *Jude* (Jew) was erased and the word *Pfarrer* (priest) was added. He also had a forged German document that stated he'd been sent to Poland by the German ecclesiastical authorities in Berlin to warn Polish priests in this area that they were obligated to follow German orders and laws.

Gottowt told me that Germans had already visited him three times, but when they heard him speak German, they believed him and only checked his documents once. Each time they left him in peace, saluting him.

"They checked my documents once because I didn't have this German catechism in my hands." He showed me the book he'd been reading earlier. "You have no idea what kind of effect it has on Germans when they see me with this open catechism and hear my Berlin accent," he said with satisfaction, as if he'd managed to pull off a good joke.

Gottowt knew that Francis, Fela, and Aunt Liba had gone to hide in a village near Wieliczka. They'd left their house the same evening we had. They'd said goodbye to Gottowt, and Francis had kissed him. She'd asked him to give me a kiss for her when he saw me.

I asked Gottowt if Francis had still been sad and pensive. He told me she hadn't been, and he'd even been surprised that while saying goodbye to him, she'd been in such a good mood. "She was chirping like a little bird," he added with a smile. Their apartment was vandalized two days after they'd left. Drunken soldiers came during the night and destroyed everything they could get their hands on.

Gottowt told me the priest who had given him the cassock was going to come get him that evening and put him in a monastery. If this worked out successfully, Gottowt would ask his priest friend if he could hide us there, too. He would send a message to us through the woman in whose home Aunt Liba, Fela, and Francis were hiding. My father knew where she lived.

"Go to your parents quickly now and tell them this," said Gottowt, looking straight into my eyes.

This raised my spirits very much, and I felt I'd found a way to save my whole family. I decided to give myself a reward for this and eat a small piece of the sausage, which was still stuffed in my pocket. I felt an uncontrollable desire to taste it. I took it out and asked Gottowt for a knife, but he didn't manage to hand it to me because at that moment loud footsteps were heard outside. He turned to me and shouted, "Hide under the bed! Quickly! Quickly!"

I dove beneath the bed with the sausage in my hand, and Gottowt lay down on the bed. I'd just managed to pull my legs in when several Germans entered the room. I couldn't see their legs because I was turned the other way. I lay under the bed as if I were dead, but I heard them speaking.

Suddenly an enormous German shepherd lurched into the room. It leaped around the bed twice, and to my horror, I saw its huge head right next to my face and its wet nose sniffing me. I closed my eyes because I was sure this was going to be the end of me. But it only tore the sausage out of my hand, gnawed on it, and then swallowed it. It was extremely lucky that this happened on the other side of the bed and nobody noticed it. The dog was clearly happy because it sniffed at me and licked my face. Then it ran to the other side of the bed where the Germans were standing. This all lasted only a few seconds, but I felt like my heart had stopped beating.

"*Wer sind Sie?*" (Who are you?) I heard a voice say in German.

"I'm a German priest," Gottowt answered in his Berlin accent.

"What are you doing here?"

"I have an order from Berlin for the local priests here that they must comply with orders from the German authorities."

"Documents," commanded the German.

I heard Gottowt open a drawer in the night table and rummage through it. Then something unbelievable happened. The German started speaking to Gottowt slowly, drawing out each word as if he were trying to remember something.

"But . . . I know you . . . from somewhere."

"Perhaps from the church in Berlin," answered Gottowt very calmly.

It was clear he handed the document to the German at this moment, because the German exclaimed with amazement in his voice, "Gottowt! Gottowt!" And then even louder, "*Donnerwetter*! Gottowt!"

It was obvious something had happened. I didn't know whether it was something good or bad.

Carefully, millimeter by millimeter, I turned my head because I wanted to see what was happening. I saw, about a meter in front of the bed, the shiny black boots of an officer as well as several pairs of soldiers' boots standing slightly farther away. The shiny boots took two steps alongside the bed and then two steps back, and the German, clearly unable to recover from his astonishment, kept repeating, as if he were talking to himself, "*Na, so was! . . . so was!*" (Now how about that!) And then . . . then came the devastating question.

"*Wie geht's Gottowt, alles in Butter?*"

Gottowt remained silent, but I understood he'd been recognized. The German laughed loudly and then asked, "*Was für ein Theater machen Sie hier?*" (What kind of play are you performing here?)

There was silence in the room.

Then the officer ordered the soldiers to leave the room and wait for him in front of the building. The dog stayed in the room and sat on the floor next to his leg.

"I didn't think I'd ever see you again, especially in such circumstances."

"How do you know me?"

I heard the German laugh again.

"Many people knew you, but I was among those who knew you the best because I admired you." As he addressed Gottowt, he used the formal form of "you" out of respect.

"For what reason?" Gottowt asked calmly.

The German, with a great sigh, answered, "Are you still asking me?"

The shiny boots came even closer to the bed, and it seemed to me that they were the ones speaking to Gottowt.

"Ten years ago"—and then he said the name of a theater and a play that I don't remember now—"you had to come back out to the stage seven times to bow. I wanted to be just like you then . . . with people clapping for me and admiring me."

Gottowt was silent, and the German told him that as a young acting student, he'd adored him, despite the fact that for his party colleagues, Gottowt was already a *Saujude*—a Jewish swine.

"Why did you admire me?" asked Gottowt.

I noticed he used the informal form of "you," like a teacher to a student. The German seemed not to have noticed this insult.

"Who else could speak onstage like you?"

At this point he began to recite a poem. It lasted about a minute, and when he stopped, he asked, "What do you think of that? Did I have a chance to follow in your footsteps?"

"Possibly. But your pathos is artificial and doesn't express real emotion. Listen to how it should be said."

Then he recited the same poem. When he finished, there was silence. Only the dog was very restless, which I could see from the movements of its paws. I was so stiff with fear that I even forgot to pray.

The German was obviously delighted because he said, "Gottowt, you were and still are unsurpassed." Then he added, "But please come with me, because we need to check a few things."

"I'm not going anywhere," answered Gottowt.

The shiny boots stood there as if unsure what to do. Then the German cleared his throat and said, "Don't be foolish, Gottowt. There has to be an investigation, but maybe you'll have a chance."

"If even my fans have turned against me, there can't be any chance for me," Gottowt said slowly, with great sadness in his voice.

"An actor right to the end, eh?"

"Right to the end."

The boots took several steps and opened the door. It was clear he gave a signal to the dog, because it ran out of the room. The door closed, and the boots once again approached the bed.

"Are you coming?" asked the German.

"No," answered Gottowt.

An explosion of gunshots deafened me. I felt a sharp pain in my ears and instinctively plugged them with my fingers. There followed several more shots, as if the entire room were exploding. Each shot shook my body as if it had struck me. I thought I'd been killed. My vision went dark. I'm quite sure that for a moment I lost consciousness, since I didn't see the German leave the room.

The first thing I saw when I opened my eyes was a pool of blood beneath the bed. It was slowly coming closer to me. It took a while before I returned to my senses enough to remember where I was and what had happened. I didn't know if I could come out from under the bed yet. I listened carefully but still felt stunned. I wanted to keep hiding there for a while, but the pool of blood was gradually coming closer to me, even though I'd moved as far away from it as possible.

At last I crawled out from under the bed and struggled to stand up. My legs buckled under me as if they weren't strong enough to carry me, and I collapsed on the floor. Only then did I dare look at the bed where Gottowt was lying. I saw a black cassock and blood . . . a lot of blood . . . I slowly stood up, not looking at Gottowt. Standing there, I closed my eyes and slowly turned my head once again toward the bed. I knew I would see something terrible. I was afraid something bad could happen to me just at the sight of him. I wanted to leave the room as quickly as possible, but I thought I should check first because perhaps Gottowt was still alive and only wounded. I opened my eyes slowly as if I were trying to stop time in order to prepare myself for what I was going to see . . . I was petrified with fear and had to summon all my willpower to open them completely.

Gottowt looked more like he was sitting on the bed than lying on it. His eyes were open and staring at the ceiling, and there was a dark hole in his forehead. The back of his head was completely covered in blood. His cassock, too. Even the wall and the sacred image above him were splattered with blood. What terrified me the most, however, was Gottowt's mouth. It was twisted in a smile as if he were alive and still laughing. There was something macabre in this dead, laughing figure.

My legs felt like they'd become rooted to the floor. I couldn't move them at all. Only then did I realize that I loved Gottowt very much. I felt a great need to approach and embrace him as warmly and lovingly as before. I couldn't, however, because I was paralyzed by fear. I covered my face with my hands. I wanted to cry, but I was unable to do this, either. I just let out wordless scream and escaped from that horrible room. I didn't think at all about the fact that the Germans could still be there.

The Germans were gone, but after running for a dozen or so meters, I remembered I'd left my bag of bread in the room, so I summoned some courage and went back for it. I knew I had to bring this bread to my parents at any cost. That's what they'd sent me for. I snatched the bread from the room, pressed it against my chest, and started running with all the strength left in my legs.

I forgot to be careful—instead of staying in the fields, I once again ran out into the streets. I passed Polish people, German soldiers, and policemen in blue uniforms. I ignored everyone and just ran and ran . . . Fear triggered new strength in me that I'd never had before. I was in shock and didn't notice what was happening around me. Even while I was running, I felt like I was still in Gottowt's room.

After a while I found myself near the grocery shop where I'd bought the loaf of bread. Only then did it occur to me that if it hadn't been for the sausage I'd been given in this shop, surely the German dog would have attacked me and torn me to pieces, or the German officer would have shot me. It was impossible to understand why the dog had been placated so easily by a piece of sausage.

I passed the shop, and there were only a few more buildings ahead of me. Nobody paid any attention to me, perhaps because I wasn't making any attempt to go unnoticed. To passersby I probably looked like a Polish child who'd been sent by his mother to get some bread. I slowly returned to my senses and once again became aware of danger.

"After these buildings, it'll be easier," I thought. I was yearning intensely to be with my parents and Lusia again.

A boy was leaning out a window on the ground floor of one of the houses. It didn't occur to me that he could pose a threat of any kind. As I drew closer, I noticed he was watching me closely.

When I was quite close, the boy started waving his hands wildly and shouting in my direction. "A Jew! A Jew! I know him! He lives in Klasno! Catch him!" He pointed at me and, looking all around him, shouted to the passersby, "He's a Jew! Catch him! Catch him!"

He was surprised that nobody grabbed me even though there were many people in the street. A few pedestrians glanced at me, but nobody reacted. I started running faster. I glanced behind me and saw that the boy was no longer in the window. I was about to slow down so I could catch my breath, but he ran into the street and started chasing me, screaming, "A Jew! A Jew!"

There were several people in front of me, but nobody tried to stop me. Someone even smiled at me.

The boy was much older than me, and the distance between us quickly diminished. I felt him coming very close. I saw a man in front of me. "Maybe he'll protect me?" I thought, but I didn't have time to ask him for help and only looked at him pleadingly.

I passed the man and heard the boy scream right behind me, "Let me go! Let me go! He's a Jew! I have to catch him!"

I turned around and saw the man holding the boy and struggling with him. I had to stop because I was completely out of breath.

"But he's a Jew!" shouted the boy.

"Why are you screaming your head off?! What harm has he ever done to you?!" the man shouted at the boy, not letting him go.

Oh, how grateful I was to him!

They grappled with each other, and I started running again. I decided to turn off the road into a field where I was less visible. It was perhaps already afternoon, but the sun was still scorching. I caught my breath for a moment in some high grass and continued onward, straight ahead, now much more carefully. There were fields all around me and several houses. I felt exhausted and decided to rest. I was also afraid that my pursuer could reappear at any moment.

Not far from me I noticed a large barn near a farmhouse. Its wide door was locked with a padlock, but next to a side door, there were some wooden stairs leading to a loft. There was no door up above, only an opening.

I climbed the stairs as quietly as a cat and peeked inside. There was a lot of hay in the loft. I lay down on it, and after a while I felt better and stronger. It made me happy to lie in the hay; I liked the smell of it. I don't know how long I lay there like that. All I remember is that I tried not to fall asleep. I also began to worry about whether I would find my parents in the spot where I'd left them.

I felt somewhat rested and was just about to leave when, from the direction of the house, I heard voices speaking in German and Polish. Someone asked in Polish, "So were there Jews here last night or not?"

A woman answered, "We don't know anything. There was a noise of some kind, but we don't know what it was."

They said something else, but I didn't understand. Someone commanded in German, "Open this barn!"

From what I'd overheard, I understood that Germans were going to check the place where I was hiding. I started digging desperately in the hay. I was already completely covered when I remembered I'd left my bread, and it could give me away. I dug myself out, took the bread, and buried myself again. Someone brought a key, and I heard them opening the barn door. They looked in the space down below; then I heard someone say in German, "Karl, go check upstairs."

My heart once again started hammering inside me. I was certain I'd reached the end of my life. I heard slow, heavy footsteps on the stairs, and then there was silence. I almost screamed in pain. Someone was standing on my chest. Even though I was quite deep in the hay, I felt an enormous pressure. I closed my eyes and clenched my teeth so I wouldn't make any noise. Fortunately, the German moved, and the weight became more bearable. He now seemed to be standing on me with one leg.

He started stabbing a bayonet into the hay. I heard the blade enter it again and again, to the left of me and then to the right. I wasn't thinking about anything, I was just waiting for the blow that would end my life. I was even afraid to breathe. It lasted only a moment, but to me it seemed like ages. Finally, the pressure on my chest decreased, and I heard the heavy footsteps of the German on the stairs. At the same time, I heard him say, "There's nobody here."

His words—*"Hier ist niemand da"*—sounded to my ears like a beautiful melody. I breathed a sigh of relief and understood that I'd escaped death once again.

I waited about half an hour more and then tiptoed down the staircase. Now I was much more cautious; I snuck through the fields stealthily and hid when I saw people in the distance. I walked around buildings and stopped, listening carefully as if I were a hunted animal. I found a stream somewhere on the way and quenched my thirst.

Soon afterward I drew near the place I'd left that morning. I pressed the bag of bread against my chest as if it would bring me salvation. I entered the bushes and looked for my parents. To my great joy, they were still in the same spot. I was bewildered by what I'd experienced, but I also felt triumphant. I'd accomplished my mission—I'd returned with bread and escaped danger.

I approached them unnoticed. Lusia and my father were sleeping, and my mother was praying. Suddenly she raised her eyes and, seeing me, screamed, "Henryk!" She reached her hands out to me as if I'd come from another world.

My father jumped to his feet and exclaimed, "Henryk, where were you for so long?" Not waiting for me to answer, he added, "We were already sure the Germans had caught you."

I wanted to tell them everything, but I didn't have the strength. I was overwhelmed by a terrible fatigue as if everything I'd experienced was only now beginning to have an effect on me. I was still in shock. I fell to the ground and could only stammer three words: "Gottowt . . . is . . . dead." After I said this, lying on the ground, I realized I was still clutching the bag of bread to my chest.

Seeing the state I was in, my parents let me rest. Later my father took me to the stream, and I drank some water. After I'd regained my senses slightly, I started telling them what I'd experienced. They listened in silence, but I saw terror in their eyes. I had the impression they didn't know what to do next. My father told me they could hear gunshots and were very worried about me.

We lay in the bushes like animals. We had no plan. We thanked God for being able to survive from hour to hour. Instinctively I felt that this situation couldn't last long and something had to happen, although I didn't know what it would be. My calmness and inner conviction that everything would be okay in the end surprised me. I couldn't imagine how we would be saved, but I felt that help would come.

My parents were also completely calm and didn't show any anxiety or despair. But our situation was desperate. In their helplessness, had they already come to terms with their fate? I fully trusted my parents and relied on them to make the right decisions, but I wanted to live and was ready to fight for my existence. I knew that if I fell into the Germans' hands, my life would come to an end.

That day's experiences and the anticipation of something new sharpened my senses. I could hear and see things very clearly at a greater distance than usual. Even my sense of smell had become much keener, and I realized I was sniffing like a dog.

At some point, even before I heard anything, my instinct warned me that someone was approaching us. Then I heard some cautious footsteps. Someone pulled the branches aside and came close to us. My parents still didn't hear anything because it was just a quiet rustling sound.

In a stifled voice, I shouted, "Someone's coming!" Automatically, in a state of extreme fear and unaware of what I was doing, I leaped into some thick bushes near us. It was just a small clump of bushes; we couldn't hide in them because it was difficult to enter. Now, like a startled animal, I plunged into these bushes, injuring my arms and legs on nettles and thorns. I felt nothing but fear.

I stopped only when I heard an unknown voice addressing my father and my father answering. I crouched in the bushes. I was stunned and couldn't understand what the conversation was about. It lasted a long time, and then there was silence. I waited a while longer and then carefully headed back to my parents. I asked God to keep them in the same place where I'd left them. My heart was pounding because I was afraid they'd been taken away. I parted the branches carefully and . . . I saw them. They were looking all around, searching for me.

My mother scolded me and told me never to run away again. She said we had to stay together and never split up. Whatever was awaiting us, we would face it together. My father wasn't angry at me; he pulled me close to him and caressed me. I was pale with fear and noticed that my hands were shaking.

My father calmed me and told me that a man had appeared and demanded money. He'd threatened them that if they didn't give him any, he would hand us over to the Germans, who were giving out rewards for such services. They paid—as he expressed it—"per head," and my father had to purchase each of us so that the man wouldn't lose out. He didn't have anything against Jews, but he needed something to live on, after all, and times were hard. My father gave him some money; then he added my mother's watch. The man scowled and said he thought he'd get more. But finally he was satisfied with what he'd received and went away. My father said the man wasn't a village peasant but an intelligent man from a city, which was evident from his clothes and the way he spoke.

This incident pulled my parents out of their state of apathy and helplessness. They started thinking about what we should do next. They feared that even though my father had paid the man, he might still turn us over to the Germans. So we needed to hide somewhere else as soon as possible. My father decided we would walk along paths near the bushes for two or three kilometers and then hide again.

We snuck carefully along the bushes and sometimes through fields. Thankfully we didn't see any people, and after a while we found ourselves at the edge of a forest. My father decided we should stop here, since there could be Germans in the forest. Once again, we pushed our way into some bushes and, exhausted, threw ourselves to the ground. We'd already eaten the bread earlier and were feeling very hungry.

We could hear gunshots in the fields, off in the distance. My father thought we should wait here at least until evening and then decide what to do next. We lay on the ground and listened carefully for anyone approaching. We knew our situation was critical and, logically speaking, perhaps even hopeless, but some new energy had entered my parents, and it was clear they had decided to fight for our lives. I didn't want to allow myself even to consider that something bad could happen to us. I realized what kind of danger we were facing, but I had stopped feeling scared. My attitude to danger had changed. Perhaps this was because I was already very tired. Maybe I trusted my parents and believed that, like always, they'd find some way to save us. Perhaps I'd become completely indifferent. I don't know why, but I felt peace and hope beginning to prevail over all my other feelings.

We lay there for about an hour when suddenly the bushes parted, and a strange figure appeared before us. It was a tall, thin old man with a gray beard that flowed down his long white shirt. He had wispy gray hair and large blue eyes. He looked like a village peasant.

He gazed at us. It was obvious he immediately understood who we were. "From Wieliczka?" he asked. None of us answered. He looked at each of us again and uttered memorable words that have resounded in my ears my whole life and that I can still hear now: "Oh my God ... you poor people ... I would do anything to help you." He said this with great sadness, and his eyes expressed compassion and pity.

My parents didn't respond; we were all amazed. We weren't accustomed to such kind words. Even Lusia looked at him with her mouth hanging open as if she thought he was a ghost.

He told us he lived nearby, and I think he mentioned a forester's lodge. He asked if we were hungry. My mother nodded. He said he'd bring us something to eat right away, and then he disappeared into the bushes.

We didn't know what to do. Could we trust him? Would he return with some Germans? Should we run away to a different spot? My parents consulted with each other and decided to wait about twenty minutes. If he didn't return by then, we would leave.

Soon the bushes parted again, and the man was standing in front of us. He handed us a container consisting of several aluminum tins piled on top of each other. In each tin there was wonderful food: soup in one, potatoes with meat in another, and apple compote in the third. How tasty this compote was! It was the best I'd ever eaten in my life; I've never forgotten the flavor of it.

The old man stood nearby and waited for us to finish eating. We gave the empty tins back to him and didn't even manage to thank him because he started speaking to us as if he felt responsible for our lives. He said we had to escape during the night because there was no chance of us surviving here. He offered to lead us through the forest to a small train station in the village of Węgrzce, and from there, together with workers on the first morning train, we could travel to Tarnów, where we could enter the ghetto. The Germans never inspected the station in Węgrzce because there weren't any Jews there. He arranged with my parents that he would come for us, and he advised us to sleep because we had a long and tiring road ahead of us.

We were satiated and reinvigorated, but sleeping was out of the question. Also, Lusia began to whine, and it was hard to calm her. Our state of excitement increased. But we didn't have long to wait because it was already beginning to get dark.

Soon night fell. We stared at the spot in the bushes where we expected to see the old man. Finally, he appeared. He was now dressed in dark clothes and had a small rucksack on his back. He told my father he had water and something sweet to eat in case we ran out of energy. He told us to follow him as quietly as possible since Germans could still be in the area. He walked as silently as a cat. It was obvious he knew the forest well, because he led us along various narrow, almost invisible paths, and sometimes along moss, tree roots, or stones.

After about two hours of walking, we were very tired, and our guide stopped so we could rest. We sat on a fallen tree. He first gave us water, and then each of us received a slice of bread smeared with a thick layer of honey. He also ate with us. He told us we now had to be especially cautious because we would be walking along paths near a road that was often patrolled by Germans.

At his signal, we got up and started following him again. My father carried Lusia and helped my mother, and our guide held my hand. He also picked me up in difficult spots. Without his help I would have fallen many times. Sometimes, for example, when we had to step on stones to cross a stream, he first led me across and then went back for my mother; then he went back again to help my father and Lusia.

It was a clear night, but the forest was pitch-black in some places. Our eyes quickly adjusted to the darkness. From time to time, we stopped walking, and our guide listened carefully. I was sniffing at the air like an animal. We walked along a highway, and every time a car approached we threw ourselves to the ground.

At a certain point, some flashing lights appeared on the highway, and our guide gave us a signal to throw ourselves to the ground. Once again, we were extremely lucky. It turned out to be a German patrol with a dog; they passed only several feet away from us but didn't notice anything, and the dog didn't pick up our scent. Later, patrols and military vehicles passed us several more times. Eventually we entered the dense forest again.

After a while I realized I was sleeping while walking. I could feel our guide's arm around me, holding me up. Every time I woke up, I fell asleep again immediately, but I kept walking somehow. The old man's arm never let me fall. We took two more breaks to rest, but it was getting harder for us to walk. Our guide was the oldest one among us, but he showed no signs of fatigue. He guided us the entire time, helped us, and encouraged us, and most importantly—he had a perfect knowledge of the terrain.

We reached the train station in Węgrzce at dawn. All of us, except our guide, were completely exhausted. There was a small station building there. We stopped before reaching it, and our guide went to check if there were any Germans at the station and how much tickets to Tarnów cost, for my father wasn't sure if he had enough money for the journey. The forester returned and told us there was nobody at the station. It turned out my father had enough money for tickets to Tarnów, so the forester went back to the station building to buy some.

The train was leaving in less than an hour. The old man waited with us at the station the entire time, as if he felt responsible for us. He comforted us, strengthened our belief in our salvation, and warned us to remain on guard. My parents thanked him profusely. It seemed to me that he wasn't a human being but an angel, and I kissed his hand, which embarrassed him very much. A few workers had gathered at the station, but they didn't pay any attention to us.

The train to Tarnów finally arrived, and our guide helped us enter a train car, after which he gave my father his rucksack and said, "There's some breakfast in here for you. May God be with you and watch over you." He blew us a kiss with both hands and walked away.

I never saw this man again. Our attempts to find him after the war were fruitless. We didn't know his name. We put a great deal of effort into finding him, but there wasn't a single trace of him. He was the noblest person I've ever met in my life. It was solely thanks to his help that we were able to survive at that point. On his own initiative and completely unselfishly, he risked his own life to rescue strangers.

I've thought of him many times in my life. At the birth of each of my children and grandchildren, I've thought of him and how he also played a role in these joyful events.

I admit that more than once I've had a feeling that he wasn't a person but an angel in human form. Sometimes I've thought that every person is capable of being an angel if he or she wants to be. The memory of him has inspired me to have faith in people throughout my entire life, and I've always carried the memory of him in my heart.

At that time, while traveling to Tarnów by train full of fear, praying to God that we'd arrive there safely, I didn't yet know what had happened to all my dear friends in Wieliczka. Later, we found out.

Aunt Liba, Francis, and Fela were shot in Wieliczka's cemetery. First Francis and Fela were murdered in front of their mother; then Aunt Liba was killed. The woman in whose house they'd been hiding had kicked them out during the massacre.

Uncle Schenker and his family, along with a dozen or so other people, hid in the tannery in Klasno. His workers, who were very devoted to him, walled them up in a storeroom. Two weeks later they managed to escape at night in a truck from Wieliczka to Bochnia, where they entered the ghetto.

Nina Armer and her family died in the gas chamber at the Bełżec concentration camp.

Jankiel and his family, and Adaś Grossfeld and his family, died there, too.

Adam was shot just like his father had been, in front of his house, along with his paralyzed grandmother, who had been dragged out of her bed.

Zylek and six hundred other boys were sent to a concentration camp in Płaszów, near Kraków. Sometime later, he fell ill there and was shot by the Germans.

These were the fates of the people I loved who were torn from life by a bestial force.

I still cry for them today.

NOTE

1. John Gottowt (Isidor Gesang) was an outstanding German film and theater actor. For many years the circumstances surrounding his death were unknown. He was born in Lwów in 1881 to an Orthodox Jewish family. He studied in Munich and Vienna, where he made his debut as an actor and adopted the stage name of John Gottowt. He lived and worked in Berlin from 1905 onward. He was an actor and director at the Deutsches Theater, which was run by Max Reinhardt, and then in many other Berlin theaters. He acted in films, including Murnau's famous film *Nosferatu: A Symphony of Horror*. After Hitler assumed power in 1933, he was forbidden from working in theater and film. He moved to Denmark and then Sweden, where his ex-wife and children lived, and unsuccessfully applied for work and permanent residency there. In 1938 he decided to move to Kraków, his mother's hometown (he still had Polish citizenship). After the outbreak of the war, he moved to Wieliczka.

TARNÓW

THE TRAIN TO TARNÓW CRAWLED along and stopped at every station, which made my parents anxious because they were afraid someone might board the train who would be a threat to us. I was very tired but felt so tense I couldn't shut my eyes. Even Lusia, who'd been carried all night long, was now sitting quietly next to our mother, not whining like usual. She stared at our mother with her big blue eyes as if she wanted to read in her face what was going to happen to us. I thought I saw fear in her eyes, but perhaps it was just my own fear, since I don't think Lusia understood the danger we were in.

We were alone in the compartment. Several people entered our train car at a small station. My parents started speaking to each other in German. They talked loudly, pretending to be arguing about something. A woman opened the door of our compartment and was about to enter, but when she heard German being spoken, she closed it and went to a different compartment. A moment later this happened again with an old man. The train started moving, but my parents didn't stop talking.

I noticed something shiny under a seat, right near the door, leaned over, and picked up a small, round Nazi badge with a black swastika on a red background, like the ones often worn by Germans on their civilian jackets. A small piece of a broken pin was sticking out of it. I showed it to my father. My mother thought we should throw it away immediately, but my father said it might help us on the way to Tarnów and, without giving any more thought to it, he pinned it to his lapel.

The first person to see it was the conductor. He checked our tickets and then saluted my father with great respect. At a larger station, many people boarded the train, and our compartment filled up. When they heard my parents speaking German and saw my father's badge, the other passengers stopped talking to each other. Some faces even looked frightened. I kept my eyes fixed on the window so they wouldn't notice me observing them.

There were many beautiful, sunny days in August 1942, and this was one of them. Normally at this time of day, I would have gone outside to meet with my friends or Francis. Where were they now? I started thinking about them and recalling what I'd done with them only a few days before. Everything seemed so far away now, as if years had passed, even though it had just been a few days.

The feeling of danger that had been consuming me disappeared, and I was overcome by a strange but pleasant bliss. Perhaps it was caused by my fatigue and the memories . . . I closed my eyes and immediately fell asleep. I don't remember what I dreamed, but it must have been something very nice because my mother told me later that I was smiling in my sleep the entire time. I don't know how long I had slept, but I felt a gentle hand on my arm and heard my mother say, *"Wir sind angekommen"* (We've arrived).

We got off with everyone else. The train station in Tarnów was full of people because two trains had arrived at the same time. People were getting on and off the trains. The only exit from the platforms led through the station building, and everyone who'd just arrived was moving toward it.

My mother said to my father quietly, "Throw that badge away now." But my father indicated with his eyes the wide-open door through which we'd have to pass. Two German soldiers and two civilians were standing there, closely watching the people passing by and ordering those with larger baggage to step aside. Some other Germans were inspecting suitcases and asking people for identity documents. A train conductor was standing there, too, collecting tickets.

"Maybe we should get on another train," said my mother.

But this was impossible because people were pushing us forward. If we'd turned back, the Germans would certainly have noticed.

"There's no other way," my father told my mother. "Speak to me in German."

I started reciting my Shema Yisrael prayer silently to myself. We slowly approached the exit with everyone else. My father didn't take off the badge with the swastika.

When we were several steps away from the soldiers, my mother said loudly to my father, *"Es ist eine unerhörte Geschichte, dass wir zusammen mit all den polnischen Arbeitern fahren müssen!"* (It's unbelievable that we have to travel with all these Polish workers!) In her voice there was outrage and even a bit of resentment toward my father. I noticed both soldiers smiling, clearly amused by my mother's words.

My father answered her calmly but loudly enough for the soldiers to hear, *"Es wird nicht lange dauern, die Gestapo hat mir einen Wagen zugesagt"* (It won't be very long, the gestapo has promised me a car).

My parents understood each other very well, and when they acted together, they always went all the way with it. This time they were acting to save our lives. Later, they were amazed by their courage. They both said it had been completely instinctual.

It was clear their conversation had made an impression on the soldiers, because they smiled even more than before. I was afraid to look at the two civilians. My father gave our tickets to the train conductor and was about to continue walking, but at that moment one of the soldiers leaned toward Lusia and asked her, *"Wie heißt du, kleines Fräulein?"* (What's your name, little lady?)

I felt my legs buckling under me from terror. Lusia looked at him and answered with one word, in perfect German: *"Fräulein."* The soldier took this as a joke, laughed, and said, with admiration in his voice, *"So klein und schon so witzig"* (So small, but already so witty). He saluted my father and then gestured to show us the way out. The two civilians raised their arms and said, *"Heil Hitler!"* My father also raised his arm but didn't say anything, pretending to be occupied with Lusia.

We entered the waiting room, and then from there, together with the crowd, we exited onto the street. Suddenly I noticed that my right leg was wet. I had peed myself from fear.

We were all amazed that Lusia had been able to give such an answer to the soldier. She was five years old and had never spoken a single word in German. Although my parents sometimes spoke to each other in this language, I doubt Lusia understood any of it. It was obvious she'd automatically repeated the soldier's last word. It was probably a total coincidence that she'd pronounced the word *Fräulein* so perfectly—just a childish attempt to copy an older person.

That's how we explained it to ourselves—but much later, for right then we didn't have time to think about it. We had to reach the ghetto as quickly as possible because while we were on the Aryan side, without any identification documents, we were in constant danger. At any moment we could be recognized as Jews and handed over to the Germans.

"Now you can throw that badge away," my mother said to my father.

"Maybe it's better to keep it until we enter the ghetto," my father said.

"No, I'm afraid. I have a feeling it'll be better if you throw it away immediately."

My father unpinned the badge and threw it in a garbage can. He knew the way to the ghetto, and at first we thought we just needed to cross a few streets to get there. There were a lot of people on the streets, and it didn't appear as if anyone was paying attention to us. None of us had typical Jewish facial features, and we were walking at the same pace as everyone else, trying not to show any anxiety. My parents were talking to each other in Polish and smiling at each other. They gave the impression of a married couple out for a walk with their children.

Suddenly we heard someone say, "Just a moment." A policeman in a navy-blue uniform was standing in front of us. He was short and thin with a pale face on which there was the flicker of a smile.

"Are you just taking a stroll, or are you headed somewhere?" he asked politely.

"A stroll," answered my father.

The policeman's smile became slightly ironic, but his voice was still polite.

"Since when do Jews go for strolls on the Aryan side?"

My parents understood we'd been recognized, and there was no point pretending to be non-Jews. Without Aryan documents, we didn't have a chance.

My father answered him, "Please let us go because we've just had some very difficult days. God will repay you."

"I'll gladly do it, but first you have to buy yourselves from me."

"We would do that, but we don't have any money," my father replied helplessly.

"In that case, I have to take you to the gestapo because it's my duty. Are you going to pay me or not?"

"We have no money," repeated my father.

"Well, let's go to the gestapo, then," answered the policeman stubbornly.

Just then my father remembered his friend who lived in Tarnów, Fessel, and told the policeman he would pay for us.

"Fessel? The one who owns the Papapol factory?"

"Yes, let's go to Papapol—maybe I can get some money from him."

The policeman agreed, and we started walking together in a different direction. We reached Fessel's factory. The policeman stood with my mother, Lusia, and me in the doorway of a building while my father continued onward to the factory. I prayed silently for Fessel to be there, for him to have some money, and for him to be willing to give it to my father.

We waited silently. The policeman was acting the most nervous. He lit a cigarette and stared tensely at the factory's entrance. We waited a very long time, which seemed to me like a good sign. Suddenly my father appeared in the factory's gateway and quickly approached us. Breathless, he stood in front of the policeman and handed him a thick envelope. The policeman opened it and ran his fingers over the money.

"Good," he said. "You can go on your way."

My father took several more banknotes out of his pocket.

"I'll give you this, too, if you take us to the ghetto, because someone else might recognize us as Jews."

The policeman took the money.

"You scratch my back, and I'll scratch yours. Follow me."

On the way, my father asked him how he'd known we were Jews. The policeman smiled and said it hadn't been hard at all. He'd watched us all the way from the train station, and everything had indicated to him that we were Jews.

"What, for example?"

"Everything. You Jews walk differently and talk to each other differently. You just behave differently, in general. Your children had scared expressions on their faces and kept looking behind them. You and your wife kept glancing sideways. But, above all—my intuition can detect a Jew from a hundred meters."

He told us he would take us to the ghetto's side entrance rather than the main gateway because it was less dangerous there. SS men and Jewish policemen stood at the main gateway all day and night, while at the side entrance it was mostly just the latter. We would have to enter the ghetto when there weren't any Germans near it.

We crossed several streets and saw the side entrance to the ghetto and a guard booth next to it. We stood in the doorway of a nearby house and observed the spot. Several people went in and out of the ghetto, but there were no Germans in sight.

After a while the policeman said, "Let's go." He led us to the entrance. Only one Jewish policeman was standing there in a cap with a yellow band. We approached him, and the Polish policeman told him we were supposed to enter the ghetto.

A small window in the guard booth opened and an SS man's face appeared in it. He pointed at us and asked, *"Wer sind die?"* (Who are they?)

Our policeman displayed presence of mind and responded in Polish, "They've been inspected and are to enter the ghetto."

The Jewish policeman translated this for the SS man and waited for his decision, but the latter just waved his hand.

"Rein!" (Enter!)

The Polish policeman turned and left us without a word. A moment later we found ourselves inside the ghetto.

Fessel had given my father the address of one of his friends in the ghetto. We were supposed to go to him and tell him Fessel had sent us. His friend's name was Eliahu Lehrhaupt, and he was the deputy chairman of the *Judenrat*. He lived at 4 Lwowska Street.

The ghetto made a very miserable impression on us. All the narrow streets and alleys we passed through were filled with poverty. People were emaciated and badly dressed, sneaking along the walls of buildings as if they might face mortal danger at any moment. I didn't yet understand why, but I soon found out.

As we walked along the streets of the ghetto, our spirits grew very heavy. We asked for directions several times and eventually found the apartment building at 4 Lwowska Street. This street turned out to be outside the ghetto. The building's main entrance door was always locked, while the building itself was inside the ghetto and could be entered through a small side door from another street, a narrow passageway, and then a large courtyard. There was a staircase next to the narrow passageway and two other staircases that could be accessed from the courtyard. It was a large three-story apartment building with many tenants.

The Lehrhaupt family lived in their own prewar apartment on one of the upper floors. They welcomed us very warmly. They were close friends of Fessel's, and it was clear they had a lot of respect for him. They gave us a room, and Mrs. Lehrhaupt prepared a meal for us. We were very hungry and tired.

After eating, we went straight to sleep—my parents lay next to each other on a narrow bed, and Lusia and I slept on blankets spread on the floor. We slept like the dead until evening, when Mrs. Lehrhaupt and her son, a young man about twenty years old, woke us for supper. I don't remember the son's name, but we immediately felt that he wanted to help us. Supper was meager: soup, a slice of bread thinly spread with margarine, and a black, dishwater-like liquid instead of coffee. Mrs. Lehrhaupt brought hot water mixed with milk from the kitchen for Lusia.

While we ate, Mr. Lehrhaupt told us the ghetto had existed for only two months and that everyone in it was suffering from extreme poverty. All people capable of working were officially employed in factories and workshops run by Germans outside the ghetto. Unfortunately, nobody knew how long these factories and workshops would continue to exist, since the hatred of Jews was growing and had already reached a level of total degradation. Nobody knew what else was going to happen here.

People in the ghetto were terrified. SS and gestapo officers came here nearly every day, shooting at people for no reason at all. The worst ones were Rommelman and Grunoff. Every time they appeared in the ghetto, several people were killed. Sometimes they came with their girlfriends. They'd keep one arm around their girlfriend and shoot at people with the other, as if they were bird hunting. They entertained themselves with murder. When the Jewish community complained about this, the officers replied that during the day the ghetto was supposed to be empty because everyone should be at work. In June 1942, there were two massive roundup operations during which thousands of Jews were taken away—rumors were circulating that they'd been taken to Bełżec and killed there. Nobody knew if the Germans were about to transport people from the ghetto again. For now, everyone was living from day to day, thanking God for each day that passed peacefully.

These descriptions were so distressing that we didn't immediately comprehend them. Our consciousness simply refused to accept them. It was difficult for us to come to terms with the fact that we found ourselves in such a terrible place.

Mr. Lehrhaupt explained to us that we were now living in this ghetto illegally, so it would be impossible for my parents to be assigned work in a factory or workshop. He warned us to be very careful and not walk in the streets. He promised he would try to obtain food ration cards for us so we wouldn't starve and would also search for somewhere for us to live. It wouldn't be easy because the ghetto was already very overcrowded.

And so it was clear to us that our situation had drastically worsened. At night, none of us could sleep except Lusia. I envied her blissful ignorance.

We didn't leave the Lehrhaupts' apartment at all during our first days there. Our hosts were very kind to us, especially their son, who did his best to help us—he found clothing for us and brought a rag doll for Lusia. Mr. Lehrhaupt spent nearly all day at the office of the *Judenrat*. After a few days, he told us there might be a room for us but it would take a while to arrange it, and he wasn't sure if he would manage to get the room since there were many other people waiting for it.

It was the beginning of September 1942. I realized that for normal children my age, the summer vacation was over and they were already going back to school. I hadn't gone to school for three years and missed it terribly. I fantasized about what it would be like after the war when I'd be able to attend school again.

At the end of the first week of September, a strange anxiety took hold of the Lehrhaupt family. They told us that people who'd been working in certain factories had received an order to stay in the ghetto and not go to work. This was a bad sign; people feared the worst. In the evening, Mr. Lehrhaupt told us the ghetto was surrounded by German soldiers, and a new roundup operation was probably about to begin.

In the apartment building at 4 Lwowska Street, bunkers were prepared for everyone who hadn't gone to work. There were many people in the building who normally worked in factories, and it wasn't clear if there was enough space for everyone in the bunkers. Mr. Lehrhaupt told us that when the time came, we should hide with the neighbors from our floor.

On the morning of September 10, we were woken up and told that we should hide. We went out onto the staircase, which was already full of people. Some were going down the stairs; others were going up. A man came up to us and asked, "Are you the ones staying with Mr. Lehrhaupt?" My father nodded, and the man told us to follow him. We hurried down the stairs.

It was quite dark in the staircase because there was only one light bulb lit on the top floor. People were pushing each other. Muffled screams could be heard.

Children were crying, and everyone was rushing. There were many old people who were having trouble walking. My mother was carrying Lusia even though she'd been able to walk on her own for a long time already. My father tried to help, but my mother didn't want to give Lusia to him; she held her tightly to her chest, as if this would ensure her survival.

A strange, intense odor struck me. The man leading us explained that Lysol, a disinfectant, had been poured throughout the entire building because everyone feared the Germans would come with dogs, and Lysol caused dogs to lose their sense of smell.

We entered the courtyard and passed through another hallway, then descended to the cellar. In the cellar there was a hole in the ground into which people were disappearing one by one. We were pulled into the hole, too. We found ourselves in a low, narrow, foul-smelling space beneath the cellar. About a dozen people were already sitting there, including small children. I remember them the most vividly because never before had I seen such terrified expressions on children's faces.

After a while, we heard shouting from various directions: "That's all! That's all! We can't let anyone else in, or we'll all suffocate!" Despite this, several more people entered, and the trapdoor was closed.

A kerosene lantern was lit, but someone immediately shouted, "Put out the lamp!" We found ourselves in total darkness. There was a trapdoor that we were supposed to open so air could enter, but nobody knew where it was. Someone said that it was probably open already, since a slight draft could be felt.

Finally, there was complete silence. From time to time, children started crying, but their mothers calmed them immediately. Lusia held my hand with both of her hands, squeezing it tightly. We sat like this, crammed in this small space and leaning against each other, for about two hours. The lack of air became increasingly unbearable, and finally a decision was made to open the entrance trapdoor slightly. It wasn't possible to do this yet, however, because something had been placed on top of it to conceal it. After a while, several people fainted.

I sank into a deep lethargy and began to hallucinate. I thought I was once again lying sick in my bed in Wieliczka. I sought the light that I'd seen then, but I was surrounded only by darkness. Lusia stopped squeezing my hand, and every so often I heard her whisper, "Mommy, I love you." I don't know how long this lasted because I was no longer aware of what was happening to me.

Suddenly someone near me hit the entrance trapdoor. We heard rustling sounds above us, and the trapdoor opened. Someone asked, "How are you all doing down there?" It was an *Ordnungsdienst* (a Jewish policeman) who lived on the top floor of the building. He told us where the trapdoor was through which we could let more air enter, and he said several people should come out of the bunker, and he would lead them to another spot.

Nobody volunteered. Only my mother agreed to leave because Lusia and I were nearly suffocating. Some people helped us climb out; the policeman closed the entrance to the bunker and slid two blocks of wood over the trapdoor. He told us to follow him quickly. He said the Germans hadn't come to this building yet but could appear at any moment.

He led us into an apartment and pushed aside a chest of drawers standing against a wall in one of the rooms. He lifted the wallpaper at the bottom edge; under it, right near the floor, there was a nearly invisible trapdoor. He opened it, and a narrow gap appeared. He told us to go inside. We crawled into the new hiding place.

We found ourselves in a tiny space where six people were already sitting. There wasn't enough room for all of us. I sat on my father's lap and Lusia on my mother's lap. There was a bit of light because the space had a tiny window and—most importantly—there was enough air. I was no longer hallucinating and began to breathe freely. I felt my consciousness becoming increasingly acute—even more acute than usual.

A middle-aged man sitting next to my mother winced with pain every now and then. Seeing my mother's questioning looks, he whispered, "It's a stomach ulcer."

People on all sides reprimanded him, also in a whisper: "Shhhh... quiet..." I felt like I was also starting to have pains in my stomach. I began to wince, too, and my mother was startled; she cast me questioning looks. I couldn't answer her because I didn't want people to get mad at me.

Lusia saved me. Hearing her whisper quietly, once again, "Mama, I love you," I realized that I also loved my mother very much. My heart overflowed with love for her, and at that very moment my stomach stopped hurting. The man next to us also seemed to feel better and smiled at me.

After a while, we heard soldiers' boots walking quickly, loud commands, and shouts. Germans walked through this apartment but didn't search it. We all sat motionless, like mummies. We even held our breath. It didn't last long; soon there was complete silence again. Only about an hour later did we allow ourselves the luxury of shifting our positions.

There was some bread and water in the hiding space. Someone divided up the bread and poured water into two cups. We took turns drinking and chewed on some bread, more to pass the time than from hunger. We were all so agitated that we didn't even feel hungry. This is how the entire day passed for us. In the evening, someone opened the trapdoor and told us we could come out because the roundup had ended. We crawled out of the hiding space and went down to the courtyard.

I remember September 10, 1942, in the Tarnów ghetto as one of the most dreadful days of my life. Not because of what we experienced while hiding but because of what happened later in the building's courtyard. Dantean scenes unfolded there. People returned from their work in factories and workshops and found their children, mothers, fathers, husbands, and wives gone. They cried, lamented, and threw themselves into each other's arms. Everyone gathered in the courtyard, asking each other who had lost whom. They asked those who had survived the roundup how it had happened and begged for even the smallest details about their loved ones who had been taken away.

Someone described what had taken place on Magdeburski Square in the center of the ghetto, where all the Jews had been forced to gather before being taken away. A few people had managed to escape from there. A selection had been made by the Germans. Women had been forced to give up their children, who were led to a different transport. Those who refused to give their children to the Germans had them torn away by force. There were some cases when enraged Germans tore infants out of their mothers' arms and, holding them by their feet, smashed their heads against the walls of buildings in front of their mothers' eyes. Several people who had witnessed this described it in detail.

Women threw themselves on the ground in despair; men stood in groups and wept loudly. A woman screamed with her hands reaching up toward the sky, "Mama! Mama! Why did they take you away? Why did you go? Oh... my life is over!" Women were sitting on the ground, crying; their faces were contorted with grief. Others were just standing there like specters, as if they'd lost their senses and didn't know what was happening. In the courtyard there was one electric light, which cast long shadows of the lamenting people in various directions. I'll never forget this image; if a person would like to try to imagine hell—it was there, in that courtyard.

I no longer remember if the bunker in the cellar, where we'd hidden at the beginning, had been discovered or not. There were many bunkers in this building, but some people had decided not to hide. They'd lain in their beds in total apathy, awaiting their fate. Many people had already run out of strength to survive even before this roundup operation began. They had, quite simply, lost the will to live. Everyone who was caught that day by the Germans was forced to go into the courtyard, and from there they were led to Magdeburski Square. Then they were loaded, like cattle, into trains that were waiting for them.

On that day, September 10, 1942, eight thousand people were transported from the Tarnów ghetto to the gas chambers in Bełżec, where they were killed.

The next day, my father fell ill with a high fever and stomach pains. He vomited constantly. In the evening a doctor named Dr. Wachtel came to examine my father and said he had dysentery, and it was necessary to quarantine him because it was an extremely contagious disease. The Lehrhaupts' son had a good idea—to put my father in the building's attic. My mother said we'd go with him. A bed was made for him from planks, and an old, shredded mattress was placed on it. Blankets were spread on the floor for us. The attic was very large and seemed much more comfortable to me than the cramped room in the Lehrhaupts' apartment.

My father's condition worsened the next day, and he had to sit constantly on a bucket. My mother kept telling us to stay away from the bucket because it was full of blood. Dr. Wachtel gave my mother instructions on how to disinfect my father's clothes and warned us to be very careful about hygiene. Hearing him say this, my father, who was lying there with a fever, started laughing and said that talking about hygiene in that attic was like telling a chimney sweep to avoid soot. The doctor reassured my anxious mother by telling her that he was sure my father would recover because he was in a good mood.

My father was ill for two weeks. Sometimes he was better, sometimes worse, but he never lost hope, and he continued to cheer us up even while he was fighting the disease. We remained with him constantly, and my mother took care of him day and night. Dr. Wachtel told us later that he couldn't understand how it was possible that we didn't catch the illness. The only person who visited us apart from the doctor was the Lehrhaupts' son. He brought us food, water, and news from the ghetto. His helpfulness and kindness moved us deeply. He was a remarkable boy—a "noble soul," as my parents said.

One day he joyfully told us he'd found an apartment for us. In the courtyard there was a closed-up shop in which some old things were stored. The Lehrhaupts' son had cleared everything out by himself, plastered the cracked walls, and whitewashed the entire place. He'd put a lot of work into it. After my father recovered, the Lehrhaupts' son led us there triumphantly. It was a large space—larger than a normal room.

People brought us several pieces of furniture and various household necessities. We were set up quite well, and we each had our own bed. The shop didn't have any windows, only a door made of a corrugated sheet of tin that rolled down from the top.

That day I went for a walk through the ghetto for the first time, promising my parents that if I saw any Germans I'd hide immediately. I looked all around as I walked. Now I understood why people were sneaking about like frightened animals. I walked along poverty-stricken streets and alleyways that looked as if their residents were extinct. Most people were in the factories, and the rest were afraid to go outside. But the desire to experience life was more powerful than fear; I passed people here and there, including children. In a courtyard they were even kicking a ball made of rags back and forth.

Once again, I felt a profound loneliness. I missed my friends and began to think about them. I soon found myself facing a tall wooden fence that separated the ghetto from the Aryan side. I noticed people standing there, talking with people on the other side of the fence through gaps between the wooden planks. I went closer and saw that the people in the ghetto were buying bread, butter, and vegetables. Everything was happening in a rush; the people were constantly looking around. One of the planks could be pushed aside, and products were being passed into the ghetto.

I knew my mother didn't have any bread for us that day. I wondered how I could get a loaf of bread from these people. I knew nobody would give me anything without money—there was no point asking for bread, since everyone would laugh at me. But I saw them haggling over every penny. I made a mental note of where this spot was and kept walking. I wandered aimlessly and looked at the ghetto. Everything was gray, neglected, and horribly squalid.

I was finally about to go home when I found myself at the main entrance gate. There was a German soldier in front of the gate and several Jewish policemen were standing on the ghetto side. One of them was speaking with a postman. Seeing me, he beckoned me over to him. I wondered whether I should run away. He beckoned to me again, and when I came closer, he took a large bundle of letters from the postman and handed it to me.

"Deliver these letters. It'll be worth it for you because everyone will give you a tip."

I took the letters and started walking around with them, constantly asking people how to find certain streets. I went to various apartments where I was welcomed by people as if I were an angel visiting them. Everywhere I went, I was given something—mostly spare change, but sometimes a slice of bread, which I put in a bag that a woman gave me. An old woman with trembling hands gave me a carrot. I thanked her but refused to take it. "Just take this, at least," she said, and kissed me on the forehead. When nobody was home, I slid the letters under the door. About two hours later, all the letters had been delivered.

I'd collected, it seemed to me, a handsome sum of money. I was sure I'd now be able to buy a loaf of bread and maybe even something more. I headed to the spot I'd seen earlier but couldn't find it. I decided to walk along right next to the fence. Suddenly I heard a voice from the other side say, "Wait! Where are you rushing off to so fast? Come here, we can do some business."

I looked through a gap and saw a boy standing on the other side with a thick bundle of newspapers under his arm.

"What do you want?" I asked.

"Buy a few newspapers and start selling them. The price of a newspaper in the ghetto is a lot higher. Then come back to me and buy some more. I'll wait for you here." Seeing my indecision, he added, "What are you afraid of? There's no way to lose money in this business."

I bought ten newspapers. I stood in the doorway of a building and called out, "Newspapers! Newspapers!" It took me only a few minutes to sell all the newspapers, at double the price, to the residents of the building in front of which I was standing. A woman asked me if the price of newspapers on the Aryan side had fallen, since I was selling them so cheap.

Because it was going so well for me, I went back to the boy, who was waiting for me on the other side of the fence. I bought all the newspapers from him. I decided to keep selling them in doorways. I went from one entranceway to another, shouting, "Newspapers! Newspapers!" Half an hour later I only had three left. People were craving news from the outside world and were looking for something in it that would give them hope.

When I left the last doorway, someone grabbed my hand from behind. I turned around and saw a Jewish policeman in front of me. He shouted, "Don't you know it's forbidden to sell newspapers in the ghetto? The Germans have already shot three boys like you. Do you want to be the fourth?" He let go of my hand and commanded, "Throw those newspapers away and get out of here!"

He shook his finger at me and shouted, "I never want to see you around here again!"

I stood there, frozen to the spot. Seeing my helplessness, he asked, "How old are you?"

"Eleven."

"You look older. Who are you trying to fool?"

"Eleven," I repeated.

A bit calmer now, the policeman nodded, and his voice became gentler. "Maybe you're telling the truth. In the ghetto people grow up quickly. All right, scram!"

I tossed the last three newspapers on the ground and ran away from the man as fast as my legs could carry me. After a while, out of breath, I slowed down. I realized I was once again next to the spot in the fence where people were buying food. I stood there and asked how much a loaf of bread cost that a man had in a basket. He told me the price. I also saw a woman who looked like an old village granny holding a large lump of butter on some cabbage leaves. Butter was a rare treat for us. We hadn't eaten butter for a very long time—only yellow, rancid margarine.

I imagined how happy my mother would be if I brought her such a present. For the amount of money I had, I could buy several loaves of bread. It took me quite a while to decide what to buy. The woman urged me, "Take this fresh butter, straight from the countryside."

Finally, I bought one loaf of bread and the butter. She wrapped the butter up for me, together with the cabbage leaves, in an old newspaper, and handed it through the fence as if it were a precious object that was hard for her to part with. I put the loaf in my bag, in which I already had a few slices of bread. I carried the package of butter carefully and found my way home.

My parents were astounded when I proudly presented my treasures to them. I told them quickly about what had happened, and we began to cut the bread.

Before my mother touched the butter with the knife, she looked fondly at it for a moment. The butter was decorated with marks from a spoon and truly looked lovely. Then my mother started spreading some on the bread, and Lusia smacked her lips because she knew the first slice would be for her. But the knife struck something hard, and it turned out to be a turnip coated with a thin layer of butter. I felt so horribly betrayed and hurt that I didn't want to put any of the butter in my mouth.

After this event, my parents forbade me from wandering off. My heart was very heavy. I didn't have anything to do to pass the time, and I missed my friends.

My father found some company for himself more quickly. There was a man named Baruch living in our building; my father spent many hours with him, talking and playing chess. They became very close friends. He was also in Tarnów "illegally." He was about forty years old. He'd left his wife and infant daughter outside the ghetto. They were from a small town near Tarnów. Right before a roundup operation during which the Germans deported all the Jews from their town, they'd hidden in their maid's house in the countryside. Mr. Baruch, however, had been unable to remain there and had managed to reach the ghetto in Tarnów.

One day, Mr. Baruch told my father he'd received a message from his wife that the maid and her family no longer wanted to let her stay in their house. He contacted a close friend who lived in Tarnów, who promised him that he would get his wife and child and help them enter the ghetto. Later he would try to obtain forged identity documents for all of them and find somewhere for them to live.

Despite his clearly Jewish name, Mr. Baruch had a very Aryan appearance. He promised my father that as soon as they were settled somewhere on Aryan papers, he would ask his friend to help us, too. This gave us fresh hope that we might manage to leave the ghetto before the next roundup operation. We discussed plans and wondered where we could hide.

One afternoon several days later, a neighbor came to us—a *shohet* (ritual butcher)—and asked my father to go with him to Mr. Baruch's apartment because he was reciting the Kaddish (the prayer for the dead) and needed ten men.

"What happened?" asked my father, alarmed.

The man told us that a terrible misfortune had befallen Mr. Baruch. His friend had driven to Tarnów with Mr. Baruch's wife and daughter; two hundred meters from the ghetto, someone had recognized his wife and called the police. All three were arrested and taken to the gestapo. Before entering, Mr. Baruch's wife put cyanide in her daughter's mouth; then she swallowed some herself. Both died on the spot.

I went with my father to the apartment in which Mr. Baruch had a small room. It was already full of men. Mr. Baruch's eyes were bloodshot, and someone was holding him up. Soon the men began to pray, and for the first time, I saw my father cry while praying. It was a long time before Mr. Baruch was able to pull himself together and then, sobbing, haltingly recite the Kaddish. This tragic ceremony was repeated twice a day for an entire week, and Mr. Baruch seemed to become increasingly devastated.

My father stayed with him all the time and tried to keep his spirits up, but he himself returned from Mr. Baruch's apartment increasingly despondent. Then a message came that Mr. Baruch's friend had been shot in the gestapo's headquarters. This noble Polish man lost his life because he had helped his Jewish friend. Mr. Baruch tortured himself with reproaches that all of this had been his fault. He felt responsible for their deaths and was unable to forgive himself.

One day someone told my mother it was possible to obtain milk with food cards. My mother gave me a jug and some cards and told me to run quickly and stand in line. I left our shop-apartment, ran across the courtyard, and entered the hallway that led to the street. It was a lovely, sunny day, and when I ran out of the dark, narrow corridor, the sun blinded me, and I shut my eyes. I only opened them after I'd taken several more steps. What I saw at that moment made my heart sink with terror. About thirty steps away from me were several Germans, and they were coming straight toward me. I stood there, not knowing what to do. At that very moment someone shouted from a window: "Run! It's Rommelman! Run!"

I spun on my heels and started running home. I heard shouts behind me: "*Halt! Halt!*" I flew like lightning through the entrance hallway and into the courtyard. I ran up to our shop and, with a sudden instinct, quickly lowered the metal door over the entrance and ran to the hallway on the opposite side of the courtyard. When I was about three steps away from it, once again I heard behind me: "*Halt!*" The sound of a gunshot rang out; the bullet flew past my head and made a hole in the wall in front of me. On the threshold of the hallway I crashed into the *shohet*, who happened to be coming out right then. A second gunshot rang out, and the bullet hit the *shohet*.

I frantically ran up the staircase and only stopped when I reached the top floor. I heard another gunshot. I saw a Jewish policeman from our building standing near another staircase, close to the covered balcony that encircled the entire courtyard on every floor. He was cautiously leaning out and looking down at the courtyard. He noticed me and signaled for me to stay quiet and come closer to him. It was the same policeman who had led us to the second hiding place during the roundup operation. I approached him, and when he saw that I was trembling from head to toe, he drew me close to him in a fatherly way, which calmed me greatly.

I looked down. The *shohet* was lying near our shop in a pool of blood. The Germans were looking around the courtyard. They stood there for a while, smoking, then headed back to the building's entrance hallway. We stayed where we were for about fifteen minutes before someone came into the courtyard and shouted, "The Germans are gone! The Germans are gone!"

People started appearing in the courtyard one by one, slowly and fearfully. I hurried down to the courtyard and lifted the door of our shop.

A strange sight met my eyes: my father was sitting on the bed with Lusia, and his hand was over her mouth. He looked at me with a confused expression.

My mother was sitting on the floor, holding her head in her hands. I said, "Mama," and then... she fainted. It turned out that my parents had been watching through a small hole in the roller door and heard the gunshots that were fired right after I'd pulled the door down. They'd seen the pool of blood in the courtyard and had been sure the Germans had shot me. They couldn't see the body.

There was no doubt that if I hadn't closed the roller door right at that moment, Rommelman would have entered the shop and killed my entire family.

After this happened, I felt even more scared of leaving home. I was overwhelmed by a growing feeling of hopelessness and loneliness. I was sad and despondent all the time, and I barely spoke. I sat on my bed for hours on end, completely motionless.

My mother told my father I was depressed and suggested summoning the rabbi, who was still frequently visiting Mr. Baruch. My father thought I was too young for conversations with the rabbi. When my mother kept insisting, he said, "Mina, you don't understand. What the rabbi tells people is philosophy. Henryk is still too young for it. There's no point burdening him with things he's unable to understand." I knew there were many things I couldn't understand. It depressed me, however, to realize that when I did begin to understand something I hadn't understood previously, it was always something bad, never something good.

One day, at my mother's urging, I went out into the courtyard and sat down on a chair. The rays of sunshine caressed my face, and I had a pleasant feeling as if a huge weight had been lifted off my heart. I sat there for about an hour in the sunlight until I sensed someone standing next to me. I opened my eyes and saw a very pretty girl about my age, maybe nine or ten years old. I looked at her curiously because I'd never seen her before. She had dark hair and green eyes.

"What's your name?" I asked.

"Ninka," she answered with a smile.

I was surprised because her name reminded me of Nina from Wieliczka. We started talking, and the more we said to each other, the more interested I felt in her. I brought her a chair from our home, and we sat together in the sun.

She told me she'd been smuggled into the ghetto from the Aryan side just the day before. She'd been hiding there with her father, but she ended up alone because the Germans had caught her father in the street. Some kind people helped her enter the ghetto. Her mother was living on Aryan papers in Lwów. For the time being, Ninka was staying with her aunt in our building. Her aunt was going to ask her mother to send someone for her. I also briefly told her my story; she listened to it intently, as if it concerned someone dear to her.

Ninka was very intelligent. She was always solemn, and her beautiful eyes looked sad. While talking to her, I had the impression she was much older. It occurred to me then that the Jewish policeman who had caught me with the newspapers had been right. The war was clearly adding years to us. I was deeply moved by the symbolism of her name. It seemed to me that Nina from Wieliczka had sent her to me so I wouldn't feel lonely.

Meeting this girl stirred in me a new desire to live, and my depression gradually passed. We spent entire days together. She felt even lonelier than I did because her aunt was rarely home—she worked in a German factory and came home late at night.

Ninka and I talked about many things and tried to understand the world. She was most deeply troubled by the following problems: Why do wars happen? Why are there so many people who hate Jews? What harm have we ever caused them? Why do they think we're worse than other people? We couldn't find answers to any of these questions, but even just thinking about them together and being able to share our thoughts with someone was a relief. One day, while I was with her in her room, I asked her where she would hide if another roundup operation began in the ghetto. "I have parents, and they're definitely already thinking about this, but what will happen to you? Who will you hide with?"

At this question, Ninka looked at me with her large, sad eyes, and said she'd hide alone.

"Come, I'll show you where. My aunt told me what to do in such a case. Nobody knows about this hiding place except me and my aunt. Swear you won't show it to anyone, because even if one day I'm no longer here, this hiding place will belong only to my aunt."

I swore she could trust me. She led me along a balcony to one of the staircases and then up the stairs to a higher floor. There was a bathroom in the hallway. We entered it, and Ninka pointed upward.

I saw a narrow shaft above us, which seemed to lead to the roof. But I couldn't see any kind of hiding space—just walls. Ninka stood on the toilet seat and pulled on a barely visible string wound around the chain that flushed the toilet. Something fluttered high above us and then fell. It turned out to be a rope ladder. Ninka grabbed it and straightened it out.

"I'll climb up first. You can come up after I reach the top and give you a signal. OK?"

I nodded, and she climbed up as nimbly as a cat, which surprised me very much because I didn't expect such dexterity from her. A moment later she was already at the top of the ladder, and then she disappeared.

"Now it's your turn!" she called out.

It took me longer; I had to stop several times because I was afraid of falling. Ninka watched my exertions from above and laughed. Finally, climbing very slowly, I reached Ninka's legs and saw that she was sitting inside a large alcove. I scrambled in, and Ninka pulled up the ladder. She told me she had practiced entering the hiding place several times with her aunt and was now used to it.

I looked around curiously. The alcove was about three meters by one meter in size. Above us there was a small glass window overlooking the roof. In the alcove there were two barrels, a bucket, and several cardboard boxes piled on top of each other. The box at the top was open, and there were bottles inside it. Ninka explained that the bottles were full of water, and there was also water in one of the barrels. The other barrel was for relieving oneself, so that it wouldn't be necessary to go down and use the toilet. A sack full of something was lying next to the other wall, and in front of it was a small bench.

"What's in there?" I asked, pointing to the sack.

"Crackers."

Right in front of my legs, in the middle of the alcove, there was a mattress and some blankets. I also noticed a bottle of Lysol.

"My aunt told me it's possible to hide here for a month, maybe even two months."

"On nothing but crackers and water?" I asked, doubtfully.

"Not only crackers. Look what's on the wall."

Only then did I notice something hanging against the wall, covered by a piece of material. Ninka lifted the material and two huge, thick smoked sausages appeared before my eyes. She pointed at a second piece of material.

"There are two more sausages under that one, but we're not allowed to touch them because we'll eat them when we hide here."

She told me her aunt had received this hiding place from a man who'd prepared it for his family, but he and his family had managed to escape from the ghetto on Aryan papers. If a roundup happened while her aunt was working at the factory, Ninka was supposed to hide here. Her aunt had brought the crackers and sausages because she was afraid the Germans might liquidate the entire ghetto, and she wanted to be able to hide here for a long time if necessary.

We sat on the bench, and Ninka told me her aunt had forbidden her from entering one of the bunkers with other people during a roundup because those hiding spots were too precarious. Several people lived in this building who worked for the *Judenrat* as well as some Jewish policemen. Ninka's aunt was afraid that if there weren't as many people rounded up for a transport as the Germans demanded, they might report hiding places they knew about in order to save their own lives.

Ninka's aunt had told her that in other ghettos there had been cases when the Germans had demanded, on pain of death, that the members of the *Judenrat* hand over Jews for a transport. Those who didn't want to reveal where people were hiding committed suicide. There were also some who yielded to the Germans and betrayed their brothers. There was no way to know what was going to happen here, in Tarnów.

Ninka became very emotional while telling me this. She was clearly more concerned about our situation than I was. Perhaps it was because she was alone and had a more acute instinct for self-preservation. I relied completely on my parents. Whatever happened to them would also happen to me. I didn't think about the future. I just lived from day to day, like most people in the ghetto.

We sat there in the alcove above the toilet, and Ninka gave me a long lecture about her aunt's speculations on the chances of surviving a roundup operation. She spoke like a grown-up and emphasized things she thought were particularly important.

After a while she looked at me, smiled, and said, "Take off your clothes." I was startled and bewildered. I didn't know how to react. I looked at her in disbelief.

She stood up and completely undressed right before my eyes. Her breasts were already clearly visible, like flower buds that were about to blossom at any moment. Her pubic area was dark, and her skin was as white and delicate as ivory.

"Well, what about you?" she urged me.

I stood up and also took off all my clothes. I wanted to embrace Ninka, but she didn't let me. She told me to sit next to her on the bench. I sat down, and she put her hand in mine. I didn't know what to do and looked at her questioningly. I was embarrassed and felt surprised that she wasn't embarrassed.

Ninka said, "When grown-ups are in love, they sit together like this."

"How do you know?"

"I saw my parents do this. They loved each other very much," she said wistfully.

I noticed her eyes were filled with tears. We sat on the bench together, naked and feeling abandoned by the whole world. I had a strange feeling that we were waiting to be reborn. I heard her whisper, "Close your eyes and begin to dream."

I did as she requested. I no longer remember what I dreamed of, but I remember experiencing something very sublime and pleasant. I felt like I was in a good, pure world and that I, too, was pure. It seemed to me that we both belonged to a better world, not the filthy one below us.

We started to feel cold, so we covered ourselves with a blanket. We continued to hold hands and sit there without speaking, deeply immersed in our dreams. I don't know how long it lasted because time stood still for me. After a while I opened my eyes and asked her, "Are we in love?"

She answered for both of us with such conviction that I had to believe her: "Of course. Very much so." And she kissed me on the mouth.

Then Ninka quickly stood up and got dressed. I did the same. She came up to me, put her hands on my shoulders, and looked straight into my eyes.

"After the war, when we're older, I'll come to you, and we'll get married."

At her request, I gave her my address in Oświęcim: 41 Jagiellońska Street. Ninka went over to the sack of crackers, took a sharp knife from it, and scratched my address into the wall. Then she dropped the ladder, and we climbed down. She pulled on the thin string; the ladder went up and disappeared into the alcove. From down below it was impossible to see it.

"Remember this hiding spot. You can use it when we're no longer here," she said.

Two days later a messenger came to them with a letter from Ninka's mother in Lwów. That very night, Ninka went with the messenger to the Aryan side by climbing a rope ladder over the fence. I stood close by and watched them leave. I'd slipped away from home while everyone was sleeping. Ninka's aunt was there, too. I stood in the doorway of a building and cried. When Ninka reached the top of the fence, she turned and waved to me.

I went home with her aunt, and we didn't exchange a single word. I saw that she was crying, too. When I got home, I lay on my bed in the darkness for a long time with wide-open eyes, thinking about Ninka.

I never saw her again. Her aunt didn't hear a single word from her, either.

My entire friendship with Ninka lasted only a few weeks, but it was very important to me. I've thought many times during my life about how there was something very deep and significant for me in this friendship. I've always felt certain, or perhaps I've only deluded myself into believing, that if Ninka had survived, she would have come to find me in Oświęcim after the war. In my life she has been a kind of supernatural phenomenon that, in difficult times, has enabled me to understand that always, in every situation, life is worth living.

I experienced this brief time with Ninka in the Tarnów ghetto as if I'd known her for many years in a normal, peaceful time.

Life in the ghetto passed much more quickly than outside the ghetto. Time lost its old, commonplace meaning for me. Only now did I understand what we'd been told by the physics professor in Wieliczka. "Time truly is relative," I thought. Life in the ghetto, full of constant danger, accelerated strangely. It was as if a person wished to pack all his experiences and all the events that await him in a normal life into the short time remaining for him on earth.

In the ghetto, nothing flowed smoothly. For us it was like a tumultuous waterfall of events. Time passed at an insane speed, but . . . not for everyone. There were also those for whom time stood still—those who had completely surrendered to fate and no longer sought ways to survive, even in their thoughts. They became apathetic and indifferent to what was happening around them. All their strength had left them, and they no longer fought to live. These people had lost all chances of survival and ended up being the first to die.

Thanks to my friendship with Ninka, I left this group of apathetic people and returned to those who were still fighting to survive. Ninka had made me realize my life was worth fighting for and inspired me not to give up. I've always been convinced that she was sent to me from heaven.

Once again, my life began to rush along and change constantly as if I were inside a kaleidoscope. Events happened one after another. I doubt I would have been able to cope with it all if it hadn't been for Ninka, who had freed me from my apathy.

Several days after Ninka left the ghetto, my grandmother, Frydzia Münz (my mother's mother), appeared in our shop-apartment. She'd come from Rzeszów, where she lived, and a Jewish policeman she knew had managed to help her enter the Tarnów ghetto. She'd heard we were here and wanted to be with us.

My mother was extremely happy, but when she saw the solemn expression on my grandmother's face, she asked, "How's Dad?"

My grandmother burst into tears, and it took us a very long time to calm her. She told us that during a roundup operation, the Germans had led the residents of their apartment building into the courtyard and shot them all there. This is how my mother's brother, Iciu Münz, had died, along with his wife and his son, Szymuś, who was my age. My grandfather, Mordechai Münz, had refused to go down to the courtyard. He sat at the table with the Talmud open in front of him, wrapped in his prayer shawl, and waited for the Germans. He was shot right there, on the spot. My grandmother had been in the countryside at the time, buying some food, and had survived thanks to this. When she returned home, all her loved ones were dead.

My mother and grandmother cried for two days straight. My father took me to visit some friends of his because he was afraid I'd fall into a state of apathy again. But at that time, I felt completely transformed and strengthened in spirit. I was no longer in danger of succumbing to apathy. Quite the opposite—I was filled with new energy and a strange feeling of anticipation.

About two days after my grandmother's arrival, a Jewish policeman came to us and asked my father if he knew Ignaś Frenkel.

"Of course," answered my father. "He's my sister's son. My sister died giving birth to him. He's five years old now. What about him?"

Someone had left the child in front of the ghetto's entrance. Hanging around his neck, on a string, was a piece of paper with the following written on it: "Ignaś Frenkel—please give him to Leon Schönker in the ghetto." A Jewish policeman had led him to the *Judenrat*. The child didn't speak or answer any questions. They thought he was deaf. I could see that my father was shocked. He immediately rushed out of the apartment. After a while, he returned with Ignaś in his arms. Ignaś had a letter in his pocket saying that his father, Zalman Frenkel, had been shot in the street—I no longer remember where—and an acquaintance of ours had sent this child to us in the ghetto. Ignaś had a seventeen-year-old brother named Arie, but there was no mention of him in the letter.

During his first days with us, Ignaś said almost nothing, but his sad eyes expressed everything. I remembered Ignaś from Oświęcim as a beautiful two-year-old child. Now he looked even lovelier. Long, golden curls fell nearly to his shoulders. His big blue eyes gazed at us as if he were an angel in a painting. He was an extremely sweet and obedient child.

We all loved Ignaś very much, but I . . . I began to adore Ignaś intensely. He clearly felt this, for he never left my side even for a moment. I took care of him and helped him with everything. I played with him all day long. I was happy when Ignaś, about a week after coming to us, smiled at me for the first time while we were playing.

We shared a bed; Ignaś slept curled up to me, with his arm around me. He never complained and was satisfied with everything. Sometimes it seemed to me that Ignaś was really an angel, not a human being. He had so much kindness in him. All the love I'd once felt for my brother, Musiu, I now showered on Ignaś, and I felt life had gained new meaning for me. He was my new brother. I loved him very much, and he loved me. I decided that after the war we would always be together.

For the time being, we never left our courtyard. Rommelman and Grunoff were appearing more often in the ghetto, killing people to entertain themselves. Everyone in the ghetto lived in constant fear. We were also afraid of another roundup operation. Everyone focused on how to survive each day. I rid myself of all negative thoughts because I was aware I was powerless and unable to prevent whatever was going to happen to us. But I had a strange feeling that nothing bad would happen to me. I thought about the end of the war and how nice it was going to be when we returned to our house in Oświęcim, and Ignaś would be with us, as well as my grandmother, since she no longer had a home of her own.

A few weeks later, a strange anxiety swept through the ghetto again. There were rumors that another roundup was about to happen. I remember an old man in our building explaining to my father that there were increasing indications that another deportation would happen soon. My father started thinking about where we could hide and discussing it with other people.

It was impossible to leave the ghetto without any contacts on the Aryan side. It was very rare that anyone had such a contact. Without one, crossing to the other side meant certain death. There were many informants, blackmailers, and extortionists who earned a living by handing Jews over to Germans. Apart from these people, there were many ordinary people who considered themselves to be decent, honest, and even pious, but who denounced Jews because of their pathological aversion to them. Jews who were outside the ghetto were soon handed over to the gestapo.

Even the truly decent people who were willing to help Jews didn't do so because they were afraid their neighbors, acquaintances, friends, or even their own family members might denounce them. This gave Jewish people the impression that most Polish people were hostile toward them or, at the very least, were indifferent to their plight.

And yet there were also some Poles who, despite all danger, risked their own lives and the lives of their family members in order to aid and hide Jews. They tried to obtain forged identity documents for them, connected them with other people who could help them, led them to hiding spots, pretended they were part of their family, and—no less importantly—felt compassion for them. They often hid them for long periods of time inside their own houses. They gave them food and experienced along with them the fear of being discovered. Despite this fear, they didn't stop helping them and didn't order them to leave their homes when circumstances became difficult or when people started spreading rumors about them hiding Jews. Sometimes they paid for this with their own lives. These were the true unsung heroes of this war.

My parents also considered crossing to the Aryan side, but they quickly abandoned this idea. We had no option but to keep hiding in the ghetto. Someone confided in my father that a large bunker had been built in our building's attic and was camouflaged in such a way that it would certainly never be discovered. My father was introduced to the people who had created this bunker. After seeing it, my father asked for us to be added to the list of people who could use it. It was an extremely well-concealed hiding place.

The attic in the building was very large and divided into sections. A door leading into one of the sections had been bricked up. This section faced Lwowska Street, outside the ghetto. The attic's ceiling was held up by beams; against a wall of the closed-off section, there were three pieces of wood forming a triangle at the base of a beam in the corner, right next to the floor. This triangle could be pulled out, and then it was possible to enter the bunker through the hole where the triangle had been. There were identical triangles throughout the entire attic, in the corners down below and up above, and nobody could possibly guess that one of them led to a bunker. This entrance could be closed from inside after the triangle was pushed back into place.

Even people who lived in the building weren't aware there was a hiding place here, for nobody ever went in this part of the attic. There was enough space for two hundred people inside it. Supplies of food were hidden in the bunker, to which everyone had contributed, and barrels had been filled with water. Three toilets had also been installed.

One night, news came that Germans had surrounded the ghetto. The entire building started buzzing with life. We ran out of the shop, not even pulling the metal door down behind us. We felt that every extra second could determine our fate. People were walking and running anxiously, not speaking to each other.

It was dark on the staircase, and we were constantly crashing into other people. I held Ignaś's hand and shielded him with my body so nobody would hurt him. On the top floor it was even more crowded. We finally reached the attic. There was already a long line of people in front of the entrance to the bunker. We each had to lie down on the floor and crawl through the hole in the wall.

Ignaś and I went in first. My grandmother was pulled in by her legs. Then Lusia was passed through; there was a terrified look in her eyes, and her mouth was hanging open. My mother said to her over and over again, "Don't be afraid, don't be afraid, I'm here with you." My father was the last one to crawl in. It was difficult for him, and we had to help him because he was a tall, broad-shouldered man. We sat down on the floor with the other people, all in a row. My mother held Lusia on her lap, and I put my arm around Ignaś and held him close to me. My grandmother sat next to my mother and gave an impression that none of this concerned her at all. Ignaś was also very calm and soon fell asleep. He must have had a nice dream because he was smiling in his sleep.

More people came, and the bunker filled up. The people who had helped us enter came in last, and they pulled the triangle back into place, which they further reinforced with an iron bar.

When everyone had settled in, someone said, "Now we have to sit silently, without moving."

The flashlights were switched off, and then there was total darkness and silence in the bunker. Sometimes a child began to cry, but the sound was immediately suppressed by the child's parents. All that could be heard from time to time were sighs and stifled coughs.

It was November 1942. The bunker at 4 Lwowska Street was awaiting its fate.

I woke up, and at first I didn't know where I was. Light was entering through several small windows with opaque panes that were on the roof. People were sitting in a row, pressed against each other. Almost everyone was listening intently as if they were expecting something to happen. Ignaś was sleeping with his head on my lap. Suddenly I heard something. A muffled thumping sound was coming from down below, as if someone were breaking down a wall. My father placed his finger on my mouth because he was clearly afraid I would say something. Only then did I remember that I was inside a bunker.

I looked at Ignaś. He was smiling in his sleep again. Soon the sounds stopped, and once again there was total silence. It was mostly older people there—those who didn't go to work and those who had come to the ghetto illegally, like us. The Germans operated with great precision. It was necessary to have a special pass even while you were waiting to die—otherwise you were headed toward death illegally. In the bunker there were also many disabled people, as well as children whose parents were at work.

An old Jew with a beard was sitting near me, praying with the Book of Psalms open in front of him. I was surprised he hadn't cut off his beard, since there had been such an order from the Germans. "How is it possible that he isn't afraid?" I thought. I observed his face and the other people's faces, too. He was the calmest one. Even calmer than my grandmother, who was looking at my mother and us children with such pity that I felt sorry for her. It was clear she was very worried about us but not about herself. We sat there in silence, each of us deeply immersed in our own thoughts.

It was about eleven o'clock in the morning when we heard some murmurs and voices on the other side of the wall. The murmurs became louder, right near the entrance to our bunker. We all froze with fear. Suddenly we heard loud blows right at the entrance. It sounded like the roar of a cannon. One, two, three... Someone was smashing the entrance to the bunker. We were sitting right next to the entrance and saw the blade of an ax. Soon the entrance was open. A Jewish policeman's head appeared in it.

He looked around and shouted, "Come out! Come out! Everyone has to come out!"

Nobody moved. We all sat there, petrified. The policeman repeated the command, but seeing that nobody was obeying him, he warned us that if we didn't come out, the Germans would come and throw grenades into the bunker. Then we would all die on the spot. We had no choice. People started climbing out through the hole in the wall.

It was obvious someone had revealed the bunker to the Germans. The attic was full of Jewish policemen, who ordered us to go down to the courtyard. They were standing on every floor and on the stairs so that nobody could escape down the hallways. We descended the stairs, trying to stay together. I held Ignaś's hand, and my mother carried Lusia. My father tried to take her, but my mother refused to let her go. Lusia's eyes had a terrified look in them again. My grandmother was clinging to my mother.

There was total chaos on the staircase. Some people were rushing down the stairs as if this would increase their chances of survival. Others were walking slowly, prodded along by the policemen. I could hear children crying. Someone swore in Yiddish. People were pushing and shoving each other.

We finally reached the courtyard. We were forced into rows, one after another, about ten people in each row. Jewish policemen surrounded us on all sides with truncheons in their hands. We stood there and waited for what would happen next. This lasted quite a long time because many people were walking very slowly, especially the physically disabled people. I didn't see anyone resist.

Suddenly, Ignaś told me he needed to go "poo-poo." I told my father. He thought for a moment and observed the Jewish policemen, as if searching for someone in charge. Finally, he went up to one of them and asked him to allow Ignaś to go "to this shop, to the bathroom," and he pointed at our home. "He'll come right back." The policeman looked at Ignaś, who was clearly having trouble restraining himself, and agreed. My father returned to us and told Ignaś, "Go back to our home and go to the bathroom, but afterward don't come back; just hide under the bed. Do you understand?"

Ignaś nodded. But my father didn't stop there and told him to repeat what he was supposed to do. Ignaś repeated, "I'll go home to go to the bathroom; then I'm going to hide under the bed and not come back."

I saw Ignaś enter our apartment. People were still coming down to the courtyard.

I looked at my mother and saw something strange happening to her. Her eyes had become unnaturally wide. She was holding Lusia in her arms and rocking her, the way a person lulls an infant to sleep. Her mouth was twisted in an ugly kind of grimace I'd never seen on her face before. She wasn't standing calmly like the others but was trembling from head to toe. I was afraid something terrible had happened to her. My father tried to calm her down, and my grandmother tried to take Lusia out of her arms, but my mother refused to let her go. She started screaming hysterically with her eyes widened in terror.

"I won't give them my child! I won't! They're going to kill her in Magdeburski Square! I won't let them take her! I won't let them!"

People who had been completely apathetic until now became enlivened. Some started shouting at the policemen, others swore at them. A policeman who was directing everyone ran over to my father and shouted at him, "Calm her down!"

My father spread his hands helplessly. "She needs some water."

"Where is there some water here?"

My father pointed at an open door close to us. The policeman took one of my mother's arms, and my father took her other arm, and they pulled her toward the door. There once had been a shop there, and now it was a restaurant for the *Judenrat*. There was a long counter inside it and a faucet.

The policeman said to my father, "Give her some water and then hide here under this counter."

I remained alone with my grandmother in the courtyard.

Suddenly I noticed a young woman, an acquaintance of ours who had recently given birth, moving closer to one of the doorways leading to the entrance hall with her baby in her arms. Nobody noticed her because there was now a great deal of motion and chaos in the courtyard. The policemen were having trouble watching over us and keeping order. They kept running up to people to shout at them or force them back into line. Meanwhile, the woman was creeping, step by step, closer to the entrance hallway, which the policemen were no longer standing near.

She was very close—only about two steps away. I watched her anxiously and thought she would succeed because none of the policemen had noticed her movements. If she reached the entrance hallway, she would be able to escape with her baby. But then I saw a policeman run over to her with a huge stick in his hand. He reached her when she was almost in the entranceway and hit her on the back with the stick. She staggered but didn't fall. She just let out a muffled scream, or rather a loud moan: "Uhhh!" He hit her again, and she moaned once more but still didn't move from the spot, as if she were trying to earn the right to leave the courtyard by suffering these blows. It was only after the third blow that she staggered, with her baby, back to her spot in the row of people.

My eyes saw all of this. They didn't want to believe what they were seeing, but they couldn't deny it because they had really seen it. The sight of this woman being beaten made me realize that if I went with all the other people, something terrible was going to happen to me. I started looking around in all directions but couldn't see any way to escape. I stared, as if hypnotized, at the stick held by the Jewish policeman who had beaten the woman. It was a piece of wood flattened on one end, normally used for beating laundry.

I also kept looking at the door through which my parents had disappeared with Lusia. I waited, expecting to see them at any moment, but they didn't come out. I didn't know what had happened to them. I was very worried about my mother, but also happy they weren't with us. My grandmother didn't say anything. She stood there calmly and didn't look scared.

The policemen began to arrange us in small groups in order to leave the courtyard. My parents and Lusia were still nowhere to be seen. At the other side of the courtyard, Ignaś appeared in the doorway of our shop! I tried to signal to him that he should go back in the shop, but he started walking in our direction with his tiny steps. I was distraught. I wanted to shout at him to go back, but it was already too late. Ignaś stood next to us and, clearly ashamed he hadn't obeyed me, took my grandmother's hand instead of mine.

"Why did you come back?" I asked him reproachfully.

"Because I was afraid," he answered in a mournful tone.

I felt extremely restless. I wanted to fight but didn't know how. They started leading us to the building's entrance hallway. They forced us through it in single file because it was narrow. Ignaś and my grandmother were walking behind me. Two children were in front of me—a brother and sister. He was about eight years old, and she was about six. He had his arm around her and was trying to comfort her. She was crying and calling out, "Mama! Mama!" Their mother must have been at work in a factory outside the ghetto.

I no longer felt afraid. I advanced mechanically, like a robot, without any emotion. I walked into the entrance hallway. On my righthand side there were stairs going up, and the main door of the building was straight ahead. A policeman was standing in front of the staircase, holding a stick.

And then something completely unexpected happened. Something I'm unable to explain to myself. With every ounce of my strength, motivated by an incredible rage, I shoved the policeman. He was a tall man and certainly very strong, but I rushed at him with such force that, taken off guard, he nearly fell backward. He tried to catch me, but I was already on the stairs. I raced up like a madman with the policeman right behind me. He shouted, "Stop! Stop!" But I didn't have any intention of stopping. I felt like I wasn't running but rather flying in the air. Some kind of superhuman force had entered me. I ran onto the balcony and then into someone's apartment with the policeman on my heels. A window was open in one of the rooms; I jumped through it back onto the balcony, ran farther up the stairs, and dashed into another apartment. I hid under a bed. I heard the policeman's footsteps on the balcony, but he'd lost track of me. He ran back and forth for a while; then his footsteps died away.

I lay under the bed and hardly breathed. I was like a taut spring, ready to leap up and escape at any moment. I watched from under the bed and listened carefully to see if anyone was searching for me. My sense of hearing was much sharper than before. I heard shouts coming from the courtyard several times; then there was complete silence. I lay under the bed for about two hours. The building remained completely silent. I decided to find out what was happening with my parents and Lusia. But I wasn't sure if the policemen had left our building.

I crept out of the apartment and, seeing nobody on the balcony, crawled all the way to the railing and looked down at the courtyard—it was empty. There were just a few objects scattered on the ground: bottles, dolls, blankets, bags, various articles of clothing, and even several open suitcases. There wasn't a single person in sight. I crept to the entrance hallway and strained my ears. Silence. As a precaution I didn't stand up—I went down the stairs very slowly on all fours. I kept stopping to listen. I realized I was sniffing the air like a dog. I was on the third floor, and it took me a long time to reach the courtyard. Nobody was there. I looked up at the balconies and windows. Everything was empty. I waited a while and then, gathering all my courage, stood up and ran quickly, staying close to the wall the whole time, to the shop into which my parents and Lusia had disappeared.

The door was still open a crack, but it was completely dark inside. It was already afternoon and quite dark in the courtyard, too. I stepped inside and asked quietly, "Is anyone here?" There was complete silence. I said, "It's me, Henryk. Is anyone here?"

Then some voices whispered to me. I recognized them as my parents' voices and sighed with relief. I ran toward the voices and heard my father say, "Here ... here ... Henryk, we're here ... bend down and come to us." I bent down and crawled to them under the counter. We were all crying.

My mother asked me about my grandmother and Ignaś. "They're gone," was all I managed to say. My mother sobbed loudly, and my father covered her mouth with his hand.

Suddenly we heard harsh voices giving commands in German right next to the shop. There were several Germans and a woman. They asked her something, and she explained something to them. She was very agitated; she was speaking hysterically and yelling in a hoarse voice. Then the voices receded. A few moments later we heard commands shouted in German again, immediately followed by a peal of gunshots in the courtyard. Then everything fell silent.

I don't know how long we sat there, petrified. Eventually my father whispered, "I have to go out and take a look. Perhaps someone needs help." He crawled out from under the counter and went to the door. He looked into the courtyard and then came back, badly shaken.

"There's no one there to help," he stammered.

We stayed under the counter until evening, when people returned from work and we heard them in the courtyard. We emerged from our hiding place. Near the shop in which we'd been hiding lay several corpses in a huge pool of blood. More and more people were arriving, wringing their hands.

I don't have the strength to describe what happened there. The lamentation and tears of dozens of people who had lost their loved ones defies description. My mother was among those who cried the hardest, and my father sat on the ground, completely shattered. I was so bewildered that I was no longer able to think. I felt like everything happening around me was just a bad dream. The bodies of the people who had been shot were taken away by gravediggers, and the blood was washed from the ground. People cried there all night long.

Only when I was lying in my bed and feeling Ignaś's absence did I realize what had happened and what a terrible misfortune had befallen us. My second brother had left me. A terrible and merciless force had taken him away. My life with Ignaś has remained a beautiful memory from a terrible month in my life.

Our bunker at 4 Lwowska Street had been revealed by Jewish policemen in order to fill the quota demanded by the Germans. It's hard for me to write about this, but it's what happened. I don't know how many other hiding places were revealed to the Germans, but ours was certainly one of the largest and most well-prepared. Without this betrayal, all the people hiding in the attic would have survived.

During that roundup operation, the following event occurred.

There was a two-room apartment on the ground floor right next to the staircase where an old, physically disabled couple lived in one room, and a woman with a child lived in the other. At night, when everyone was woken up to go to the bunker in the attic, the woman and the child left the apartment. The old couple weren't able to leave as quickly as they had. Suddenly several people entered their room. It was the family of one of the high-ranking officials of the Judenrat, who lived in this building.

This family had been planning to hide with us in the attic bunker, and everyone in the building knew about it. We felt safer because of this. It felt like a guarantee that our bunker wouldn't be reported to the Germans. Now this family, instead of going with everyone else to the attic, entered the old people's apartment and ordered them to leave immediately. They went in the room where the woman and child lived, and two Jewish policemen started blocking the door of the room with a wardrobe.

"We want to hide here, too," said the old people.

"You have to go upstairs," answered one of the policemen.

The wardrobe was pushed in front of the door, and the old couple slowly walked up the stairs to the attic and hid in our bunker, according to the plan. When the bunker was discovered, the two old people very indignantly told their neighbor, the woman who lived in the room next to theirs, that the family of a Judenrat official was hiding in her room—and now they understood why.

There was a great deal of chaos while everyone was going down the stairs, and nobody paid any attention to the old couple. They walked slowly, stair by stair, holding hands. I saw them, too. When they reached the bottom of the stairs, they took advantage of the fact that the policeman standing there was distracted for a moment, and instead of going to the courtyard, they slipped back into their apartment. They went up to the wardrobe and begged the people in the room to slide it to the side so they could hide in the room, too. But nobody answered. Seeing no alternative, they climbed inside the wardrobe and hid there.

On Magdeburski Square, the Germans conducted a selection during which children were separated from their parents. The woman who had been living in this now concealed room fell into a frenzied rage when her child was taken from her and started screaming in German: "You're taking my child away from me, but you're allowing the people hiding in my room to live! Shame! Shame!"

An SS officer approached her and said, "Come and show us where this room is."

The woman led them to her apartment. The wardrobe with the two old people inside it was moved to the side, and the people in the room were ordered to come out into the courtyard. They were shot there. Those were the gunshots we heard near us, and it was their bodies we saw after leaving our hiding place under the counter. The old people remained safe.

This is how we survived the roundup operation in the Tarnów ghetto when twenty-five hundred people were sent to their deaths in Bełżec. There were two angelic souls among them—my grandmother, Frydzia Münz, and Ignaś Frenkel.

The days and weeks following the roundup were very difficult for us. We felt as if our whole world had collapsed. We had already witnessed other people experiencing this after the previous roundup operations we had survived in Tarnów, but a person is incapable of imagining what it's really like until he experiences it himself.

My mother cried for days and nights on end. The only thing in the whole world that kept my mother alive was Lusia. I don't know what would have happened to my mother if Lusia had no longer been with her. Lusia stroked my mother's head and kissed her every chance she got. I went through phases of complete apathy to outbursts of anger and rage. I tormented myself with reproaches that I might have been able to save Ignaś. I had dreams at night and daydreams during the day of Ignaś and I escaping together and living happily, free of all danger.

Later, after my parents had returned to their senses slightly, they tried to talk with me and raise my spirits, but to no avail. People told me that my misery would pass and I would come to terms with fate. But this hasn't happened. I've never come to terms with Ignaś's death.

A profound state of mourning overwhelmed the entire ghetto. Extreme poverty, a lack of food, illnesses—it all intensified. Murders were happening in the ghetto more frequently. We feared we wouldn't survive the winter. It was clear to everyone that if a major change of some kind didn't soon occur that would stop the Germans, we were all going to die. More and more people tried to obtain Aryan identity documents or help of some kind from outside, but with very little success. We didn't see any chance of leaving the ghetto and saving ourselves. We were all condemned to annihilation.

There were people who, out of desperation, escaped from the ghetto without any help from outside, believing that even a slim chance on the Aryan side would be better than waiting to die in the ghetto. These people were the first to die. They were very quickly recognized as Jews and brought to the gestapo, where they were shot. Sometimes entire families died this way.

The Tarnów ghetto was like a huge, merciless, automatic killing machine that was advancing and destroying everything in its path.

In January 1943, something completely unexpected happened that changed our fate. One night someone started pounding on the main entrance door of our building on Lwowska Street, outside the ghetto, and shouting in German: "*Öffnen! Öffnen!*" (Open up!) They alternated this word with our surname: "Schönker! Schönker!"

As I've previously mentioned, this entrance door was always locked. The Jewish policeman who lived on the top floor had a key to it and was allowed to open it only in the case of a fire or some other emergency. Someone ran to get him. When he saw through the peephole that an SS soldier was standing on the other side, he opened the door. The SS soldier was surrounded by people wearing striped uniforms, and a military truck was parked in the street.

The people asked where Mr. Schönker lived. The Jewish policeman pointed to our shop on the other side of the courtyard. The SS soldier told him to go home and not tell anyone about what he'd seen. He could lock the door again in half an hour.

Human specters started walking toward us one after another. They were emaciated and resembled skeletons more than people. My father ran into the courtyard to help them, because some were too weak to walk. I looked at them and couldn't believe my eyes. I'd never seen people in such a state.

My father talked with them by the entrance door and seemed to understand what all of this meant, but my mother and I stared at them, bewildered and confused. Several men who couldn't walk at all were lifted out of the truck. The door was locked again, and the military truck drove away with the SS soldier inside it.

Our little shop filled up entirely with men. If I remember correctly, there were seventeen of them. Frightened, they sat next to each other quietly on the floor as if they were inside a bunker during a roundup operation. Finally, one of them started talking.

We found out they'd just come from a work camp in Stalowa Wola and were on their way to another camp in Płaszów, near Kraków. We'd heard about the camp in Stalowa Wola already. People were dying there like flies from the heavy work, constant beatings, starvation, and exhaustion. Leon Salpeter, one of my father's close friends, who had run a pharmacy in Kraków before the war, was now in the Płaszów camp and was running a pharmacy there, too. Thanks to his important position, he was in close contact with the Germans. Some of his acquaintances in Stalowa Wola had pleaded with him to help them leave that terrible camp. They wanted to go to Płaszów.

We'd also heard about the Płaszów camp. It was a work camp that had been established in the summer of 1942. It was believed at that time to be relatively safe. Jews worked there in factories and workshops, manufacturing things for the German military, and were convinced it was in the Germans' interest to respect this camp. A group of Jewish scientists and engineers even worked there on various military projects that were important to the German war effort.

After receiving this plea for help, Leon Salpeter had bribed some Germans, and they had sent an SS soldier in a truck to transport Salpeter's friends to Płaszów. On the way it was necessary to provide them with immediate aid so they could gain some strength, for they were too weak to reach Płaszów. Salpeter had been informed of this by telephone and had been asked if he knew of somewhere they could rest for a few days. He knew our address in the Tarnów ghetto. He had given it to the driver and suggested they go to us.

My mother immediately started boiling some potatoes in a huge pot, and then she cut half a loaf of bread into this watery potato soup. We didn't have any other food. All the men were exhausted, frozen, and famished. They warmed themselves up in front of our small iron stove.

Then my parents washed and bandaged their wounds, and I helped, too—I boiled water and brought it to them in bowls. Bandages were made from bedsheets, and it took a long time to help everyone. It was already morning when we fell asleep, utterly exhausted. It was very crowded. The men slept on our beds, and we lay on the floor, pressed together like sardines.

I woke up at noon. My mother was making potato soup again. Our guests were sitting on the floor. Some were drinking hot water. Our home looked like a hospital. Nearly everyone had some part of their body bandaged—arms, legs, noses, and even ears. These men had been condemned to death, but through a miracle they'd managed to escape from the hell of Stalowa Wola.

My mother complained to my father that there wouldn't be any more food the next day, and they wondered what to do. Nobody except the Jewish policeman who lived on the top floor of our building knew there were so many people in our home. The metal door remained pulled down over the entrance with only a narrow gap left at the bottom for some air to enter.

I looked at these people with pity, but I noticed that nearly all of them seemed to be feeling better. They were talking to each other in whispers, and some were even smiling. They looked like wounded men after a battle.

I heard one of the older men say to another, "I have a daughter named Ninka. She's twenty-six years old and is hiding in Otwock, near Warsaw. I want to reach her. She's the only one who can take care of me."

This reminded me of my friend Ninka. I decided to visit her aunt in the evening, after she returned home from work. Maybe now she knew if Ninka had managed to reach her mother in Lwów.

But Ninka's aunt wasn't there. Some other people were now living in her room. They told me that a week before, the Germans had taken her straight from the factory where she worked. I realized there was no longer anyone I could ask about Ninka. She had come to me from nothingness and had returned to nothingness.

On my way home, I thought about her and was overcome by nostalgia and longing. It seemed to me that years had passed since she'd left the ghetto, even though it hadn't really been very long. Then it occurred to me that the hiding place where I'd been with Ninka now belonged to me. After all, that's what she'd told me.

I hurried to the bathroom in the hallway. I turned on the light and locked myself in. I stood on the toilet seat, as Ninka had, and found the string that released the rope ladder. I scrambled up the ladder to the alcove where I'd sat with Ninka. Everything was just as we'd left it.

I took down three sausages that were still hanging on the wall and left one of them, to have it as an emergency supply but also because I was afraid I wouldn't be able to carry all of them. I put the sausages in the sack of crackers. Then I pulled the ladder back up and tied the sack to it. I slowly and carefully let the ladder down. It was a very difficult task for me because it was heavy, but I managed to do it. I wondered whether I should call my father to come and carry the sack, but eventually I decided to drag it along the ground by myself.

"What's that?" asked my mother when she saw me struggling with the sack.

"See for yourself," I answered.

My parents were amazed. I told them about Ninka and the hiding place above the toilet. When I finished, everyone in our room, even those who were extremely weak and tired, started clapping as if they were at a theater. A joyful atmosphere filled our home, and my mother started to cook bread soup with sausage in it. We now had enough food for everyone.

The military truck was going to come back for the men in five days. The leader of the group suggested we join them and travel with them to the camp in Płaszów. He tried to convince my parents that it would be the only chance of survival for us. Płaszów was considered to be a privileged work camp. People had heard that there were even entire families there. Here in Tarnów we were awaiting certain death. My parents agreed because they knew we no longer had anything to lose.

On their last day with us, our guests took baths and shaved. They tried to make themselves more presentable. My mother washed and dried their clothing over the stove. The group's leader had a list of all the men and the German order for them to be taken to Płaszów. The driver who had brought them had given this document to the leader so they would be able to prove who they were in case something happened while they were with us. Our family was now added to the document.

The truck came for us during the night. The policeman from the top floor opened the building's main entrance door again, and we all climbed into the vehicle. While I was walking past him, he suddenly embraced me and kissed me. It was the same policeman I'd been with on the balcony when Rommelman had shot the *shohet* and nearly killed me. Now I could see he was sad to see me leave. He said to me in Hebrew, *"Chayim veberacha."* Then he helped me get in the truck.

"What did he say?" I asked my father after we had settled ourselves inside the vehicle.

"He told you in Hebrew: 'May you live long and be blessed.'"

I asked my father if a blessing from a Jewish policeman was worth anything. My father said he believed that a blessing given in good faith was always worth something. The truck started moving, and soon we left Tarnów.

I felt as if some part of me stayed in the ghetto. My emotions were deeply stirred, and tears filled my eyes. The monotonous journey lulled me, and soon I fell asleep. I don't know how long I slept.

I was awoken by my father saying loudly, "This is Bochnia! My father lives here!" And then he said, "Please tell the driver to stop at the entrance of the ghetto. We'll get out here."

Someone shouted to the driver in German. The truck stopped. We got out in front of the ghetto's entrance gate—my parents, Lusia, and me. There were only two Jewish policemen standing there. They allowed us to enter the ghetto without any trouble. It was a cold night; we stood in the street, not sure where to go. One of the policemen approached us and told us to go to the post office because it served as a gathering place for new people who had just arrived. At that time, in January 1943, the ghetto in Bochnia was already very overcrowded.

He explained how to get to the post office and told us there was a large room there where we could stay until we found a more permanent place to live. We walked to the post office with mixed feelings. We didn't know what awaited us in this town.

My father told us later that when he realized we were passing through Bochnia, he was struck by an impulse to get out there. Perhaps it was longing for

Grandpa Józef, whom he hadn't seen for a long time. We knew he was in the ghetto in Bochnia, which he'd managed to reach from Kraków.

This sudden decision by my father saved our lives. There's no doubt we wouldn't have survived in the Płaszów work camp. And we also later found out that if we'd stayed in the Tarnów ghetto, we would also have died.

The final liquidation of the Tarnów ghetto began on September 2, 1943. Seven thousand people were sent to Auschwitz, three thousand to Płaszów, and one thousand to Bełżec. Many Jews were murdered in Tarnów's Jewish cemetery.

Fessel, my father's friend who owned the Papapol factory—the man who had saved our lives by buying us from the Polish policeman—didn't survive the war. Leon Salpeter was also killed, and everyone in the truck in which we traveled to Bochnia probably died, too, since very few people survived the Płaszów camp.

At that time, we felt abandoned by God and humanity. There was no help for us from any direction. People in the ghetto frequently asked, "Has God really forsaken us?" They couldn't understand why Eternal and Merciful God, in whom they believed so devotedly and passionately, would allow something like this to happen. To this day there are many people who are unable to understand this. It has caused many people to lose their faith in God.

My father, my mother, and I never asked ourselves such questions because we always had a feeling we would survive, and we believed there must be some higher explanation that we couldn't understand. Did this feeling arise, perhaps, from the fact that we refused to resign ourselves to death? Did we instinctively feel that if we accepted death as inevitable, we would be taking the first step toward surrendering to it?

We survived, but deep pain remained with us for our whole lives. This pain accompanies nearly everyone who survived, day and night. Only a few have managed to overcome the pain within themselves. It's a riddle to me how they've accomplished this. I've always felt helpless and defenseless against this pain. I've never been able to fight it. Perhaps I haven't wanted to. Sometimes I've wondered if I wish to punish myself for the fact that I'm still alive while so many others whom I loved are gone. I don't feel guilty for their deaths, but sometimes it seems to me that perhaps I subconsciously feel the need to suffer so that I can, in this way, feel connected to them.

Figure 1. A portrait of Izaak Aron Schönker (1848–1932) painted by his grandson, Leon Schönker.

Figure 2. Fanny (Feiga) Schönker, Henryk Schönker's grandmother.

Figure 3. Fryderyka Münz, Henryk's grandmother (his mother's mother).

Figure 4. Józef Schönker, Henryk's grandfather.

Figure 5. Leon Schönker, Henryk's father.

Figure 6. Mina Münz, Henryk's mother (left), and her sister, Lida (right).

Figure 7. Henryk Schönker in Zawoja, 1933.

Figure 8. Liba Hofstetter, née Schönker, Leon Schönker's sister.
Photo from the collection of Gołda Tencer-Szurmiej's "Shalom" Foundation.

Figure 9. Arie Frenkel, Henryk's cousin, 1938.

Figure 10. Józef Schönker's villa on Jagiellońska Street (now called Jagiełły Street) in Oświęcim. During World War II, it was taken over by the German army; then it became the headquarters of the Arbeitsamt (employment office).
Photo from the collection of Tadeusz Firczyk.

Figure 11. Klaśnieńska Street in Wieliczka. The Schönker family lived on the upper floor of the center building. Nina Armer's family lived in the house on the right-hand side (the entrance to their shop was on the ground floor).
Photo: Robert Sotwin.

Figure 12. The building on Klaśnieńska Street in Wieliczka that served as a temporary shelter for the Schönker family.
Photo: Robert Sotwin.

Figure 13. Wieliczka, March 1942. Jewish children at a Purim performance organized by the Jewish community. Henryk Schönker is in the fourth row, seventh from the left (in a cap). Nina Armer is behind him and slightly to his left.
Photo from the collection of the Jewish Historical Institute in Warsaw.

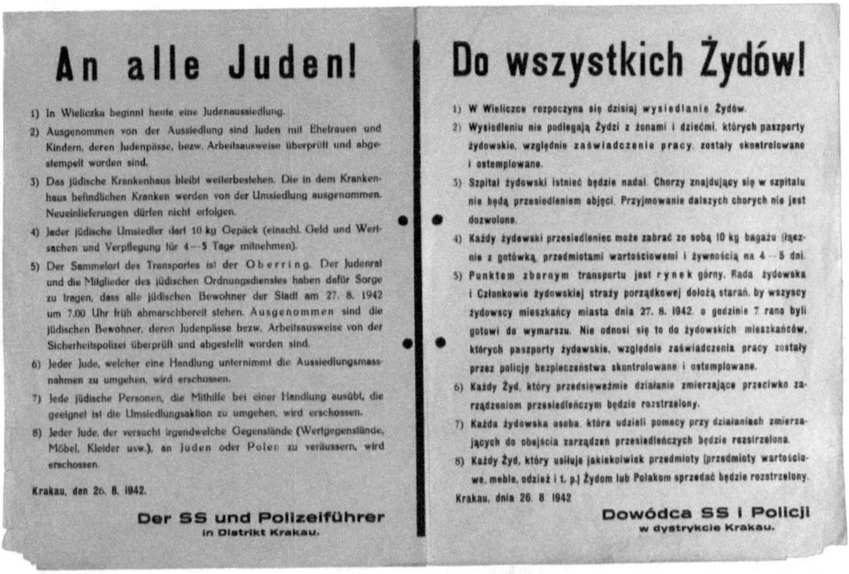

An alle Juden!

1) In Wieliczka beginnt heute eine Judenaussiedlung.

2) Ausgenommen von der Aussiedlung sind Juden mit Ehefrauen und Kindern, deren Judenpässe, bezw. Arbeitsausweise überprüft und abgestempelt worden sind.

3) Das jüdische Krankenhaus bleibt weiterbestehen. Die in dem Krankenhaus befindlichen Kranken werden von der Umsiedlung ausgenommen. Neueinlieferungen dürfen nicht erfolgen.

4) Jeder jüdische Umsiedler darf 10 kg Gepäck (einschl. Geld und Wertsachen und Verpflegung für 4—5 Tage mitnehmen).

5) Der Sammelort des Transportes ist der Oberring. Der Judenrat und die Mitglieder des jüdischen Ordnungsdienstes haben dafür Sorge zu tragen, dass alle jüdischen Bewohner der Stadt am 27. 8. 1942 um 7.00 Uhr früh abmarschbereit stehen. Ausgenommen sind die jüdischen Bewohner, deren Judenpässe bezw. Arbeitsausweise von der Sicherheitspolizei überprüft und abgestellt worden sind.

6) Jeder Jude, welcher eine Handlung unternimmt die Aussiedlungsmassnahmen zu umgehen, wird erschossen.

7) Jede jüdische Personen, die Mithilfe bei einer Handlung ausübt, die geeignet ist die Umsiedlungsaktion zu umgehen, wird erschossen.

8) Jeder Jude, der versucht irgendwelche Gegenstände (Wertgegenstände, Möbel, Kleider usw.), an Juden oder Polen zu veräussern, wird erschossen.

Krakau, den 26. 8. 1942.

Der SS und Polizeiführer
in Distrikt Krakau.

Do wszystkich Żydów!

1) W Wieliczce rozpoczyna się dzisiaj wysiedlanie Żydów.

2) Wysiedleniu nie podlegają Żydzi z żonami i dziećmi, których paszporty żydowskie, względnie zaświadczenie pracy, zostały skontrolowane i ostemplowane.

3) Szpital żydowski istnieć będzie nadal. Chorzy znajdujący się w szpitalu nie będą przesiedleniem objęci. Przyjmowanie dalszych chorych nie jest dozwolone.

4) Każdy żydowski przesiedleniec może zabrać ze sobą 10 kg bagażu (łącznie z gotówką, przedmiotami wartościowemi i żywnością na 4—5 dni.

5) Punktem zbornym transportu jest rynek górny. Rada żydowska i Członkowie żydowskiej straży porządkowej dołożą starań, by wszyscy żydowscy mieszkańcy miasta dnia 27. 8. 1942. o godzinie 7 rano byli gotowi do wymarszu. Nie odnosi się to do żydowskich mieszkańców, których paszporty żydowskie, względnie zaświadczenia pracy zostały przez policję bezpieczeństwa skontrolowane i ostemplowane.

6) Każdy Żyd, który przedsięweźmie działanie zmierzające przeciwko zarządzeniom przesiedleńczym będzie rozstrzelony.

7) Każda żydowska osoba, która udzieli pomocy przy działaniach zmierzających do obejścia zarządzeń przesiedleńczych będzie rozstrzelona.

8) Każdy Żyd, który usiłuje jakiekolwiek przedmioty (przedmioty wartościowe, meble, odzież i t. p.) Żydom lub Polakom sprzedać będzie rozstrzelony.

Krakau, dnia 26. 8 1942

Dowódca SS i Policji
w dystrykcie Krakau.

Figure 14. SS notice about the displacement of Jews from Wieliczka.
From the collection of the Historical Museum of the City of Kraków.

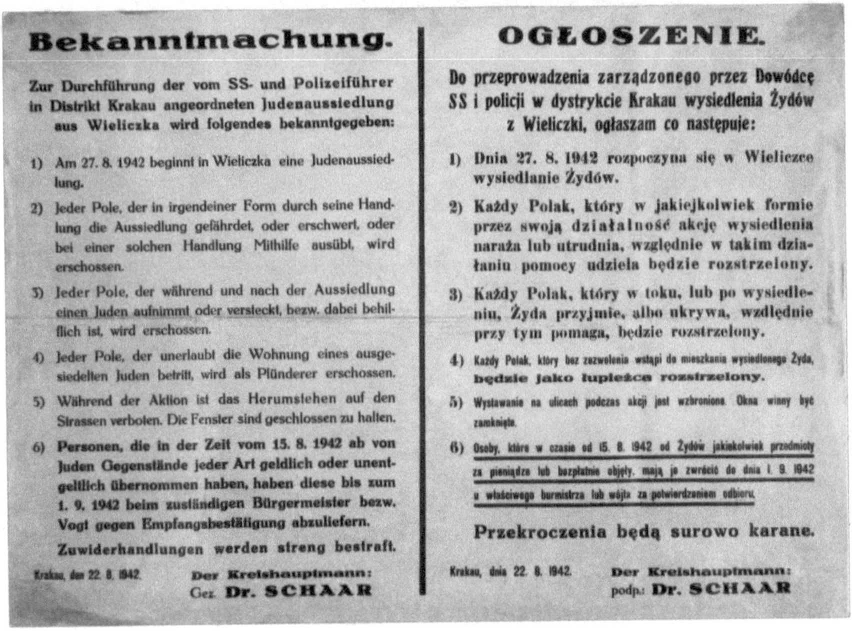

Bekanntmachung.

Zur Durchführung der vom SS- und Polizeiführer in Distrikt Krakau angeordneten Judenaussiedlung aus Wieliczka wird folgendes bekanntgegeben:

1) Am 27. 8. 1942 beginnt in Wieliczka eine Judenaussiedlung.

2) Jeder Pole, der in irgendeiner Form durch seine Handlung die Aussiedlung gefährdet, oder erschwert, oder bei einer solchen Handlung Mithilfe ausübt, wird erschossen.

3) Jeder Pole, der während und nach der Aussiedlung einen Juden aufnimmt oder versteckt, bezw. dabei behilflich ist, wird erschossen.

4) Jeder Pole, der unerlaubt die Wohnung eines ausgesiedelten Juden betritt, wird als Plünderer erschossen.

5) Während der Aktion ist das Herumstehen auf den Strassen verboten. Die Fenster sind geschlossen zu halten.

6) **Personen, die in der Zeit vom 15. 8. 1942 ab von Juden Gegenstände jeder Art geldlich oder unentgeltlich übernommen haben, haben diese bis zum 1. 9. 1942 beim zuständigen Bürgermeister bezw. Vogt gegen Empfangsbestätigung abzuliefern.**

Zuwiderhandlungen werden streng bestraft.

Krakau, den 22. 8. 1942.

Der Kreishauptmann:
Gez. Dr. SCHAAR

OGŁOSZENIE.

Do przeprowadzenia zarządzonego przez Dowódcę SS i policji w dystrykcie Krakau wysiedlenia Żydów z Wieliczki, ogłaszam co następuje:

1) Dnia 27. 8. 1942 rozpoczyna się w Wieliczce wysiedlanie Żydów.

2) Każdy Polak, który w jakiejkolwiek formie przez swoją działalność akcję wysiedlenia naraża lub utrudnia, względnie w takim działaniu pomocy udziela będzie rozstrzelony.

3) Każdy Polak, który w toku, lub po wysiedleniu, Żyda przyjmie, albo ukrywa, wzdlędnie przy tym pomaga, będzie rozstrzelony.

4) Każdy Polak, który bez zezwolenia wstąpi do mieszkania wysiedlonego Żyda, będzie jako łupieżca rozstrzelony.

5) Wystawanie na ulicach podczas akcji jest wzbronione. Okna winny być zamknięte.

6) Osoby, które w czasie od 15. 8. 1942 od Żydów jakiekolwiek przedmioty za pieniądze lub bezpłatnie objęły, mają je zwrócić do dnia 1. 9. 1942 u właściwego burmistrza lub wójta za potwierdzeniem odbioru.

Przekroczenia będą surowo karane.

Krakau, dnia 22. 8. 1942.

Der Kreishauptmann:
podp.: Dr. SCHAAR

Figure 15. SS notice about the displacement of Jews from Wieliczka.
From the collection of the Jewish Historical Institute in Warsaw.

Figure 16. John Gottowt, Germany, 1920s.
Photo: Deutsches Filminstitut, Frankfurt am Main.

Figure 17. Portrait of John Gottowt painted by Leon Schönker, Wieliczka, circa 1941.

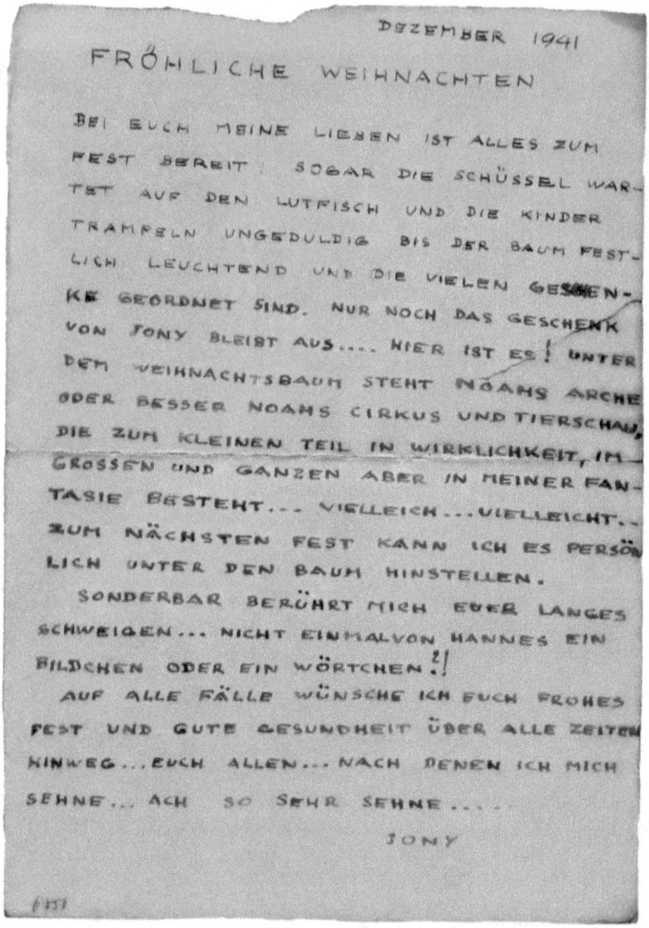

DEZEMBER 1941

FRÖHLICHE WEIHNACHTEN

BEI EUCH MEINE LIEBEN IST ALLES ZUM FEST BEREIT: SOGAR DIE SCHÜSSEL WARTET AUF DEN LUTFISCH UND DIE KINDER TRAMPELN UNGEDULDIG BIS DER BAUM FESTLICH LEUCHTEND UND DIE VIELEN GESCHENKE GEORDNET SIND. NUR NOCH DAS GESCHENK VON JONY BLEIBT AUS.... HIER IST ES! UNTER DEM WEIHNACHTSBAUM STEHT NOAHS ARCHE ODER BESSER NOAHS CIRKUS UND TIERSCHAU, DIE ZUM KLEINEN TEIL IN WIRKLICHKEIT, IM GROSSEN UND GANZEN ABER IN MEINER FANTASIE BESTEHT... VIELLEICH... VIELLEICHT.. ZUM NÄCHSTEN FEST KANN ICH ES PERSÖNLICH UNTER DEN BAUM HINSTELLEN.

SONDERBAR BERÜHRT MICH EUER LANGES SCHWEIGEN... NICHT EINMAL VON HANNES EIN BILDCHEN ODER EIN WÖRTCHEN?!

AUF ALLE FÄLLE WÜNSCHE ICH EUCH FROHES FEST UND GUTE GESUNDHEIT ÜBER ALLE ZEITEN HINWEG... EUCH ALLEN... NACH DENEN ICH MICH SEHNE... ACH SO SEHR SEHNE....

JONY

Figure 18. John Gottowt's last letter to his family in Sweden, written in Wieliczka, Christmas 1941:

At your house, darlings, everything is ready for Christmas: even the serving bowl is waiting for the fish to be put in it, and the children are stamping their feet impatiently for the tree to start sparkling with festive lights and for numerous presents to be handed round. But one present is missing—from "Jony" . . . It's here! Noah's Ark is under my Christmas tree, or rather Noah's circus with an animal show. . . . Perhaps . . . perhaps next Christmas I'll be able to put it under your Christmas tree in person.

I'm quite worried by your long silence . . . Not a single picture, nor a single word, from Hannes?!

I wish you all a merry Christmas and good health at all times . . . I miss all of you . . . all of you . . . so very much . . . Love Jony.

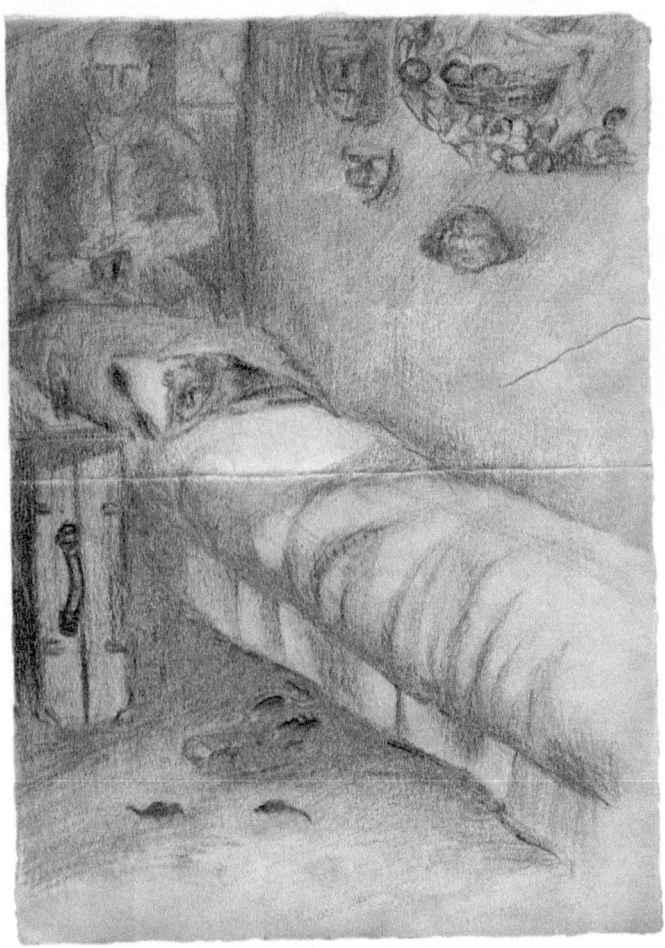

Figure 19. A drawing of the room in which Gottowt lived in Wieliczka and where he was murdered in the summer of 1942 (with a portrait of him painted by Leon Schönker hanging above the bed). A continuation of the letter:

Longing doesn't leave me even in sleep ... And so, as you can see, I'm falling asleep peacefully in my bed already at eight o'clock on this holy Christmas Eve next to a burning candle. Only mice are carousing in the empty room and waiting impatiently for me to extinguish the candle so they can eat some scraps ... In my dreams I'm able to fly ... My longing carries me to you at lightning speed ... I'm with all of you even when you can't see me, I dance with you around the Christmas tree, I take a crumb from each plate ... how delicious they taste ... but alas, I must leave again.

I embrace you all and am so happy I was able to see you. Even if it was only a dream ...

(English translation based on a Polish translation by Piotr Filipkowski from the German original)

No:	Name	Vorname	Geb.Datum	Nationalität:
3933	Sieradzki	Perla	26. 5.19	Palästina
3934	Skowronska-Przygorka,Hinda		27. 3.15	"
3935	Skowronska	Marian	31. 5.40	"
3936	Solowiejczyk	Aleksander	2.12.34	"
3937	Solowiejczyk	Eliasz	8. 9.03	"
3938	Solowiejczyk	Margot	19. 8.07	"
3939	Spett	Arnold	3. 5.98	USA
3940	Spett	Martin	2.12.29	"
3941	Spett	Rosa	29. 9.32	"
3942	Spett-Leisten	Sala	19. 5.93	"
3943	Spiegel-Segall	Fanny	13. 2.06	Palästina
3944	Spiegel	Golda	15. 1.38	"
3945	Spira	Feiwel	23. 5.33	Paraguay
3946	Spira	Israel	12.11.91	"
3947	Spira	Perla	19. 6.91	"
3948	Szajnberg	Gustav	1. 7.15	Palästina
3949	Szczupak	Josek	1. 5.23	"
3950	Szejn	Dawid	29. 8.11	"
3951	Szejn	Jochwet	26.11.36	"
3952	Szeps-Picyoz	Ida	6.6.12	"
3953	Szerman-Rozenwayn,Szyfra		5. 6.89	"
3954	Szladow	Adam	15. 2.38	"
3955	Szladow	Icek	16. 2.40	"
3956	Szladow	Nuta	15. 8.13	"
3957	Szladow-Lichtenstein,Rachela		25. 1.17	"
3958	Szochet-Gronen	Malka	28. 7.11	"
3959	Szop	Chaim	1. 7.06	"
3960	Szop	Dawid	26. 9.33	"
3961	Szop	Hermann S.	1. 4.44	"
3962	Szop-Rosensztrom,Rywka		11.11.09	"
3963	Schneck-Storch	Bela	31.12.96	"
3964	Schneck	Jozef	11. 4.27	"
3965	Schneck	Stefan	22. 9.31	"
3966	Schönker	Arie	14.12.25	"
3967	Schönker	Fanny	23. 8.36	"
3968	Schönker	Heinrich	14. 2.31	"
3969	Schönker	Josef	1. 4.72	"
3970	Schönker	Leo	24. 1.03	"
3971	Schönker-Minz	Mina	25.12.05	"
3972	Schönker-Schwarz,Regina		9. 8.76	"
3973	Schwartz-Bratter,Amalia		19. 4.12	"
3974	Schwartz	Melchior	12. 3.09	"
3975	Schwieger	Anatol	22. 5.25	Chile
3976	Schwieger-Kalisz,Julie		25. 1.03	"
3977	Schwieger	Julius	3.12.94	"
3978	Schwieger	Rita	11. 7.26	"
3979	Steinberg-Schechter,Anna		11. 2.11	Palästina
3980	Steinberg	Henriette	29. 5.36	"
3981	Steinberg	Jakob	14. 9.39	"
3982	Teichtal-Münz	Leontyna	5. 5.07	"

Figure 20. A fragment of "Weiss's List," which includes the Schönker family, Bergen-Belsen, 1944. This list, which was stolen from the camp's head office by a prisoner named Joseph Weiss, a Jew from Holland, contained the names of 349 prisoners held at the camp known as the Aufenthaltslager, who were waiting to be exchanged for German prisoners of war.

Figure 21. A small portrait of Irena Gitler (owned by Irena Landau) drawn with pastel by Leon Schönker on September 11, 1944, in Bergen-Belsen. Of the numerous works of art created by Leon in the camp, including large oil paintings on canvas, this small sketch on paper is the only one that has survived.

On December 31, 1943, Józef Gitler-Barski, Irena's father, wrote in his camp diary: "The Germans have discovered our painter. From time to time, they take him to their canteen and order him to paint portraits of them (apparently some send them afterward to their families)."

As documents found in Germany have revealed, Adolf Haas (the commander of the Bergen-Belsen camp) and other SS officers faced serious repercussions because of these portraits. At the end of January 1944, Haas had to report to the SS headquarters in Berlin and was interrogated about this matter. He confessed that he and some other officers had been painted by "a Jewish prisoner—these paintings were intended as Christmas gifts."

On March 31, 1944, Haas received a letter from Obergruppenführer Oswald Pohl, head of the SS Main Economic and Administrative Office and concentration camp inspector:

> *I have ascertained that you and many other SS commanding officers in the Aufenthaltslager Bergen-Belsen commanded a Jewish prisoner to paint portraits of you. This fact, which you have not denied, is so dishonorable for an SS officer that it quite simply leaves one speechless.... I am sending words of the harshest condemnation to you and your officers and hereby order all portraits painted by this Jew, without exception, to be burned immediately. I order you to convey the content of this letter, as my opinion in this matter, to all SS officers who took part in this act. A report confirming the incineration of the paintings must be submitted to me no later than 30 April 1944. (Berlin Document Center, SS-Personalpapiere Adolf Haas)*

Leon Schönker faced no consequences for having painted the portraits, but Adolf Haas was removed from his position as commander of the Bergen-Belsen camp on December 1, 1944, and was sent to the Balkan front, where he died.

Figure 22. The Agrochemia factory owned by the Schönker family, Oświęcim, 1930s. *Photo from the collection of Mirosław Ganobis.*

Figure 23. Aron Hollender and his wife, Ela (née Silbiger, sister of Rachela—Edward Ochab's wife), with their children, Roma and Maniek, Kraków, 1945 or 1946.

Figure 24. Lusia, Mina, Leon, and Henryk Schönker in their house, Oświęcim, 1946.

Figure 25. From the left: Regina Kupperman and Mina Schönker, with Lusia Schönker standing below them, Krynica, 1947 or 1948.

Figure 26. Henryk Schönker with his mother, Kudowa-Zdrój, 1948.

Figure 27. From the left: Roman Maksymowicz, Kazimierz Paw with their friend Raźny on his shoulders, and Henryk Schönker, 1948.

Figure 28. From the left: Kazimierz Paw, Roman Maksymowicz, Raźny, and Henryk Schönker, Oświęcim, 1948.

Figure 29. Romek Maksymowicz and Henryk Schönker, Zakopane, winter 1948–1949.

Figure 30. Henryk with his parents, sister, and dog, Baca, in front of their house in Oświęcim, 1949.

Figure 31. Mina Schönker and Karol Rydzoń, the Schönkers' chauffeur, posing with the Humber bought from the English consul, Oświęcim, 1949.

Figure 32. Henryk, Mina, Lusia, and Leon Schönker at home, Oświęcim, 1952.

Figure 33. Self-portrait by Leon Schönker, 1952.

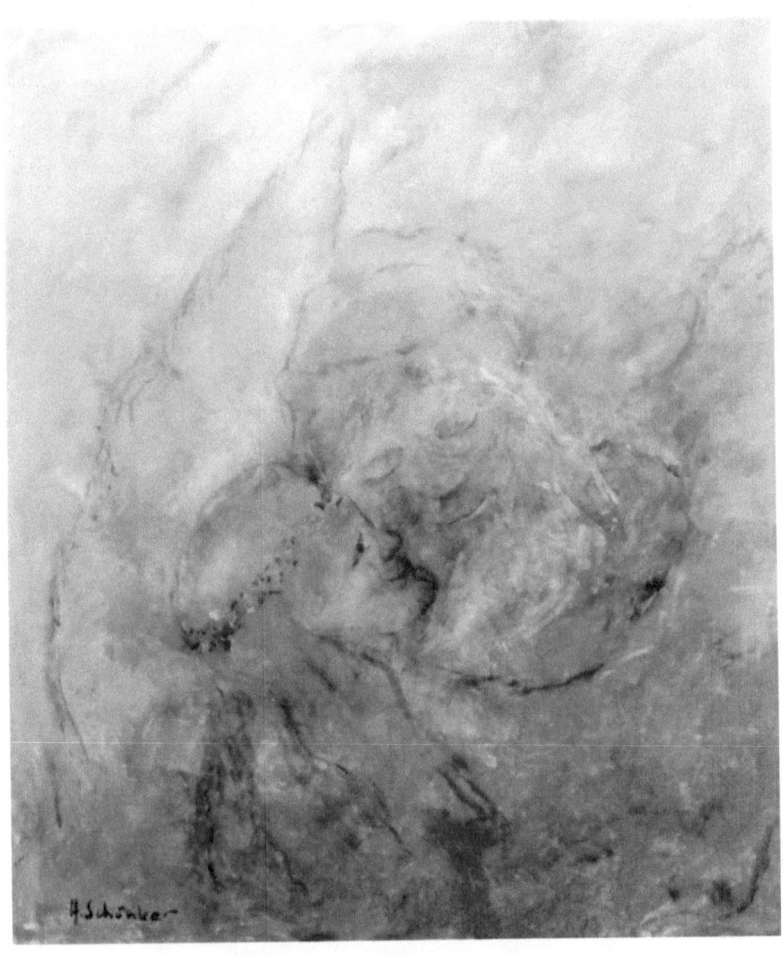

Figure 34. A painting by Henryk Schönker, *A Kiss from an Angel*, oil on canvas, 1988.

BOCHNIA

THE POST OFFICE IN BOCHNIA's ghetto was closed, but its large room served as a shelter for homeless people, of which there were many. People woke up when we entered. They looked at us curiously as if they were expecting someone they knew; then they went back to sleep. We looked around for a free spot, but the room was packed, and we could barely even enter because people were lying side by side across the floor.

Finally, thanks to someone's help and after waking several people so they would move over, we found a space right next to the door. Several times during the night, people went in and out of the room, and each time my father and I had to stand up so the door could be opened. I slept on somebody's lap. In the morning we were able to see how truly overcrowded the room was. Despite this, we thanked God we had a roof over our heads.

It was a pleasant winter day. Everyone went into the street and formed a long line. We stood in line, too, and each of us received a slice of stale bread and some artificial coffee. We took turns drinking it from a pot that someone had lent us.

Then my father went to look for my grandfather, and we stayed at the post office so we wouldn't lose our spot. At noon my father returned and joyously announced that he'd found my grandfather and his wife, Regina, healthy and in good condition. They had a room to themselves not far from the post office. They were very happy that we'd come to Bochnia. They had talked for several hours, but then my grandfather had ordered my father to return to the post office so he wouldn't miss the next meal. A lineup formed again in the street, and we received soup and potatoes. It turned out that the Jewish community was providing this homeless shelter with three meals per day.

We found out that the ghetto in Bochnia had been created in March 1942. The first roundup operation had taken place on August 24 of that year, thus more or less at the same time as the one in Wieliczka, and it had also lasted three days. There had been a selection, and whoever wasn't employed at that time in a factory or workshop was sent—people later found out—to Bełżec, where they were murdered immediately. After the roundup, the ghetto became a work camp. In November 1942 there was another roundup; anyone without employment and women with children were sent to Bełżec, and invalids in the hospital and children in the orphanage were shot on the spot.

After this second roundup, registration began of foreigners and people possessing permits to travel to countries outside of German-controlled territory.

Whoever didn't have official employment tried desperately, through the *Judenrat*, to obtain it in factories or workshops that were run by German companies and were supplying the war effort.

The people in the post office were mostly refugees who had managed to survive roundups in other ghettos and nearby towns. There wasn't any trace of fear among these people; everyone was waiting for some kind of miraculous rescue. There was something inexplicable in their calmness. Or does fear perhaps also require a strength of spirit, which had been taken from them by what they'd experienced and witnessed?

In the afternoon my father took me to visit my grandfather Józef. He and his wife lived in a small room in which there was only one bed, and another small fold-out bed was set up at night. My grandfather was emaciated and had aged a lot since the last time I'd seen him. He was sixty years old, but now he looked more like an eighty-year-old man. His hair had turned as white as snow. He and Regina had miraculously survived the last roundup, hidden in a bunker in the building where they lived.

In answer to Regina's questions, I had to tell her in great detail about Adaś and his family, with whom I'd spent so much time in Wieliczka. Adaś's father, Iziu Grossfeld, was Regina's son. I told her about my last visit to their home, when I didn't find anyone there. She cried silently, and I also started crying.

"Maybe you have something from Adaś… some kind of souvenir?" she asked.

I shook my head. I regretted not having taken one of the bags of stamps that were lying on the desk—I could have given it to her now. I told her about the stamps, and she stopped crying. She began to gaze off into the distance as if she could see the past.

"You know, Iziu collected stamps his whole life," she said, smiling. "He told me that stamps symbolized life for him because they're a reflection of it. He loved them. He believed that when a person loves something, his life becomes prolonged because the object of his love that he leaves behind is also part of his life."

I didn't understand what she was saying, but I caressed her hands, and she kissed me.

My grandfather discussed the situation in the ghetto with my father. He thought nobody would survive unless a radical political change happened. The Germans' cruelty during the last roundup was something completely unimaginable for a normal person.

"People won't want to believe something like this could happen. They're going to say it's an exaggeration, because how is it possible to murder small children in an orphanage and invalids in a hospital? Callously, mercilessly, without any emotion . . . as mechanically as mowing grass! Will anyone ever be able to understand this?!"

My grandfather's voice broke, and it was obvious he was having trouble controlling himself. In his opinion, we shouldn't delude ourselves about the future. The only flicker of hope lay in the fact that ever since an SS officer named Müller had become the ghetto's commandant, the situation had improved. People were saying he was the best commandant so far, compared to all the previous ones. Under his control, the Germans hadn't committed any murders or rapes in the ghetto and in fact rarely even appeared in it. It had become much easier to obtain employment; food supplies had also increased. Of course, the situation could change at any time, but these moments of relative peace were important.

We found out that my father's uncle, Chaim Schenker, was also in the ghetto. He had managed to survive the roundup in Wieliczka and was now living in the Bochnia ghetto with his wife and children. My mother's sister, Lida Teichtal, was also here with her son, Menek, and her daughter, Tosia. Her husband had escaped to Russia. She was supposed to follow him there, but she hadn't found a way to leave and had remained in Kraków. Later she'd gone to Brzesko and from there to Bochnia.

We returned to the post office, overjoyed by the news about our relatives. My grandfather suggested to my father that he sleep in his home for the time being. In the evening, my father went there, and we stayed at the post office. At night I was cold because wind was blowing in through the door; someone let me share his blanket.

The next day we had another huge surprise. My father decided to go to the *Judenrat* and took me with him. Suddenly on the street we ran into — Hochman!

He and my father stared at each other, unable to believe their own eyes, and then they fell into each other's arms, pulling me into their embrace. Hochman still had long hair, which now fell nearly to his shoulders and was even whiter than before. He was also very hunched over, as if he were carrying a heavy weight. They bombarded each other with questions. We sat on a low wall and told each other about our experiences.

Hochman told us that during the roundup in Wieliczka, he had been painting the interior of a church. Several days before the roundup, he had started walking around to churches, presenting himself as a painter and offering his services for a very low fee, accommodation, and food. He had found work quickly. Nobody knew he was Jewish. He spent two months painting a church and was highly praised for his work. After it was finished, he was afraid to wander around in the area because the roads were dangerous, so he decided to enter the ghetto in Bochnia. There he found work as an orderly in an orphanage.

During the roundup operation in November 1942, Germans entered the orphanage. Several dozen children lived there, including many babies. Without saying a single word, they went from bed to bed, killing each child with a bullet to the head. The entire staff was also murdered.

Hochman hid behind some bushes in the garden during the massacre. Afterward he had to take the dead children's little bodies off the beds so they could be taken to the cemetery along with the corpses of other people who had been murdered during the roundup operation. He washed the blood off the floors and beds.

With trembling lips and a strange grimace on his face, Hochman told my father, "Leon, it was something so terrible that I can't even describe it to you." After he said this, he started to cry on my father's shoulder. This was the first time I'd ever seen him in such a state. My father was also deeply shaken. He started breathing rapidly like after intense physical exertion. It took them a long time to calm down.

Hochman told us he was still living in the orphanage, which was now empty. Apart from Hochman, nobody was allowed to enter it.

Hochman was struck with an idea while talking to us. Before the war, someone had started building a small wooden house close to the orphanage but hadn't finished it. Only the frame of the house was standing there with a roof on it. Hochman thought it might be possible, with a bit of work and some materials, to finish one room, and then our family could live there.

We went to have a look at the house. Its wooden frame stood on a cement foundation. The exterior walls had been started, but there were wide gaps between the boards and deep pits instead of a floor. The roof was partially covered with red tiles.

My father decided to finish a large room in the house—the room that was the closest to completion. I don't know how he obtained the materials, but he worked there every day with Hochman and a friend from the ghetto. They received permission to do this from the *Judenrat*.

One day after breakfast, the man responsible for maintaining order at the post office shouted, *"Achtung!"* Everyone stood at attention. We were in our spot right next to the entrance. I raised my head and saw an SS officer in the doorway with two civilians. They entered, followed by three SS men. Müller, the commandant of the ghetto, had come for an inspection. One of the civilians was the leader of the *Judenrat*, and the other was his deputy. They were answering Müller's questions and explaining something to him.

My heart started hammering inside me. From my experiences in the Tarnów ghetto, I'd become accustomed to running away at the sight of an SS man. But everything happened so quickly that there was no time to run away. Everyone stood at attention while they continued talking right next to us. I was very scared, but after a short time, I realized the conversation was quiet and sounded rather normal. Müller listened attentively to the leader of the *Judenrat* and nodded. I felt my fear beginning to leave me and raised my eyes to Müller.

He was very thin and tall with an angular face, high forehead, thin neck, and large Adam's apple that bounced when he spoke. He was wearing a green uniform that looked like it had just been picked up from the tailor's—it didn't have a single wrinkle and fit him perfectly. His tall, black boots shone like a mirror. It was the first time I'd ever seen an SS officer acting calmly around Jews. It seemed very strange. I didn't know what to think of it, and I was anxious because I knew the situation could change at any moment.

My father was standing off to the side. At a certain point, Müller, to my even greater surprise, addressed him.

"Wie heißen Sie?" (What's your name?)

He used the formal, polite form when addressing my father, *Sie*, rather than *du*, the familiar form. An SS officer addressing a Jew with *Sie*—this was something completely extraordinary in the ghetto. How could an officer who believed he belonged to the *Herrenrasse* (master race) address a Jew this way? Was this just a prelude to them beating my father? After all, the Germans liked such games and surprises. They enjoyed taking people off guard with their brutality.

But nothing like that happened. This conversation was clearly something quite out of the ordinary, since the leader of the *Judenrat* was staring at both men in surprise. My father introduced himself. Müller asked him what his profession was, and my father answered that he was a painter. Müller nodded and then, without another word, went out into the street followed by the SS men and the Jewish men from the *Judenrat*.

People told us later that Müller did such inspections from time to time in the ghetto. But he never spoke to anyone apart from the people from the *Judenrat*. We didn't attach any importance to this event and soon forgot about it.

A few days later, my old friend from Kraków, the violinist with whom we'd lived on Dietla Street—Birnbaum—appeared in the post office. He came with his wife, whom I had known as his fiancée. Now she was even prettier. Her long blond hair seemed to be spun of gold.

We were very happy to see each other again. I asked him where his violin was. He didn't answer; he just looked at me sadly. But I was curious and repeated the question. He told me a German had smashed it on his knee during a search of his apartment in Kraków, and Birnbaum hadn't played since then.

I knew how attached he'd been to his violin, and tears came to my eyes. Birnbaum noticed this and told me not to cry because even if a person stops playing music, he can still hear music inside himself.

"In fact, all of life is music," he reassured me with a smile, and then he patted my head with a fatherly gesture.

"But never again will I hear music as lovely as the music you played," I said, to explain how upset I was.

Birnbaum smiled again and promised that after the war he would invite me to his home and play just for me.

"And if I don't survive," he added, "there will be others after me whom you'll be able to listen to. Even better musicians than I am, more talented. Because you know, Henryk, music can never really be destroyed."

These were the last words I heard Birnbaum say. I don't know what happened to him or whether he survived the war.

Soon our room was ready, and my father proudly led us there. It was quite difficult to enter the room because we had to walk across boards laid over pits where the other rooms were supposed to be. We got water from a well and used a carbide lamp for light. The toilet was in the garden behind the house. We were happy to have a home of our own again.

My father was given work as an upholsterer in a workshop outside the ghetto. He left in the morning and came back in the evening. Our situation improved greatly because my father bought food and smuggled it into the ghetto. Every day we waited impatiently for him to return from work. It was the most exciting moment of the whole day for us. My father had a string hanging around his neck, with which he would pull several potatoes or a piece of pumpkin out of a trouser leg. He would hide pieces of bread or sometimes even butter in the sleeves of his jacket, and eggs under his hat. We all helped him undress very carefully so that nothing would break or spill; even Lusia helped us do this.

Once my father brought a jar of marmalade in his trousers, and we were overjoyed. Another time a bag of flour he was carrying under his hat burst, and he arrived completely white, like a baker. One day he was carrying a loaf of bread on his back, under his coat, and at the ghetto's entrance gate one Jewish policeman turned to another and said, pointing at my father, "That guy hunches more every day."

It was decided that I should learn upholstery, too, so my father could take me to work as his assistant. In the evenings, after supper, I had to sew stitches on an old sack with a very long, thick awl that was curved at the end. It went well, and my father was pleased with my work. But he was unable to find a job for me.

One day Hochman took me to the orphanage, which was empty but which he was still guarding. He said he wanted to show me something. The orphanage was in a villa surrounded by a large garden. Inside the villa there were rooms with white, child-sized beds made of iron. Large windows adorned with curtains created a pleasant impression. Everything was very tidy. There was no indication whatsoever of the horrible tragedy that had recently happened here.

Hochman led me from one bed to another and told me whom they had belonged to. He remembered all the children vividly—what their names had been and how they had behaved. He told me how he had dressed, bathed, and fed them and how they had laughed and cried. He was able to tell me something specific about each child. It was obvious he loved them all like his own children. He didn't have any children of his own.

At one point, he stopped talking and looked at me pensively, with a keen gaze, as if he wished to gauge whether I was capable of understanding what he was saying.

"I'm alive and breathing, but my life ended along with these children's lives," he said. Then he pointed at one of the beds. "This is the bed I wanted to show you. You're young, and perhaps you'll survive the war. If you do, tell others about this."

On the bed's guardrail there was dried blood that Hochman said couldn't be washed off. He'd tried to wash it with many different substances because the Germans had commanded him to do so, but the stain remained. On the other beds, the blood had washed off, but on this one it hadn't. Even when he'd managed to wash some of the blood off and the stain had become lighter, the next day it was the same, as if blood were constantly flowing from the bed's guardrail.

"The walls were whitewashed again because they were covered in blood and remnants of the children's brains, but the beds were only washed—we weren't told to paint them. I've tried to cover this stain with whitewash, but it keeps coming back."

"Who slept here?" I asked.

Hochman told me it was a beautiful two-year-old girl whom someone in the orphanage had named Ora, from the Hebrew word *Or*—light. When she laughed it was like a heavenly light was filling the entire room. She had been brought to the orphanage one day by a Polish railway worker who had found her standing next to the train tracks. It looked as if her parents had thrown her out of a train that was transporting them to their deaths. She had been in the orphanage for only a few months, but the entire staff adored her.

Hochman started to cry. I felt very sorry for him. Sobbing and struggling to speak, he continued, "While the children were asleep, Germans came and . . . shot them all. I felt every bullet as if each one struck my heart. I was sleeping in a separate room. When I heard the Germans entering, I jumped instinctively out the window and hid in the bushes. I wanted to come back and die with them, but fear overpowered my will."

Hochman took a rag out of his pocket and wiped his eyes with it, but he didn't stop crying. I embraced him, and we wept together.

"A human being is weak, so very weak," he mumbled over and over again, as if he felt guilty that he was still alive.

He clearly felt that life was a luxury he didn't deserve.

After a while, he grew a bit calmer and, pointing to the little bed next to us, said, "I wanted to show it to you because perhaps it's important for someone to find out about this blood that can't be washed away. Maybe it's the only reason I survived—to tell people about it."

Hochman looked very solemnly into my eyes and said, "Promise me that if you manage to survive, you'll tell people about it. Do you promise?"

I nodded because I was too overcome with emotion to answer, but I was uncertain if I'd ever have the strength to do it. I imagined the children being killed. I heard their cries, screams, wails. I could see their terror. They looked at me with their silent, uncomprehending eyes, which, in the last moments of their lives, asked, "Why? Why?"

I couldn't bear it anymore and ran out into the garden. Hochman followed me. He showed me the spot in the bushes where he'd hidden. The bushes weren't very dense, and if the Germans had searched the garden, they would certainly have found him. I told Hochman this and tried to convince him that clearly fate had wanted him to survive.

"Yes, but I don't know why," he answered.

It was very troubling for me to see this old, broken man crying in front of me like a child.

While writing about this, I've suddenly realized that only now, after so many years, am I able to describe it.

I returned home very saddened and disturbed by Hochman's story and by what I'd seen. I was surprised by my own lack of fear. I was only twelve years old and wanted to live. Today it seems to me, quite simply, that I just didn't want to think about what could happen to me. I resigned myself to fate with a strange conviction that I'd be protected from evil. I think most people in the ghetto probably felt the same way.

A huge surprise was waiting for me at home. As soon as I entered, someone embraced me and kissed me on both cheeks. It was my cousin Arie, Ignaś's brother—a tall, blond boy with prominent cheekbones and a crew cut. I don't remember whether he'd finished high school, but I knew he was a very good student and a decent, reliable boy. My mother always told me to try to be like him. Arie, like Ignaś, was deeply loved by the whole family. After the Germans shot his father, Zalman Frenkel, he found out where we were and decided to try to reach us. We were his closest relatives who were still alive.

Arie cried when he heard what had happened to Ignaś, but eventually he grew calm. After this, he never mentioned Ignaś again. I asked him about Ignaś once, but he answered that his memories of his little brother were sacred for him, so he didn't want to talk about them with anyone.

A deep friendship soon grew between us, and we began to treat each other as brothers. My parents also considered Arie a member of our family. My bed was turned into a bunk bed; I slept up above and Arie down below. My father tried to find a job for Arie, but despite his efforts, he couldn't find any work for him because an increasing number of people were pouring into the Bochnia ghetto. At that time, our ghetto was relatively peaceful.

The list of people waiting for work was growing constantly, and there were very few available positions. People believed the situation was safer for them if they had jobs. Everyone lived with a foreboding of imminent danger because nobody knew how long the peace in our ghetto would last or when the Germans would begin another roundup. My father started looking for a hiding place for us, but he couldn't find anything suitable.

One summer afternoon I was standing with my cousin Menek behind our house, where the only cherry tree in the entire ghetto stood. The last two cherries were hanging high among the leaves. We gazed at them longingly and wondered how we could pick them. Suddenly someone ran up to us and told Menek he had to go home immediately because travel documents had arrived from Palestine for him, his mother, and his sister. We made a pact that I owed him one cherry and would give it to him after the war.

Later I found out that his father, Akiba Teichtal, had escaped to Russia and joined General Anders's army. He had traveled with the army to Tehran and from there had reached Palestine. After a great deal of effort, he had managed to send his family a permit to enter Palestine. The Germans had found his family in Bochnia and now told them to prepare to leave Poland. The Germans planned to exchange them for German prisoners.

Two days later, Aunt Lida left the ghetto with Menek and Tosia. We were very attached to them and felt much lonelier after they left. From then onward my father stopped searching for a hiding place for us and started thinking about other ways to save us.

At that time, rumors were circulating in the ghetto that there was a route along which people were being smuggled to Hungary. People said that Jews weren't being persecuted as severely in Hungary as in Poland. But it was very expensive and dangerous. We didn't have any money, so this wasn't an option for us.

Another way was to obtain foreign documents—a visa to enter another country or an affidavit from Palestine. The Germans registered people who had such documents and from time to time sent them off in unknown directions. Unfortunately, not many people managed to get such documents, and they were also very expensive. Only a few families in the ghetto obtained affidavits from Palestine. The world was indifferent to what was happening to us.

One day Chaim Schenker confided in my father that he possessed such an affidavit for his entire family but was afraid of registering because nobody knew where the Germans were sending these people. My father asked him to lend it to him for a few days and made a photocopy of it outside the ghetto that was the same size as the original.

In the center of the document, there was a space where the family members were listed who had received permission to enter Palestine. My father covered this space with another piece of paper and wrote the names of everyone in our family on it. He added Grandpa Józef and his wife. Arie was listed as my brother. I remember my father using watercolor paints to make the piece of paper with the list of our names match the color of the photocopy.

Then, when the new list of names was lying on the photocopied document, my father took a photo of it with a camera he'd borrowed from a friend and dropped the film off to be developed. He received a photograph of the affidavit listing our names that was the size of a postcard.

Then he tried to find out where Aunt Lida had gone with her children. But all he managed to establish was that they'd traveled by train toward Kraków.

In the evenings, my parents had long discussions about whether we should register or not. Grandpa Józef was hesitant because—as he expressed it—how could we voluntarily head into the unknown? The whole matter was eventually dropped because news began to circulate in the ghetto that over one hundred

American citizens had been shot in the Montelupich Prison in Kraków. This made my parents decide to abandon the plan, and my mother even began to mourn her sister and her sister's children.

One day my father was summoned to the office of the *Judenrat* and was ordered to stand at the ghetto's entrance gate the following morning. A soldier would come and take him to Commandant Müller, who had some work for a painter and remembered having met one in the ghetto.

Müller explained to my father that he wanted a large insignia made that would hang in his office. He wanted a huge skull and crossbones and some gothic lettering embroidered on black velvet with silver thread.

Müller asked my father to draw this Nazi insignia and lettering on the velvet with white chalk so that the embroiderer, who was already waiting in the room, could stitch it according to his drawing. He also ordered my father to sit next to the embroiderer while she worked to make sure she didn't make a mistake and to correct the drawing if the chalk rubbed off.

My father got down to work, and the drawing was soon ready. The embroiderer started working, and my father sat near her, watching her hands. The work progressed slowly because Müller wanted the embroidery to be very thick, which meant several layers of stitches. The insignia was 120 centimeters wide and 100 centimeters tall, so it required a great amount of work. My father sat all day next to the embroiderer and explained to her where the stitches should be. In the afternoon they were given a hot meal in the kitchen, and before finishing their work for the day, they were given a small supper. In the evening my father was taken back to the ghetto. Every day passed this way.

One time, Müller called my father to his office and started talking with him about art, which, it turned out, he was very interested in. My father was careful with his words so as not to offend the SS officer in any way, for he was aware he might have to pay for it with his life. So he spoke slowly and often stopped in the middle of a sentence to think carefully about what to say.

Müller was interested in knowing what my father thought of modern art and particularly the works the Germans were destroying, which they called *entartete Kunst* (degenerate art). These were primarily works by German expressionists. My father suspected that Müller possessed such paintings and was hiding them. It was a dangerous topic, and my father vacillated as much as he could.

After a while, Müller started laughing and told my father he could speak to him freely and had nothing to fear. This surprised my father, but he continued to be very careful about what he said. From that moment onward, they talked every day, and the conversations became longer. Müller conducted these conversations as if he needed my father to know that he, personally, had nothing against Jewish people. He also ordered food to be given to my father that he could take home with him, and this helped us greatly. We shared it with my grandfather and his wife.

The work for Müller was nearly finished, however, and we knew we'd once again be facing hardship and danger.

My father decided that on the last day, he would ask Müller to arrange employment for Arie and me as assistants in the upholstery workshop. My father didn't seek work for my mother because she didn't want to leave Lusia alone. Finally, it was decided that if Arie and I found work and there was a roundup one day in the ghetto, my mother and Lusia would hide with my grandfather in his house.

One day I urgently needed to go to the bathroom, but it was occupied. Unable to wait, I squatted in the garden, near the pit where we tossed our household garbage. There were many scraps of paper lying around, and I reached out to grab one. To my surprise I saw that I was holding the photograph of the affidavit my father had prepared not long before. I didn't know he'd thrown it away after deciding there was no point in pursuing the matter. I decided to give it back to him.

After my father returned from work in the evening, I showed him what I'd found on the garbage heap. My father admitted he'd thrown away the photograph, but now he began to reconsider the matter. As he later said, an instinctive feeling hinted to him that he shouldn't throw it out after all. Müller's insignia was supposed to be ready the following day, and my father's work there would be done. It was as if someone were telling him, "This is your last chance to clarify this situation."

My father decided that if Müller seemed to be in a good mood that day and my father had a chance to speak with him, he would ask if it was worthwhile for us to submit the document and if he knew where they would take us.

The next day the embroiderer made the final stitches, and the completed work was ironed and spread out on the table. It looked truly impressive. Müller entered the room where my father and the embroiderer were waiting for him, and they presented him with their work. He was very pleased and stroked the black fabric as if it were an infant.

Then, like every other day, he started talking with my father in his office on various topics connected to art. He was in a good mood and expounded at length on how impossible it was for art to develop only in one direction and how freedom was necessary for its development. Unfortunately, the politicization of art was spreading throughout the world, which consequently would lead to its suppression. It was a very risky subject, and my father remained silent the entire time, waiting for an opportunity to bring up the matter he wished to discuss.

After a while, Müller told my father that if he had a personal request of any kind, he could ask him. My father replied that he wished to ask him for some advice, for he had an affidavit for Palestine but didn't know if he should register or not, because he was afraid of where we might be sent. Müller answered that if my father possessed a foreign document, he should register as soon as possible.

And then an astonishing thing happened. Müller got up from behind his desk and started pacing around the room nervously. In a reprimanding tone of voice, he said he was surprised by this question because it indicated my father didn't realize what kind of situation he was in. Then he asked, "Are all Jews so naive? Nothing awaits you in the ghetto except annihilation." He told my father he had no influence on this at all. The orders came from above. A new roundup operation could happen any day.

"What kind of question is that, anyway—is it worth leaving the ghetto with foreign documents? It's your only means of survival!" he exclaimed.

"But . . . but there have been various rumors," explained my father.

"I know; I've heard them. I don't know what happened then, but I know what occurs now after registration. Everyone gathers at a special internment camp for foreigners and waits there for formalities to be settled. Then these people are sent abroad, either through Switzerland or Sweden."

"But I only have a copy. I've lost the original."

"It doesn't matter if you have the original document or a copy. All that matters is whether they want to accept you in Palestine or not. We have German citizens there. There'll probably be an exchange, or maybe you'll get there some other way."

My father had the impression that Müller wished to help him. Suddenly he stood in front of my father and, shaking his finger at him, shouted, "This is your one and only chance at survival; don't you understand?!"

Seeing his agitation, my father answered obediently, "I understand."

"All right, so I wish you a safe journey," Müller said with a smile. He shook my father's hand in farewell.

My father was driven back to the ghetto. The driver gave him one more large package of food.

That evening my grandfather and his wife came to our house for a hearty supper, during which my father told us about his conversation with Müller.[1] After discussing it for a while, my father and grandfather decided we would register.

The next day my father went after work to visit Chaim Schenker, who had the original affidavit for his whole family. My father told him everything and suggested we register together. Chaim promised he would think about it and give my father an answer in three days. After three days had passed, he told my father he'd decided not to register because, in spite of everything, it still seemed too uncertain, and he would try to reach Hungary.

Hochman also refused, even though my father offered to make a document for him just like ours. He wasn't afraid; it seemed like he had lost the will to fight for his life. He didn't even want to discuss it with my father.

New people were constantly arriving in the ghetto. We already knew this tactic of the Germans from Wieliczka. Even though the ghetto in Bochnia was considered a labor camp, there was a growing number of people in it without employment of any kind. It was clear to my father that this state couldn't last very long.

Three days later, my father went to the office of the *Judenrat* where, following the Germans' orders, Jews with foreign passports or visas for other countries were registered. My father registered himself there and submitted the photograph of the forged document.

A few days later, we were informed that we had to wait at the ghetto's entrance gate the following morning at nine o'clock. We were allowed to take two suitcases, and my grandfather could take one. We were all very excited because we were aware a huge change was about to happen in our lives.

Arie gave me his wallet, which contained identity documents bearing his real surname—Frenkel—and asked me to throw away all the documents and hide the empty wallet. There were also various papers and photographs in it. I really liked his wallet. I thought the war might end soon and Arie would need these papers and family photos. But he was afraid to take them with him in case they revealed he wasn't really my brother.

I wanted to save the wallet, so I looked for a good place to hide it. Finally, I climbed the wooden frame that supported the roof of our unfinished house and placed the wallet on one of the beams, right beneath the roof's tiles. I was sure nobody would find it there, at least until someone finished building the house. That would surely be after the war. I told Arie about this, but he just smiled at me and said nothing.

The next morning, we waited at the ghetto's gate as we'd been instructed. Hochman accompanied us there. He and my father were both deeply moved, as if they realized they were looking at each other for the very last time in their lives. There were a few other people there, too. A military truck pulled up, and we climbed into it one by one. My father got in last, after saying goodbye to Hochman and kissing him. I put Lusia on my father's lap and waved goodbye to Hochman.

He was standing in the ghetto's gateway with his white hair flowing behind him like a prophet. He blew me a kiss and shouted, *"Derech tslecha!"* This meant in Hebrew—as my father later told me—"Have a safe journey!" Neither my father nor I had ever heard Hochman utter a single word in Hebrew before that moment.

The truck transported us to the train station. Soon a train that was headed toward Kraków arrived, and we were ordered to board it under the escort of several SS men. We took up two compartments. I gazed at the fields, trees, and villages that flew past the train windows and felt like I was sitting inside a kaleidoscope. There, outside, was a beautiful world to which I wasn't accustomed and in which I no longer belonged. The vast sky and far-off horizon were enchanting.

I had a strange sensation that I'd been invited to visit another world. Normal people lived in this strange world who didn't have to wait for death every day. There were certainly people among them who suffered—but among us, everyone was suffering. I looked at the passing landscapes and thought to myself that despite everything, the world was beautiful. I wanted this trip to last as long as possible because I was afraid of its unknown destination.

We got off the train in Kraków. The station was full of people, and once again I felt surprised to see people freely going wherever they wished. The SS men quickly led us out of the train station, and we got in another truck, helping each other up. The tarpaulin was lowered, and we couldn't see where we were going. After a very short time, the vehicle slowed down and then stopped. We heard the scraping sound of a gate being opened.

We were ordered to get out of the truck. Everything happened without any shouting. We found ourselves in the courtyard of a prison that was several floors high. We were told to put our suitcases on the ground, off to the side, and we were arranged in a line against a wall. In front of us stood a machine gun mounted on a tripod. There was nobody near it, but the sheer sight of it instantly filled us with terror. Then an SS man came and, smoking a cigarette, started pacing around the gun.

We stood there for several minutes but nothing happened. My father and grandfather, as well as some other people, began to pray quietly. I also recited Shema Yisrael—the only prayer I knew. I recited it over and over to myself and regretted I didn't know any other prayers. Arie put his arms around me, and my mother put her hand over Lusia's eyes. We were certain this was the last moment of our lives. But time passed and nothing happened. We stood there for about half an hour. Strangely, after a while we stopped feeling afraid.

Two Germans came and ordered us to follow them. They led us to the prison's main building. We walked down long corridors and up a staircase to one of the higher floors, until we were standing in front of a cell. We were ordered to enter it. It was quite large, and half of it was taken up by a wooden platform covered with straw. Some neatly folded blankets lay next to the wall. We sat down on the platform and waited for what was going to happen to us. We were all excited but barely spoke to each other. I felt like I was in a daze.

After a while the cell door opened, and two large pots of food were brought in on a cart. They gave us some soup, buckwheat groats, and bread with margarine. My father asked one of the Germans where we were, and he answered, "Montelupich." And so we found ourselves in Kraków's famous prison, the very name of which filled people with horror.

The hours in the cell passed quickly, and night soon fell. I slept curled up to my father and had strange dreams that I no longer remember, but they must have been pleasant because I woke up late in the morning feeling very fresh and well rested. My mother said I'd been smiling in my sleep, and she didn't want to wake me, even though everyone else had already gotten up. The food cart came in again. We were given bread with margarine and artificial coffee. There was enough food for us not to feel hungry, and nobody complained. We realized we were being given special treatment.

After breakfast we were informed that we'd be leaving the prison in an hour. Once again, we became filled with a feeling of excitement and anticipation—we hoped something good awaited us. Some people were praying. My grandfather was reciting psalms. I satisfied myself with my usual prayer.

An hour later we were led back into the courtyard, and each of us received a package for the journey that contained two bottles of water and several pieces of bread with marmalade. We were told we'd be fed during the trip. We were given back our suitcases, which must have been searched because they weren't shut properly. We were transported by truck to the train station, where we were handed over to several SS men who were to escort us. Nobody told us where we were going or how long the journey would last.

After a while, a long express train with elegant Pullman coaches arrived at the station, and we were ordered to board it. It had been a very long time since any of us had traveled in such a train. This time we were also given two compartments, which the Germans locked with a key. They pasted stamped pieces of paper on the outside of our compartments, and the train left the station.

It was July 10, 1943.

Today I can say with total certainty that Müller's advice for us to register ourselves for foreign travel saved our lives. A month later, on August 15, 1943, the final *Aktion* was carried out in the Bochnia ghetto. Nearly all the Jewish people who had survived the two previous roundup operations were sent to the camps in Płaszów and Trzebinia. Only 120 people were allowed to remain in the ghetto and were given the task of collecting and separating Jewish belongings. After completing this work, these Jews were also sent to the same camps on October 1, 1943, and Bochnia was declared *judenrein*—cleansed of Jews.

Chaim Schenker and his family were killed. Lulek and Muszka, whom I had admired so much in Wieliczka, were also sent to their deaths. Our beloved friend Henryk Hochman—a wonderful person, outstanding artist and sculptor, and pupil of Rodin—was shot with a group of people in Baczków, a village near Bochnia.

This time, fate had allowed us to escape from one of the most terrible murderers operating during World War II—Hauptsturmführer Amon Leopold Göth.[2] He led the liquidation of the ghettos in Tarnów and Bochnia, while also serving as the commandant of the work camp in Płaszów.

Once again, sheer luck had saved our lives.

NOTES

1. Franz Josef Müller, commandant of the ghetto in Bochnia, was brought to trial in Kiel, Germany, after the war and was acquitted in 1969. The verdict was appealed in 1970, and he was sentenced to twelve years in prison for crimes committed in 1942–1944, including participation in the liquidation of the Bochnia ghetto and the selection and shooting of Jews.

2. SS-Hauptsturmführer Amon Goth (1908–1946) was a war criminal. From February 1943 to September 1944, he was the commandant of the camp in Płaszów. He was in charge of liquidating the ghettoes and forced labor camps in Bochnia, Tarnów, Kraków, and Szebnie. After the war he was sent back to Poland by the American forces and sentenced by the Supreme National Tribunal to death by hanging.

BERGEN-BELSEN

THE TRAIN WAS GOING VERY fast. I wondered where we were headed and what was going to happen to us. Landscapes I hadn't seen for a very long time were flying past the window. My parents and Arie were looking out the window with such curiosity that it seemed like they were traveling by train for the very first time in their lives. Our train compartment was elegant; it occurred to us that if the Germans were treating us this well, surely nothing bad was going to happen to us.

The train only stopped at large stations. Women wearing white caps were standing on the platforms, and when our train pulled up they handed cups of tea to us through the window. We passed through Czechoslovakia and then found ourselves in Germany. There was a lot of commotion on the station platforms; we could see many soldiers, and we noticed buildings here and there that had been damaged by bombings.

At one of the large stations, we were ordered to go onto the platform, where we received dinner from a cart that was parked there with big pots on it—a bowl of potato soup and a plate of pasta with vegetables—which we ate in our compartment. We were filled with fresh hope.

Only my grandfather remained sad and pensive. Not even his wife managed to cheer him up. In response to my father's observation that the Germans were treating us like human beings for the first time, he merely remarked that "too well doesn't bode well." I thought to myself that my grandfather was old, and old people always had a dark view of everything.

It was already late afternoon when the train arrived at a large, covered platform that was full of soldiers.

"They're all heading to their deaths," said Arie.

"How do you know?" I asked.

"I don't know, but I just feel it," he answered.

At one of the stations, all the children, including Lusia and me, received a glass of hot milk. This had a very calming effect on me; I curled up to Arie, who gently kissed me several times on the forehead, and soon fell asleep.

My father woke me up, saying we were getting off the train. It was night, and the platforms were poorly lit. I read a sign: Hannover. I pointed it out to my grandfather, but he couldn't see things clearly that were far away. I told him what it said, and he rejoiced. He ran up to my father and said we were clearly going to be exchanged since we were close to Hamburg, from which it was possible to sail anywhere in the world.

We were ordered to go to another platform and board a train that was waiting there. Only now did we discover that another train car full of Jews had been traveling with us. From snatches of conversation, we found out they were from Warsaw, Lwów, and other ghettoes, where they'd registered as foreigners or holders of foreign travel permits.

We all boarded an ordinary local train. The Germans urged us onward but were very calm. There weren't any lights inside the train, and it moved much more slowly than the previous train. My grandfather grew sad again. My father conjectured that perhaps we were going somewhere to spend the night, and they would transport us to Hamburg in the morning, but my grandfather just waved his hand and didn't say anything else. Arie fell asleep on my shoulder.

We got off the train. Several floodlights lit up a spot where we were told to stand. Trucks were waiting for us. We had to put our suitcases aside—we were told they'd be given back to us later. Finally, two SS soldiers got in our truck and pulled the tarpaulin down. It was almost completely dark. We were ordered not to speak. The truck started moving; this change in the situation made me extremely anxious, and I clung to Arie's arm. He had begun to tremble.

Suddenly the vehicle stopped, and we heard German voices. One of the soldiers guarding us got out of the truck. The tarpaulin was raised, and someone outside shone a flashlight on us. The soldier got back in, and the truck started moving. This time the tarpaulin wasn't completely pulled down, and I saw that we were traveling down a wide road. On both sides of the road there were tall poles with bright lights at the top and a double barbed-wire fence with rows of barracks behind it. There were no people in sight.

"A ghost town," Arie said to me.

"*Schweigen!*" (Silence!) one of the German soldiers shouted.

The truck slowed down and turned sharply to the left. We drove through a wide gate. When we got out of the truck and walked into a large open area, we were blinded by a bright light. There were over a hundred of us. Nobody shouted at us; nobody hurried us along. In front of us, there was a long row of tables with typewriters on them. A civilian sat behind each table. An SS soldier told us we had to register ourselves there.

Next to each table there was a board with the name of a country written on it—South American countries, Palestine, the United States, and various other countries. We were overwhelmed with joy and excitement. We were sure these men were emissaries who were going to take us abroad with them. Long lines formed in front of some tables—mostly for South American countries. We stood where there was a sign that read *Palästina*.

We soon found out, however, that the people behind the tables were Jews from this camp who had been given the task of registering us. I noticed that each of them had on the lapels of their jackets the flag of a country that indicated their citizenship.

Our turn came. A form was filled out for each person with our personal information, and in the space for "citizenship," we wrote *Palästinensisch* (Palestinian). Only now, from this man who was writing on the typewriter, did we find out where we were.

"You're in a camp for people who are going to be exchanged. The official name of the entire camp is Aufenthaltslager Bergen-Belsen, and this section is called Speziallager für Ausländer (Special Camp for Foreigners). You'll be interned here until you're exchanged, like the rest of us."

Then we were told to wait. Lusia was the calmest; she played the entire time with a rag doll she'd had since Wieliczka. It had been the last gift from Francis.

My father tried to reassure my grandfather.

"You'll see—everything will turn out well. An internment camp isn't the worst thing. Someone will surely agree to accept us."

My grandfather smiled and replied with skepticism in his voice, "You're luckier than I am because you believe in an illusion."

"Why do you think it's an illusion?"

"Because there's nobody in a foreign country willing to fight for us, to protest and shout, to rouse the world for us. Who's going to buy our freedom? People only care about themselves and their own politics."

"Do you think the whole world is evil?" asked my father.

"Not the whole world," answered my grandfather. "Only those who have something to say in this world."

After our registration was completed, we were taken to some barracks—men were separated from women. We were each assigned a bunk bed. People were already living inside the barracks; we tried to be quiet so we wouldn't wake them.

I was given an upper bunk. There was a straw mattress on it as well as a blanket and pillow. I was very tired and fell asleep as soon as I lay my head on the pillow.

It seemed to me that I'd only just fallen asleep when someone started waking me up. I heard my father saying urgently, "Quickly, quickly, at seven o'clock all the beds have to be made, and everyone must report for roll call."

There were several dozen people in our barrack. There was an iron stove in the middle of the room. An old man with narrow, slanted eyes slept in the bunk below mine. Eventually I found out he was a rich man, a Jew from Mexico whom the war had taken by surprise while he'd been on a business trip in Poland; apparently, he worked in the oil industry. He was ill and spent all day lying on his bunk. A few other old people in our barrack remained lying down all day long and didn't go for roll call, which happened once or twice a week in the large open area where we'd stood when we first arrived.

The *Lagerältester* (supervisor) of our camp, whom we chose ourselves from among the camp's inmates, reported to an SS man, and the latter counted the rows of people. We all stood at attention while being counted. There were fifteen or sixteen hundred people interned in our camp at that time.[1] Then the *Lagerältester* and *Blockältester* (the man in charge of our barrack, also chosen by us) entered the barrack and counted the ill people. The SS man reported something to an officer, and then the roll call ended. We were allowed to wear our own clothes, and some people even dressed elegantly. The women stood close to us, in separate rows.

After the roll call, lines formed in front of each barrack, and we were given breakfast: three hundred grams of bread that also had to last us for supper, a small portion of margarine, a spoonful of fruit preserves, and some artificial coffee. Lusia also received a plate of watery milk with noodles in it.

Between breakfast and lunch, which was served in the middle of the afternoon, we could spend our time however we pleased. For lunch there was soup and a few potatoes. I noticed that everyone watched the hands of the man who served the food—but he performed his camp job masterfully. His name was Rafael Wald, and he had a wonderful feel for how to stir the ladle and plunge it into the soup so that everyone received the same amount. Nobody ever felt treated unfairly by Wald, which was quite unusual in such conditions.

On the first day, I tried to figure out exactly where we were. There were about a dozen barracks surrounded by a lot of empty space, as if there were plans to build more barracks. The entire area was surrounded by a double row of barbed wire. People moved freely between the barracks. There were many children there, all very calm and serious. They didn't play, which surprised me since until then it had seemed to me that children were capable of playing in any conditions. There weren't any Germans in our camp. We only saw them at roll call and through the barbed wire, on the camp's main road.

Suddenly I heard a familiar voice behind me: "Henryk!" I turned around. My cousin Menek was standing in front of me. We leaped into each other's arms. It turned out that Aunt Lida and her children were here, too. We immediately rushed to her barrack. My aunt was very happy, but she complained that there wasn't enough food being distributed in the camp. She told us they hadn't begun sending people to be exchanged yet, but everyone was constantly talking about it. Everyone was waiting for someone to buy their freedom.

"We have to be thankful for what we have," she said, "because there are other camps all around us where things are much worse."

That morning I saw hundreds of people in striped uniforms marching in columns along the camp's main road. It looked like they were heading off to work. I could hear shouts and commands. I stood at the barbed-wire fence and watched in astonishment as columns of gaunt, emaciated people staggered past. Many of the faces were marked by suffering, while other faces expressed resignation and indifference.

Arie ran up to me.

"Henryk, where have you been? I've been looking for you for ages. Everyone has to be in our barrack because the barrack supervisor has something important to say on behalf of the Germans."

I thought that perhaps our moment of liberation had finally come, and the Germans were about to announce it to us. We sat on our bunk beds. A man spoke loudly about how we needed to be patient, and how those of us who had just arrived should find some sort of activity for ourselves, for our own good, until it was time for us to be exchanged, so that time would pass more quickly and we wouldn't think about food all day. There was no doubt that someone in the world would buy our freedom, most likely the countries for which we possessed documents. Nor was there any doubt that the Germans wanted to exchange us for their citizens who were interned in foreign countries, for otherwise they wouldn't have brought us here and wouldn't be providing us with food without forced labor. Then he informed us of the camp's rules and regulations, which we had to follow without exception.

"You see," said my father to my grandfather, "everyone here is very hopeful."

In a surprisingly sarcastic tone, my grandfather said, "It'll be easier for them to die than me."

"Why?" asked my father, puzzled.

"Because dying with hope is always easier," answered my grandfather with a faint smile, as calmly as if he were talking about the weather.

We slowly got used to our new situation. Most of the people in our camp were Polish. A small number were from other countries. Apart from the Mexican man who lay on the bunk beneath me and whose name I don't recall, there was a sick, old man—an engineer named Lindenbaum from Romania. He spoke Polish very poorly and was more fluent in German. People said he also worked in the oil industry. In our barrack, these two men were called "the oilmen." I started looking after them.

The Mexican lay in his bunk nearly all day. Sometimes, when he was feeling a bit better, he would get up for an hour or two. I washed his face, brushed his hair, helped him get dressed, and walked with him around the barrack or outside for several minutes. I also brought him food, and sometimes, when he felt weak, I fed him. Lindenbaum, the engineer, was in better condition and could get out of his bunk by himself, and he often even stood in line for food. But sometimes he was so weak that we had to bring him food and help him eat.

They were both unable to go to the latrine, which was quite far from our barrack, so I brought a bucket for them. I wasn't the only one who did this. A few other boys also helped the invalids, and I followed their example. I felt responsible for my "patients" and was happy to have something important to do.

Dinner was the culminating moment of the day. Sometimes there was a piece of meat floating in the soup, and we would chew it for a long time since it was a shame to have to swallow it. The greatest delicacy was soup with noodles in it, which was served very rarely. Sunday was a special day because we received a slice of sausage, which they called *Blutwurst*, and three sugar cubes; the dinner was also better.

I had one more activity—I played roulette. My neighbor in the next bunk bed, an engineer whose name I can't remember, claimed in all seriousness that he'd invented a system for the game in which one would always win, on condition that the game was played for a long time. Everyone in the barrack had already heard his lecture on this topic, and nobody wanted to play with him because they all thought he was obsessed.

One day he asked me to play with him. He begged me so insistently that I finally agreed. He suggested we play for grams of bread. I was afraid I'd lose and then wouldn't have anything to eat, but I decided I'd allow myself to play only until I'd lost half a day's ration.

Instead of a spinning ball in a round basin with numbers on it, we rolled dice. The roulette was drawn on paper, and buttons served as chips. We played all afternoon and the engineer lost half a kilogram of bread. Of course, he was unable to pay it to me. He wrote down my winnings, and we agreed to play again the following day.

And so, my mornings were almost completely taken up by caring for my patients, the "oilmen," and I spent my afternoons playing roulette. The engineer kept losing. This continued for several weeks until he admitted, to the delight of the entire barrack, that his system was worthless. He owed me sixteen kilograms of bread. I didn't see a single gram of these winnings, but he promised to give me the bread after the war, with interest.

My father also soon found a way to keep himself occupied. An architecture student had brought a large box of pastels with him. He drew pictures all day long, and my father asked if he could draw with him on some paper the *Lagerältester* had managed to obtain. My father drew beautiful portraits with the pastels. Soon other people joined them, and the entire group painted and drew for several hours every day. They gathered in a spot outside our barrack, which everyone started calling "the Academy."

Arie studied English all day. Someone had brought Langenscheidt self-study materials. These were English lessons in workbooks, which were passed around among people in various barracks.

Long discussions were held about politics and other topics. Everyone tried to find ways to occupy themselves so that time would pass more quickly. In these difficult conditions, there were people who nobly sacrificed their time for the benefit of other prisoners. There was a teacher from Warsaw named Mrs. Gitler who started a school for children on the bunks inside a barrack. They wrote with pencil stubs on the wooden boards of the bunks.

New transports were constantly arriving at the camp. These were people who had already lived through terrible experiences. For example, one of the women traveling to the camp had felt certain they were being transported to their deaths and had thrown her small child out the train window, thinking she might save the child this way. All night long she screamed in her sleep: "Give me back my child! Give me back my child!" People woke her up and tried to calm her, but she would start screaming again as soon as she fell asleep.

There was also a large group of about thirty people who all claimed to belong to one family. Their surname was Róża, and they were from Warsaw. They had forged documents from a South American country. Every morning they sat in a secluded spot next to the barrack, and one of them taught each person, one at a time, what his name was, when he was born, and how he was related to all the others. Then they would tell each other various details from their family life and their shared experiences.

In fact, nobody in the camp told anyone else about how they had received foreign passports, visas, or other documents. It was clear that only some of them were genuine, and the rest had been acquired through illegal means. Many of the people claimed to be Palestinians, but I don't remember if any of them had ever really been to Palestine. I knew only five people whom I can confidently say possessed real documents—my aunt Lida Teichtal and her children, the Mexican in the bed beneath me, and Lindenbaum, the engineer. But there were probably a few others.

Our camp for interned foreigners was completely isolated from the other camps in Bergen-Belsen. We realized we were in a very privileged situation, for people in our group managed to have brief conversations from time to time with prisoners in the other camps.

We found out that the entire camp in Bergen-Belsen had been built not long before we arrived—in April 1943. It was meant to be a large camp for people destined to be exchanged. Five hundred prisoners had been sent from other concentration camps to construct the camp, and there were plans for it to be further expanded. The Germans were clearly counting on the fact that they would be able to exchange a large number of people.

The conditions were terrible in the prisoners' camp (*Häftlingslager*). Many people died, and the number of prisoners was steadily decreasing. They gazed at us as if we were in paradise.

But after several months, our food supply also began to worsen. Our bread ration was decreased to 250 grams per day, and soup was served less often. Children no longer received milk with noodles. We were very hungry. The men suffered more than the women.

Cigarettes were distributed once a week—only a few per person. It would have been better if they hadn't been given out at all, because then all the smokers would have been forced to quit. Some people were completely unable to bear the lack of cigarettes and exchanged bread for them. They were the first ones to become swollen from hunger. My father stuffed straw and sawdust from his pillow into his pipe and smoked it. He was a tall, broad-shouldered man, and hunger tormented him very much; his daily ration was the same as mine, and I was also very hungry. My mother sometimes came to our barrack and gave him a piece of her bread, but my father refused to take any food from her.

One morning during the roll call, which now happened on a daily basis, we were told that Adolf Haas, the camp commandant, would come to inspect us the following day.[2] We spent the entire day washing the floors and cleaning the barracks. The latrine was also cleaned and scrubbed with Lysol, which not only served as a disinfectant but also covered up all other smells with its sharp, pervading odor. It reminded me of our bunkers during the roundup operations in the Tarnów ghetto.

Commandant Haas and some other officers inspected the barracks, asked questions, and even listened to requests from our *Lagerältester* to increase our food and fuel rations. Haas didn't say anything in response; he just nodded. The officers walked around together, talking. I was standing nearby and suddenly imagined all the SS officers lying on a wide cart—dead and naked. The image was so vivid that it was difficult for me to return to reality.

While passing my father's bunk, Haas noticed two portraits hanging on it that my father had drawn with pastels on paper. He stopped and looked at them for a while, and then asked who had drawn them. Our barrack supervisor pointed at my father. "Name?" asked Haas. Then he ordered my father to wait by the gate the following morning at eight o'clock for a soldier to come and get him.

From then on, a soldier took my father every morning to a building outside the camp, where he painted pictures on the walls of the officers' casino. After completing this work, he began to paint portraits of Haas and other SS officers. He was given oil paints, canvases and frames, and all other necessary supplies. He also received a two-course dinner and a large piece of bread with margarine.

The significance of this for my father can only be understood by someone who has also nearly starved to death. Sometimes my father brought one or two pieces of bread for us, smuggled under his clothes. However, he was usually inspected when returning to our camp. My father especially tried to bring food to my grandfather, who was growing weaker every day.

A painting studio was set up for my father in the officers' building. It was a spacious room with several easels in it, and there was a small room off to the side that had been turned into a storeroom for the painting materials. One of the studio's doors led to a small outdoor area adjacent to the officers' kitchen. My father noticed that every morning about a dozen twenty-five-liter pots of milk were delivered. After being unloaded from a truck, the pots stood there for about an hour before they were carried into the kitchen.

One time my father ran out of his studio and, seeing nobody nearby, grabbed one of the pots, quickly carried it inside, and hid it under the canvases in the storeroom. He drank this milk as soon as he found a safe moment to do so. He drank several liters of milk throughout the day, and the next day he exchanged the pot for a full one.

He repeated this procedure almost daily for several weeks, until a day when the truck arrived with the pots of milk and a fat cook came running out of the kitchen with an angry look on his face. He showed the driver a pot that was standing off to the side, which my father had exchanged the day before. It was clearly not full, and the cook made a huge fuss about it. The driver apologized and explained something to the incensed cook. It took him a long time to calm him down.

My father was now too afraid to continue drinking the milk, and throughout the following week he drank milk from the pot that was still in the storeroom until it turned sour. He poured the rest of it down the sink and left the empty pot near the kitchen. That was the end of my father's milk adventure. By drinking the milk, he quickly gained weight and regained a lot of strength.

We also benefited from my father's painting work. His next order was to paint the walls of a large room in the officers' casino. My father painted on a scaffold, and because the Germans constantly urged him to work more quickly, he requested some help. He needed someone to hand him paints while he was on the scaffold, mix the paints, and wash the paintbrushes. He was told to find two children as assistants. My father brought Arie and me to help him for a short time. Unfortunately, we didn't receive any dinner, only two slices of bread and a glass of watered-down milk, but my father shared his food with us, and it helped us a great deal.

My father also started stealing scraps of newspaper from the bathroom, which were hanging there to be used as toilet paper.

In our barrack there was a man named Mr. Gitler, the schoolteacher's husband—a very kind and intelligent man who tried to keep up everyone's spirits. From time to time he performed a "spoken newspaper" from the various bits of news that reached us from other camps, which we named *Tramwaj* (Streetcar). It filled a very important function in the life of the camp because it was our only source of news from the outside world. Mr. Gitler presented the news and commented on all of it in a very humorous way; he managed to find a spark of hope and encouragement in every piece of news. The presentations took place in the evening, when everyone was lying in their bunks.

From the time when my father began to paint in the officers' casino, *Tramwaj* became more frequent and in-depth. We all waited anxiously for each new issue. Mr. Gitler patiently and lovingly assembled the pieces of torn newspapers that my father brought, hidden in the lining of his jacket or under his hat. He tried to draw conclusions not only from what was written there but also from what wasn't mentioned. From *Tramwaj* we found out what was happening on the front.

One day Commandant Haas, while posing for a portrait in his armchair, said to my father in a calm tone of voice, as if he were speaking of something very trivial, "Mr. Schönker, please do me a favor and stop stealing our toilet paper."

My father remained silent from fear. He didn't know what to say.

"*Versprechen Sie?*" (Do you promise?)

My father came to his senses and said that sometimes he took paper from the bathroom to clean his palette, but if it caused a problem, of course he wouldn't do it anymore.

From that day on, some unseen hand put *Das Reich* and *Völkischer Beobachter* newspapers from the previous day in the pocket of my father's overcoat that was hanging in the entrance hallway. The German who inspected my father on his way out, handing him over to the soldier who led him back to the camp, saw these newspapers but said nothing.

Now Mr. Gitler was very busy all day long. He took notes, made clippings and arranged them as if he were a newspaper editor. We all waited for the evening editions of *Tramwaj* in our barrack.

While painting portraits of the SS officers, my father complained to them several times that there was severe hunger in our camp. But this didn't lead to any change in our situation. After the incident with the newspapers, my father told Haas, while painting him, that if our food rations in the camp weren't increased, soon we would all die of starvation and exhaustion. Haas said that our daily food rations were calculated according to how much a person needed in order to live.

My father answered, "The calculation is wrong, and the proof of it is in those who have already died and those who are swollen from hunger and will soon follow the others to the grave. You, sir, are the only person in this camp with the power to change the situation, and that's why I entreat you to increase our food rations."

"Please believe me; I must follow my instructions. Besides—your *Aufenthaltslager* receives larger food rations than the other camps here."

While saying this, Haas shifted slightly, and my father had to correct his position, which forced him to stop painting for a moment. After resuming his painting, and seeing that Haas had grown calm, he said, "You, yourself, sir, referred to our camp as an *Aufenthaltslager*—in other words, a 'holding camp.' But we won't be held here very long waiting to be exchanged for German prisoners of war because we'll all starve to death. The camp thus defeats its own purpose."

Commandant Haas waved his hand dismissively and smiled at my father for the first time.

"These are times, now, when one shouldn't be making long-term plans. What do you think about that, Mr. Schönker?" Adolf Haas was clearly in a good mood that day.

My father thought for a moment and then answered, without pausing in his painting, "I think that whoever wants to stay alive must also think about the future."

The conversation ended on that note. The food rations didn't change, but the soup served to us became slightly thicker, and sometimes pieces of meat were floating in it, and children once again received watered-down milk with noodles in it (only twice a week). In our daily portion of bread there was now more flour and less water.

My father painted Haas and other SS officers until January 1944. During this time, he completed fourteen large oil portraits.

There were twenty-five hundred people in our camp. One day, near the end of October 1943, we were told that we all had to gather in the roll call area at nine o'clock in the morning and that the names of the first people to be sent on an exchange would be announced. We became very excited. At last someone had thought about us. Our brothers abroad hadn't forgotten us!

After a while, a vehicle arrived with German officers in it. After they got out, one of them announced through a megaphone that all the people whose names were called had to stand in front of the camp's gate. They shouldn't bring anything with them because they would be given everything they needed.

Names started to be called—first several people I didn't know, and then the entire Róża family. I prayed inwardly for our family name to be called out, but it wasn't, even though we waited several hours. The crowd of people gathering at the gate grew larger. Trucks arrived and started taking them away. In total, eighteen hundred people were called that day. Aunt Lida and her children remained in the camp, as well as my patients—the oilmen.

After a while, a card arrived from Katowice addressed to our *Lagerältester*. It contained simple greetings but was signed by his friend who had been taken away in this transport. Clearly someone had been asked to send the letter for him or it had been tossed out of a train window. It turned out that this entire transport from our camp had been taken to Auschwitz and, immediately after arriving, had been murdered in the gas chambers.[3]

We didn't know what had happened. There were discussions and conjectures. My father tried to extract information from the German officers he was painting, but with no luck. Today people know why this transport was sent to Auschwitz. It turned out that German diplomatic posts in neutral South American countries had received lists containing the names of people in our camp who had identity documents from these countries. They had checked in the Ministry of Foreign Affairs if the documents possessed by these people were genuine or not. After receiving a negative response—the people were sent to Auschwitz. We were saved solely by the fact that the Germans were unable to verify Palestinian documents.[4]

One morning in late autumn 1943, an open military vehicle drove into our camp, and an SS officer got out of it with a prisoner in civilian clothing. The officer summoned our *Lagerältester*. When he appeared, the officer told him he'd brought a very famous person named Professor Ajzenman, and we needed to look after him and make sure no harm came to him. He required special care because he was suffering from amnesia and was unable to speak. Doctors hoped he would recover from this condition if he were among other Jews. If Ajzenman started talking, we had to inform the *Scharführer* (squad leader) at roll call.

The officer left, and Professor Ajzenman remained with us. By chance he was brought to our barrack and given the bunk beneath mine. The Mexican man I'd been taking care of was in the camp's infirmary at that time, and when he came back, he was given a bunk closer to the stove.

After Ajzenman's arrival, many men from our barrack and the other barracks tried to engage him in conversation, but he never responded. He lay on his bunk all day long with a frightened look on his face. People spoke to him in various languages, trying to calm him, but he didn't react. It was obvious he found all these attempts to communicate with him very unpleasant. I felt sorry for him, so I shouted at everyone from my top bunk to leave him alone. But some people, not having anything else to do, treated it as a kind of sport and tried to prove themselves capable of bringing Professor Ajzenman back to life.

One night I was awoken by the sensation of someone jabbing me in the back. I opened my eyes. It was dark in the barrack, with only a little light coming from the fire burning in the iron stove. My bunk was close to the stove, and my eyes quickly grew accustomed to the darkness. I began to distinguish the contours of other bunks and the men sleeping on them beneath blankets. I sat up and looked around, but there was nobody near me. I thought I must have been dreaming and lay down again. A moment later I felt, this time without any doubt, someone jabbing me in the back.

I looked down at Professor Ajzenman. His leg was pressed against the boards beneath my straw mattress, and he was signaling for me to come down to him quietly. I slipped from my bunk like a cat and kneeled next to him so that my face was close to his. In broken Polish he asked me, in a whisper, to summon our *Lagerältester*.

"Now?" I asked.

He nodded.

I tiptoed quietly to the *Lagerältester*'s bunk and gently woke him. He hurried over to Professor Ajzenman and told me to go back to sleep. I was the only one to see them because everyone else was sleeping. I don't know how long they talked because I fell asleep quickly.

I didn't tell anyone about this. However, it was clear now that our *Lagerältester* had shared Professor Ajzenman's secret with several trusted people, for I noticed them conversing discreetly. By that afternoon rumors were beginning to circulate in our barrack. In the evening it was decided to put a stop to them. The barrack door was closed and, with Ajzenman's permission, our *Lagerältester* told everyone about their conversation and asked them to leave Ajzenman in peace from that moment onward and not to speak about him with anyone.

It turned out that Ajzenman was really named Cudyk Mendelsohn, and he didn't have any connection whatsoever with the real Professor Ajzenman. He was a completely uneducated person. Before the war he had run a vegetable stall in the Jewish district of Warsaw. Later he had worked for an undertaker. Nearly everyone spoke Yiddish in Warsaw's Jewish district, and this was Mendelsohn's mother tongue. He spoke Polish very poorly. During the war, he'd started working as a gravedigger in the Warsaw ghetto. One day, while transporting a corpse on a cart, he had searched the dead man's pockets and found foreign documents bearing the name Ajzenman. By chance, the person in the photograph on the identity documents looked similar to him. The real Professor Ajzenman had come to Warsaw for an academic conference, and the war had taken him by surprise there, making it impossible for him to leave Poland. Presumably he'd been afraid of reporting to the Germans and had gone to the ghetto along with other Jews, where he'd been shot.

The gravedigger, no longer having anything to lose, had reported to the Germans as Ajzenman. He had no idea the Germans had been looking for this professor already for some time because the foreign academic community was willing to pay a large sum of money for his freedom. All diplomatic posts in Poland had been told to look for Professor Ajzenman, but nobody had been able to find him. When the gravedigger reported to the Germans as Ajzenman, it caused a huge sensation.

Mendelsohn figured out that Professor Ajzenman was an important person for whom the Germans had been searching. He was overcome by fear that he would be exposed, which would mean instant death. He knew that if he said anything, the Germans would immediately realize he wasn't the man they were looking for. So he had decided to stay quiet and pretend to be mentally disturbed. He didn't answer any questions. He appeared to have lost his memory and his ability to speak.

The doctors concluded that he'd been through some very difficult, traumatic experiences, and they sent him to a mental hospital. He was given various tests there, and after a while he was sent to another hospital, but the treatment there wasn't successful, either. There were moments when, no longer able to endure all the medical procedures, he tried to take his own life—but each time the Germans saved him. Finally, they decided to send him to our camp to live among Jews, in the hope that among his own people, he would recover his memory and his ability to speak. And that's how he had ended up at Bergen-Belsen.

When the *Lagerältester* finished telling the story of the gravedigger from the Warsaw ghetto, there was a long silence, which was broken finally by Ajzenman, who said in Yiddish: "*Un itst vil ikh hobn mayn ru, gornisht mer. Ir farshteyt mikh, Yidn?!*" (And now I want peace and quiet, nothing else. Do you understand, Jews?!)

Everyone promised not to bother him anymore and to keep the entire matter a secret. Each of us went up to him and shook his hand. Several people kissed him. Ajzenman was so overcome by emotion that he cried. For the first time in ages, he was able to be himself.

The next day, life continued in our barrack as usual. Ajzenman was silent, and everyone left him in peace.

After a while he also found some work for himself. He became very good at scraping the nearly invisible residue from the empty soup kettles. He even made special tools for himself—he polished spoon handles on a rock, bent them, and patiently scraped the kettles clean, getting several extra spoonfuls of soup from each of them. Because there were about a dozen kettles, he managed to get more or less a full bowl of soup for himself this way. The others were tolerant of this but also a bit scornful. Despite how hungry we were, people considered this behavior degrading.

At the beginning of 1944, we were again told that the Germans would summon people who were going to be exchanged. One of my friends from the camp was called first, along with his family. I prayed to God that I'd hear our surname and we'd be sent to Palestine. But we weren't on the list.

A small, seemingly insignificant incident occurred then that had an impact on one family's fate. The Gletzer family was called: a man, his wife, and their young son—a very beautiful, joyful child with blonde curls, similar to Ignaś. Perhaps that was why I liked him very much and sometimes played with him. The little boy stood at the gate with his parents. Suddenly a ball fell out of his hands and slowly rolled toward Haas, the camp's commandant, and stopped right at his feet. Before his parents could react, the boy ran to get his ball, looked at Haas's shiny boots, then raised his beautiful little head, gazed for a moment at that fat officer, and ran back. None of the Germans moved or uttered a word. The German with the megaphone was about to begin reading out the names, but Haas raised his hand, interrupting him. He said something to his adjutant, and the latter ordered the Gletzer family to return to their spots. They were very disappointed that this trivial incident had destroyed their chance at freedom.

This time about three hundred people were called. Their belongings were later placed near the gate and taken away by some other prisoners. It surprised us that nobody from Palestine was ever called. We regretted not being among the lucky ones who were able to leave.

It was not until much later that we found out that the first transport of eighteen hundred people had gone to Auschwitz and had been sent directly to the gas chambers, and the second transport had gone to Theresienstadt and from there, after a while, also to Auschwitz.

Our camp had now become nearly empty. About 450 people remained in it. We were moved to another, smaller camp.

The winter of 1943–1944 was very severe. The iron stove was too small to heat the entire barrack. We kept blankets wrapped around us at all times and slept in our clothes. The Germans, however, still treated us relatively well. We waited for our exchange, but it never happened. New transports of people didn't arrive, either.

Our strength was declining, but we lived with the remnants of hope that the war would end one day. Squadrons of heavy American and English bomber planes were flying over our camp more often, heading toward Hannover and Hamburg. At night, far away on the horizon, we could see the glow of fire and flashes of light. We knew Hannover was being bombed, several dozen kilometers away. At first the planes flew over us only at night, but later they also flew during the day, with nothing stopping them. When they passed over us, a siren wailed in the camp, and everyone had to remain in the barracks.

One day, through the window we saw one of these huge planes explode in the air and several parachutes appear in the sky. Another time our camp was shot at by a solitary fighter plane that flew low over the barracks and released a shower of bullets. Two people were slightly wounded, and the Germans took them to a hospital in Celle.

During one of these flights, Lindenbaum the engineer died. At first, I thought he was just sleeping. It was only when he didn't respond to my questions that I realized something had happened to him and called other people over. A doctor who was a prisoner with us in the camp examined him and confirmed he was dead. I was very sad, and it took me a long time to get over his death.

Arie helped me. He was my teacher now and gave me lessons as if I were in school. We spent entire days together. Often while studying, at my request he wandered off topic and described to me how beautiful it was going to be after the war because we'd be able to eat as much bread and potatoes as we wished, until we were completely full. That was our greatest dream at the time.

My grandfather also made a huge effort to keep me busy and distract me from dark thoughts. He started teaching me how to produce superphosphate. He explained everything to me in the tiniest detail, as if I'd soon be running our factory in Oświęcim. He drew the machines and equipment for me, explained how it all worked, and wrote out chemical formulas that, despite his thorough explanations, I couldn't understand. He quizzed me constantly, and these lessons pulled me out of my apathy.

We noticed that the people who lost hope and fell into apathy and depression were the ones who were in the most danger. To a certain extent, a person was capable of programming himself: either to fight for life, giving his body the best chances at survival that were possible in those conditions, or to meet his own death and accept it without a struggle.

The people in our barrack refused to give up. They found ways of filling our evenings with entertainment. It turned out that imagination and humor were powerful forces that could help a person survive any situation. After the lights were turned off, we lay on our bunks in the darkness and listened while someone—a different person every night—described an extraordinary culinary experience he'd had.

He'd tell us, for example, how he'd gone to a famous restaurant in his town, whom he'd gone there with, what the occasion had been, how everyone had been dressed, how they'd behaved, how the restaurant had looked and how the table had been set. After this introduction, he gave a detailed description of the dishes that were ordered and served. Finally came the culminating moment—a description of the flavor and aroma of each dish and how they'd been consumed. In our imaginations we could clearly see the restaurant, the food, and the people, and we were able to smell and taste these wonderful dishes. We could hear the conversations that took place there. The boundary between imagination and reality vanished. We lay silently on our bunks and listened as if we were hypnotized. We felt we were taking part in these feasts along with the man who was describing them for us. Some of the men in our barrack described meals with such mastery and hypnotic power that afterward we actually felt satiated, as if we'd eaten to our hearts' content.

Then came the second part of the evening when various anecdotes, skits, and humorous stories were presented. My father recited, in Yiddish, *Khelmer narunym* (The Fools of Chełm). It was a very long story full of piquant scenes from the lives of Jews in Chełm, which—I don't know why—had entered Jewish folklore as a town of simpletons. My father was often asked to repeat this story, and he told it about a dozen or so times with many variations. Each time, everyone laughed as if they were hearing it for the first time.

These culinary and humorous evenings helped us greatly, and I'm convinced they saved many of us. The women also had their own culinary activities—they invented recipes for various wonderful dishes, cakes, and pies. My mother had a thick notebook filled with recipes.

Unfortunately, even this, our sole entertainment, ended after a while because in the evenings we began to hear screams from the camp next to us, which was designated for people who were unfit for work. New transports of Jews were constantly arriving there, and every morning a dozen, or even several dozen, corpses were carried out. We couldn't make any contact with these prisoners because they didn't come to the kitchen. They were even more cut off from the world than we were.

One morning, after breakfast, I went with Arie to look at the camp next to us. A prisoner was standing opposite us, next to the barbed wire. He was very thin; his striped uniform hung on him like on a coat hanger. I felt like I was looking at a ghost... But his facial features seemed familiar to me. He raised his hand and waved at me as if he were greeting me. At that moment I recognized him—it was the Lehrhaupts' son who had helped us so much in the Tarnów ghetto. I waved back and smiled at him to let him know I recognized him. But he remained very sad; his face was full of suffering and sorrow. At least that's how it seemed to me. I wanted to help him somehow, to give him something, to comfort him by saying something nice, to hug him. But there was nothing I could do for him. I was powerless.

We stood there for a long time in silence, staring at each other. After a while he began to cry, and I cried with him. Only two rows of barbed wire separated us, but I felt like we were in different worlds.

"You know each other?" asked Arie.

I nodded, still crying. Then the Lehrhaupts' son stopped crying, and a mournful smile appeared on his face. He waved to me several times in farewell and then shuffled off to his barrack. I cried for a while, until Arie put his arm around me and led me to his bunk. There, I told him about this kind, noble-minded boy. Arie told me he doubted I'd ever see him again, for his face had been marked by death. I went to that same spot by the barbed wire every day for a while, but I never saw him again.

From January 1944 onward, new transports of Jews from Holland, Greece, and other countries were constantly arriving at a camp near us. They were also supposed to be exchanged. The Germans called them *Austauschjuden*—

"exchangeable Jews." Unlike us, they were forced to work, but they wore, like us, their own clothing. They had to wear a yellow patch with the Star of David on it, which is where the name of their camp came from: Sternlager (Star Camp).

On the other side of our camp was the most terrible camp in Bergen-Belsen—Lager für die Arbeitsunfähigen—the camp for people who were unfit to work. From March 1944 onward, transports of sick and emaciated prisoners began to arrive there from other concentration camps. They were just hollow shells of human beings. They made a terrifying impression. Arie, Lusia, and I often stood near the barbed wire and stared at these unfortunate people.

When one of them needed to go to the latrine, two other people had to support him, and then all three started walking like in a film projected in slow motion. There was no medical care there, and the hygienic conditions were terrible. They were given almost no food and didn't have any blankets. It wasn't possible to last more than a few days in that camp. The people brought there were primarily those whose health and strength had been completely depleted in other concentration camps.

My mother shouted at us not to look at this horrifying sight. But we kept going back to the barbed-wire fence as if something were forcing us to engrave this sight in our memories. Even today I still sometimes dream of it at night, and then I scream in terror. Every morning, many naked, skeletal corpses were carried out of there. They were thrown onto wide carts and taken to the crematorium. This is the camp in which the Lehrhaupts' son was imprisoned.

Not far from there, at the beginning of July 1944, another camp was built—for Hungarian Jews. Their transports came straight from Hungary, also intended for exchange. It was known that transports sometimes left from there, headed abroad; this gave us hope that someone might think of us, too.

At that time, we didn't know that a decision had been made in March 1944 to turn Bergen-Belsen into a concentration camp. The weaker and older people started dying from starvation. My father was now so weak he could barely walk, and my grandfather spent most of the day lying on his bunk or sitting on it and staring at the floor. My mother and Lusia managed to keep going somehow, and Arie and I did, too.

Arie was now intensively studying art history from a book someone had lent him. He said that art could liberate a person and suggested that I study with him. I refused because I preferred to spend my time in the company of other people. Learning about art made Arie very happy, and it often seemed to me that he was living in another world. He was as hungry as everyone else but seemed to suffer less. He talked about art with such excitement that it seemed as if he wasn't in the camp at all and wasn't affected by the lack of food. Only when I asked him about it directly did he look at me for a moment and, returning to reality, say, "Yes, I'm hungry too."

Aunt Lida and her two children, Tosia and Menek, were also holding on somehow. We were still receiving sugar cubes once a week, and Aunt Lida kept a hidden stash of them for emergencies—she felt she didn't need them yet. We didn't know what the future held for us or how right she would turn out to be. At that time, we didn't realize things could be even worse.

Wishing to save their strength, people lay on their bunks nearly all day long. Roll calls were happening every day now. Everyone stood in front of their barracks in rows; each of us held his spoon and food bowl made of red tin. We were counted every time by the same soldier, who reported to the *Scharführer* about the state we were in. This soldier, an Austrian, seemed to be a decent person, for he never shouted at us. It was clear that beating us wasn't allowed, for only from time to time, when an SS man became irritated, would someone receive a few kicks seasoned with expletives. Or if we spent too long bathing, we could get hit with a baton. In comparison to what was happening in the camp right next to us, we were living in paradise.

While this Austrian was counting us, he would wobble back and forth while he walked; he probably had a physical disability of some kind. There was a phrase he often repeated and that everyone waited to hear during the roll call because it cheered us up. When counting the rows of women, if he heard even the faintest murmur of a conversation, he always scolded them by saying, *"Haltet die Schnäbel, alte Gänse!"* (Shut your beaks, you old geese!) It was funny for us because he himself walked like a duck.

One time during the morning roll call, the *Scharführer* announced that a special roll call would be held the same day at four o'clock. Everyone had to be in their best clothes, bathed and shaven, and the entire camp had to be perfectly clean. There was going to be a visit from the International Red Cross.

We were overjoyed. Someone had finally taken an interest in us! After the roll call, exclamations could be heard from all sides: "What luck! What luck!"

We were all very excited. We became very busy making ourselves look relatively decent. The barracks were tidied up, and a special team cleaned the whole camp. Ajzenman was the only one who didn't do anything at all, and after lunch we noticed that several new stains had appeared on his shirt and trousers alongside the several dozen old stains that were already there.

When it was time for the roll call, everyone lined up in the yard. Most of the people now in our camp were registered as Palestinians, just like us and Aunt Lida. Since the beginning, none of the Palestinians had joined any of the transports. We were sure something had happened; perhaps the English authorities had finally agreed to allow us to enter Palestine, and someone was willing to buy us from the Germans. Many people were saying the world wasn't as evil as we'd thought. I was stunned by how everything in a person's life can change in a single moment.

Arie was strangely calm. He spoke with my father about what was happening and finally remarked, "Perhaps the people in our camp will survive. But this won't clear the consciences of all the influential people in foreign countries who could have freed us from this hell but didn't."

We stood in rows, and several SS men examined the yard to see if it was clean. Then we were ordered to stand with our families—women, children, and men together. This in itself was something unusual. Our excitement increased even more. We were sure we were all going to be exchanged. We stood there in silence for about an hour. My grandfather stood next to us, supported by my father and Arie. I was surprised to see that they looked sad.

At last, an elegant car drove through the camp's open gate and stopped close to our rows. An SS man shouted, *"Achtung!"* Everyone stood at attention. Commandant Haas, some other officers, and a woman got out of the car. Haas pointed at us as if he were inviting the woman to take a close look at us. The woman looked around, surveying the whole camp with one long gaze. Haas pointed at us again, but the woman shook her head. They discussed something for a while; then Haas turned to one of the officers, who shouted at us in a commanding tone: *"Ajzenman! Austreten!"* (Ajzenman! Step forward!)

Ajzenman remained in the row right behind us and didn't move.

The officer repeated his command, but Ajzenman still didn't move.

Finally, someone nudged him and said, "Step forward; they're calling you."

Ajzenman responded in Yiddish, his voice breaking, *"Ikh . . . gey nisht, ikh hob moyre."* (I'm . . . not going, I'm afraid.)

The officer started looking around and shouted more loudly, "Ajzenman! Ajzenman!"

Ajzenman was trembling with fear and refused to step forward, but someone pushed him from behind. We were all dressed in clean clothes, the men were shaven, the women's hair was neatly brushed, and some of the women were even wearing scarves across their shoulders, but Ajzenman looked terrible—unshaven and dressed in dirty, stained clothing. It was obvious his clothes had never been washed. His trousers were too wide for him and hung on him like a sack. The string he used to hold them up was badly frayed.

Terrified, Ajzenman was pushed in front of us. The woman opened her arms to greet him. He was forced to walk toward her, and she took several steps toward him. Only now did we notice she had a Red Cross badge on the lapel of her suit. They met halfway. The woman grasped his hand in a warm, friendly manner and said something to him, but Ajzenman remained silent. She was clearly aware of his state, for she didn't try to say anything else to him; she just observed him carefully. A horrified look appeared on her face.

She approached the group of officers and looked reproachfully at Commandant Haas, as if she were asking him, "What have you done to this man?" There was accusation in her eyes. Commandant Haas lowered his head in shame. I felt astonished while watching this scene because it had always seemed to me that SS officers were incapable of feeling shame.

They talked to each other for a short while; then one of the officers summoned our *Lagerältester* and told him that Ajzenman had to wait at the gate the following morning at eight o'clock—well washed and with his hair brushed, wearing elegant clothes and a tie.

"How could you allow him to come to roll call in such a filthy state?" he hissed.

"But how were we supposed to know this roll call concerned him?" the *Lagerältester* explained.

The roll call came to an end. Once again, our hope had been in vain. We were all disappointed, and some people cried.

A search began in the men's barracks to find a decent suit for Ajzenman. Finally, an elegant gray suit was found that fit him perfectly. Someone gave him a shirt, someone else gave him some shoes, and my father offered a red tie with white spots. Underpants, socks, a beautiful belt—everything was prepared for him.

Next came the more challenging part of our task. We had to shave and wash Ajzenman, who defended himself like a lion because he couldn't stand water. He explained that he'd just shaved a week before, and that his skin hurt when he washed it. Despite his resistance, he was bathed and shaved. Four men who were still relatively strong took care of these procedures, which lasted until late at night.

There was a rabbi named Lewin in our barrack. He was a very dignified man who comforted his fellow prisoners every day. He inspired many of us with fresh hope. The night before Ajzenman's departure, the rabbi sat all night long and wrote the names of everyone in our camp inside a prayer book, between the lines of the prayers.

At six o'clock in the morning, there was a lot of commotion near my bunk. Ajzenman was woken up, and once again the difficult procedure of washing and dressing him began. This time he allowed everyone to do what they wished with him. There was only one thing he refused—to wear a belt instead of his frayed string.

Meanwhile, a car pulled up at the gate with a soldier inside it who called out Ajzenman's name. We had to give up on the belt. Ajzenman was given back his favorite string to hold up his trousers, and then he calmed down. Rabbi Lewin slipped the prayer book into a pocket of his jacket and implored him to do everything he possibly could for us once he was abroad. The German by the gate once again called out, "Ajzenman! Ajzenman!" He was led out of the barrack—just like a groom to his wedding.

When Ajzenman was in the doorway, he suddenly remembered something. He came over to my bunk, gestured to me impatiently, and said, *"Henryk, shnel, gib mir mayn marmelad!"* (Henryk, quickly, give me my fruit!) Ajzenman always gave me his portion of fruit preserves to hide for him because he was afraid someone would steal it. I kept it hidden, wrapped in paper, inside my straw mattress. Now I dug it out and handed it to him. He put this paper package full of fruit preserves in the pocket of his elegant suit jacket and ran out of the barrack. I scrambled down from my bunk and ran after him. Ajzenman had clearly resigned himself to his fate, for he was walking away by himself.

The gate was open, and an SS man was waiting there impatiently. At the gate, Ajzenman stood for a moment, turned to us, and waved in farewell. He got in the car with the soldier and they drove away.

A while later, our *Lagerältester* was taken away to be interrogated. We were all very worried and expected the worst. Some people in the camp believed we were all about to be killed, since they were convinced that as soon as Ajzenman's deception came to light when he was abroad, the Germans would take revenge on us. The *Lagerältester* returned a few hours later. He was pale and slightly shaken, but nothing bad had happened to him.

During the interrogation, the Germans had asked him if anyone in the camp had been aware that the man posing as Ajzenman had really been someone else. The *Lagerältester* had firmly denied it, explaining that Ajzenman's strange behavior had been attributed to the fact that he wasn't of sound mind. After all, that's how the Germans had presented him when he'd first arrived at the camp. We didn't notice anything suspicious about him. The interrogators finally accepted these explanations. At the same time, the *Lagerältester* found out how the Germans had made complete fools of themselves and what had happened later to Ajzenman.

After long negotiations, the professor's ransom had finally been paid, and he was supposed to be handed over by the Germans near Lake Geneva in

Montreux, Switzerland. A special delegation was waiting for him there to give him an official welcome with an orchestra, flowers, and speeches.

The car in which Ajzenman was traveling drove to Montreux and stopped in front of the delegation. The orchestra was playing, and people were cheering. In this delegation there were people, of course, who knew Professor Ajzenman very well. The SS officers got out of the car with Ajzenman, and then it was immediately clear that the man was someone else. There was great consternation, and the Germans were accused of deception. The German officers justified themselves by explaining they'd had no idea this man was someone else. In the end it was decided that Ajzenman should remain abroad, and the disgraced SS men returned to Germany.[5]

The *Lagerältester* told us the Germans were very angry and told him several times that if this hadn't been a special camp, they would have sent all of us to our deaths.

One day a soldier came for my father and said he'd received an order to take him to the workshop in the administration building because someone wanted my father to paint a portrait of him. This time it turned out to be a high-ranking SS officer from Berlin who served as a liaison between the gestapo headquarters there and the Bergen-Belsen camp.

My father painted him in various positions—standing and sitting in an armchair. The officer came to our camp once a week and constantly demanded a new painting. My father found out that this was the person who inspected the files and identity documents of every prisoner in our camp. He was the one that decided who left on transports and who remained in the camp.

One time he told my father, while posing for a portrait, that everyone in Berlin was surprised that nobody abroad was interested in us. This special camp was starting to seem pointless, and he wasn't sure what decisions would soon be made about it.

My father told the *Lagerältester* about this. It was clear our camp was in a dangerous predicament. But there was nothing we could do to inform people outside Poland about our desperate situation.

After finishing a series of portraits of the officer, my father was ordered to paint the officer's dog. It was an enormous dog that, at its master's command, stood on a small podium and stayed completely still. My father felt as if he were painting a statue and not a living creature. He'd never seen such a well-disciplined animal. He told Arie about it, and Arie remarked that surely the dog belonged to the SS, too.

The portrait of the dog turned out very well, and the officer was delighted. He decided that my father should paint another picture, this time of him sitting in an armchair with the dog next to him. My father tried to stretch out his work on this last portrait as long as he could because he was fed very well on days when he was painting. But he couldn't take any food with him because he was carefully inspected before he left. Nobody was putting newspapers in his pocket anymore, either, so we didn't know what was happening on the fronts. Vague news reached us from time to time that the Germans were going to be defeated and the end of the war was approaching. My father also sometimes managed to read something on the newspaper scraps that served as the officers' toilet paper.

One day, when my father was putting the final touches on the last portrait of the officer, the officer said to him, "I must admit I'm surprised, because someone from a foreign country has finally shown some interest in you. What do you say about that?"

My father's heart started hammering inside him, but he tried not to show it.

"I don't see anything strange in it. It was clear to me from the very beginning that it would happen."

The officer seemed amused.

"It seems to be true, then, that Jews are better at predicting the future than other people. And that's why they're also so"—he nodded several times, as if he were searching for the right word—"dangerous."

The conversation came to an end, and the soldier took my father to the camp. Right after he passed through the gate, my father noticed a strange excitement in the camp. People were standing in groups, absorbed in lively discussions. It turned out that several hours earlier, a soldier had come to the camp and announced that packages had arrived for us from abroad.

Our names were called. We each received a large package and had to confirm with our signatures that we'd received them. There was a large white tag on each package printed with our names and the address: *Aufenthaltslager für Ausländer, Bergen-Belsen*. The sender was written in the upper corner: the Swedish Red Cross.

We opened these packages with hands trembling from excitement. They turned out to contain high-calorie food items—precious treasures such as condensed milk, smoked meat, lard, jam, crackers, sugar, coffee, cocoa, chocolate bars, vitamins, medicine, cigarettes, and tobacco...

Shrieks of joy rang out on all sides. We'd become millionaires. Such incredible luck had befallen us! People were overcome with emotion, and some were crying. In total, our family received five packages of wonderful food! We were very happy. The camp's doctor warned us to be careful and not to eat too much at once, because it could have fatal consequences for us.

For several weeks our lives revolved solely around the contents of these packages. Nobody talked about anything else apart from the marvelous taste of these treats that had fallen from heaven. We became much stronger and began to foster new hope.

It was clear to us that Ajzenman was the only person who could have arranged, in some unknown way, for these packages to reach us. Everyone in the camp blessed him. There was another clue that he had sent us these packages. Some of the names had been misspelled, with vowels replaced by other vowels. They looked like typescript errors, but it was clear to us how they had occurred. Rabbi Lewin had printed our names in the prayer book in Hebrew letters without vowels, since vowels are often left out in Hebrew.

After a while, we received more packages! This time they were sent by the Swiss Red Cross. We woke up at night and touched the packages to make sure we weren't dreaming. The incorrect vowels in some names were the same as before. Now it was absolutely certain these names had come from the prayer book Ajzenman had been given. Over a short period of time, my family received ten packages of food. And what incredible food!

There's no doubt these packages saved our lives—and in a twofold way. First of all, without this additional high-calorie nourishment, none of us would have physically survived the war. Secondly, it's highly probable that our camp, in which several hundred people remained, would have been liquidated without this interest expressed from abroad. This means that all of us would have died in the gas chambers of Auschwitz. We owed our lives to Ajzenman.

We wondered how he did it, and we came up with various theories. Only after the war did we find out what had happened. Apparently, the gravedigger, after various interrogations in Switzerland, was granted asylum in Sweden. From the very first day of his new life in Sweden, a country completely foreign to him, this simple man began to act with extraordinary determination and strength as an emissary of our camp. There wasn't a single bureaucratic office in Stockholm that he didn't attempt to visit in an effort to get help for us. Someone accompanied him each time and translated what he said in Yiddish.

In each office, Ajzenman begged people to help us. He described what was happening to the Jews in Poland and what was happening in our camp. When people didn't listen to him, he shouted and got angry. But nobody was willing to do anything for us. He was brushed off with empty promises that his requests would be conveyed to the Ministry of Foreign Affairs and perhaps, through diplomatic channels, it might be possible to influence the Germans.

Ajzenman tirelessly renewed his efforts. One day he met a Jewish man named Gilel Storch from Finland.[6] He had escaped to Sweden at the beginning of the war. Storch was an intelligent and wealthy man who devoted all his time and energy to organizing aid for Jewish people in the territories occupied by Germany, and particularly those imprisoned in concentration camps. He cooperated with international Jewish organizations and tried very hard to arrange emergency aid. Unfortunately, his efforts were completely in vain. He then limited his activities to attempting to send food packages to starving people in concentration camps in Germany. But he was unable to get official permission for this; he was told by Sweden's Ministry of Foreign Affairs that there weren't enough funds for it. Then he met Ajzenman, and this encounter brought a change to the situation.

Storch presented Ajzenman as an eyewitness. Despite the fact that he spoke in Yiddish and his words were translated, his descriptions were so dramatic and authentic that everyone who listened to him was deeply moved. These presentations finally convinced official agents. Funds were approved, and a campaign was carried out to send packages to concentration camps in Germany.

In total, forty thousand packages of food were sent by the Swedish Red Cross after an understanding had been reached with the Germans. Our packages were sent directly to us according to the names written in the prayer book. These packages undeniably saved many people's lives. They were like life preservers thrown to drowning people.

A rich man in the camp vowed that if he survived the war he would find Ajzenman and reward him abundantly. After the war, this man found him in Sweden and kept his promise. He also offered him various jobs in his companies. However, Ajzenman wished to continue doing what he enjoyed: running a vegetable stall. His vegetable business was very successful, but he continued to hold up his trousers with a string instead of a belt. He died many years later in Sweden. I'm certain that the real Professor Ajzenman would have been proud of him.

One day—when it was raining, as if the heavens were crying—my neighbor from the bunk beneath me, the elderly gentleman from Mexico, died. After Ajzenman left, the Mexican returned to his old bunk because he wished to be near me. Shortly before his death, he talked with me, and nothing indicated to me that he was about to leave us. He asked me to hold his hand, which I did. I didn't see anything out of the ordinary in this, for he often asked me to hold his hand. I noticed, however, that his facial features seemed to have become somewhat sharper. His hand felt cold, and his eyes were staring straight ahead, as if made of glass. Someone approached him and checked his pulse; then he closed his eyelids.[7]

"That's the way of the world," the man said and patted me on the head. I climbed up to my bunk and cried.

I was already accustomed to death, for people were often dying all around me. I saw the most corpses on the main road in front of our camp. Carts and wagons loaded with naked corpses were pushed and pulled along the road every day by prisoners in striped uniforms. I saw the intertwined arms, legs, heads, and torsos of dozens of people. Sometimes it seemed to me that they were still alive and in agony. They reminded me of the reproductions of Hieronymus Bosch's paintings of hell that I'd seen in Arie's book.

The conditions surrounding us were getting worse. More and more carts heaped with corpses were pulled and pushed along the camp's main road to the crematorium. It was said that the crematorium was no longer large enough to burn all the corpses, so they were being thrown into mass graves behind the camp.

On March 5, 1945, my beloved grandfather, Józef Schönker, suffered a cerebral hemorrhage and died a few minutes later. He was seventy-two years old. We mourned him very deeply.

In December 1944, Adolf Haas was removed from his post, and the new commandant of the camp in Bergen-Belsen was SS-Hauptsturmführer Josef Kramer.[8] He was highly experienced in organizing and carrying out mass killings. In Bergen-Belsen he reached the peak of his career as a mass murderer. People called him "the Beast of Bergen-Belsen." Right after being appointed as the commandant, our camp for interned foreigners was transformed into a concentration camp, along with all the consequences of this.

There were over fifteen thousand people in Bergen-Belsen at that time. As the front drew closer, the Germans organized "death marches" of prisoners evacuated from camps. Thousands of people collapsed from hunger and exhaustion during these marches, and those who were unable to go any farther were shot. Twenty thousand prisoners from many different camps, including Auschwitz, Buchenwald, and Sachsenhausen, were sent to Bergen-Belsen. Thousands of prisoners arrived from all directions.

Everyone who managed to survive these marches reached Bergen-Belsen with the last remains of their strength, in a state of complete exhaustion. No steps were taken to create even the most basic living conditions for them. There were no rooms to sleep in, no sanitary facilities, and no food. They were abandoned in the camp, outside, often even without any water. People were dying in massive numbers; epidemics broke out. It was impossible even to keep up with throwing corpses into mass graves, which were always open. The boundary between life and death had been obliterated.

Our camp still remained completely isolated from the others, but it was becoming smaller. There were only three or four hundred of us left. We were no longer counting the days, but rather the hours, until our liberation or death. We knew the Allies were approaching the camp. We lay on our bunk beds all day long, often overcome by apathy and indifference.

Arie fell ill. His leg became swollen and filled with pus, right above the knee. This was a common ailment in the camps, called phlegmon. The swelling increased until a doctor decided that Arie's leg needed to be cut open to release the pus. After various negotiations, Arie was finally allowed to undergo an operation in the infirmary, which was in the neighboring camp. My father carried him there on his back and several hours later carried him back. My father himself couldn't believe he was still capable of such strength. Arie was as white as a sheet, but his leg was well bandaged.

We all hoped it would be over and Arie would soon recover. Every few days my father carried him to the infirmary to change his bandage. The Germans didn't allow any of us to accompany my father. We stood at the barbed-wire fence and watched my father slowly advance one small step at a time, and we prayed silently for him to have enough strength. Arie clung to my father's neck and gave him encouragement. The same happened on the way back. We were afraid they would both collapse, but some kind of extraordinary strength had appeared in my father.

Arie was so emaciated that he weighed about half his normal weight. Strangely enough, he was never despondent. He believed he would recover. He even made plans to write a book about our camp after the war titled *Futile Hopes*. He once told me he wasn't sure about the title, but the entire book was already in his head.

Unfortunately, Arie's leg didn't seem to be healing. It was better for a little while, but then pus started collecting in it again. He didn't receive any medicine because there wasn't any. He began to lose hope in his recovery, and said that he clearly had accomplices in heaven, and they were calling him to them. We tried to comfort him, but he became increasingly solemn and immersed in his own thoughts.

One month after his first operation, there was a second one, and then it was necessary to repeat it several weeks later. The doctor said it was a miracle that Arie was still alive and hadn't contracted blood poisoning. His emaciated body had endured all of this somehow. During a high fever, Arie called out, "Mama! Mama!" Then his fever subsided, and better days followed.

Our situation became increasingly tragic, because our camp's supplies were completely disrupted. We received hot food only once every few days. After a while, hot food was no longer served to us. A few raw rutabagas and turnips were thrown to us through the camp's gate as if we were cattle. Our camp was privileged, for in the other camps the prisoners didn't even receive this much.

Unfortunately, we didn't get the chance to await the liberation of Bergen-Belsen. Even though the Germans now found themselves in a terrible situation, they still believed we were of some value to them and felt it was necessary to guard the treasure they perceived in us right until the last moment. We were evacuated from the camp on April 10, 1945.

We stood by the camp's gate at a specified hour without any personal belongings except our food bowls. All day long I'd had a strange foreboding that something terrible was going to happen. At the SS men's order, we lined up in a column together with our families. We were led through the gate and to the camp's main road. I'll never forget, for the rest of my life, what I saw there. Every ten or twelve meters, there was a pile of naked corpses. Each pile was about twenty to thirty meters long, six to eight meters wide, and two to four meters high.

Death itself no longer had any effect on us because we'd become completely accustomed to it. But we'd never seen anything like this before. Those faces contorted in convulsive spasms, those glassy eyes, those twisted, intertwined bodies lying on top of each other—dead, defiled human remains.

My mother led Lusia along and covered her eyes, and she begged me not to look. Only the first pile of corpses frightened me. The next ones we passed seemed to me like statues carved from stone. Perhaps it was my instinctive way of protecting myself from this sight.

Arie, held up by my father and me, walked in the middle of the column, hobbling on one leg. My father was afraid of carrying him because he didn't want the SS men to notice he was ill, since we didn't know how they might react.

Arie told me, "Don't turn away; look at these piles of corpses, Henryk, and remember them well, for this is the final summation of the war and of Nazi ideology."

Trucks were waiting for us behind the last pile of corpses, and we were ordered to enter them by climbing a ladder. Something terrible happened then. Arie, aided by my father, climbed the ladder very slowly, which irritated an SS man standing near us. He started shouting at him. This didn't help, since Arie couldn't move any faster. The SS man lost patience and kicked Arie's swollen leg. Arie screamed in pain and fell from the ladder to the ground, where the enraged SS man continued to kick him. My father threw himself in front of Arie and shielded him with his body, explaining that he was ill. As a result, he was also kicked several times and showered with curses. Some people jumped down to help Arie and lifted him into the vehicle. My father also managed to get to his feet and climbed the ladder into the vehicle. We stood there, petrified.

Finally, prodded by the SS man's shouts and curses, we also scrambled up. Even my grandfather's wife managed, through some kind of miracle, to climb up the ladder with my mother's help.

They took us to a train station in the small town of Celle. A freight train was waiting for us there. My family entered the same train car as Aunt Lida and her children, and my grandfather's wife, Regina. We carried Arie. He didn't know what was happening to him. It wasn't crowded; we were all able to sit on the floor, and even lie down. Later, turnips and rutabagas were thrown into each car, and two buckets of water were put inside as well as two buckets for waste. We were told we'd be given some food during the trip.

My mother and father took care of Arie. Lusia cried, cuddling close to me. I felt as if I were the one who'd been kicked. Some people in the freight car said they regretted not having been left in Bergen-Belsen to die in peace. We weren't even hungry anymore, just very weak. We felt certain the Germans didn't want to send us to our deaths, for if they'd wanted that, they would have left us in Bergen-Belsen.

I watched my parents put wet compresses on Arie, and I sighed with relief when he fell asleep. However, in his sleep he once again began to rave deliriously.

At last, the door was shut, and the train started moving. We didn't know where they were taking us, but our sudden departure from Bergen-Belsen can be compared to being saved from a sinking ship.

From January to mid-April 1945, roughly thirty-five thousand people died in Bergen-Belsen. In March alone, over eighteen thousand prisoners died. The Bergen-Belsen camp was liberated by the English on April 15, 1945. There were sixty thousand prisoners then—living corpses, sick and in the throes of death. The English army was helpless in the face of this catastrophe. Despite their efforts, massive numbers of prisoners continued to die.

I can still see the piles of corpses on the camp's main road in Bergen-Belsen, and at night I can still hear Arie's moans, which turn into quiet weeping.

NOTES

1. The chronology of events in the Bergen-Belsen camp and the general numerical data are based on Eberhard Kolb's book *Bergen-Belsen from 1943 to 1945* (Göttingen: Vandenhoeck & Ruprecht, 1996). This book contains many clarifications and precise numerical data about all the subcamps in Bergen-Belsen, as well as the transports of Jews that arrived there from all over the world.

2. SS-Hauptsturmführer Adolf Haas (1912–1945) was a war criminal who served as deputy commandant of the Sachsenhausen concentration camp and the first commandant of the Bergen-Belsen camp (spring 1943–December 1944).

3. See Eberhard Kolb, *Bergen-Belsen from 1943 to 1945* (Göttingen, Germany: Vandenhoeck & Ruprecht, 1996), 71.

4. See Christopher R. Browning, Richard S. Hollander, Nechama Tec, eds. *Every Day Lasts a Year*. (Cambridge: Cambridge University Press, 2007), 59.

5. The *Politisches Archiv des Auswärtigen Amts* in Bonn contains documents concerning Ajzenman from the administrative office of Heinrich Himmler, SS head commandant and Reich minister of the interior. The documents are letters written in 1944 in response to letters from the minister of foreign affairs in Berlin. This shows that Ajzenman's case was discussed on a very high level. These letters were found in a file in the Ministry of Foreign Affairs' archives that concerned the exchange of civilian prisoners, with this annotation: Palestine. These documents show that Ajzenman (actually Cudyk Mendelsohn) was sent from Bergen-Belsen on September 23, 1944, to an internment camp in Kluczbork run by the Swiss Red Cross, in order to be exchanged for German prisoners. He was probably given an exit visa in Kluczbork and went abroad from there.

In the archives of the Jewish Historical Institute in Warsaw is an account written by Szymon Kraus in the Warsaw ghetto, which describes Germans shooting a group of Jewish cemetery workers, including Cudyk Mendelsohn, on April 19, 1943 (the first day of the uprising in the Warsaw ghetto). Meanwhile, an issue of the *Bulletin of the Jewish Historical Institute* published in 1975 features an excerpt from a diary written by Józef Gitler-Barski in the Bergen-Belsen camp in December 1943 and the first half of 1944, which includes conversations he had with a fellow prisoner named Cudyk Mendelsohn, who had been a gravedigger in the Warsaw ghetto. However, "Weiss's List" (an official list compiled in 1944 of the names of all the Jewish prisoners in Bergen-Belsen waiting to be exchanged) doesn't include the name Mendelsohn—but Chaim Ajzenman is listed. All of this confirms that Cudyk Mendelsohn wasn't shot on April 19, 1943, in Warsaw, and that he traded identity documents with Ajzenman on that day and assumed his identity.

6. Gilel (Hillel) Storch (1902–1983) was a Lithuanian Jew who arrived in Sweden as a refugee and—thanks to his extensive diplomatic contacts—organized many campaigns to save Jews during the Holocaust (Storch also led the Swedish branch of the World Jewish Congress). One of the many things he managed to accomplish was the delivery—through the Red Cross, either directly from Sweden or via Portugal—of about 170,000 food packages to specific people imprisoned in Nazi concentration camps and forced labor camps. Most of the packages were sent to the Bergen-Belsen camp, but the Germans distributed only a small number of them (after the camp was liberated, most of the food packages were found by British troops in the camp's storerooms). Storch was also engaged in Raoul Wallenberg's mission in Hungary as well as the rescue of twenty-five thousand concentration camp prisoners, including eleven thousand Jews. The prisoners were transported to Sweden in the final weeks of the war in special white buses

bearing the Red Cross symbol (the initiative was led by Count Folke Bernadotte, vice president of the Swedish Red Cross).

7. Józef Gitler-Barski, a prisoner at the Bergen-Belsen camp, wrote in a diary he kept while he was there that Jakub Grand, a Mexican, died January 27, 1945 (J. Gitler-Barski, *"Aufenthaltslager* Bergen-Belsen: Dziennik Więźnia," *Jewish Historical Institute Bulletin* 95, no. 3 [1975]). His official first and last name—Jacob Granat—appears on the bureaucratic list known as "Weiss's List," which contains the names of all the prisoners in Bergen-Belsen in 1944. The diary kept by Gitler-Barski, who was in the same barrack as Leon and Henryk Schönker, is an important supplement to this chapter. The same people and themes appear here (for example, the packages from the Red Cross, the *Tramwaj* spoken newspaper, scenes from the prisoners' everyday life, etc.).

8. SS-Hauptsturmführer Josef Kramer (1906–1945) was a war criminal. He served as adjutant to Rudolf Höss, commandant of the Auschwitz concentration camp (until November 1940), and then head of the Dachau concentration camp and commandant of the Natzweiler camp. From May 8 to November 25, 1944, he was the commandant of Auschwitz-Birkenau. From December 1944 he was the commandant of the Bergen-Belsen camp, until its liberation on April 15, 1945. That same year he was sentenced to death by a British military court.

TRÖBITZ

I HAD ONE GREAT DESIRE throughout the war: to live. I tried not to let myself consider any other outcome. I never doubted that life was still worth living, even in such inhumane conditions. I wanted to live, regardless of the circumstances in which I found myself.

But on the first day of our evacuation from Bergen-Belsen, I experienced a spiritual crisis. Something broke inside me. Up until then I'd believed life to be such a precious treasure that it was impossible to measure its value. But it became clear to me that there was a limit to life's value within each person. I felt myself swiftly approaching this limit. I started to feel afraid that I, too, could face the question of whether life was worth living.

I looked around. It was very dark inside our train car. There were narrow windows on two walls that gave a bit of light, but not enough to illuminate the entire train car. Everyone was lying on the floor, pressed close to each other. Nobody spoke. The children weren't even crying. My grandfather's wife, Regina, the oldest person in the car, had become indifferent to what was happening around her. She stared endlessly at the ceiling, and the expression on her face, which resembled a mask, never changed.

Arie was moaning. I moved close to him and tried to talk to him, but he didn't answer. My mother put a wet compress on his forehead. Someone had given her a shirt to use for this. Arie mumbled something from time to time, but he remained semiconscious. The steady clatter of the train's wheels soon lulled everyone to sleep. I kept watch over Arie. Something was forcing me to listen to his moans. Perhaps I'd been struck by the awareness that I needed to listen carefully in order for his moans to be engraved in my memory forever.

Late in the evening, the train stopped at a small station. The door of our train car was opened from the outside, and each of us received two slices of bread and some hot, rather thick soup—a real treasure for us, since we hadn't put anything hot in our mouths for several days. We felt that someone was trying to keep us alive.

My father said this to Regina to comfort her, but she rebuffed him skeptically that even if someone cared about our survival, the chances that we'd survive were very slim. Someone else remarked that the soup didn't prove anything, for the Germans, with their pedantic bureaucracy, could also be transporting us to the gas chambers. Someone accused him of being a pessimist, but he replied that if you look at things realistically, you can't help being a pessimist.

After the soup and bread, everyone was slightly invigorated. The train started moving again, and conversations could be heard on every side, even some laughter.

Night fell and everything was quiet again. Everyone fell asleep, including me. I woke up a few times because Arie was shouting, "Mama! Mama!" My mother comforted him.

In the morning I woke up; I could sense that the train wasn't moving. There was a gray light in the car. I looked at Arie. He was smiling at me, completely conscious. I was about to say something to him, but he put his finger to his lips and whispered, "Don't wake them, for sleep gives them strength." We lay silently next to each other and looked into each other's eyes. We were both deeply moved.

A few hours earlier, it had seemed to me that Arie was dying. I'd felt tears flowing down my cheeks. He'd clearly understood I was crying because of him, for he wiped my tears away with his hand and kept smiling at me. His smile poured new life energy into me.

Suddenly we heard voices outside. The door slid to the side, and a soldier told us we could get out, but we weren't allowed to walk farther than five meters from the train. Arie, Regina, and a few others stayed in the car. Aunt Lida didn't want to come out, either, but my parents persuaded her very forcefully to come out with us. I wanted to stay with Arie, but he asked me to go outside, for him, and so I climbed out with the others.

My parents and Lusia stood near the freight car with their eyes closed, inhaling the fresh air. Several SS men with rifles were guarding us on both sides of the train. We stood in a field, and there was a light mist rising around us. We felt cold even though each of us was wearing two shirts and a sweater. We were also very hungry. Someone—an optimist—remarked that it was a good sign that hunger had returned to us.

People went between the train cars to relieve themselves. The buckets full of excrement were also dumped out.

A young SS man standing near me, about twenty-two years old, swore loudly: *"Donnerwetter!"* Then he shouted, *"Stinkende Juden!"* (Filthy Jews!)

Almost at the same moment, a woman dropped her walking stick, and my father bent over to pick it up. The German soldier noticed the watch on his wrist and shouted, *"Gib her die Uhr!"* (Give me that watch!) My father hesitated, and this caused him to be kicked several times. He took the watch off and gave it to the SS man while he was still being kicked.

I was standing near my father, trembling from head to toe. I felt terribly debased on his behalf—humiliated that he'd had to follow the German's order and hadn't been able to defend himself against such a scrawny weakling. In normal times, my father could have crushed him with one hand. But now, in the course of two days, my father had been kicked twice. When he'd defended Arie, I'd been very proud of him, but now I felt as if someone had spit in my face.

Then everything was the same as before. People were walking alongside the train or standing and looking around. I thought about the watch—a Longines watch with a large black face. I knew my father loved this watch. It had been a birthday present from my grandfather; the following was engraved on the back of it: "For my dear Leon, from your father," and the date. It was a precious keepsake; it was the last remaining object from our former, better times, and the only proof that those times had ever existed.

We ended up staying there for several hours because the track next to ours, on which trains were traveling in the opposite direction, had been bombed at some point ahead of us. We had to wait because military transports were going along the other track in the same direction as us, and then later they would go on our track. I saw such a transport as it passed us—it had platforms bearing tanks and cannons covered with tarpaulin and cars full of soldiers; it was a long train with two locomotives.

We sat near the tracks and happily inhaled the fresh air. On the other side of the train there was a forest, and the long-forgotten fragrance of trees reached us from it. My father returned to our car and carried Arie to the door.

"How do you feel?" I asked him.

"Much better," he answered, and he raised himself on an elbow. He was extremely emaciated; his skin was hanging on him. He stuck his head out of the train car and looked around with curiosity. I could see that he was suffering, for his face was contorted with pain, and he emitted muffled moans.

Soon news spread that we were still waiting for two military trains. Our *Lagerältester* was summoned to the transport commander, an SS officer, who ordered him to distribute food. Each of us once again received two slices of bread and some hot tea. The food was carried from car to car because many people were now too weak to stand in line.

Finally, the military transports passed us. We returned to our train car, the door was shut, and the train continued onward. We started slicing the turnips we'd received at the beginning of our journey. Everyone received only one thick slice, for we decided to save these remaining scraps of food.

The train stopped again two hours later; after a while it rolled in one direction, then in the other. We had no idea where we were or where we were headed. Some thought the Germans were sending us to be exchanged—others said that perhaps the Germans wanted to exploit the remnants of our strength in a weapons factory. But nobody said any longer that we were traveling to our deaths.

I asked Regina what she thought about it. She told me she didn't know where the others were headed, but she was going to God. She said this with great solemnity and confidence. I also wanted to ask Arie, but I stopped myself because I lacked the courage.

After several hours of moving, stopping, and maneuvering, the train arrived at a station. The doors were opened, and we were allowed to leave the train cars. Once again, we were given some hot soup and a slice of bread. We enjoyed every mouthful. We ate in silence and concentration like people performing a sacred ritual.

At this station, news began to circulate that we were headed to Theresienstadt. Someone had overheard a conversation between the commander of our transport and a railway worker at the station. We weren't very affected by this news because we didn't know if it was good or bad. But those who had been hoping we were going to be exchanged were very disappointed.

The train started moving again, but—to our surprise—we were now going in the opposite direction. The next day we found out that the tracks had been bombed, and we had to take a different, indirect route. In the morning, the train stopped in a forest, and we were allowed to get out. My father put Arie on his back, and we all climbed out of the train car together.

Never before had I realized how much pleasure fresh air can give a person. Arie squinted, and it took him a long time to get used to the daylight. He looked around in amazement as if he were seeing a forest, a train, and people for the first time in his life.

"It's beautiful here," he said.

Before he managed to finish this sentence, I saw people throwing themselves to the ground next to the train. I didn't understand what was happening, but my father shoved me to the ground, shouting, "Airplanes!" Right then a fighter plane with red stars on its wings flew over us very low, shooting.

I rolled down the railway embankment and fell into a hole in the ground. Someone leaped onto me and covered me with his body. A moment later we heard a series of gunshots again that sounded like the rattling of a toy. With a loud drone-like roar from its engine, the plane flew low over us with a second one right behind it.

I was pressed to the ground and couldn't move. It was very uncomfortable, and I was afraid I was going to suffocate. The man lying on top of me began to tremble—clearly from fear, for he was mumbling quietly, "Jesus Christ, *helft mir* (please help me)." We lay like this for a long time, and eventually I felt like I was barely breathing.

Finally, someone next to us shouted, *"Alles vorüber!"* (They're gone!) The German stood up, and then I did, too.

I looked at him while he brushed off the sleeves of his uniform, and I recognized him immediately. It was the same SS man who'd taken my father's watch and kicked him the previous day. He looked at me and, as if to give himself some encouragement, growled, *"Verfluchte Scheiße!"* (Fucking hell!) Expletives were clearly his usual mode of expression, but in moments of danger he shook with fear and called out to God for help.

Until then I had felt humiliation and pain as a result of what I had seen this German do to my father. Now I remembered what my friend Jankiel from Wieliczka had said when a small boy had insulted me. Jankiel told me, "What? You're letting yourself be offended by that little shithead?" I looked scornfully at the SS man who, looking up at the sky, cursed again, and quickly walked away. From that moment on, I felt something like triumph, for this SS man was shaking with fear, and I wasn't.

We barely moved that day. The train stood still for many hours at a time or rolled slowly back and forth. Once again, we each received two slices of bread and some tea. Later we ate turnips and rutabagas, chewing each bite for a very long time, like cattle. Many people fell ill with dysentery. All the train cars stank of excrement. And we were crawling with lice.

Lice had preyed on us in the camp, too, but we'd had enough strength to deal with them there and had often succeeded in defeating them. Here, in the freight cars, lice had completely taken over our bodies and clothing. We all had hundreds of them on us. I could see long rows of them on the seams of my shirt and beneath my collar. Our emaciated bodies were covered in bites. When our train stopped for a longer amount of time, anyone capable of leaving the train cars focused on one thing once he or she was outside—flicking off lice. They were annihilated one by one. They popped when we squeezed them with our fingernails and left a trail of blood—our blood, which they'd sucked out of us. We did this every day, and they kept returning to us in droves. I don't know where they were coming from; after all, they couldn't reproduce so quickly and in such great numbers. Strangely, we grew accustomed to the lice along with everything else, and after a while we didn't even feel them biting us.

My father took care of Arie, and my mother looked after Regina, who had fallen into a state of total apathy. It was impossible to wash ourselves, but my mother wiped Regina with a damp rag. My father did the same for Arie. He seemed to be getting better, but he was still very weak, and walking was out of the question for him. His leg had become inflamed again.

My cousins Menek and Tosia slept all day long, curled up close to their mother. My father told me I should wake them up often, because they might fall asleep and never wake up. Every day Aunt Lida gave her children two sugar cubes each, which she'd saved from the rations in the camp.

On the third day, two people in our train car died. They fell asleep and never woke up. At a small station somewhere, we were ordered to carry their bodies out of the train and lay them on a cart. Dead people were also brought out of other cars. We were so used to corpses at this point that the sight of them made no impression on us at all.

Many people were waiting for a train at this station, mostly soldiers. There were many young boys—nearly children—among them. As they looked at us, their eyes nearly popped out of their heads from fear; they didn't understand who we were. Surrounded by SS guards, terribly emaciated, and dressed in rags—we looked like living corpses that had risen from our graves and would soon return to them.

That day our train continued to move back and forth aimlessly because many tracks had been bombed and were being repaired in a hurry. Once again, we waited for military transports to pass us.

We were promised we would receive some hot soup in the evening, but it turned out the station where we were supposed to receive it had been bombed, and a fire had broken out. Despite this, efforts were still being made to keep us alive—we were each given a very thin slice of bread and a tiny portion of fruit preserves. It was clear we were still being viewed as valuable merchandise that could serve the German regime in some way.

We asked ourselves many questions: At the camp in Theresienstadt, where we were headed, were they finally going to exchange us? Was there perhaps a meeting point and would we be handed over to the Red Cross? Was there, after all, someone out in the world, somewhere, who took pity on us?

At this station we noticed that, in addition to the fire, something else was happening, for the SS men from our convoy were becoming very agitated. It seemed as if they had received some important news from the approaching front. But we didn't know what was going on.

The next morning, our train entered a large station. The car doors were opened, and a strange sight met our eyes. There were several platforms, all of which were crowded with people despite the early hour. Almost everyone had a rucksack or some kind of bundle. Some were carrying cardboard boxes with string tied around them or old, shabby suitcases. Everyone was dressed in ragged clothing and looked terrified, as if something unfortunate had just happened to them or as if they were running away from something terrible. A train pulled up to one of the platforms; everyone swarmed into it like locusts.

There was no order or discipline whatsoever. Everyone was fighting to board the train as if their lives depended on it. They forced their way into it, but only a few managed to get inside because the train was already full when it arrived. We could see through the windows that there was no space in it, at all. Nobody paid any attention to women or children. Shrieks and curses could be heard. A few minutes later, the train started moving in the direction we had just come from. A crowd of disappointed people remained on the platform.

There were some German soldiers standing on one of the platforms. They were smoking and barely speaking to each other. They seemed deeply immersed in their thoughts. One of the soldiers, who was clearly drunk because he was staggering and barely keeping his balance, started singing the German national anthem in a loud, hoarse, drunken voice: *"Deutschland, Deutschland über alles . . ."* The others standing with him began to laugh, but then they grabbed the drunk soldier and covered his mouth.

We stared in amazement. And so these were the *Übermenschen* who wanted to conquer all of Europe? A train slowly rolled up to their platform, this time nearly empty, but with soldiers leaning out the windows. It was clearly a military transport. All the soldiers boarded the train, and it started moving in the same direction in which we were headed.

After a while, another passenger train arrived at the station, and the crowd instantly lunged at it. People were shoving each other in order to board the train, knocking each other down, even trampling those who were lying on the ground. Everyone fought viciously to get closer to the train's doors. Children and packages were handed through the windows. Some people shoved others off the steps of a train car and took their places. An old woman fainted, but nobody cared, and she was nearly trampled.

The train departed, leaving even more people on the platform than before because new people were constantly arriving. We had never seen anything like this. We watched the panic-stricken people fighting each other for places on the train. We didn't feel sorry for them, but neither did their unhappiness fill us with joy. On the contrary—we saw them as poor, pathetic people, and we felt superior to them.

When things calmed down a bit on the platforms, the SS men from the convoy started giving us orders. The dead were carried out of the cars, and our buckets were filled with water. The train, however, didn't move. The car doors were open, but we weren't allowed to leave.

At one point we noticed an old man in a railway worker's uniform emerge from the station's building and walk quickly toward our train. Our convoy's commander met him halfway. He hurriedly straightened his hat that had a skull on it, and it was clear from how fast he was walking that he was feeling anxious. He looked similar to the skull on his hat, which is why we nicknamed him Totenköpfchen (Skull). They met close to our train car and began a lively argument.

We understood that the railway worker was the station master, and he was trying to explain why there was no soup here for us. He explained that the town had been bombed, and it hadn't been possible to prepare any soup; the town's residents themselves had nothing to eat today. Our commander shouted at him and refused to accept any excuses. He went up so close to the railway worker that their noses almost touched and shouted in his face: *"Ich habe einen Befehl diese Leute lebendig ans Ziel zu bringen und nicht tot!"* (I've been ordered to deliver these people alive, not dead!)

The railway worker's face turned red, and he began to tremble. Totenköpfchen hissed at him: *"Ich mache Sie dafür persönlich verantwortlich, Herr Bahnvorsteher!"* (I'll make you personally responsible for this, Station Master!)

Our train was switched to a side track, and then we were allowed to leave the cars. We waited for about two hours and then some carts with pots full of hot, steaming soup were brought onto the platform. The soup was rather thin, but there were potatoes floating in it and even small pieces of meat. I remember it perfectly; I'll never forget, for the rest of my life, the taste of that soup. It strengthened us not only physically but also spiritually.

I noticed that more people were now clambering out of the train cars, and it was becoming crowded on the narrow platform next to our train. The Germans were having trouble keeping an eye on us; they were shouting and waving their rifles in the air. The only people allowed to go to the station were those who were ordered to bring buckets of drinking water, and this was only if they were accompanied by SS men.

People in our train car commented on what the commander of our convoy had said about having orders to deliver us to our destination alive. Some claimed this was irrefutable proof that we were still of some value to the Germans. Others were of the opinion that what Totenköpfchen had said only revealed that the Germans had some plans for us, but it was impossible to know what they were.

An emaciated human skeleton lying next to a wall of the car raised himself up on one elbow and slowly said, drawing out every word, that in his case, Totenköpfchen wouldn't be able to carry out his order since he wasn't going to arrive alive. After saying this he burst into derisive laughter, as if he were playing a prank on someone with his imminent death. Later, I sometimes talked with my father about this man. Indeed, he died that very day.

At about the same hour as the man's death, his friend, who was traveling in another train car but often came to visit us while the train was stopped, snuck under the cars, and slipped away into the forest; perhaps he wanted to reach a village and beg for food. On the way back, he encountered some SS men from our convoy in the forest. They ordered him to stop, but he ran away between the trees. They shot him. Someone remarked that these two friends had arranged to go together into the afterlife.

Our stops were getting longer. We traveled mostly at night, and during the day we stopped for many hours at a time. Large formations of English and American bomber planes were flying high overhead. We were now able to recognize these Boeing B-29 Superfortresses majestically gliding across the sky, leaving tails of long white clouds behind them.

On the fourth day we weren't given any food. We ate only turnips and raw carrots that were thrown into the train cars at a station. I noticed that fewer people were getting out of the train cars during our stops, and those who did were acting and moving very strangely, as if overcome by lethargy. The children, like me, were the strongest among us, relatively. The Germans from the convoy were also becoming more nervous and agitated. They erupted with shouts and expletives at the slightest provocation.

Arie slept constantly, and I had to keep waking him up. He was calm, but his leg hurt, and he raved deliriously at night. His leg had become much more swollen; the inflammation was getting worse. Nearly all day long, I was busy keeping Arie, Menek, and Tosia awake. Lusia was in the best condition of all of us. My mother never took her eyes off her. She spoke to her constantly in a soft voice. She told her we would soon arrive at someone's house, and we would be given very good food there. Lusia was now seven years old. She often pointed at people who were lying down and asked me if they were alive.

That night I woke up because the train had stopped. It was a very clear night, and a bit of moonlight was coming into our train car through the small windows. I looked around. Everyone was asleep, lying very close to each other. It was cold. Thankfully there were some blankets in the train car. I was about to cover my head with the blanket when I heard a rustling sound near the wall. I looked in that direction and was astounded by what I saw.

A married couple was sitting there. The man was holding a knife and using it to cut thick slices of smoked bacon, which he was balancing on his knees. It was a large piece of meat, at least two kilograms. He gave his wife one slice and began to eat a second one. Pretending to be asleep, I watched them from beneath my half-closed eyelids. I wondered if I should go up to them and ask for a slice of meat. I gave up on this idea because I was afraid of waking other people, and I didn't know what would happen then. It was obvious they were eating at night because they wanted to hide it from us.

I told my father about it the next morning, during one of our stops. He listened to me silently and then told me not to talk about it, so that their meat wouldn't be confiscated by the SS men.

"That bacon belongs to them," my father said. "And it's nobody's business how they got it."

Throughout the entire fifth day our train stood in a firebreak in a forest because the tracks both in front of us and behind us were damaged. Our food ration for the whole day was two slices of bread and tea. That day we also ran out of turnips and carrots. Some people asked if they could be allowed to go into the forest or to a village, but the Germans refused. They weren't hungry because they'd brought enough food for themselves. They were completely indifferent to our starvation and slow, agonizing deaths. Every morning they repeated to us that anyone who wandered too far from the train would be killed.

We lay in the train cars almost all day. We heard bombs exploding nearby several times. Sometimes fighter planes flew over us, too, but they didn't shoot at us. I slept less than the others because I felt that I needed to pay careful attention to Arie, who often asked me for water. That day I woke Menek and Tosia less often because it made no difference; they immediately fell asleep again. Aunt Lida slept almost all the time.

It was a lovely spring day. At midday I left the train car to get some fresh air. The forest was only a few meters from our train. The thick, mossy undergrowth looked like a magic carpet. I had a strong desire to lie down on this moss and look at the treetops. Suddenly someone placed a hand on my shoulder. It was

Poldek Fiszelberg, Menek's cousin. He and his family had been with us at the camp in Bergen-Belsen, and we had become friends. They also possessed foreign papers of some kind. Now they were traveling on the same train but several cars away from ours.

Poldek was about a year older than me. He was even thinner than I was but very lively; he always had something to say. He suggested we try to find some food together by sneaking into the forest and going to one of the nearby villages. He heard the SS men say the train would definitely stay here until the following evening, maybe even longer, until the tracks were repaired. Poldek was from Katowice and so he spoke German as perfectly as anyone from Germany. He eavesdropped on the conversations between the SS men in our convoy all day long. He told me that if we didn't try to find some food, our parents would starve to death.

I told him that this plan was very dangerous and we could both die, just like the man who had been shot the day before. But Poldek tried to convince me that this was our only chance to save our lives and our parents' lives. His parents were already so weak they couldn't leave the train car.

"Why don't you go alone?" I asked him.

"Because I'll have to watch out for the Germans, and two pairs of eyes are better than one," he answered calmly.

He was convinced we would succeed in our mission if we went together. He had heard that some people from our transport had already snuck off to villages and managed to bring back some food.

"But maybe they had to pay for this food in some way, for example with diamonds or gold. What do we have to exchange for food? Nothing but our filthy trousers," I objected.

"Don't be afraid," answered Poldek. "As soon as we're in a village, we'll think of something."

I couldn't make up my mind. I told him I had to think about it and would give him an answer the following morning.

I thought about it all day, carefully considering our situation. Everyone was saying the front must be very close now, since our train was going back and forth. And the previous day it had been clear at the train station that people were fleeing in panic, as if danger were close by. So why should I risk my life?

On the other hand, I imagined myself bringing back bread and butter, just like I did in the Tarnów ghetto. Why shouldn't I take a risk now, too? My mother was also climbing out of the train car less often. Should I really not take the chance to help her? And perhaps if I managed to bring a few slices of bread, they would give some strength to Arie, who was in the worst condition of us all. And what about me? I was still getting by somehow, but I was terribly hungry. The hunger pains were becoming increasingly difficult to bear.

I kept returning to these same thoughts. It occurred to me that I shouldn't make a decision about this by myself, for my life didn't belong only to me, but also to my parents. I imagined how deep their despair would be if something bad happened to me. Late at night, hungry, cold, and bitten by lice, I decided I couldn't do it. "If Poldek wants to do it, he can go alone or find someone else to go with him," I thought. Then I curled up next to my father like a cat.

The next morning Poldek came and brought some news. Nearly all the SS men from the convoy were sleeping in a nearby village and hadn't come back yet. We were being guarded by only two SS men on each side of the train. When they looked away, it would be easy to sneak into the forest. The day before, Poldek had heard one German telling another where the villages were located.

"We have to go straight toward that hill covered in trees, and from there we'll be able to see the edge of the forest. Right beyond it is one village, and to the right of it is the other village. The German said it takes twenty-five or thirty minutes to walk there through the forest. It's an ideal opportunity for us. What do you say?" he asked me urgently.

I opened my mouth to say I had decided not to go, but at that moment I heard my own voice say: "OK, let's go!" I was very surprised to hear myself say this—it came out spontaneously, against my will.

Poldek joyfully patted me on the shoulder and said, "I knew you weren't a coward." But seeing my bewilderment, he looked me in the eyes and asked me what was wrong.

"I'm not so sure I'm not a coward," I replied.

He looked at me solemnly. "Don't be afraid. Up there, above us, there's someone who'll watch over us."

It was strange, but I had a similar feeling at that moment.

We decided not to waste any time and to sneak away from the transport right away. Many people were wandering around and sitting on rocks in front of the train, on the side where the car doors were open. It was very easy to reach the forest from that side of the train, but we had to go the other way.

We returned to our train cars and told our parents we were going to look at the locomotive. Then we met again, slid beneath the train, and pressed ourselves to the ground. Two SS men were standing and talking to each other a few meters from us.

We lay there for a while, but they didn't move. Poldek gave me a signal to crawl back out, but at that very moment, the SS men started walking away from us. I slid out from under the train and crawled toward the forest on my elbows and knees, never letting the Germans out of my sight. Soon I was among the trees. My heart was hammering inside me, not from the effort but from excitement. Poldek waited a moment and then did the same. There was silence all around us. We started walking slowly toward the hill.

My senses were extremely heightened; the smell of the forest intoxicated me. Soon, panting heavily, we reached the top of the hill, which turned out to be higher than we'd guessed from the train. We headed down the other side and could see the spot off in the distance where the forest ended. We quietly broke some branches and leaned them against trees as signs because we were afraid we might get lost on the way back. The forest became denser. We walked slowly and in complete silence, stepping carefully so our footsteps wouldn't be audible. We constantly looked around. Sometimes we stood still and gazed at the trees around us. We didn't know their names, for we hadn't had any opportunity to learn them, but we admired their beauty.

The forest seemed very majestic; there was harmony, order, and peace here. It was hard for me to believe we now found ourselves in the midst of this wealth of light, shade, and greenery. I began to listen carefully to the forest. It seemed to me that the trees were talking to each other.

"You're walking with your head in the clouds!" Poldek scolded me. "Get a grip on yourself! We're not going for a stroll." He was walking in front of me as stealthily as a cat and kept turning around to urge me onward.

Suddenly he squeezed my arm. We both stopped abruptly. We could hear voices and laughter ahead of us. We threw ourselves to the ground and pressed our heads against the moss. We waited until the voices died away. We started crawling forward cautiously. About a dozen meters onward, we discovered that we were lying in front of a well-camouflaged military vehicle with massive wheels and thick tires. It was a large trailer that could be attached to another vehicle. Everything was quiet.

We were overcome by curiosity and crawled under the net that was camouflaging the trailer. The undergrowth in this part of the forest was so abundant that we were completely submerged in it. We stopped crawling when we reached the side of the trailer. It had two windows. Poldek kneeled and propped himself on his elbows. He signaled to me to stand on his back. Slowly stretching myself upward, I was able to reach the window.

What I saw inside took my breath away—across from me, along the entire inner wall of the trailer, there were pieces of meat hanging on hooks. Some were raw, others were smoked. On the right-hand side, there was a stove, and in the middle of the trailer there was a long table and two stools. Some meat and sliced vegetables were lying on the table. Under the hooks with meat on them hung net bags containing loaves of bread. I couldn't see any people. I could easily enter through the window, take a piece of meat or some loaves of bread, and hand them through the window to Poldek. I even selected the best piece of meat in my mind—the one that would be the easiest to carry.

I climbed off Poldek's back and told him in a whisper what I had seen inside the trailer and that I would hand these treasures to him. He nodded in agreement, and I climbed onto his back again. I didn't think about how risky this was; I focused on carrying out the task quickly and successfully. I carefully climbed up to the window. I was just about to put my leg on the windowsill when I realized it had gone numb. I tried again, but I lost my balance and fell onto Poldek. We tumbled to the ground. This saved us, for at that very moment two German soldiers appeared near the table, talking to each other in a lively way. While falling, I caught a glimpse of them, but they didn't see me. They had obviously been sitting quietly on the other side of the trailer.

We were so frightened that we lay motionless for several minutes with our noses pressed to the ground. Voices and laughter reached us from inside the trailer. We crawled carefully from under the net and stood up only when we were far from the trailer, shielded by trees. Sneaking from tree to tree, we went around this mobile military kitchen in a large semicircle. We were afraid of running across the military unit it belonged to. But the forest around us was empty, and we soon found ourselves at the edge of it. Cultivated fields stretched in front of us. Some looked as if they had just been plowed. Not far from us there were some small houses with red roofs.

We chose one of the farms, shook the dirt and moss off our clothes, and walked toward it through the fields. We tried to act normal, as if we were German boys, but we didn't pass anyone on the way. Poldek ordered me not to speak under any circumstances, for even one word from me could reveal we weren't German.

We entered the garden in front of the house and knocked on the door. After a while, a young, sturdy woman appeared on the threshold holding a small child. She looked at us and asked who we were. Poldek began to act very abashed and awkward; he didn't say anything and kept shifting from one foot to the other. I knew he was pretending, because he'd never acted that way before. Suddenly someone called out from inside the house. The woman turned and shouted that she was coming, and she gestured to us to follow her.

She led us to a large kitchen where an old man was sitting. He was clearly the one who had called her. He looked surprised when he saw us and gave the woman a questioning glance. She was looking at us. Only now did Poldek explain that we had been evacuated from Hannover and that our train was parked not far from here. We were very hungry and were looking for something to eat. The woman looked at us kindheartedly and then asked me why I was so frightened. Poldek saved me from this difficult situation by explaining I had experienced a shock during the bombing and hadn't recovered from it yet.

We sat down at the table and the woman gave each of us a large bowl of hot soup and a slice of fresh black bread. While setting the bowl of soup in front of me, the woman stroked my head. Oh, that soup! I lack the words to describe how delightful it was. We'd forgotten that something like this even existed. The old man and the woman sat across from us and watched us eat. After a while the man said he'd heard that Hannover had been bombed, but he didn't know people were starving there. Overcome with emotion, he exclaimed, *"Das ist eine Schweinerei!"* (It's an abomination!)

When we finished eating, the woman asked us if we wanted some more. We both immediately nodded. Our bowls were filled again. We were in heaven! This time we tried to eat more slowly and remember our manners, but we were unable to hide our voracious appetites. After we'd finished, Poldek thanked the woman profusely, and we got up from the table. For the first time in a very long while, I felt wonderfully satiated. I was unable to think about anything else. Poldek displayed more presence of mind. He asked whether we could have some more food for our parents, who were in the train.

The woman said there were potatoes in the field, and she told us we could fill our pockets with them. She also gave us some matches so we could light a fire and bake them. I felt grateful to these people. I knew that if they'd known who we really were, they probably would have treated us differently, but this didn't change the way I felt about them.

We went to the field the woman had indicated, where two women were working. Three sacks of potatoes were lying off to the side. I looked at them as if hypnotized. Finding half a potato in my soup had made me feel incredibly lucky, and here in front of us—sacks full of them! Poldek approached one of the women and told her we'd been given permission from the farmer's wife to take a few potatoes. She looked at us suspiciously, but then she smiled and said, *"Bitte sehr,"* pointing to one of the sacks. The farmer's wife was standing in the doorway and had waved at the women to let them know it was fine.

The women returned to their work in the field, and we filled our pockets with potatoes. Each potato was a precious treasure, but unfortunately we couldn't fit very many of them in our pockets. I was so excited that I forgot I wasn't allowed to say anything and shouted, "Poldek, put them under your shirt!" Both women ran up to us, and one of them called out in Polish, in an astonished voice, "My God! Are you Polish?"

They were so happy they almost started kissing us. They turned out to be Polish women who had been sent to Germany for forced labor. They told us to take another half a sack of potatoes in addition to what we had in our pockets. They partially emptied one of the sacks and helped Poldek put it on his back. But he wobbled and fell to the ground. They wanted to take more potatoes out of the sack so it would be lighter, but I told them I'd try to carry it. Soon it was on my back. It was very heavy, but I didn't fall. Poldek held me up from behind.

We effusively said goodbye to the Polish women. One of them said, "May God guide you," and the other added, "and watch over you." They both made the sign of the cross in the air behind us and waved, just as people bid farewell to their loved ones. They had tears in their eyes.

We walked slowly toward the forest. We were overflowing with joy and pride. Now everything depended on whether we would manage to carry the sack to the train. I turned out to have more strength left in me than Poldek did, so I didn't have to switch with him. I was surprised to discover I had so much strength. But Poldek helped me a lot by supporting the sack from behind. We often stopped to rest. After a while, the sack started to feel heavier and our pace slowed. My back ached all over; I clenched my teeth and tried not to think about the pain.

We couldn't be as careful as before, because it was difficult to carry the heavy sack and look around at the same time. We were both panting from the exertion. Suddenly we heard a loud shout: *"Halt! Hände hoch!"*

I felt my heart stop beating. The sack of potatoes fell to the ground; I went numb with fear. We stood there with our hands raised, unable to see anyone in front of us. Two figures in uniform emerged from behind some trees with rifles pointed at us. They approached us cautiously as if we posed some kind of threat to them. They were SS men from our convoy. They asked us what was in the sack. Poldek told them it was potatoes. They looked inside and glared at us.

"Don't you know that stealing is forbidden?"

"We didn't steal the potatoes. They were given to us at the farm in the village," Poldek stated very calmly.

"Why did they give them to you?" asked one of the SS men curiously.

"They felt sorry for us."

"Why do you speak German so well?"

Poldek replied that he was from Katowice, and German was his native language.

"And did you have permission to leave the transport?" asked the SS man in a menacing tone of voice.

"No," said Poldek uneasily, and he immediately added, "But we were very hungry."

After thinking for a moment, the SS man sent the other one to inform the commander and ordered us to sit on the ground. I had a feeling that if they didn't shoot us on the spot, it meant we were destined to live.

Soon the SS man returned and announced that the commander was still in the village, and nobody knew when he was going to come back.

"What are we going to do with them?" asked the first one.

I sensed that our fates were in the balance—life or death. At that moment Poldek whispered to me: "Cry!" I started pretending to cry because I was too scared to really cry. Poldek also started wailing.

The SS men stood in front of us, seeming to relish our crying, for they started grinning at each other. Finally, the first one, who was of a higher rank, shouted, *"Verschwindet!"* (Get out of here!) He didn't have to tell us twice. We jumped up and were about to run, when the SS man added: *"Zusammen mit dem Sack!"* (With the sack!) We grabbed our treasure and started running away with it, dragging it behind us. I looked back, terrified. The SS men were watching us and laughing as if they had played a prank on someone.

We dragged the sack along the ground for about fifty meters and then stood there, breathing heavily. We rested for a while, and Poldek helped me put it on my back again. Now it seemed lighter to me. Poldek held it up from behind, and I could hear him breathing hard from the effort.

"I was praying the whole time," he said.

"I didn't hear anything."

"I was praying in my soul, while on the outside I was pretending to cry."

"Why didn't you really cry?" I asked him out of curiosity.

"Because when you're face-to-face with death you don't cry anymore."

Soon we were close to the train. Two SS men were lighting cigarettes about twenty meters from us. Then they started walking in our direction. We pressed ourselves to the ground, holding the sack between us. Now I began to pray in my soul. They passed us and moved farther away.

We slipped under the train and emerged on the other side. Nobody had noticed us, and we tried to hide our excitement. Not far from our train car, we bumped into my father. He reached his arms out to me joyfully and exclaimed, "Where were you for so long? I couldn't find you anywhere!"

I dropped the sack in front of him and opened it. My father was dumbstruck. We told him where we had gotten the potatoes and what had happened to us on the way. Then we divided them up. My father took off his shirt and poured half the potatoes into it. There were too many and it was impossible to make a bundle, so he put a few potatoes in the pockets of his trousers and jacket. He tied up the rest of the potatoes in his shirt. We gave Poldek half the potatoes in the sack, and he hurried off to his train car with them. Our pockets were also loaded with potatoes. We felt happy and rich.

Luck was on our side that day. My father found a piece of rusty tin next to the train tracks. It turned out to be part of an old locomotive headlight. My father used a nail and a rock to punch some holes through it and told us it was going to be both a potato grater and a stove. We peeled a few potatoes, and my father grated them into two bowls full of water. Then he lit a fire under the piece of tin, and soon we had two bowls of thick potato soup. We took turns eating from them. There weren't many people left in our train car apart from our family. Several had died, and some had switched to other cars to join their families or friends.

From that day on, my father cooked potato soup every day while the train was stopped, and I helped him make it. Everyone in our car ate it, and there were many days when it was our only meal. The train barely moved during the day. All train travel in that region had come to a standstill because of the constant bombing of tracks and stations. Squadrons of bombers and fighter planes flew over us, but our train was never attacked. Chaos and confusion were increasing at the stations. There were no longer any meals waiting for us. The potatoes Poldek and I had brought back from the farmer's house saved our lives.

Unfortunately, Arie got a high fever again and lost consciousness for many hours at a time. He was visited by the doctor who had been with us at the camp and had taken care of Arie there. He examined him and said the phlegmon had flared up again and there was nothing to be done about it. All we could do was wait until we arrived somewhere. There was no medicine here to cure Arie. We had to keep putting wet compresses on his forehead and all over his body. It didn't help, however; the fever didn't subside.

At night my parents took turns watching over Arie. They changed his compresses and stroked his head, but Arie didn't regain consciousness. It was clear he was in extreme pain. For the next few days, we were occupied solely with taking care of Arie and making potato soup.

Our train went back and forth, unable to escape the Allied forces. The Russians were approaching from one side, and the American and English armies from the other. We were caught in the middle and were waiting for liberation, which never came.

We kept switching directions and traveling past the same train stations and towns over and over again. Someone remarked that our train was like a ghost—it kept disappearing and reappearing. Sometimes the train waited for military units to pass. Some stations we'd passed through not long before were now completely destroyed by bombs. We barely received any food. I don't know how people were staying alive. An increasing number of people were dying. Many lay in the same spot all day, feverish and lethargic. We didn't know (or perhaps I was the only one who didn't know) that typhus had broken out in the train cars.

One night, more than ten days after we had evacuated Bergen-Belsen, the train stopped. The doors were opened. It was clear that a long stop was expected. Arie regained consciousness and started to say something. My father lit a match. I went close to Arie because he called my name. Suffering was no longer visible on his face. He took my hand and squeezed it firmly. I put my ear to his mouth, but he was silent. My father ran to get the doctor. He examined Arie and then left the train car with my father. I stayed close to Arie, holding his hand. I felt tears flowing down my cheeks.

The doctor told my father that he had to operate on Arie immediately, otherwise he wouldn't live to see the morning. His condition was critical, but an operation could give him a chance at survival.

And so, in the middle of the night, by the light of a candle, the doctor cut open Arie's leg with a pocketknife. Arie lost consciousness right at the beginning. I don't know if he screamed because I plugged my ears and ran out of the train car.

When I returned, I fell asleep immediately. I felt my father cover me with a blanket. I was awoken by shouts. At first, I thought I was still dreaming. I wasn't sure if I had really woken up. It seemed like I had slept for only a moment. I sat up and looked around—early morning light was coming through the open door. And so, I must have slept for several hours. Everyone was asleep in the train car, including Arie. My mother was sleeping next to him with a wet rag in her hand. Lusia was holding a food bowl and sleeping curled up to my mother. My aunt was sleeping with her arms around Menek and Tosia. My grandfather's wife was moaning quietly as if she were in pain or having a nightmare.

Someone outside the train shouted: "They're leaving! They're leaving!"

I scrambled out of the train with the blanket wrapped around me. Several people were standing there and pointing into the distance. I looked in that direction and saw the SS men from our convoy. They were walking along the track in single file and were already quite far from our train. They became smaller and smaller until they disappeared in the morning mist.

Suddenly we heard a whistling sound above us, followed immediately by a second one, then a third and a fourth. Then there was silence. We stood there, bewildered. Somewhere in the distance we could hear echoes that sounded like thunder.

"What is it?" I asked someone, frightened.

"Artillery," he answered, gazing up at the sky.

Then the whistling sounds came again, and we could hear rumbling very far away.

"Those are explosions," the man standing next to me explained. "They've been rumbling for several hours now. Haven't you heard them?"

More people were coming out of the train. They were rubbing the sleep from their eyes, listening carefully, and looking around. They stood in one place or moved very slowly; some were leaning on each other. They looked like ghosts that had emerged from the forest.

We were alone. I noticed a freight car nearby, parked on tracks parallel to ours. I ran over to it because I thought there might be food in it. The door wasn't closed completely. Half the car was empty, and in the other half, there were boxes piled up to the ceiling. I went up to them. Each box was labeled: *"Munition. Kaliber..."* Terrified, I leaped out of the freight car and told everyone about it.

A group of men gathered, and they started pushing this freight car away from our train. They stopped only when it was very far from us. I helped them push it because I wanted to be useful. I don't know how the men were able to push it at all, since they were now mere skeletons, barely able to stay upright. We walked back slowly, looking up at the sky and listening intently to the whistling of bullets flying past us.

There was a hill next to our train, and someone pointed at it. I raised my head and saw three people on horses. They stood there on the hill, observing the train and us. They were soldiers but in a kind of uniform that was unfamiliar to us. Someone shouted, "Russians!" We stood there in complete silence, unable to move; we stared at these three soldiers as if they were otherworldly apparitions. We didn't feel any joy. There was just the solemnity of the moment and anticipation of what was going to happen next.

They were also completely motionless, staring at us. Then they rode their horses down the hill and approached, looking around carefully. They had machine guns strapped across their backs. They started talking to us, but it was hard to understand them. Someone who knew Russian ran up to them. They asked who we were and if there were any German soldiers in the train.

Those people who still had some strength emerged from the train cars. Some asked the Russians for food. The soldiers opened their small rucksacks and handed out what they had. Our leader asked them for help, pointing to the people who were peering out the doors of the train, too weak to come out. Others crawled out of the train cars like giant lizards.

Then something incredible happened. People stood up straight, each as well as he could, some leaning on each other, and started singing the anthem of the

Zionist movement—"Hatikvah" ("The Hope"). This handful of rescued Jews who were starving, nearly dead, dressed in rags, and barely able to stand, sang this anthem of hope and liberation with deep emotion and solemnity.

I also stood up straight and tried to sing along even though I didn't know the lyrics. The Russians sat on their horses and watched us in amazement.

The majesty of this moment intoxicated me. I felt like I was in heaven. When the song was over, there was total silence. Everyone who had been singing was very excited, but there were also people who were unable to come out of the train cars on their own and watched us with indifferent gazes from a lying position, no longer capable of feeling any kind of emotion.

Then, after consulting with each other briefly, the Russians told us to go to a small town nearby that had just been abandoned by the Germans. We could enter the houses and would certainly find something to eat in them. But we had to wait for permission from their commander, who was somewhere behind them. Then the whole patrol galloped away.

I ran to our train car to tell Arie we were now free. He was lying with his eyes closed. My parents were next to him. I shook him by the shoulder and shouted, "Arie! Arie! The Russians have come!" But he didn't move. My father took my hand. I saw that my mother was crying and Lusia was wiping her tears away.

"Arie's dead," my father said. Only now did I notice that he was crying, too. Such a sudden shift from the greatest happiness to the greatest unhappiness was too much for me, and at first I didn't understand the meaning of my father's words. The news of Arie's death struck me like a blow to my head. I didn't cry. I was so shocked that I couldn't feel anything. I was speechless and had lost my ability to think. My father put his arm around me and held me very close to him. It was only after a while that I began to sob quietly.

This is how Arie Frenkel—my cousin, friend, and brother—died. His death occurred at the very moment we were liberated—on April 20, 1945.

The people outside the train were now making more noise; we could hear occasional and somewhat tentative shouts of joy. But most of the people in the train cars continued to lie in a profound state of apathy.

I don't know how long we had been sitting next to Arie's body, removed from the entire world, when I heard Poldek's voice calling me to come out. I hesitated and looked at my mother.

"Go see Poldek. You can't help Arie anymore," she said.

"Now Arie will be able to help you, instead," added Regina.

"How can he help me?" I asked her, astonished.

"You'll find out when the time comes," she replied from the corner where she was lying.

Poldek called to me again, and I felt I had to go to him because life was out there. In here, there was only death. He told me there was a small town very close by; some people from our train had already gone there and brought back food. It was clear the inhabitants had fled, for the town was completely empty. He suggested we go there together.

The first small, one-story houses were very close. We entered one of them. The door wasn't even closed all the way. We walked slowly through the entrance hall and found the kitchen. On the table there were still plates with scraps of food on them and a pot of coffee. Everything indicated that the inhabitants of this house had left in a hurry. Everything was in disarray. Wardrobes were hanging open, and the floor was scattered with objects, which showed that the people living here hadn't even had time to pack their belongings.

We went back to the kitchen and started looking for food. Poldek opened some little doors on two cupboards, and I looked around for a pantry. I noticed a large clay pot on a table by the window that was full of melted, congealed lard with dark brown bits of pork rind floating in it. I plunged my hands into the lard and brought them to my mouth. Poldek slapped my hand very hard. "Are you crazy?" he yelled. I looked at him, confused. "If you put that lard in your mouth, you'll die!" he said emphatically.

He explained to me that we couldn't eat large amounts of lard at once and that we had to accustom ourselves to it very slowly because our bodies were too weak to digest it. He had heard the doctor warning people about it. Seeing that I wasn't moving, he pulled me away from the pot of lard and helped me wipe off my hands with a cloth. We found pots of soup, potatoes, and carrots on the stove. We ate these cold. It was our first feast after regaining our freedom.

That day I learned to ride a bicycle, and it made me feel very proud. We found two bicycles at the house. Poldek got on one of them and began to ride.

Seeing me standing there uncertainly, he asked, "What's wrong with you? Why aren't you riding?" He helped me position myself on the bike's seat and told me to start pedaling. He ran next to me, holding my bike, while I pedaled and tried to keep my balance. After a few practice sessions, he let me go. I fell but wasn't hurt. I fell a few more times, but finally I was able to ride by myself. It was so enjoyable that it was hard for me to part with this bike.

On our way back to the train, we passed many people from our transport. When we reached the train, we discovered it was now almost empty. Soviet soldiers were standing next to it, giving orders. The dead had to be laid on the ground near the train. Several bodies were already lying next to the tracks, and Arie was there, among them. He was almost naked because he had been undressed during the operation. We were allowed to go to the town now, but my father didn't want to leave Arie's body; he was given permission to bury him next to the train tracks. Someone brought two shovels, and a grave was dug for Arie.

It turned out that the town was called Tröbitz, and it was close to Dresden.[1] Nearly all the residents of Tröbitz had fled as the front approached, and on the day we arrived, none of them could be seen in the streets. Many houses were already occupied by our people. After a short search, we found a free house that had several bedrooms and a garden. Aunt Lida and her children were with us.

In the house we found bread, margarine, fruit compote, and jam. I was still feeling full and only drank a bit of compote; I noticed that everyone was eating very little. Our bodies had become unaccustomed to food. Some of us started feeling unwell. My father said it was best for us to eat often and in very small amounts. My mother made tea for everyone, and it helped us feel better.

Then we started bathing ourselves and changing our clothes. Everything we were wearing was thrown away, and we took new clothing from the wardrobes. The house had a bathroom with a bathtub in it, and there was also a large tub for washing clothes. We took turns going into the bathroom to scrub ourselves with a thick brush. At first we enjoyed the hot water, but later our bodies turned red and began to hurt. It was hard to get completely clean because the dirt was deeply embedded in us. Later we lay on the beds and sofas, feeling completely exhausted. There were enough beds for all of us; clearly a large family had lived here.

After some time, my father and I went to inspect the entire house. In addition to the jars in the kitchen, we found a whole cupboard full of canned food. There were crackers and biscuits in it, too. In the cellar we found several large bottles of pure grain alcohol with vanilla beans in it. My father sniffed it but didn't try it. He never drank alcohol. We also found a pantry in which there was a piece of smoked meat, some coffee, and lots of raw vegetables.

We started dividing up the clothes we had taken from the wardrobes, but nobody wanted to get out of bed. I sat with my father at the kitchen table and drank some hot coffee with him. Everyone else was sleeping. It was early afternoon. I told my father I was going to sleep, too. I didn't feel hungry, but I was incredibly weak and tired. My father also looked exhausted, but I could tell he wanted to watch over us because he said he would keep sitting in the kitchen for a while. I got up from my chair, but at that moment the door opened.

A Soviet soldier was standing on the threshold; he swiftly glanced around the whole room. He marched up to my father and asked, *"Kak tvoya familiya?"* (What's your name?) My father didn't understand the question and thought the Russian soldier was asking where his family was, so he gestured toward the room where my mother and Lusia were sleeping. The soldier repeated his question, and my father repeated the answer. Suddenly the soldier pulled out a pistol with a long barrel. The expression on his face became threatening.

"*Kak tvoya familiya?*"

He aimed the pistol at my father. Seeing that my terrified father wasn't reacting, he hissed, "*Ya tebya zastrelyu!*" (I'm going to shoot you!)

I noticed his eyes were bloodshot; he was obviously drunk. I shouted in Polish, "We're Jews from Poland!"

The Russian looked at me in surprise, and then at my father. I saw that he understood.

"*Zhidy?*" (You're Jews?) he asked.

My father gave him a broad smile, which the Russian interpreted as confirmation. He went up to my father, shook his hand, and slapped him on the shoulder. Then he checked the rooms without saying a word and put the pistol back in its holster. Only now was it clear to him that my father hadn't understood his question. He went up to my father and, pointing at himself, said his last name, and then, pointing at my father, asked, "*A ty?* (And you?)"

My father introduced himself and added, "And my family is over there." He pointed to the bedrooms. Then he described how we'd been liberated that morning from a transport of people evacuated from the Bergen-Belsen concentration camp.

I don't know how much this soldier understood, but he nodded good-naturedly and repeated in a reassuring tone of voice, "*Khorosho . . . khorosho*," as if he wished to placate my father after having just threatened him with a pistol.

Then he asked, "*Vodka est?*"

"Yes!" my father exclaimed triumphantly, and he sent me to the cellar to get a bottle. After my father filled a shot glass for him, the soldier sniffed it and then put a bit on his tongue to taste it, but didn't drink any. He stood up and took a tumbler out of the cupboard. He filled it to the brim with the alcohol, put it in front of himself, and sat down at the table with a solemn expression on his face as if he were carrying out a religious ritual.

Only now did I notice he was carrying a small bundle on his back. He took an onion out of it; then he took a penknife out of his pocket and used it to peel the onion and slice it. We watched him in silence, not interrupting him. He ate a slice of onion and drank some alcohol. Then he ate another slice of onion and drank a bit more of the alcohol. It was clear he was delighted, and each of his movements testified to the fact that he often conducted this ceremony. Soon he had eaten the onion and drunk the entire glass of alcohol. He wiped his mouth with his hand and said to my father, greatly satisfied, "*Spasibo . . . ochen' khorosho.*" Then he stood up and shook our hands in farewell. My father wanted to give him the bottle, but he refused, explaining that he was on duty.

That was our first meeting with this Russian soldier. Later he visited us almost every day and, repeating the same ritual, solemnly drank one bottle of alcohol after another. Each time he brought us a gift of some kind—usually clothes or food. Once he brought my mother what he called a ballroom gown. He was very proud of this gift. It turned out to be a nightgown, but my mother didn't tell him that and only thanked him warmly.

Over time he and my father learned to communicate with each other and became friends. He was a kind, good-natured man. I remember him trying to convince my father that we shouldn't return to Poland because of the extreme poverty there, and that we should go to the Soviet Union, instead. He believed my father could have a fine career there as a painter.

He said, "*U nas vsego mnogo*" (Everything is plentiful with us), and spread his hands wide to emphasize his words. He had been a medical student in Moscow before being sent off to war.

On that first day of freedom we all went to bed very early and slept for two full days and nights, with short breaks to eat.

On the third day I got up and put on some clothes I found in the house. The jacket and trousers were too large, but I rolled up the sleeves and trouser legs. My mother was bustling around the kitchen. I happened to notice a little door to a cubbyhole in the entrance hall. There was a scale inside it. I pulled it out, and my mother weighed herself. She was a forty-year-old woman of average height. She weighed thirty-six kilograms!

I don't remember how much I weighed, but my mother screamed in fright, "Oh my! Henryk, you must eat a lot now!"

After sleeping for two days, I felt much stronger and refreshed. My father wasn't in the house, for he had gone outside to look around. I decided to go out, too. The very thought that I was now a free person and could go wherever I wished filled me with euphoria.

"A new and beautiful life awaits me, the life I've always dreamed of," I thought joyfully. I felt as if I had woken up from a long, terrible nightmare. I had rid myself of the Nazi torment, constant fear, danger, life on the brink of death, uncertainty, hunger, and suffering. "Everything will be fine now," I said to myself with relief.

When I left the house, spring sunshine washed over me. It was very pleasant, and the air was filled with the fragrance of flowers. I stood in the garden, intoxicated by the smell. Flowers, grass, trees—it all swirled before my eyes. There was pure beauty all around me. I went out into the street. People from our transport were standing there. I asked them how to get to the center of town, and then I walked there, whistling a tune.

On the way I met more of our people, who were talking with two Soviet soldiers. I stood near them because I thought perhaps they were talking about something that might interest me, too, but it was difficult for me to understand them. One of the soldiers gave me a friendly pat on the back and smiled at me. I smiled back at him and continued on my way.

I approached the main road. Long columns of trucks full of soldiers were driving along it. I stood with some of the other people from our transport, and we waved at them. They smiled and waved back at us. Someone near me shouted, "*Za pobedu! Za pobedu!*" I looked at him questioningly, and he explained to me that this meant "Here's to victory!" We waited there for quite a long time, until the columns passed and we were able to cross the street.

The houses became more frequent and closer together. Soon I found myself in the center of town. There was nobody in the streets; I only saw a patrol of two or three soldiers from time to time. On the way I noticed several shops, but they were all empty and vandalized. I decided to search for a grocery store on side streets. I thought that if I didn't find one, I would start looking for food in houses, because I was afraid that what we'd found in our house would soon run out.

I found myself in front of a shop that had a sign above its door that read *Lebensmittel Warenhandlung*, which meant it was a grocery store. But the door was shut, and a large padlock was hanging on it. My attempts to open the door were fruitless. I decided to ask a soldier for help.

I looked around until I saw two soldiers with submachine guns. I ran up to them and tried to ask them in Polish to open up the shop for me. But they were hurrying somewhere and only smiled at me. I ran alongside them and explained to them what I wanted. They stopped, and one of them said to me threateningly, "*Net, net!*" He waved his hand to shoo me away. The other one, seeing my confusion, came up to me, patted me on the head, and said something I didn't understand. They left me on the sidewalk and walked away.

I wondered what to do. A few steps away from me, I saw a soldier walking slowly and watching the patrol disappear in the distance. "This soldier will certainly have time," I thought. I put the friendliest expression on my face that I could manage and approached him.

He looked at me and asked, "*Shto takoye?*" (What do you want?)

I told him about the shop and the padlock on the door. The soldier was about twenty-five years old with a fat, ugly, rough-featured face. He was strongly built with broad shoulders, like a bear. I thought it would be easy for him to open the shop. He stood and listened to me attentively. He seemed to understand what I was saying, because he nodded.

I took him by the hand and was about to lead him to the shop, but then he started talking to me as if he wanted me to help him with something. He kept repeating the same thing to me, and I translated his words into Polish to be sure I had understood him, and asked him if my translation was correct. Finally, after repeating it a few times, I understood what he was asking me to do.

He wanted to visit someone in the next house, but he was afraid of the patrols that were going around, searching the houses from time to time. He asked me to stand guard in the entrance hall; if a patrol entered the building, he wanted me to pound on the door several times. Under no circumstance was I allowed to enter the apartment, or he would be very angry at me. If I did this favor for him, afterward he would go with me and open up the shop. I agreed.

We walked together until we were standing in front of a house that was divided into separate apartments. The soldier took a piece of paper from his pocket with something written on it; I could tell he was checking the address. Then we entered the entrance hall and started ascending the stairs. There were doors leading to apartments on both sides. The soldier went up to a door on the left-hand side, signaled to me to be quiet, and then listened very intently. The staircase was completely silent, and no sounds were coming from the apartment, either. He turned to me and once again forbade me from following him into the apartment. He also pointed to a spot where he wanted me to stand guard and watch the entrance door of the building. He turned the doorknob cautiously; the door was unlocked. He winked at me and disappeared into the apartment.

I stood there on guard, like a soldier, and waited for him to come out. I waited a very long time, but the Russian never reappeared. I began to fear that something bad had happened to him. I didn't know what to do. I went out to the street several times to see if a patrol was coming, but the street was empty. I didn't want to enter the apartment because the soldier had forbidden this categorically, and I was afraid of him. I waited a while longer and then finally decided to abandon my sentry post and leave. I had no choice but to forget about him helping me.

I went down the stairs to the entrance door, but then it occurred to me that I could force the Russian to come out. All I had to do was pound on the door a few times, like he told me to do if a patrol came. Then I could tell him some soldiers had entered the hall but had gone out again right away. I thought that if he didn't come out, I would know for sure that something bad had happened to him and would run to get some help.

I went back to the apartment door and hit it twice with my fist; then I also kicked it. I stood back because I was sure the door was about to fly open, and the soldier would rush out. But nothing like that happened.

I heard the crash of a window breaking and the sound of shattered glass falling to the sidewalk. Then there was a loud thump as if someone had jumped from the window into the street. I ran to the building's entrance door to see what had happened. Before I reached it, I heard someone running away. I stuck my head out the door and saw my soldier. He was running as if possessed and disappeared around a corner. I went into the street and stood there, astonished. Above me there was a broken window, and the street below was covered in shards of glass. I didn't understand what had caused him to panic like this or why he hadn't come out the apartment door.

I hesitated, undecided. I told myself that ultimately it was none of my business and decided to leave. I took a few steps, but again I was struck by the question: "Why didn't he go through the door?" I was overwhelmed by irrepressible curiosity. I went back to the apartment door. I turned the doorknob. It wasn't locked. I pushed it open a crack and listened carefully. It was silent in the apartment.

I slipped into the apartment's entrance hall, leaving the door slightly ajar behind me. I moved forward cautiously. I tiptoed and stopped to listen every two or three steps. I peeked into the kitchen and two rooms. The entire apartment was in a state of disarray as if it had been abandoned in a hurry. I entered a bedroom. A wardrobe on the right-hand side of the room was wide open, and clothes were scattered all over the floor. In the middle of the room, there was a wide bed with an iron frame, and clothes, evidently taken from the wardrobe, were strewn all over it. The broken window was on the left-hand side of the room. There were shards of glass all over the floor and an overturned chair under the window.

I was about to leave the bedroom when I noticed something strange. Two thick cables were tied to the bed—they looked like telephone cables. They disappeared somewhere beneath the clothing that was lying on the bed. I went closer and tugged on one of them but couldn't pull it out. I noticed two other, similar cables also tied to the head of the bed. I started throwing blouses, trousers, and underwear off the bed. There was a bedspread under them. With one quick movement, I pulled it off the bed.

What I saw there took my breath away. I recoiled in horror. In front of me lay the naked body of a young girl, and the bed around her was soaked in blood! Her eyes were closed, and her tattered shirt was bunched up beneath her chin. Her hands and spread legs were tied to the bed with the cables. She looked like she wasn't breathing. Her blonde hair was spread out on a pillow. It was a gruesome sight. I was in shock. I saw the corpse of a young girl in front of me, but that blood ... The blood between her legs was very fresh and seemed to still be flowing from her body.

I wanted to run away, but I stood there petrified, completely unable to move. Finally, I somehow managed to pull myself together. The girl's head was lying to the side; I turned it gently so it was straight. Her face was swollen and covered in bruises. Her lips were split, and there was a dried-up trickle of blood in the corner of her mouth. She had been severely beaten. I saw a rag in her mouth, so I pulled it out. Her breasts seemed to rise slightly when I did that. I put my ear to them but couldn't hear anything. I picked the bedspread up off the floor and covered her naked body with it. There was a mirror on a chest of drawers. I grabbed it and brought it close to her mouth. It fogged up. She was breathing! I had seen this done many times in the camp to check if someone was dead.

My hands were shaking, and I began to panic again. "Get out of here! Get out!" I thought. But then a different thought struck me: "You mustn't! You mustn't run away, Henryk!" I realized this girl's life depended solely on my help. I said to myself, "There's nobody here who can help her, so I have to do it!" I urged myself onward: "Hurry up, Henryk; do something! Save her! You must!"

I felt a huge burst of energy inside me. I no longer felt afraid. I struggled with the cables to untie the girl but couldn't manage. I ran to the kitchen and found a sharp knife. I cut through the cables, though it was extremely difficult.

The girl was completely inert. I put a pair of white underwear between her legs and pressed them together. I slapped her cheeks lightly several times, but she didn't react. I ran to the kitchen again and returned with a pot of water. I sprinkled some on her face, but it didn't help, either. Only when I scooped some water in my hand and splashed it in her face several times did she begin to show some signs of life. She started breathing slowly and opened her eyes. They were blue and looked clouded over. She stared at me with an uncomprehending gaze. She started looking around the room without raising her head. It seemed like she didn't know where she was. Her face was contorted with pain.

She slowly regained consciousness. She seemed to understand from my actions that I was trying to help her, for, mumbling with difficulty, she asked me to give her some cotton wool and told me where I could find it. When I brought it, she pressed it between her legs, and I supported her back because she was too weak to sit on her own. I told her to keep her legs pressed together. Then I held a glass to her mouth and gave her some water.

When she was finished drinking, she asked me, *"Wer bist du?"* (Who are you?)

In broken German I told her I was a Jew from Poland and that we had been liberated from a transport here in Tröbitz. She nodded to show that she understood. Then she wanted to know how I had come to be inside this apartment. She spoke slowly in a monotonous, lethargic tone of voice, the way people speak when they've grown tired of life. People in the camp who had lost their will to live spoke this way.

It seemed to me that her face was still swelling up. She looked terrible. Her eyelids and the areas beneath her eyes were one large, dark spot. At first I thought it was a shadow, but then I realized they were bruises. At her request, I brought a basin full of water and towels from the bathroom. I helped her wash since she was unable to do it by herself.

Her legs were completely covered with blood, and the towels immediately turned red. I carefully ran a wet towel over her body. Her entire body was in pain. I pulled the bloodstained bedsheet out from under her and threw it on the floor. I replaced it with a clean towel. I dried her off and covered her again with the bedspread. Her eyes expressed gratitude. She didn't say anything, but I could see that she was fully conscious and aware of what was happening to her. Then I made some wet compresses for her face. I offered to bring her something to eat from the kitchen, because I had seen bread and fruit preserves there, but she shook her head.

She asked me to hold her hand. I gave her my hand, and she grasped it convulsively. She put her arms around me so tightly that I had to sit down on the bed. She lay her head on my shoulder and started sobbing loudly and uncontrollably. The sound of her crying was incredible, almost nonhuman, like the howl of an animal. I was deeply shaken by it. I instinctively drew her closer to me. I felt very sorry for her.

I realized I had heard such crying before. I tried to remember where and when I had heard it. She held me in a tight embrace, as if I were her brother or father, and continued to cry. Her blonde hair covered my shoulder. We sat there with our arms around each other, and I remembered where I had heard such nonhuman cries that were like the howling of a wounded animal. It was in Tarnów, after the first roundup operation, when people came back from the factories outside the ghetto to find their children and parents gone.

It took her a long time to calm down. I asked her timidly what had happened, and she began to tell me about it. She spoke in a quiet voice, interrupted by sobs and whimpers. Her first words were: *"Das war schon der vierte Soldat der mir das angetan hat."* (He was the fourth soldier to do this to me.) She stopped, then added a moment later: *"Er war der ärgste."* (He was the worst one.)

When the war ended, she had been away in another town. When she came home, she discovered that her parents had fled. She went to her aunt's house and hid with her in the cellar together with her aunt's father and two children. The Russians had taken over the town, so they were afraid to go out on the street. Yesterday she had returned home to get some food because there was nothing left to eat at her aunt's house. Two Soviet soldiers stopped her in front of her apartment building. They led her into her apartment, and it was here . . . here that they had attacked her.

She started sobbing again on my shoulder. She was covered only by the bedspread. I got up and brought her some clothes. I helped her get dressed. She continued to describe what had happened.

Before they left, they tied her to the bed with a telephone cable and pushed a rag into her mouth. Then another soldier came. She lay on the bed, unable to move or make a single sound. After that, a fourth soldier came. She didn't know what happened to her after that because she lost consciousness.

I told her she should leave the apartment immediately because others might come. She tried to get off the bed but was unable to take a single step even with my help, and I was too weak to carry her. So we sat there with our arms around each other while she kept sobbing. I could tell she was craving human warmth. I was willing to carry her, but I didn't know what to do after that.

I was reminded again of the ghetto in Tarnów, when Nina and I had sat in the hiding place. Only now did I understand why she had told me to undress and why we had sat there together naked, with our arms around each other. She had wanted to feel the warmth of my body.

I asked the girl why her aunt hadn't come to find her when she saw that the girl hadn't returned. She replied that her aunt wouldn't come out of the cellar for anything in the world, for she was terrified of the Russians. I told her that if her aunt knew what state she was in, she certainly would come.

The girl stopped crying, looked at me, and mumbled, "*Vielleicht* . . ." (Perhaps . . .)

Her face was continuing to swell up. She asked me to hand her some cotton wool and turn around. She replaced the blood-soaked cotton between her legs and tossed the used cotton into the basin full of water next to the bed. The water in the basin turned red, and the balls of cotton looked like blood clots.

I wondered how to arrange some help for her and suggested that I tell my father about the situation. She refused but then asked me to go to her aunt and tell her to come and help her.

I hesitated. I was afraid to enter a cellar where Germans were hiding. Seeing my indecision and clearly understanding how I felt, the girl reassured me that I had nothing to fear, because nobody was in the cellar except her aunt with her two children and her old father, who was physically disabled.

I finally agreed to do it, and she wrote the address for me on a piece of paper. She explained how to get there. The cellars of some adjoined houses were connected by holes in the walls so that it was possible to escape if one of them was bombed. One of these holes was covered with an old mattress. I needed to push it aside and crawl through the hole into the next cellar, where the people were hiding.

I didn't spend very long thinking about it because I felt I needed to help her at any cost. I promised to do what she had requested as quickly as possible. I was already at the door when she asked me what my name was.

"Henryk," I told her.

She thought about it for a moment, and then a gentle smile appeared on her face.

"Henryk is 'Heinrich.'"

"And what's your name?" I asked.

"Helga." And she immediately added, looking at me imploringly, "Heinrich, don't leave me alone. Come back here with my aunt."

It was the first time someone had ever called me Heinrich.

She shouted after me, *"Heinrich! Ich danke dir!"* (Thank you!)

I felt a strange responsibility for her as if I had an old, very important commitment to fulfill. I knew I had to hurry because there was no way to know what else might happen. The streets were empty except for Soviet military vehicles that passed from time to time. I walked down two short streets and found the address the girl had written for me. I went down to the cellar. It was quite dark, but I easily found the mattress leaning against the wall. I pushed it aside and saw a hole in the wall, near the floor.

I knelt down and carefully stuck my head through the hole. There was more light in the next cellar; it seemed to be coming from somewhere up above. An old man with a cane was sitting against a wall, and next to him there was a woman and two boys. One of them was my age, and the other was about eight years old. They all looked very frightened.

Without entering, I said, *"Ich komme von Helga."* (I've come from Helga.)

Nobody answered. They stared at me as if I were a ghost.

"Ich komme von Helga," I repeated.

The aunt asked, *"Na und wo ist sie?"* (And so, where is she?)

I described what had happened to Helga and insisted that the aunt go back with me immediately because Helga couldn't be left there alone. They all remained silent, and I could see terror in the woman's eyes. Then her whole body started trembling and, gesticulating nervously, she said, *"Ich gehe nicht, ich gehe nicht, ich gehe nicht."* (I'm not going, I'm not going, I'm not going.)

I begged and pleaded with her as much as I could, but the more I spoke to her, the more she refused. I addressed the woman's father, but he remained silent. He stared at the wall with lifeless eyes. I was helpless.

I was about to go back through the hole in the wall, when the older boy said calmly, *"Ich gehe mit dir."* (I'll go with you.)

"Better than nothing," I thought. We went out into the street together. He stopped as if he had remembered something; he asked me to wait for him and ran back into the house alone. He returned a few minutes later, pulling a large wooden wagon. We didn't speak to each other on the way, because he was very tense; he kept looking around. I could see he was very scared.

We finally reached Helga's apartment building. The street was empty. We entered her apartment with the wagon. We hurriedly dressed Helga in men's clothing: a shirt, jacket, and trousers. We put my cap on her head, and her cousin tucked her hair under it. Now she looked like a boy. We also found some sunglasses for her, and then we carefully put her in the wagon. The boy took some food from the kitchen, and then we left the apartment with Helga.

On the street we pulled the wagon behind us, pretending we were having fun. On the way we passed several Soviet soldiers, who just smiled at us. Helga's cousin was as white as a sheet, and I tried to reassure him by smiling at him. The residents of the town were nowhere to be seen. Helga said that many of them were still here but were hiding.

I had the impression that the fresh air was having a good effect on Helga. It was obvious she was starting to feel better. I thought to myself that in this war everybody was capable of returning to life and of overcoming every kind of evil and every kind of pain.

We walked very slowly because it was hard for us to pull the wagon, but finally we reached Helga's aunt's house. Once we were in the hallway, Helga climbed out of the wagon and, leaning on our shoulders, took her first steps. She was unable to take more than a few steps, however. We slowly and carefully helped her descend the stairs to the cellar. This caused her pain, but there was no other way. When we reached the bottom of the stairs, Helga leaned against the wall above the hole that led to the next cellar and gave me her hand in farewell. I clasped her hand, and she said in a strangely altered voice, *"Heinrich, du sollst wissen, mein Dank wird dich dein ganzes Leben begleiten."* (Heinrich, please know that my gratitude will accompany you throughout the rest of your life.)

I smiled at her.

"Leb wohl." (Take care.)

"*Du auch.*" (You too.)

Her aunt pulled her into the cellar, and the boy went back upstairs with me to get the food from the wagon. Before we said goodbye to each other, he told me the train station was nearby and that a freight train was parked there, on a side track. In the third car, there was some excellent condensed milk. He said he would go and get some pots for me and that I should take the wagon and fill it up with this milk. My parents would surely be very pleased if I brought them such a present.

"You're giving me this wagon?" I asked in disbelief.

He nodded and added, "It's not mine, anyway. It belongs to the neighbors."

He turned and ran upstairs. He soon returned with a huge clay pot. It was very heavy, and there was another pot inside it.

"You can use the small pot to pour the milk into the larger one," he instructed me.

He smiled at me in farewell and quickly ran back to the cellar.

Now I was alone, and I took a deep breath. I went into the street with the wagon. Two drunk soldiers passed me. I smiled at them, and one of them saluted me. I knew it was only a joke, but it still made me feel proud.

I followed the boy's directions and found the train he had told me about. I went to the third car. The door on one side was slightly open. I pulled myself up and climbed inside. The freight car was full of enormous wooden barrels. One of the barrels was open. Inside there was a thick, yellowish liquid, the likes of which I had never seen before in my life. I dipped my finger in it and tasted it cautiously. It was wonderful! I stuck all my fingers into the barrel and licked them clean.

There had been tubes of condensed milk in the packages we had received in Bergen-Belsen from the Red Cross. It had tasted the same, but here there were colossal amounts of this milk! It reminded me of Nina Armer from the grocery shop in Wieliczka because the flavor of this milk was similar to her "little cows," but even better.

"There's clearly a lot more sugar in it," I concluded with the confidence of an expert.

The huge clay pot stayed in the wagon, and I used the small pot to pour this heavenly liquid into it until I had filled it right to the brim. Then I put some more milk in the small pot and also placed it in the wagon. I took off my jacket and covered the pots with it because I didn't want anyone to see them. I carefully pulled my precious treasure home. I imagined how happy all the famished people from the Bergen-Belsen transport would be when I told them about the milk. I prayed to God that nothing would happen to me on the way home, and I even recited the Shema Yisrael prayer three times, which had been my secret weapon against all forms of evil for a long time.

At last I reached home and was met with great joy. My mother poured small amounts of the milk into bowls right away, and everyone smacked their lips, unable to get enough of this thick, wonderful, heavenly liquid.

Soon afterward, my father filled the wagon with pots and started telling the other people from our transport about the treasure I had found. I returned to the train car with some of the others, and we poured as much condensed milk as we could from the barrels into pots, buckets, and even washbasins. There was so much of it that people kept returning to get milk for several days. The milk helped many people regain their strength more quickly because there was concentrated energy in it. And it helped others, including me, endure the difficulties that were still ahead.

In the very first days of our freedom, we found out that what was tormenting us wasn't just ordinary fatigue but a serious illness that had broken out while we had still been in the train cars, and here, in Tröbitz, it was now continuing to develop and spread. It began with intense shivering and a high fever. The afflicted people's faces would become red and swollen. About a week later, they would succumb to severe nervous disorders.

Our doctor seemed to be ill, as well, because I no longer saw him. Perhaps this was why the nature of the illness became clear to us only after several days. Apparently, it was a Russian military doctor who first confirmed that a typhus epidemic had broken out among us.

Menek was the first to fall ill, and then Aunt Lida soon afterward. They both had a high fever and sometimes lost consciousness. They hallucinated, tossed and turned on their beds, and shouted as if they had gone mad. We tried to help them, but our resources were very limited since there wasn't any medicine. We cared for them as well as we could.

The condensed milk helped very much. We poured it through their stiffened lips—a few spoonfuls every hour. There were days when this was their only nourishment—it was the only thing keeping them alive. Menek often called out to me in a completely normal voice, but when I ran over to him I saw that he was unconscious. Sometimes his gaze and voice seemed completely normal, but he was uttering sheer nonsense.

After a while, the Soviet army set up a quarantine for those who were ill, where they waited either to recover or die in total isolation. The quarantine was situated in former German military barracks where a hospital had been set up.

There's no doubt that many people were saved thanks to this. Russian military doctors arrived in Tröbitz and decided who needed to be quarantined. The number of places in the hospital was limited.

Menek started to feel better, and it was clear he was on the road to recovery. But Aunt Lida was still unconscious.

We, the healthy ones, were very careful about hygiene. We bathed twice a day and constantly changed our underwear and clothes. We didn't care if the clothes were the right size for us or not, and we often burst out laughing because we looked like circus clowns. My mother did laundry all day long, and my father helped her. We prayed to God that we wouldn't succumb to this terrible illness. After all, many people hadn't caught it even though they were caring for those who were ill. It was as if they were immune to it.

One day Aunt Lida was taken away to be quarantined. I remember this day very well. In the morning I left home to see if the Russians were handing out bread or some other kind of food, which happened almost every day. I approached the main road. Military trucks full of soldiers were driving along it. I saw a boy running off into the fields and a Soviet soldier chasing him. The soldier overtook the boy and knocked him to the ground. The boy's cap fell off his head, and then I saw that it was a girl. Her hair blew around her in the wind. The Russian threw himself on top of her and tried to rip off her clothes.

A military truck stopped near us, and a tall, powerfully built female Russian soldier got out of the driver's compartment. She ran over to the soldier and tore him away from his victim. Rising with his face contorted with rage, he swore viciously at her. Then she punched him in the face so hard he fell backward. He got up quickly and then bent down as if he were going to jump. But she was standing in front of him with a pistol aimed directly at him. He froze and stared at her as if he were coming to his senses. Blood was flowing from his nose. Meanwhile, the girl had picked herself up from the ground and was running off through the fields. Three soldiers jumped out of another vehicle, grabbed the soldier beneath his arms, and carried him off. The female soldier put her pistol away, spat on the ground, and shouted, "Scum!" Then she climbed back into her truck and drove away.

An hour later I returned home with a loaf of bread I had received from Russian soldiers who were distributing bread in the street. As I approached our house, I saw my aunt being carried away on a stretcher and placed in a peasant's wagon. My parents were standing in the doorway with their arms around Menek and Tosia. Everyone was crying and wiping tears from their eyes. I joined them and started crying, too. We watched as the driver whipped the horse and the wagon drove off into the distance. We were very afraid that we were saying goodbye to Aunt Lida for the last time.

Menek recovered completely. It was confirmed by a Soviet military doctor who was visiting invalids in their homes. This made us very happy, and that day we went to the hospital to visit my aunt. We weren't allowed to enter the barracks where the ill people were lying. We could only stand at a window and try to see her through it. Inside the barrack there were rows of wooden bunks; Aunt Lida had a good spot near the window. But she hadn't regained consciousness yet. We returned home disheartened.

That same evening, I started shivering uncontrollably, and the next day I became feverish. My parents kept hoping it might be just a common cold because my condition was constantly changing during the first few days. Sometimes I felt better, sometimes worse. The doctor was unable to visit us. Then my fever rose to over forty degrees Celsius.

By the time the doctor came, it was already clear I had caught typhus. My face was now swollen, and I had brown spots all over my body. The doctor also determined that my spleen was very swollen, and he told my parents I would be taken to the hospital as soon as a space became free there. I wouldn't have to be taken to the hospital if my condition improved; I was young and had a relatively strong body, so there was hope that I would overcome the illness on my own. He left some pills for me, though he admitted they weren't very effective. My parents pleaded with him not to take me to the hospital since I would have better care at home. But he said it would depend on my condition.

It was very difficult for me to swallow, so I was mostly fed condensed milk. I'm convinced it was solely thanks to this milk that my weakened body was able to fight this terrible disease.

During my second week of illness, I lost consciousness. I uttered inarticulate noises and mumbled strange, disconnected words. I tossed and turned on the bed, screaming. My parents held me down because they were afraid I would fall off the bed.

Oddly, I've never forgotten the visions, hallucinations, and chimeras that haunted me at that time. I was unconscious but felt as if I were living another, otherworldly life. All the people I had lost were with me once again. I saw them so clearly that I reproached myself for ever having thought they had left me. Everyone was alive, laughing and shaking hands with me.

Francis asked me a question I couldn't understand. She was running with me across a meadow, and then she disappeared into nothingness.

"Where are you? Come back! Come back!" I shouted after her.

Nina Armer shook my arm and begged me to wake up. I explained to her that it wasn't a dream and there was nothing for me to wake up from, but she started crying. With a cheerful smile on his face, Ignaś asked me for something, but I couldn't understand what it was. He disappeared and reappeared again. One moment he was sad, the next moment happy. The images flew past me quickly, and sometimes they stopped and refused to change. Most often I saw Arie. I asked him about something, and he answered. It was very important to him that I understood what he was saying, but I couldn't make it out.

People were constantly visiting me—in various poses, with faces contorted with grief or joyfully smiling. They shouted, gesticulated, spoke to me, and showed me things. Sometimes these images were calm and full of harmony, but other times they were disturbing or irritating. The figures crowded around me, demanding something from me. I made a superhuman effort but still couldn't understand what they wanted. I sat on my bed drenched in sweat, screaming.

My parents watched over me all night long. Sometimes I woke up and was aware of their care, but then I would fall into a new abyss. Gottowt appeared, surrounded by my friends from Wieliczka; they were acting out a scene from a play for me. I was once again in the bunker in the Tarnów ghetto, and someone put his hand over my mouth to stop me from screaming. I managed to transport myself somewhere else through sheer willpower. Mirages with wonderful colors were swirling around me while I stood with my hands raised to the sky.

I remember once seeing Arie lying next to the railway tracks, covered with a white bedsheet. It was precisely where I had seen him for the last time in real life. I understood he was dead, but I wanted to see him alive again, just once, at any cost. I started screaming, "Arie, wake up; don't leave me! Live a little while longer!" I thought that since I had managed to transport myself from place to place through sheer force of will, perhaps Arie would fulfill my wish and live again. I pulled the sheet off him. His naked body was lying under it. It was so horribly emaciated that I recoiled in terror. Then I leaned over to get a better view of his face. Maybe it wasn't Arie? But I recognized him . . . yes, it was him. He opened his eyes and smiled at me. He had a charming smile. He gave me his hand and rose from the ground.

The image was so clear and realistic that I was convinced it was really happening. It seemed to me that all my previous experiences had just been a bad dream, and this was the sole reality. Oh, how happy I was! Arie was alive, and we were together! How could I ever have thought it was otherwise?

Then suddenly I regained consciousness and saw my parents' faces hovering over me.

"Arie! Arie!" I screamed, but he was gone. I realized all of this had only been a hallucination and Arie truly was dead. Reality was merciless and left no room even for illusion. I lost consciousness again.

From then on, I only had unpleasant visions. I was plagued by nightmares about a terrible struggle in which I was caught. I didn't want to fight, but something was forcing me to take part in this battle. I no longer wanted to live and called out to heaven to free me from this life. I begged and pleaded for heaven to take me.

A bright light was approaching me. It was now so close that I closed my eyes, but then it receded from me again. I wanted to chase after it, but I couldn't move. Someone was explaining something to me, trying to persuade me of something, but I didn't want to listen. I wrenched myself from someone's embrace and was about to run into the light. I called out to the light so it would come back and take me into it, but nothing happened.

I was convinced that real, true life was there, in that light. Now I was pleading with the light to take me, but someone was holding me down, as if with iron shackles, to keep me from running toward that brightness. I fought to free myself, but I was too weak. Then I regained consciousness again and felt a cold compress on my forehead and my mother's hand. I opened my eyes and saw my mother crying. I felt sorry for her but was unable to say anything to comfort her.

I remained in this state for about eight days. I distinctly felt that I didn't want to live in this world because it wasn't worth it. There was nothing but disappointment awaiting each person, even in sleep. Joy and happiness were mirages that faded quickly, and longing for them lasted the rest of one's life. And once evil has been encountered, it relentlessly inflicts a person and remains with him throughout his entire existence. Why should I fight for my survival when there, in that wonderful light, nothing but goodness awaited me? Unfortunately, I was unable to reach this goodness.

One day I woke up as if from a deep coma. I had an uneasy feeling in my stomach and realized I needed to go to the bathroom. But I had forgotten how to say it. I made a huge mental effort to recall it and finally, with great difficulty, blurted out one word: "Shit!" My parents were thrilled to hear me say something after so many days of delirious raving, screaming, and incomprehensible mumbling. It was my first clearly articulated word since I had lost consciousness.

I heard my mother exclaim, "Henryk's speaking! Henryk's speaking!" Everyone came running from all sides to help me—my mother with a chamber pot, my father with a washbasin, and Menek with some sort of kitchen pot. Even Lusia and Tosia pushed their way past everyone else to see me. I relieved myself, smiled at everyone, and once again sank into oblivion.

I regained consciousness on a stretcher while I was being taken to the hospital barrack to be quarantined. The fresh air intoxicated me. I opened my eyes and saw the beautiful blue sky. My parents were walking next to me and holding my hands as if they were bidding me farewell. The doctor told them my condition was very serious, and they needed to be prepared for the worst. I heard what he said and understood everything, but didn't react. I was placed in a wagon, still on the stretcher. The last image I remember seeing was my parents' crying, grief-stricken faces; they said goodbye to me and stroked my head. Then I lost consciousness again.

I don't know how many days I remained unconscious or what happened to me during that time. All I remember is that I constantly struggled with something, and it was very difficult for me. And then one day I felt that my battle had come to an end—the path I was meant to follow was marked out for me. It was the first time I had woken up in about two weeks; it felt as if I were emerging from a long and lethargic sleep. I was fully conscious and felt much better.

I looked around curiously to see where I was. I thought I was still in Bergen-Belsen. The barrack was similar, and the bunk beds looked exactly the same. But then I realized it was impossible because, after all, we had been liberated. I was lying on a lower bunk next to a window. I felt extremely weak but managed to prop myself up on my elbows. I looked out the window and saw greenery and trees. But I still couldn't remember where I was.

I noticed someone on the bunk next to mine who looked familiar. At first, I couldn't figure out who the person was. She was lying there with a shaved head, gazing at me. We stared at each other silently for a while. Then she asked, "How do you feel, Henryk?" At that moment I recognized her. It was Aunt Lida. I told her that I felt fine.

"But, Aunt Lida, where are we?" I asked.

"What, you don't know?" she said, as if greatly surprised by my question. Then she explained, "We're on a ship, and we're sailing to Palestine."

"But, Aunt Lida," I objected, "I can see trees and greenery outside the window, and they don't grow in the sea."

Aunt Lida was unfazed. "It just seems like that to you. We're sailing to Palestine. Kiwek"—her husband—"is waiting there for me. He sent me travel documents."

My parents were told that the worst had passed and I was feeling better. They came to the window and gazed at me with joyful faces. They tried to communicate with me through hand gestures. I could see they were happy, and it raised my spirits. From then on, I remained conscious and aware of everything that was happening to me. My condition improved day by day.

It turned out that my parents had made a special request for me to be placed next to my aunt. They expected her to take care of me since her physical condition was better than mine. Unfortunately, she was suffering from a nervous disorder and didn't know where she was. I tried to help her understand what was happening to her. She couldn't comprehend why everyone in our barrack, except the doctor and nurses, had shaved heads. I told her it was obviously because of lice, but she declared that this was impossible since she had never had lice. She was clearly suffering from memory loss—she couldn't remember what she had experienced just a short time before.

I was terrified the same thing was going to happen to me. "This typhus is a horrible disease," I thought. I started testing my memory by checking what I could remember from the past. I felt like I could remember everything. This reassured me, but my instinct told me there was still something unpleasant ahead for me.

The worst thing wasn't the illness itself—it was the mental and nervous complications that often accompanied it. I witnessed this among other patients in the hospital. I thanked God that it hadn't happened to me—at least so far. I was only having slight trouble coordinating my hand movements, but the doctor told me this would pass. I hoped to recover very soon. I promised myself that I would soon be going on bike rides around the area with Poldek Fiszelberg.

Two days later a nurse came to help me get out of bed. We discovered that I was unable to stand on my own; the floor seemed to be buckling beneath me. I felt like I wasn't standing on firm ground, but rather on something very unstable that was going to collapse. Everything was undulating and spinning; there was no way to stay on my feet. At first the doctor and nurses thought it was because I was weak, but then they discovered that my sense of balance had been severely damaged. Walking by myself was completely out of the question. If support was taken from me, I fell immediately. I also noticed that my hearing had worsened, and I was having trouble communicating with people.

My parents were informed of this, and now their faces in the window looked solemn and worried. They waited anxiously for my condition to improve.

I practiced walking several times a day, as if I had forgotten how to do it. I felt dizzy and nauseated, but I had to keep doing these exercises. Two nurses would hold me under my arms and take about a dozen steps with me from one side of the barrack to the other. They tried to let me walk on my own, but each time I fell to the floor. Days passed, but there was no improvement. Meanwhile, Aunt Lida recovered and was sent home.

Eventually the typhus outbreak was defeated, and there were only a few convalescents left in the hospital. My parents were allowed to visit me now. They came in to see me, wearing white hospital gowns.

One evening I woke up. A doctor was speaking to my father in German and explaining something to him next to my bunk. I strained to listen, but I was only able to catch a bit of what they were saying. From what I understood, the doctor was explaining to my father that my case was particularly severe, and it was impossible to predict at that point how it would develop. Normally I should have recovered by now. Because there weren't any signs of improvement, it seemed as if there might have been permanent and irreversible damage to my sense of balance. My father asked if one day I would be able to walk on my own, and the doctor replied that it was impossible to predict anything at that moment, and my recovery might take a very long time.

Then the doctor said something I didn't understand.

"That's terrible," my father muttered.

"Yes, it might be terrible," the doctor agreed.

They walked away from my bunk, and I could no longer hear what they were saying. I felt as if I had just received a hammer blow to my head. I was overcome with despair. I couldn't bear the thought that I was now facing such a terrible outcome. "What does it mean that I'll never be able to walk again?!" I asked myself. "Am I going to be stuck in a wheelchair as if paralyzed? Will I be unable to stand on my own legs?"

I was in shock. I decided to go back to sleep so I could escape from reality. Then I started sobbing quietly because even sleep was impossible for me. "Oh, what a merciless world this is," I thought. But this state of despair didn't last long; soon I was struck by other thoughts. They became fiercer and struck me like a hammer, punishing me with reproaches. I felt like I was being tortured in a pillory.

"Why are you raising your hands in despair? Why are you complaining? Just think of how many dangerous situations you've managed to survive in your life. It's all behind you now! Giving up at this point would not only be cowardice but practically a crime committed against yourself! Stop complaining! Just think of one thing: how you can help yourself. Helping yourself recover is the most important thing. Gather some strength and faith, and don't let yourself doubt even for a moment that you're headed in the right direction. You're always headed the right way, even when you don't realize it!"

"But how? How am I supposed to fight? How can I help myself?" I asked myself.

I noticed a small sign on the wall near me, under a lamp that burned all night long. Someone had hung it a few days before, but I hadn't noticed it until now and hadn't read what was written on it. Now I slowly began to read it: *"Immer wenn du denkst es geht nicht mehr, kommt von irgendwo ein Lichtlein her."* (Whenever you feel like you can't go on, a new ray of light always appears.)

This had a profound effect on me. "Will this light perhaps reach me, too?" I wondered, and it lifted my spirits. I started feeling better, but questions once again appeared in my mind: "And so, what can I do to help myself?" I started wondering about this, and I was struck by the answer.

I lowered my legs to the floor and, holding the edge of my bunk with both hands, slowly took one small step. Then I managed to take a second one, and a third. I felt dizzy and had to take short breaks. The floor seemed to be rippling beneath me, but I gripped the bunk very tightly and, clenching my teeth, kept going. I managed to take several steps! I felt new strength growing inside me and joy overwhelming me. I told myself, "Henryk, not everything is lost."

From then on, I got up every night and walked around my bunk several times. When I couldn't go any farther, I sat down and waited for the dizziness to subside. I felt nauseated and was drenched in sweat from the exertion. But I didn't give up. I was amazed at my own progress when, after a few nights, I was able to take a few steps without holding the bunk. It was clear to me that I was going to defeat the illness.

One day the nurses who were walking with me around the barrack let go of my hands to see if I was able to stand on my own. They were ready to catch me if I fell. I smiled and told them they didn't need to worry about catching me because I had no intention of falling. They stared at me, surprised. Then I took ten steps entirely on my own! The barrack was completely silent for a moment. Suddenly everyone—all the patients and nurses—started shouting joyfully and applauded for me.

"People don't realize how lucky they are to be able to walk by themselves," I thought, and then I sat down on someone's bunk. The nurses and other patients approached me, congratulating me and shaking my hand. Someone informed my parents. Everyone hugged me, and my parents cried. They wanted to lift me up in the air on a chair, but a Russian doctor came in right at that moment and was so happy that he put me on his shoulders and started dancing with me.

From that day on, I recovered very quickly. My weak hearing didn't improve, but it didn't seem very important to me at the time. A week later I was already home. I was welcomed like royalty; even the Russian soldier came—the medical student who had visited us on the first day of our freedom. He was a frequent guest at our house.

I found out from my parents that I also partially owed my recovery to this man. When my condition had been at its worst, he had brought a bottle of old red wine to me that he had found in the cellar of an abandoned house and told my parents to pour a spoonful of this wine into my mouth several times a day; he assured them it would make me stronger. My parents were convinced that the condensed milk from the freight train and this wine had saved my life.

The war officially ended during my illness. My father told me people were very happy at the news, but there were no outbursts of joy or cheering because everyone was too weak and sad. But as for me—I felt like I had just been reborn. Everything in nature seemed far more beautiful than it had ever been. I looked around as if I were seeing everything for the first time in my life. I gazed at the fields and trees and inhaled the fragrance of the grass; the beauty surrounding me seemed completely amazing. I couldn't get enough of the flowers. I often stood and stared at them for a long time.

Those colors... The colors were far more intense than I remembered. Everything was so bright and vivid. I wondered why I had never noticed the colors before. I felt like they were speaking to me, hinting at something loftier and more important—something I needed to understand in order to begin a new, better, and happier life.

I was happy, but at the same time, I felt like I was in a state of mourning. I didn't try to rid myself of this feeling, nor did I want to. It represented something very precious and sublime to me, something almost holy. I didn't talk to anyone about this feeling, but I sensed that it had become part of my heart and would always be with me. I hadn't forgotten any of my beloved friends and relatives who had left me, and now they dwelled in a kind of shrine that I had built in the deepest, most intimate recesses of my consciousness. They continued to live there with me, and our love for each other grew even stronger.

One day at the end of May or beginning of June 1945, my parents told me that we were going home—to Oświęcim. Aunt Lida, Menek, and Tosia decided to go with us and get off the train in Kraków. Once again, we found ourselves on a train. But this time it was a normal passenger train, and we were traveling as free citizens.

We were all very excited and full of hope that perhaps some of our family members had managed to survive the war, and we would be reunited with them. Even Regina's mood changed. She became livelier and kept sighing while raising her eyes to the sky.

Unfortunately, our hearts weren't meant to stop weeping, even for a short time. The blessing the rabbi had given my father at the beginning of the war at the train station in Oświęcim—for my father, his wife, and his children to survive the war—came true with tragic precision. Apart from us, no other members of my father's large family had survived; his parents, his siblings, and his siblings' children had all perished during the war. Arie was the last one to die—right at the very moment of liberation! He died as my father's son, but it was impossible to deceive fate. His death—perhaps because I had witnessed it intimately—was so tragic for me that I've never been able to recover from it, and often relive it.

We returned like castaways from another world. We had some bread and condensed milk that my mother had put in jars. It was all we possessed, apart from suitcases with clothing in them. We went home filled with hope that we were going to build a new life for ourselves.

We had a pleasant trip. The train wasn't very crowded; we were alone in our compartment almost all the way to Oświęcim. It was clear that nobody else was returning. The closer we came to our hometown, the more our excitement grew.

We suggested to Aunt Lida that she get off the train with us in Oświęcim, but she refused because she hoped there were some survivors from her husband's family—she wanted to return to Kraków to find out.

Regina seemed indifferent. Sometimes she mumbled incomprehensible words to herself and gazed up at the sky. Several times I thought I saw tears in her eyes. I had never seen her cry, even when my grandfather died. It had seemed very strange to me in the camp, but my father explained that her tears had evidently all dried up.

I now felt like I had crossed through a gate into some other world. Just like after I had recovered from my illness, everything seemed new, beautiful, and spellbinding. I looked out the train window at the passing landscape and kept reminding myself that it wasn't a dream. I was still weak after my illness, but the excitement was giving me strength.

Lusia hugged our mother and asked if it was true that we would never be hungry again and that we would be able to eat as much bread as we pleased from now on.

We arrived in Oświęcim at noon. The train stopped at the Oświęcim station very briefly, so we had to hurry. We quickly said goodbye to Aunt Lida and her children. A railway worker helped us lift Regina out because she was barely able to walk. We were the only people getting off the train here. The platform was empty. We slowly went through the station's main hall and out into the street.

It was a beautiful, sunny day. Before the war there had always been many people here—rushing around, getting in and out of horse-drawn carriages, and selling ice cream, lemonade, and soda water with fruit syrup, which I liked very much. There had been a lot of noise and commotion everywhere. But now there was complete silence. It felt as if the whole town was asleep.

We stood in front of the train station not knowing what to do. My parents wanted to go to our villa to see if we could enter it. But it was over two kilometers away from the station, so it was impossible to walk there with Regina. We looked around helplessly. My mother noticed a peasant wagon parked near us.

My father approached the driver and asked him if he would take us home; he agreed even though we didn't have any money. On the way to our house, he talked constantly about what had happened here while we were gone.

We crossed a bridge over the Soła River and entered the town. We saw Haberfeld's house on the right-hand side and the restaurant on the ground floor where the ill-fated office for emigration to Palestine had been located. We turned right and entered Oświęcim's main square. There were very few people here, too, but I noticed that some shops were open. Jagiellońska Street looked exactly how I remembered it. From time to time, we passed Soviet soldiers.

At last the wagon pulled up in front of our villa. We discovered that the civic militia was now using it as their headquarters. A policeman suggested to us that we go across the street to my grandfather's villa, which was empty. The driver parked the wagon in front of my grandfather's garden gate. My father and the driver carried Regina into the villa. The driver tried to help us in every possible way. My father thanked him and gave him his necktie as a gift.

It turned out that my grandfather's villa had been used as a hospital by the Germans until very recently. All the rooms were in terrible disarray. There were soiled bandages and pieces of cotton wool scattered all over the floors. There were iron hospital beds in every room. The bed that used to belong to my grandfather and Regina was still in one of the upstairs rooms. When Regina heard this, she wished to lie down in it immediately. We all helped her ascend the stairs. She lay down in her bed, and a blissful expression appeared on her face.

We tidied and scrubbed two rooms. Suddenly the front door opened, and a rather short, thin old woman entered, carrying a loaf of bread. It was Mrs. Szczerbowska, our neighbor. Someone had told her we had come back. She greeted us very warmly and, in a slightly embarrassed manner, handed us the loaf of bread and said she had brought it for us because she was sure we were hungry. Seeing our overjoyed faces, she hurried home and came back with a large pot of hot soup. We found out from her that nobody else from our family had returned.

The visit from this noble, good-hearted woman greatly lifted our spirits. I still remember every detail of that visit.

My parents and I continued to clean the rooms for a few more hours, until we had returned them to a relatively acceptable state. After all this exhausting work, I felt like I was going to collapse, so I went to bed. That night I had a pleasant dream. Someone was stroking my head and comforting me. I thought I could hear bells ringing.

When I woke up in the morning, the house was full of commotion; strangers were walking through the rooms. My heart started pounding. I sensed that something serious had happened. I got up and called my mother. She entered my room and told me Regina had died during the night. We were all very distraught. Regina had returned home only to die in her own bed.

My parents went to the cemetery in a horse-drawn wagon to bury Regina. Lusia started crying, so my mother took her with them. Since there was no space for me in the wagon, my father told me to stay home.

The horror of war, which I desperately wished to forget, returned to me. I felt terribly lonely and abandoned by the entire world. I decided to walk to the river—to my usual spot, which I used to love so much. Behind the garden of my grandfather's villa, there was a road that led to the path along the river, which was bordered by beautiful trees. The riverbank was very pretty, partially overgrown with bushes. Everything was just as I remembered it.

From far off I could see someone sitting in my old spot. He was perfectly still, like a statue, and was looking up at the sky. I drew closer and sat down several meters away from him. The Soła River was flowing past in front of me. I looked at the river, fascinated by the sight of it. I realized at that moment how often I had dreamed of being able to sit once again on its bank. After a while I looked at the motionless figure close to me. I saw his face only in profile, but at once it seemed familiar to me.

He seemed to feel my gaze; he turned his head and looked at me. Suddenly his face brightened. He struggled to say something, and eventually he managed to articulate several words.

"I...I knew...I knew you'd come back," he stammered in a scratchy voice that was choked with emotion.

Then I recognized him. It was Aleks the Stork!

We leaped to our feet and fell into each other's arms.

"How did you know I'd come back?" I asked.

He pointed at the sky and stammered, "The birds...the birds told me."

We both had tears in our eyes. I felt very happy. Once again, I had a friend.

NOTE

1. One of the three transports from the Bergen-Belsen camp on April 10, 1945 was sent to Theresienstadt. There were about twenty-five hundred Jewish people in it who possessed passports and other documents from South American countries, the United States, and Palestine or were "stateless" (born in Germany but stripped of German citizenship). On April 23, 1945, the prisoners in this transport were liberated by the Red Army in the small German town of Tröbitz, roughly ninety kilometers north of Dresden. About six hundred people died during the trip and shortly after being liberated, mostly from typhus and starvation. This transport is sometimes referred to as the "ghost train."

RETURN TO OŚWIĘCIM

OŚWIĘCIM WASN'T THE SAME TOWN I had known before the war. Without Jewish people it seemed cold and empty, like after a flood or some other kind of cataclysm.

The day after we got home, my father took me by the hand, and we walked to the Auschwitz-Birkenau camp. The terrain hadn't been cleaned up yet. We saw rubble, long rows of barracks, and objects of various kinds scattered across the camp's wide roads. The barracks seemed to me like they were crying.

My father stopped walking and began to recite the prayer for the dead—the Kaddish. I reminded him that at least ten people needed to be present when the prayer was recited, to which he replied that the wise men who established this rule hadn't been aware of the terrible things that were going to happen in this world. He could recite the Kaddish by himself now because everyone who had died here was reciting it along with him.

During the first days after our return, my parents walked through Oświęcim, looking around as if they were seeing the town for the first time in their lives. They walked silently, the way people walk through a cemetery, and gazed at the buildings as if they were tombstones. From time to time they would stop in front of a house, and my mother would weep, covering her eyes with her hands. My father would put his arm around her, and I would stand next to them helplessly. There was nothing I could do to help them because I was struggling to hold back tears, too. In front of the Schenkerówka near Mały Rynek (the Small Square), my mother started sobbing hysterically, and her body was shaking convulsively.[1] I had never seen her in such a state. My father calmed her and stroked her head, but he was also very upset. His glasses fogged up every few seconds, and he kept taking them off and wiping them nervously with a dirty handkerchief.

At first I seemed more resilient than my parents, but later I experienced a difficult time, too. I was haunted by memories and anxiety of various kinds, predominantly at night. Something always distracted me from these sad recollections, however. It was May, and the days were beautiful, and every so often I came across glorious lilac bushes in full bloom. Oh my God, how fragrant they were! I couldn't understand how such beautiful and delicate flowers could exist in such a brutal world. I have no doubt that the sight of them helped me maintain spiritual balance and strengthened my resolve to never succumb to the profound sadness I saw my parents experiencing.

Other Jews who had miraculously survived the Holocaust slowly started returning to Oświęcim. Some of them stayed, but there were others who, when they saw that none of their loved ones had survived, immediately left this town where every street, alleyway, and house held memories for them. They said they were unable to live in a cemetery.

The resurgent Jewish community gave us the illusion that Jewish life could be rebuilt in Oświęcim. The people who were returning told us that their first days back at home were similar to ours. They walked around the town like mentally deranged people, crying uncontrollably. But they quickly recovered and returned to their normal lives, each according to his or her profession, disposition, and abilities. The Polish inhabitants of Oświęcim warmly welcomed their Jewish neighbors back to the town. Old friendships were renewed, and new friendships were formed. The Jews of Oświęcim didn't feel like strangers in their hometown.

Acquaintances told my father that our artificial fertilizer factory, Agrochemia, had been taken over by a Red Army unit, and there was no point even going there because a guard was standing in front of it, not letting anyone in. Agrochemia was located about three kilometers from our house, in an area called Kruki. From a distance, we could see many soldiers wandering around it. They were walking aimlessly between the factory buildings or sitting on the ground in small groups. They looked like boy scouts who were about to light a campfire.

The factory still smelled of superphosphate. As we approached the entrance gate, I detected some other strange odor mixed with the smell of fertilizer. My father started to sniff the air, too. But there was no time to talk about it because a guard with a submachine gun blocked our way and asked, *"Shto takoye?"* (What do you want?)

My father tried to explain to him in Polish, with the aid of gestures, that he was the owner of the factory. The guard first shook his head, then told us in broken Polish-Russian that we couldn't sleep there. I nearly burst out laughing, but my father elbowed me in the side, then tried again.

"Goslar, the superintendent of this factory, lives here. I want to talk to him. Or his wife," my father said.

But this didn't work, because the guard replied in a decisive tone, *"Niet Goslar, niet Goslar."* Then he straightened his machine gun.

This was a sign that the conversation was over.

My father went to the town hall to ask what he could do to make the army leave his factory. He was told there that everything depended on the Soviet military commanders of the town. He was advised to go to them with his request, but at the same time, he was warned that the Soviet officers' attitude toward people attempting to reclaim their property was very severe. One of the clerks at the town hall added, "They're running things here as if they owned the whole town."

My father wondered if it was worth going there at all. He was, after all, a capitalist who was well known throughout the entire town. At that time rumors were circulating in Oświęcim that capitalism had ended in Poland. But seeing that this was the only way to regain his factory, two days later he decided to present his request at the Soviet military commanders' headquarters.

He went there with a heavy heart and presented the identity document that had been given to him in Tröbitz stating that we had been liberated from the Bergen-Belsen camp and were Palestinians, which of course wasn't true. To my father's astonishment, he was received very well there. Our alleged foreign nationality made a great impression on the Soviet commander. He was very polite, and my father received two documents without any trouble: an order for the commander of the military unit occupying Agrochemia not to cause any damage to the factory or make any changes to the premises, and a document "issued to the Director of the English Agrochemical Factory, Mr. Leon Schönker, giving him permission to search for his furniture in the town of Oświęcim."

Seeing the impression his alleged English citizenship made in the Soviet military commanders' headquarters, my father also showed the document from Tröbitz at the town hall.[2] He expected special privileges of some kind and—no less importantly—an increase in his personal safety. Nobody at the town hall looked at his document. My father was a well-known and highly respected citizen of the town, so he was taken at his word.

A few days later, a Soviet military commander informed my father that he had issued an order for the Soviet army to leave the factory and hand it over to my father as the legitimate owner. Soon afterward we were informed that my father was supposed to go to the factory to officially accept it. From far off we could see that the factory was empty; the army had already left it. Goslar's wife was waiting for us by the entrance. She threw herself into my father's arms so violently that they both staggered, and I was afraid they would fall.

They wept for a while; then my father asked, "What's new?"

To which she responded in a strong but trembling voice, "Sir, the Russian army filled your entire factory with crap!"

We stared at her in amazement. Mrs. Goslar took my father's arm and led him to the factory's main production hall. I followed them. Once again, I caught a whiff of that strange odor, which now seemed to have a more concrete, specific source.

We entered the hall, plugging our noses. A strange sight met our eyes. Nearly the entire floor was covered with wooden boards. Before the war, these boards had been used for loading sacks of superphosphates into wagons. But now they were lying on the floor in about a dozen layers, one on top of another.

"What's going on here?" asked my father.

"They crapped here," answered Mrs. Goslar, this time in a normal voice.

The Russian army had turned the factory's production hall into a latrine. After filling it with one layer of feces, they had spread boards over it and started a new layer.

We stared at it in amazement. It took my father a long time to come to his senses. Finally, he declared that this seemed to him like the greatest invention of our century.

An officer arrived with an adjutant and handed my father a document to sign. My father showed him the production hall and told him it wouldn't have been long before they would have to climb a ladder to relieve themselves. The officer smiled, slapped my father on the shoulder, and said, *"U nas vsego mnogo."* (Everything is plentiful with us.) Then he left.

Our life in Oświęcim slowly returned to normal. My father's employees resumed their work very eagerly. They were the same people who had worked at Agrochemia before the war, and they were all very attached to their workplace. The filth was painstakingly mopped up, and the factory was scoured, which made Mrs. Goslar happy. She poured cologne throughout the unfortunate production hall and exclaimed with delight, "Heaven on earth! Heaven on earth!"

My father found a business partner who lent him money to purchase raw materials to produce the first batch of superphosphate. The enterprise was extremely successful. Local farmers' horse-drawn wagons parked in front of the factory in a line several hundred meters long. Many of them didn't have any money, so they traded things for the fertilizer—flour, potatoes, and even chickens. My father paid back his partner and from then on ran the factory by himself. The residents of Oświęcim expressed their appreciation for him reactivating Agrochemia so quickly. Everyone was happy about it and told my father many times that the factory was sure to be successful, for "where water once flowed, water will flow again."

I started attending the Stanisław Konarski Junior High School and took extra lessons at the same time so I could catch up on what I had missed. It turned out there were many other pupils like me. I was the only Jewish pupil at my school, but there were others who had similar gaps to mine because their education had been interrupted during the war for various reasons.

I was told to sit on a bench with another boy my age. His name was Romek Maksymowicz. He was about my height and had beautiful blond hair, just like I had always wanted to have. My hair had been curly and as stiff as wire since growing back after I had typhus. It was impossible to straighten it; pomade had no effect.

During my first days of junior high school, I felt very unsure of myself. I worried about how the other students would treat me. I was afraid of antisemitic remarks, jokes, and insults. During the war I had lost contact with Polish people, and now I didn't know what to expect. Romek clearly understood how I felt, for he always tried to cheer me up, and this reassured me.

None of the other students said anything offensive or antisemitic to me, with the exception of T. He was taller than me and Romek and looked much stronger than us, too. I was fourteen years old then and wise enough not to take things to heart. But Romek reacted differently. When T. insulted me in front of the whole class, Romek went up to him and demanded that he apologize to me.

"And if I don't, what will you do?" asked T. stubbornly.

"If you don't apologize to Henryk, I'll challenge you to a fistfight. Whoever's on the ground first will have to apologize to the other. If you lose, you'll apologize."

The whole class was petrified. T. couldn't dismiss the challenge or else he would seem like a coward. He had to make a decision quickly. After a moment of reflection, he chose the fistfight. They decided to have it in the cellar during the lunch break. I couldn't allow this to happen. I tried to persuade Romek that it didn't make any sense and that we were no longer little children. But Romek didn't listen to me. There was a lot of excitement in our classroom.

On the lunch break, everyone went down to the cellar. I made one more attempt while descending the stairs. I told Romek I was willing to shake T.'s hand and tell him I forgave him. Romek shook his head, thrust his chest out and proudly declared, "Don't bother, Henryk. The fight's going to happen because that insult calls for revenge." I saw that this made a huge impression on everyone, especially our female classmates.

Romek and T. stood facing each other in the cellar. Another classmate served as referee and declared that they weren't allowed to poke each other in the eyes or hit with an open hand. He also pointed out that kneeing below the belt would immediately disqualify them. The fight would continue without any breaks until one of the opponents fell to the ground. In short, it was a duel the likes of which had never been seen at the Konarski Junior High School.

A signal was given, and the fight began. The whole class surrounded us, shifting nervously from one foot to the other. It turned out that T. was indeed stronger, and Romek managed to avoid some very hard punches solely thanks to his agility. He made use of dodges that completely surprised T., who was quite heavyset with awkward movements. I was afraid, however, that one of T.'s vigorous blows would hit Romek and knock him out. At one point, T. slipped, and Romek, taking advantage of the situation, attacked him with a powerful right hook followed by an uppercut. It took T. a while to come to his senses, and then Romek helped him to his feet, like a gentleman.

T. turned out to be an honorable fellow. He came up to me and said loudly, smiling, "I'm sorry." This gesture convinced me that not all antisemitic remarks were an expression of a deeply rooted hatred of Jews. Laughing at Jews and mocking them was, for many people, simply a habit they had learned at home.

Later I also got to know Romek's close friend Zdzisiek Mróz, who was the best student in our class. My third friend, not as close to me as Romek, was named Wiesiek Kała. He also had nice, wavy hair. He was tall and, according to all the girls, very handsome. He also played the accordion beautifully.

I've always remembered our very first conversation. One day, after a religion lesson, he came up to me and said, with amazement, "So you Jews had Moses, too?" It was more of a statement than a question. He had learned this astounding fact during our religion lesson when the priest had described how Moses, leader of the Jews, had led them out of Egypt. I stood there, so dumbfounded that I only managed to say, "Yes, imagine that."

Agrochemia continued its production unceasingly. Superphosphate was sold in the spring and autumn. After several seasons my father had enough money to achieve his greatest aim at that time—namely, to rebuild my grandfather's villa.

In 1939, right after the war had broken out, my whole family had fled to Kazimierz Dolny. My father had stayed in Oświęcim because he wanted to send all the precious treasures he had spent his life collecting—antique furniture, silver, porcelain, paintings, an old tapestry, and carpets—to Kazimierz Dolny by boat. It turned out to be impossible, however, so he put some of them in a storeroom at the factory and ordered the door to be bricked over. Only Goslar and his wife knew about it. After the house was renovated, all these things were returned to the villa. Some of the furniture was found in other houses in Oświęcim. Our home became like a museum.

The first person to return to us was our housekeeper from before the war, Stanisława (Stasia) Knapik. She was a very pious old maid, over the age of forty. She went to church twice a day to pray. This wasn't difficult for her, since the Salesian Church was on our street, only a few hundred meters from our villa. She had no friends in Oświęcim and helped my mother all day or worked alone. My parents always said that we could rely on Stasia. She was very devoted to us, and we all treated her like a member of our family. She made sure that I prayed every morning, and this caused problems between us, since sometimes I neglected to do so. There were many mornings when I barely had time to get dressed and raced off to school without breakfast. Stasia shook her finger at me then, but she always managed to hand me a nicely packed sandwich as I flew out the door.

She had more trouble with Lusia than with me. My sister often snuck out of the house without breakfast. Then Stasia would run after her or take her breakfast to the school. Despite Lusia's promises that she would never do it again, the situation kept repeating itself. People sometimes asked us if Stasia was well, because they saw her running down the street, shouting, "Come back! Come back, you sneaky little devil!"

One day my father hired a caretaker named Stefan Blachura and his wife to work in our villa. They lived in an outbuilding of our villa. Stefan became a very important person in my life because he had once been a professional ping-pong player. I think he spent a lot more time training me in ping-pong than taking care of our house. He was of the opinion that he should do only the more difficult work, and his wife could do everything else. Stefan was also very fond of soccer and at some point had passed an exam to become a soccer referee. Because of this he was able to help me get cheap tickets for major league games. Soccer and ping-pong were my favorite sports.

My parents didn't mind our friendship because they knew I always needed to have someone close to me. When I was alone I became pensive and sad. Sometimes I couldn't shake off the horrible memories that haunted me and oppressed me like a dark specter. My parents and I never talked about our wartime experiences. They were so tragic and painful that we carried them inside ourselves silently.

One day an old man with a large suitcase arrived at our house. It was one of my father's relatives who had just returned from Russia. His name was Leiser Dawid Schenker. Before the war he had owned a small haberdashery factory in Kraków. His whole family had died, and now he had nothing to return to and nowhere to live. He had heard that we had survived, so he came to us. My parents immediately invited him to live with us, and he agreed.

Leiser Dawid told my father he had brought something valuable with him. We all stood around his suitcase, and he very proudly took some packages from it. To our surprise they were filled with... nails. Apparently in Russia, where he had survived the war, he had been told that everything was lacking in Poland, and nails were worth their weight in gold.

A short time later, my mother happened to find out that her aunt, Genia Sternhel, had survived the war and was living in a homeless shelter in Silesia. My parents immediately went there and brought her back to our house. She was given her own room, and our other maid, Stefcia, was always at her service. She was a thin, petite, slightly hunchbacked old woman with trembling hands and thin, gray hair. She looked like a puff of wind could knock her over. Perhaps that's why the windows in her room were always closed. She was about seventy years old but looked more like ninety. She was always dressed in black and refused to wear any other color. She spoke in a faltering, trembling voice.

Aunt Genia had survived for two years by hiding in a wardrobe in a Polish home. She had remained inside the wardrobe day and night. She was allowed to come out into the room only once in a while, after dark. In our house she prayed all day long. It was her only activity. Every day she repeated to my mother how grateful she was that my parents had taken her from the shelter. My mother told her she was a *tzaddeket*—a female *tzaddik*. She liked me very much and often stroked my head while whispering blessings over me.

Mr. and Mrs. Lieberman also lived with us in our villa. Before the war they had been wealthy owners of a tar paper factory and well-respected citizens of Oświęcim. They had returned from Russia penniless, and my father invited them to live with us. They moved into an upstairs room with an attached kitchen, and we built a separate entrance for them and stairs at the side of the house. They were very dignified people, and their refined manners always amazed me.

Because the Germans had burned down the Great Synagogue in 1939, after the war the remaining Jewish people of Oświęcim renovated a small, one-story building that had belonged to the Jewish community council and set up a synagogue in it. People prayed there on Saturdays and holidays. Often, however, it was impossible to gather the necessary ten people for prayers, and so on holidays my father brought acquaintances there so that there would be a *minyan*.

Oświęcim's Jews didn't take an active part in Poland's postwar political life. But my father and Leiser Dawid spent their evenings having long discussions and making predictions about how the political situation was going to develop and what the Provisional Government of National Unity, created on June 28, 1945, was going to achieve. It was led by Edward Osóbka-Morawski, the leader of the Polish Socialist Party. My father was an optimist and thought that even though Stanisław Mikołajczyk, the leader of the Polish People's Party, was now only the minister of agriculture, he undeniably had the most support in the country and so his party would receive the majority of votes in the next election and assume power together with the Polish Socialist Party, which would lead to democracy and liberalism. Leiser Dawid was decidedly of the opposite opinion. He said that anyone who hadn't spent time in Russia was unaware of what Fonye Ganev was capable of. *Fonye* was a nickname for Russians, and *ganev* meant "thief" in Yiddish. This is what Leiser Dawid called the Russian government and communist party.

A measure of the political powers that were going to rule Poland was the national referendum on June 30, 1946. Three questions had to be answered concerning the abolition of the senate, preservation in the constitution of the economic system based on the agricultural reform of 1944, and the establishment of Poland's western borders on the Oder and Lusatian Neisse Rivers. I remember the Polish Workers' Party's posters hanging throughout the town, declaring in huge letters, "Trzy razy TAK to Polaka znak" (A real Pole votes YES three times). At that time, there was a lot of discussion about how to vote. Voting yes three times meant handing over power to the communists, although not everyone realized this. The referendum's results were falsified with the very active help of security agencies that were under total Soviet control, and "three times YES" obtained the majority.

Leiser Dawid explained to my parents that we all needed to be prepared to leave the country because when the communists assumed power, people like him and my father wouldn't have a chance in Poland. My father was slightly angry at Leiser Dawid for having such a pessimistic view of everything and said they shouldn't automatically dismiss changes and reforms in the country.

"Besides, I'm very busy now rebuilding my factory, and I don't have time to think about such things. I don't want to leave Poland—my home is here, my factory is here, and the graves of my ancestors are here."

The Provisional Government of National Unity existed only until February 1947, when Osóbka-Morawski submitted his resignation to the newly elected president, Bolesław Bierut. The parliamentary election was rigged, and there was even talk of "miracles in the ballot boxes." A coalition of the Polish Workers' Party, the Polish Socialist Party, and the Polish People's Party took power in Poland.

Leiser Dawid walked around his room very agitated, gesticulating, and shouting in Yiddish, *"Kh'hob gezogt! Kh'hob gezogt!"* (I told you so! I told you so!)

My father calmed him down by telling him that not everything was lost because Mikołajczyk had a lot of support in the country. "A lot of support! A lot of support!" my father yelled, as if he were trying to convince himself of it.

"Leon, you're very naive!" shouted Leiser Dawid, outraged.

"Poland is a country thirsting for freedom and democracy. That's why Mikołajczyk is sure to win the election! He'll win! He'll win!" exclaimed my father.

My father once told me that if a wise person is wrong, it's worse than a hundred stupid people. I considered my father to be a wise person. Unfortunately, he was shamefully mistaken.

Old and new members of the Polish Workers' Party started filling all the important positions in Oświęcim. My father had always been held in high esteem by all the residents of the town, including members of the Polish Workers' Party, but now some of them were beginning to treat him with disdain.

A struggle for power against Polish underground forces had been ongoing since the end of the war. We were constantly hearing reports of various "gangs" attacking bureaucratic offices or militia stations. The authorities responded severely—with mass arrests, death sentences, and secret murders. Under the pretext of fighting against communism, hundreds of robberies and murders were committed. They were also committed on Jews—ordinary people who had nothing to do with politics. It was quite peaceful in our town, however, and despite feeling some anxiety, we tried to lead normal lives.

Agrochemia was developing very well. My father hired more people, but at the same time he followed Leiser Dawid's advice not to allow the factory to expand too much. At that time, I was unable to understand this, and one evening, before going to bed, I asked Leiser Dawid for an explanation.

I said, "A larger factory means that more people will have jobs. What my father's doing is good for people, so why should they be angry at him for this?"

He only replied, however, with a Jewish saying: *"Tsu gut iz halb narish."* This means, "If you do something too well, it's half stupid."

The factory absorbed my father entirely. Many things needed to be renovated or rebuilt, so he was busy arranging things and sending people around Poland. He constantly had new ideas, kept improving production and managed to keep everything going somehow, despite how difficult it was to obtain the things he needed to keep the factory running. On the grounds of Agrochemia he set up a factory that produced tiles from animal horns. The Bacutil company in Bielsko used the tiles to manufacture combs and the tips of horns to make buttons.

My father always had superphosphate ready to sell in both the spring and autumn. There wasn't as much of it as before the war, but there was always a lot being produced in the factory. All the employees worked hard and helped the factory develop as much as they could. They admired my father's perseverance. Moreover, wages at Agrochemia were higher than in other factories in Oświęcim, and the social conditions were better.

My father decided to buy himself a car with money he had earned from the factory. As far as I recall, the mayor was the only person in Oświęcim who owned a car at that time. It wasn't easy to get one. New cars weren't being sold— a person had to satisfy himself with a used one.

The news that Mr. Schönker wished to buy a car spread beyond Oświęcim. Gabriel, a worker at his factory who was entrusted with special errands because he had a motorcycle, rode around the nearby towns, announcing this news. Some people in these other towns offered their cars, but my father's newly hired chauffeur, Mr. Rydzoń, refused all of them, saying he couldn't drive in such a box, tin can, or chamber pot. My father trusted him completely. Sometimes if he liked a car he would cast a questioning glance at Rydzoń, but Rydzoń would say, "Sir, you deserve a real car, not an old clunker like this."

In Kraków at that time there was a regional liquidation office that was selling the belongings of Governor Hans Frank. They had one of his cars there—a long, sleek Mercedes limousine. My father went to Kraków with Rydzoń and bought this car. The price was very high because the liquidation office considered it to be a museum piece. The car was in good condition and my father was ready to pay any price for it because—as he said—it would certainly make Hans Frank spin in his grave.

In the year 1947, there was an important event for the residents of Oświęcim. On March 11, after nearly a year of preparations, a trial began in Warsaw for the former commandant of the Auschwitz concentration camp, SS-Obersturmbannführer Rudolf Höss. Warsaw was still in such a destroyed state that it was difficult to find a room large enough for such a trial. In the end, the headquarters of the Polish Teachers' Union were used—up to five hundred people could fit in its hall. The audience at the trial consisted mostly of former prisoners of the camp.

Rudolf Höss was sentenced to death by hanging on April 2. The court acquiesced to a petition submitted by former Auschwitz prisoners for the execution to be carried out on the camp's grounds. The execution was scheduled for April 14, but it was postponed by two days because there were fears the residents of Oświęcim would attempt to lynch Höss while he was being transported through the town.

There was a great commotion throughout Oświęcim. Everyone was talking about it in the streets; people were very excited. On the day of the execution, we went to school earlier than usual because we wanted to see the condemned man being driven past. Suddenly, someone shouted, "Here they come!" We all raced to the window. Several cars passed quickly. We didn't see anything else, but we were still very excited.

German prisoners of war built the wooden gallows. Before the execution, Höss asked for a priest. Father Zaremba, a Salesian priest from Oświęcim, recited a prayer for the dying next to the gallows. Höss was hanged near the camp's headquarters.

In 1947, the Polish government, at the request of former prisoners, decided to turn the Auschwitz concentration camp into a national museum to commemorate the martyrdom of the Polish nation and other nations. The law concerning the establishment of the museum was passed on July 2, 1947, even though the museum had already officially opened on June 14. Delegations from many countries came to Oświęcim. Everything took place very ceremoniously, and the town's residents, including my father, took an active part in this event. There was an air of excitement in the entire town.

After the ceremony, my father held a big party in our villa. Many foreign guests were invited, most of whom were quite well known. My mother, Stasia, and two other maids cooked and baked all week long. Tables were nearly buckling under the weight of the food. Stasia's face was constantly flushed, and after a while my mother collapsed into an armchair and couldn't get up. But everything turned out well.

The party lasted until late at night. There were discussions on various topics, including politics and the economy. New acquaintances were made, and business cards were exchanged. I have a particularly vivid memory of a certain American Jew of Polish origin. He talked with my father for a long time. He was interested in everything and asked my father a lot of questions. He was very friendly and apologized for speaking in such broken Polish. When my father asked him what he did in the United States, he answered that he was an intermediary in trade—anything could be bought through him. He gave my father his business card on which was printed that he sold everything "from a fingertip to a battleship." My father liked this business card very much. I could tell that this friendly American had impressed him.

In 1947, another event took place that was significant for Oświęcim's residents. Father Piotr Tirone, a priest and the general catechist of the Salesians, decided to pay a visit to our town. People called him the "Black Pope."

The Salesian priests enjoyed great respect and esteem in Oświęcim, even among communist party members. The town was proud of the vocational school they ran, called the Salesian Institute. The Salesian priests asked my father if Father Tirone, the famous priest, could be driven to Oświęcim from the Czechoslovakian border in my father's car. My father instructed Rydzoń to drive to the border with the priests to pick up Father Tirone, to remain at his disposition day and night throughout his stay in Oświęcim, and then to take him back to the border. Father Tirone's visit became a huge religious demonstration in Oświęcim. There were processions every day, and the whole town took on a festive appearance.

The massive processions were, in fact, a protest against communism, which had been spreading in our town and throughout the rest of Poland. Many people who had never participated in religious life were now walking in the processions. The communist authorities viewed all of this suspiciously but didn't openly oppose it.

The Polish People's Republic was supposed to take care of its citizens and make their lives easier. Unfortunately, in reality the opposite was true. Earnings were low, and basic supplies were growing scarcer. Life was becoming more difficult. My family had no trouble obtaining supplies because we had money. Someone would often deliver kosher meat to us from Katowice, or a Jewish ritual butcher would visit us. For holidays, Stasia and my mother would buy a goose or even two geese at the market. I remember my mother or Stasia blowing into a goose's rump at the marketplace to see if it was yellow, which was very important because it would indicate if the goose was fat. The word "cholesterol" was still unknown at that time. We liked fattening food. Everyone—not only us—who had survived the war craved fatty and high-calorie nourishment.

I remember the first train trip I took alone—to Kraków, with Romek. We were fifteen years old. We sat in Noworolski Café in Kraków and each ordered five pieces of cake. We had no trouble eating them. After nearly starving to death in the Bergen-Belsen camp, I couldn't get enough cake.

Later we started going to the cinema in Katowice. There was only one cinema in Oświęcim, and it screened films that didn't interest us very much, but in Katowice there were several cinemas and such wonderful films! I remember a film about Jesse James—a cowboy film, and in color! We watched it many times, and I liked it more each time.

My parents liked Romek very much. Of course, I didn't tell my mother that we sometimes went to a restaurant to play pool. We would always order a quarter of a liter of vodka, to make things merrier. We played in the Radwan Restaurant located in the former home of Mr. Haberfeld, who had owned a liqueur factory before the war that was famous all over Poland. Haberfeld and his wife had gone to New York in 1939 to see the World's Fair, leaving their daughter in Oświęcim. The war broke out, and their daughter died in the Holocaust. After the war, Haberfeld and his wife never returned to Oświęcim.

Sometimes I thought about all of this while playing pool, but I never told Romek about it. Memories of the Holocaust accompanied me at all times, regardless of what I was doing. The Holocaust was like a second, secret existence for me.

I didn't experience any antisemitism. From time to time I thought I encountered it, but it usually just resulted from my complexes, which I hadn't yet rid myself of. This doesn't mean that antisemitism had disappeared in Poland. Quite the contrary—sometimes it even seemed to be increasing. It's impossible to generalize, however, because many Polish people not only rejected antisemitism but strongly condemned it. Once in a while it seemed to me that people were helping me precisely because I was Jewish. Perhaps through such behavior toward me they wished to atone for the sins committed by others.

I considered leaving Poland many times. In 1947 I nearly left for England. My father's uncle, Eber, Grandpa Józef's half brother, lived in London. He wrote many letters to my father saying it would be better for me to live in England and finish high school, and then study at a university there. He was even willing to pay for my education. We thought about it for a long time and finally decided I should do this.

I applied for a passport and was granted one; then I went to the British consulate in Katowice to apply for a visa. Soon the consulate informed me I could pick up my passport and visa. Uncle Eber enrolled me in Brighton College.

I couldn't sleep all night before my visit to the consulate because I was thinking constantly about my trip. In the morning, my father didn't go to the factory and said he'd also had a sleepless night. During breakfast I noticed there were tears in his eyes. I was also having difficulty holding back my tears. I stood up from the table and shouted, "I'm not going!"

And that was the end of the plan to send me to England.

―⁂―

In the year 1948, everything seemed to be going well for us. My father refused to see the black clouds that were swiftly approaching. He chose to ignore them, despite other people's warnings. He had lost a sense of reality, in general, and didn't see what was going on around him and the direction in which the political situation in Poland was headed.

Aron Hollender, my father's cousin, visited us one day. He had just returned from Russia and wanted to leave Poland as soon as possible. My father tried to convince him to stay and rebuild a life for himself here. Aron didn't want to even hear about it and answered each of my father's arguments with one statement: "Ivan will soon have all of Poland under his control, and I've had enough of him."

My father showed him our home with pride, but Aron just shook his head with disdain. "Leon, you're not going to take a single nail from here."

"I don't want to go anywhere, this is my home, and it's where I'm staying," my father answered.

"I didn't know you were so naive."

"Why am I naive?"

Aron looked straight into my father's eyes and said, "Because you have no idea what Ivan is capable of."

"Ivan who?" asked my father. "Ivan the Terrible?"

"Believe me, Leon, Ivan the Terrible could learn a lot from the Ivan of today."

The conversation ended on that note. I could see it gave my father a lot to think about, for Aron was saying the exact same thing as Leiser Dawid.

The creation of the state of Israel on May 14, 1948, was an event of profound significance for Jewish people all over the world. Now they began to feel safer, for if they found themselves faced with danger they had a place that would shelter them.

Polish Jews felt euphoric. They constantly emphasized what a great contribution Polish Jews had made to the creation of the state of Israel. Among the thirteen ministers in the first government established by David Ben-Gurion, six were from Poland. At that time the Soviet Union, and, by association, the Polish People's Republic, was on friendly terms with Israel because, first, Israel had "thrown off the shackles of English imperialism" and, second, the communist bloc hoped that through Israel's help it could gain influence in the Middle East, which was something the Soviets had been dreaming of for a long time. Israel's government was also very left-wing.

An Israeli legation was opened in Poland in a great rush.[3] It had no financial support, so it requested aid from Jewish people living in Poland. One of its problems was the lack of a vehicle. Israel Barzilay, representing the legation, was supposed to submit a letter of credence to President Bierut soon, and it wasn't appropriate for him to drive there in a borrowed car or taxi.

That same day, Dr. Moshe Karmel, who served as vice-consul at the Israeli legation in Warsaw, phoned my father and asked him to visit the legation. The next day my father drove to Warsaw and returned with a long list of requests for aid. One was particularly urgent—a car was needed. My father decided to give them his Mercedes. I remember how it was quickly tuned up and decorated with gold-trimmed blue curtains. My father said the curtains made the car look more dignified.

My father, Leiser Dawid, Stefan Blachura, and I waited in front of our villa's garage for Rydzoń to come from Katowice. My mother, Aunt Genia, and Stasia stood on the upper terrace. The car finally arrived, and Rydzoń said to my father, with tears in his eyes, "Sir, it would be better if this state of Israel hadn't been created, because then we wouldn't have to give away this beautiful car."

"But I'm proud and happy that the first Israeli consul will deliver his letter of credence with this car," said my father, straightening up as if he were the one who would be delivering the letter. He added, "Let's not forget that this car used to belong to Governor Hans Frank. This is history's revenge."

In response to this, everyone except Rydzoń started clapping. He was close to tears. I also felt sad about losing the car but supported my father's decision. The creation of the state of Israel was a cause of great joy for all Jews in Poland. Why should I be sad, then? Leiser Dawid was very pragmatic about it and thought they would probably only need to borrow the car for a short time, until they became more organized. He was right, for not long after this, the legation acquired a large American car.

From then on, my father was a frequent guest at the legation; he became acquainted with the consul and became very close friends with the vice-consul, Dr. Karmel. My father helped them with many things. His first project was to collect money from Jews all over Poland to aid Israel. With all the money he managed to collect, he bought a ship's load of grain. War was raging in Israel at that time, and there was a lack of supplies—food was being rationed, and buses were being searched to ensure that food wasn't being smuggled out of the *kibbutzim*. People in Israel were living in harsh conditions with severe food shortages.

At the request of the legation, President Bierut granted permission for all salvaged Jewish books that could be collected in Poland to be sent to the National Library in Jerusalem. A vast transport network was established. Books were hauled out of attics and cellars. Professor Schneerson from the Hebrew University of Jerusalem traveled to Poland to oversee the entire operation.

My father financed the project. One day he asked me to travel to Warsaw by car with Rydzoń, withdraw twelve million złoty from a bank, and take it to Professor Schneerson in his hotel. I was only seventeen years old at the time and was surprised my father was entrusting me with such an important mission. My father told me I was already almost an old man because of what I had experienced during the war.

Through Dr. Karmel, my father had bought a beautiful English car from the English consul—a Humber Super Snipe. Rydzoń and I set out the next day in this car, and Leiser Dawid joined us at the last minute. When the bank clerk saw the check, his eyes popped out of his head. He looked at me and then at the check several times, told me to wait, then disappeared through a door. It was quite a while before he appeared again. He asked me where the money should be sent. I replied that I would take it with me in cash. He had an expression on his face as if he didn't understand what I had said.

"You wish to take twelve million złoty with you in cash, sir?" he asked incredulously.

"Yes," I answered modestly, pointing to two suitcases on the floor next to me.

The clerk once again disappeared through the door. This time I had to wait even longer. At last, he reappeared with an assistant who was pushing a cart loaded with packages of money. I packed them into the suitcases, and we went to the hotel where Professor Schneerson was staying. We gave him the suitcases full of money.

I had accomplished the mission and breathed a sigh of relief. We went out into the street. There was a group of people standing around our car, staring at it. One of them said, "This car surely belongs to a comrade from the party's central committee."

"Why do you think so?" asked another.

"Because there's no diplomatic number on it, and it couldn't possibly belong to a private entrepreneur."

We got in the car, but I managed to overhear the rest of the conversation.

"Maybe you're mistaken," remarked another guy.

"I'm not mistaken, because private entrepreneurs are a dying breed, and soon they'll completely disappear."

That was the first time I heard that private businesses were dying out.

"Don't worry," I told myself. "It's just some good-for-nothing's opinion."

That same day my father received many phone calls from the legation and other grateful people. Everyone was very happy, including my father.

The newspapers were full of articles stating that all the shortages on the market were temporary and the sooner Poland fully adopted socialism, the sooner these troubles would end, and there would be an abundance of everything. But other newspaper articles soon appeared declaring that the shortages were being caused by profiteers on the black market and also, in part, by private businesses, which only focus on making profits for themselves rather than supplying the masses. Members of the town council in Oświęcim reassured my father that this didn't concern Agrochemia and his business dealings. He wasn't worried in the slightest. My mother told my father to be careful, but he ignored her warnings because—well, what did women know about business? Furthermore, he had just bought two more factories—a large, empty building in Bobrek, a village near Oświęcim, in which he planned to manufacture glue, as far as I can recall, and a small glue factory in Częstochowa. He was in his element.

Leiser Dawid believed that the entire transitional economy was useless and the country was drowning in bureaucracy. The more bureaucrats and stifling restrictions there were, the fewer products there were on the market. My father said he didn't want to analyze the system because he was only interested in the well-being of his factory; as long as it was developing well, he was satisfied. Leiser Dawid stood his ground. He said that filling positions with people who were clueless about the economy was a quick route to bankrupting the entire country.

"How can a country go bankrupt?" I asked.

"It can," replied Leiser Dawid, "but in this political system, nobody will publicly admit that the country has gone bankrupt."

"But that's impossible. How can people live in a bankrupt country?"

"That's right, it's impossible to understand, but I saw it with my own eyes in Russia. I thought it would be the same in Poland. I understood it was different only when I was returning to Poland in a freight train and met a Russian who was traveling with us on fake identity documents. Everyone knew about it, but nobody said a word. I asked him why he wanted to leave Russia so badly that he would risk his life to do so. He replied that after he had been sent to paradise on a business trip, he decided to leave Russia at any cost. 'Where was this paradise?' I asked. He answered that it was in Lwów. Only then did I realize what kind of country I had been living in."

Leiser Dawid nodded, as if to make sure I had understood everything.

"So why, Uncle, did you lug that suitcase full of nails here?" I asked, not giving up.

"You're right, it was unnecessary, but when a person is subjected to brainwashing for years on end, he no longer knows what he's supposed to think." Leiser Dawid stopped for a moment to reflect; then he added, "But there's no way of knowing if they might still be of use someday."

"Leiser Dawid, I think you're exaggerating," my father said.

"Leon, believe me, I'm not exaggerating in the slightest. The things I saw in Russia . . ." He waved his hand and made a face as if there was nothing more to say on the matter. But my father remained unperturbed.

Like my father, I was satisfied with my life. I had friends, was doing well in school, and was well liked. My frequent trips with Stefan to soccer games began to stimulate my imagination. My secret dream was to play on a soccer team.

During the breaks at school, nobody was talking about anything else but the upcoming soccer tournament. Even the girls were excited and watched our practice sessions. However, something unexpected happened right before the first game. The organizers decided our class's team was too strong, and they transferred Morończyk, the best player in the whole school, from our team to a different one. We were devastated. Morończyk wouldn't be able to cheat because someone from the Soła soccer club in Oświęcim and someone from the Garbarnia soccer club in Kraków were going to watch the final game. We gave each other encouragement, and the girls cheered us on. We promised each other we would do our very best to win.

Finally, the day of the tournament came. The final game was between our class and the class with which Morończyk was playing. The game started with a powerful attack on the goal I was defending. A strong shot. I stopped the ball. I was filled with extraordinary confidence. I played marvelously. Our opponents, with Morończyk in the lead, were very powerful. I've never understood how I managed to catch all those shots. I lunged to the left and right, and leaped almost to the top of the goalpost as if my legs were on springs. I felt something unusual happening inside me; I was invincible. There were many spectators, and I received energetic applause. Every time I defended the goal, my girlfriend, Hanka Wesołowska—the embodiment of modesty, delicacy, and good manners—jumped for joy.

I no longer remember what the score was, but I clearly recall that we were one goal ahead. Suddenly Morończyk dribbled the ball marvelously past all our defense players. I found myself alone with him. It looked like I had no chance of defending the goal. With an instinctive impulse, I lunged forward and caught the ball from right under Morończyk's foot at the very last moment. Normally a goalkeeper tries to fall sideways at the player's feet so as not to be kicked in the head. But there wasn't time—what I did resulted purely from reflex. Morończyk leaped over me and helped me get up, giving me an appreciative pat on the back. The applause I received has resounded in my ears my whole life.

After the soccer game, the man from the Soła soccer club approached me and asked if I'd like to play on their team. Of course, I agreed immediately. At the end of our conversation he said, "Henryk, you played wonderfully." I felt as proud as a peacock. My whole class congratulated me, and Hanka kissed me in front of everyone—which was really something. She turned as red as a beet afterward, but the whole class applauded her.

A short time later I went to a youth camp organized by Ichud—the only Jewish political party legally functioning in postwar Poland. Its aim was to build a Jewish state in Palestine. The communist authorities allowed Ichud to create about seventy *kibbutzim* in Poland, where young Jewish people could be trained to work and fight in defense of Israel. Over two thousand youths stayed in the *kibbutzim*. The government of the Polish People's Republic generously gave them 40 million złoty. Ichud sent young people to Israel—illegally before the creation of the state of Israel, and legally after its creation. Right after the Jewish youths arrived, they were conscripted into the army and fought in battles against the Arabs. Some died, and many were wounded.

The Ichud camp provided preliminary preparation for the departure to Israel. I liked it there very much. I met other young people there, and their enthusiasm began to infect me. We spent our time listening to ideological lectures, holding discussions, going on excursions, and doing drills and sentry duty. We didn't sleep in tents but in buildings that had been constructed by the Germans during the war. We were outside in the fresh air all day long. It was a wonderful vacation!

In the middle of the camp, set slightly apart from the buildings, there was a very tall flagpole with the Israeli flag at the top of it. Sentry duty was performed day and night, four hours at a time, by a girl and boy together. My turn came. Our shift was from three to seven a.m. We stood there with wooden rifles on our shoulders. My partner was beautiful, and her eyes were very alluring. After an hour of duty, we decided to rest a bit off to the side, in some bushes. We kissed, nothing more—God forbid—but what heavenly kisses they were ... Hot, tender, thrilling—unforgettable. After a while we returned to the flagpole and saw, to our horror, that the flag had disappeared, and in its place there was now a pair of underwear flapping in the wind. Before I could do anything about it, our friends surrounded us on all sides, bursting with laughter. The camp's commander punished us by ordering us to spend three whole days peeling potatoes in the kitchen. And I acquired the nickname "Goofball."

One day my father showed up. Without uttering a single word, he took me by the arm and led me to the room where I slept.

"Pack your bags," he said curtly.

"What happened?" I asked, startled.

"I'll tell you in the car," he said in a very solemn tone of voice.

I was afraid something bad had happened. I packed my backpack with trembling hands and went to check myself out of the camp. But it turned out my father had already done it for me. We got in the car, Rydzoń greeted me, and we left. Everything happened so fast that it looked like a kidnapping. I didn't even have time to say goodbye to my companion from sentry duty.

"All right, tell me what's going on," I said, raising my voice. My patience was running out.

"What's going on is that I'm not willing to sacrifice you and let you risk your life in the war in Israel. We stayed together during the entire war and survived solely by a miracle. I can't let you leave."

I could see he was close to despair. I didn't say anything, and he added, "I'll do everything to help Israel and give everything I have, except you." He was nearly crying as he said this. I looked into his eyes and saw that they were moist. I'd rarely seen him in such a state.

What could I do? I sank into my own thoughts and barely spoke for the whole trip. I was sad and had pangs of conscience. For a long time afterward, I felt guilty that I hadn't gone to Israel to defend the country. It must have been obvious that something was bothering me, because one day a local priest named Father Adolf Baścik approached me on the street and asked me why I was so dejected. He listened to me silently, and then, looking straight into my eyes, he said, "It's clear that things were meant to happen the way they did. An angel is watching over you. The greatest proof of it is that you survived this terrible war. Who knows what would have happened to you if you had gone to Israel? Perhaps your father's love for you saved you. You should be thankful for it, not sad."

His words helped me greatly at that time.

—ɷ—

In 1949, I celebrated my birthday by inviting some of my classmates to a party at my house. I decided to surprise my guests by playing my violin for them.

My sense of hearing had been so badly damaged by typhus that I was expected to become deaf eventually. My parents took me to see an expert in Kraków. After examining me, he told me I should start playing an instrument—but not a very loud one. It could slow down the hearing loss. And so, I started playing the violin. It was difficult for me because I could barely hear any of the higher tones. But my mother urged me to keep playing, so I continued taking lessons.

My friends arrived for my party; there were about eight of us. After singing "Sto Lat," we sat down to eat.[4] We washed everything down with vodka that I had taken from the icebox in the kitchen. The atmosphere was wonderful. Stasia had prepared a real feast. Everyone admired the silver platters, pitchers, dishes, and goblets and were also very impressed by our old tapestry. A friend who had never visited me before said that if the road to communism looked like this, it was a road worth following. Everyone laughed, and the atmosphere was very joyful.

Sensing it was the culminating moment of my birthday party, I brought my violin to the table. I slowly opened the case, took out the violin, and placed it on my shoulder. My guests were waiting excitedly, and—copying the pose of Mr. Birnbaum from Kraków, whose playing used to enchant me—I played a short melody. My friends showered me with applause. Suddenly someone said something to my friend Raźny, who was an extremely impulsive boy. It had obviously been something insulting because Raźny, without a moment's hesitation, grabbed my violin and smashed it over the boy's head. He fell backward but didn't lose consciousness. My beautiful violin, on the other hand, flew into pieces. I was horrified, and my friends were, too. It took Raźny a while to return to his senses. Then he was extremely ashamed and started apologizing profusely.

I told my parents my violin had fallen on the floor, and someone had stepped on it accidentally. My father made a face as if he didn't believe me, and my mother stood there silently, covering her face with her hands. Then she said in a slow, solemn tone of voice, "This is a very bad sign. Difficult times are coming for us."

One day my father received a phone call from a lawyer named Łoziński in Warsaw, who asked my father to visit him as soon as possible because he had something very important to tell him. My father summoned Rydzoń and traveled to Warsaw. The next day he returned home and, seeing our curiosity, took us—my mother, Leiser Dawid, and me—into his office and closed the door. He made us promise to keep what he was going to tell us a secret and not breathe a single word to anyone about it.

Łoziński had a relative or friend in the Polish Ministry of Foreign Affairs who had informed him that the ministry was seeking discreet and unofficial contact with the Israeli government. It was decided that Łoziński should entrust this task to my father, who, as everyone knew, had close, private contact with Israel's legation in Warsaw. My father had to pledge complete discretion.

The proposition was as follows: the Soviet Union was willing to supply Israel with a large number of weapons at a very attractive price. A man from the Soviet Union's Ministry of Foreign Affairs had presented this offer and asked to make unofficial contact with the Israeli government through a trustworthy intermediary. The entire matter had to remain a secret. In the case of information being leaked or failure of the transaction, the Soviets would deny everything.

My father decided to convey this information privately to Dr. Karmel, at his home. The latter told my father he would ask the Israeli Ministry of Foreign Affairs to send someone to Warsaw to be presented with the details of this proposition, because although it was possible to send information by encrypted telegram, they should rely solely on personal contact in such an important matter. The proposition was very serious and attractive, since Israel was in the midst of a battle for its survival.

An envoy from the Israeli government immediately traveled to Warsaw, and my father introduced him to Łoziński. Łoziński introduced the envoy to a man from Poland's Ministry of Foreign Affairs. There was a meeting with a Russian emissary, and, after becoming acquainted with the details of the offer, the Israeli man traveled to Stockholm (the Israeli legation there was considered more secure than the one in Warsaw) in order to send an encrypted report to Israel. A few days later he returned to Warsaw and conveyed a negative answer from the Israeli government. It turned out that even in the challenging situation they currently found themselves in, they weren't interested in accepting the Soviets' offer because they feared Israel would then find itself under the protection of the USSR. Thus, the entire matter came to an end.

A short time later, my father came home from the factory in a very agitated mood. He locked himself in his office and phoned somebody. I tried to eavesdrop through the door but couldn't understand what it was all about. My father was speaking into the telephone in a raised voice, nearly shouting. I had the impression he was arguing and trying to persuade somebody of something. My mother chased me away from the door and told me that if my father wanted to be alone, we should respect his wish.

He finally emerged from his office, and my mother asked everyone to come to dinner. My parents, Lusia, Leiser Dawid, and I sat at the table together. After a while, my mother asked my father what had happened. My father said the tax office was creating a very unpleasant situation for him.

"What now?" asked my mother.

"They're going after me again," my father replied.

"But this isn't the first time," said my mother, serving some compote. "Why is it upsetting you so much?"

"So far they've only taken trivial amounts of money from me. Now it's a lot more. An enormous surtax is being imposed on Agrochemia. I don't know how I'm going to manage." My father was very upset.

Only then did I find out that the tax office had been harassing my father's company with surtaxes for a while already. They hadn't been large amounts of money, so my father had allowed his lawyers in Kraków to take care of them every time. The lawyers had written appeals but had told my father that if they were rejected, it wasn't worth going to court because there was no real chance of winning a court case against the tax office. And so my father had paid the demanded amounts, and every time he thought they would leave him in peace afterward—but he had always turned out to be wrong. The tax office continued to make new demands.

At that time, I heard from a friend that there were rumors circulating in Oświęcim that Agrochemia was going to be nationalized. I told my father about this, but he reassured me by telling me not to listen to rumors. He told me the factory met all the requirements the government imposed on private businesses. So there was no reason why the factory would be taken away from him.

"Poland isn't Russia," he continued. "Law exists here, and it's on my side." However, I saw anxiety in his eyes.

Soon afterward, I found out about my father's plan to emigrate from my friend Ignacy (Itzhak) Stieglitz from Bielsko. I wasn't surprised at all—such a plan suited him, because he was still living with the trauma of his failed plan to help the Jews of Silesia emigrate at the beginning of the war.

My father wanted a group of Jews from Poland to establish a *kibbutz* in Israel called Kfar Bierut (Bierut Village). There was already a *kibbutz* there called Kfar Masaryk, and a *moshav* (a cooperative agricultural community) called Kfar Truman in the center of Israel.[5] Why couldn't they establish a *kibbutz* or *moshav* called Kfar Bierut, then? Its founders would immediately receive passports. President Bierut could go to Israel and lay the foundation stone for the Korczak House. It would be a very prestigious ceremony and a major propaganda event for Poland, so this plan had a good chance of being realized. He was only telling me this now because he hadn't wanted to bother me, since we would probably stay in Poland. After a moment of reflection, he added, "At least for now..."

"Why do you say 'for now'?" I asked.

"It's impossible to predict how things will turn out here," he answered.

THE REGIONAL PUBLIC SECURITY OFFICE IN KRAKÓW TO THE DISTRICT PUBLIC SECURITY OFFICE IN BIAŁA KRAKOWSKA:

Please send us a detailed character description for citizen Leon Schönker, resident of Oświęcim, owner of an artificial fertilizer factory.

Schönker undertook an initiative to establish a colony in Palestine called "Bierut."[6] With this aim he compiled a list of 80 families, Polish citizens of

Jewish nationality, who planned to leave Poland for Palestine. Most of these families are of the mercantile and profiteering class (unverified). Under the pretext of creating this colony, Schönker intends to liquidate his factory and transport his machines out of Poland. Negotiations in connection with this matter have been in progress for several months between the Israeli legation and citizen Schönker.

We have also become aware that citizen Schönker has somehow obtained American or English citizenship, and privately finances an orphanage in Oświęcim.

Consequently, an intensive investigation of citizen Schönker should be initiated with particular attention given to information concerning his factory: (a) why the factory hasn't been nationalized, (b) which foreign factories or agencies the factory has been in contact with, and who purchases the products manufactured by the factory, (c) who is employed by the factory.

It is necessary to establish citizen Schönker's past: (a) where he lived until 1939, (b) his social and political activities during that time, (c) where he lived during the period of the German occupation and what he did, (d) what citizenship he possesses (if he's a foreigner, how he acquired foreign citizenship), (e) who his contacts are within Poland and abroad, and what kind of social and political activities he is currently involved in.

Kraków, 28 January 1949

At the beginning of 1949, the factory stopped producing superphosphate due to a lack of raw materials. My father said these were only temporary difficulties and would undoubtedly pass, because there was a great need for fertilizers, and his wholesale customers and local farmers would certainly complain to the authorities and ask them to allow Agrochemia to continue production.

Not long after our conversation about this, a man arrived at our house late one afternoon and said he wished to speak with my father about an urgent matter. My mother told him my father was staying longer at the factory that day, and she didn't know when he would come home.

"In that case I'll try to reach him by telephone," the man said.

My mother led him into my father's office and showed him the phone. "My husband's work phone number is—" she began, but she didn't manage to give him the number because he smiled and said he already knew the factory's phone number.

My father came home right away and, after greeting the man, invited him into his office and closed the door. Their conversation lasted over an hour. My mother brought them coffee and cookies, but as soon as she entered the office, they stopped speaking.

After the stranger left, my mother asked, "What happened?"

I noticed she seemed nervous. My father never kept any secrets from my mother, so he asked her to come into his office. I slipped in after her. Now I could see that the calm state my father had seemed to be in so far had only been a mask.

"What happened?" my mother asked again.

I could tell my father's agitation was affecting her, even though she had no idea what it was about.

"Nothing has happened—but it could happen," my father answered.

We sat down and my father began to talk. The man who had visited him was an officer from the Public Security Office in Kraków.[7] He told my father his visit to our house was an unofficial visit and asked my father to keep it a secret. My father glanced at me, and I nodded to let him know that I understood.

"What it comes down to is that they want to take my factory away from me and, in exchange, allow me to emigrate to Israel."

The UB officer told my father that it was no longer possible for companies such as Agrochemia to remain in private hands. He explained that they were aware of my father's contributions to Oświęcim, which is why they were offering to settle this matter amicably, without creating a fuss of any kind. It would be best if my father packed up his belongings and left for Israel. My father tried to explain how difficult it had been for him to start Agrochemia and how much he had invested in it so that it could develop to its present capacity. The officer responded that all of this was clear to them, which is why they were treating my father in a privileged manner. He ended the conversation by stating he hadn't come to threaten my father. He asked him to think about the offer and to treat the meeting as a private, unofficial visit.

"Did you give him some kind of answer?" my mother asked.

"Of course. I told him I didn't agree."

"And what did he say to that?"

"Nothing. He apologized for having taken up my time, and the conversation came to an end."

My mother was alarmed and told my father he shouldn't have answered so quickly. He should have spent some time thinking about it before responding.

But my father was of a different opinion. He thought it was a perfidious offer with no legal basis. In Poland, there were still laws protecting people, and it wasn't possible to take away people's businesses, even if it was what the UB wanted. They had no right to confiscate any of our property. I was feeling anxious about the situation, but I knew life would go on. "We'll see how this all plays out," I thought.

Leiser Dawid came from Katowice that evening. He was very happy. As soon as he entered our living room, he stretched his arms out to us and dramatically announced that we should congratulate him. My parents congratulated him, and we all embraced him. I didn't understand why everyone was so happy and why we were congratulating him. I asked him if he was getting married. Everyone laughed. He had visited his lawyer in Katowice and found out that his passport application had been approved. I had no idea that Leiser Dawid had applied for a passport. It was quite common for Jewish people to do this secretly. Nobody wanted other people to know they were trying to obtain a passport because if the application was rejected—which frequently occurred not only for families but even among individual applicants—the person would have difficulties later in his community. Such people were viewed with suspicion by the authorities and were no longer treated as legitimate citizens. I understood Leiser Dawid and wasn't angry at him. I wasn't surprised, either, that his passport application was approved. An old, deaf bachelor couldn't be of any use to the Polish People's Republic.

After supper my father shut himself up in his office with Leiser Dawid, and they discussed our family's situation. I don't know exactly what Leiser Dawid told my father, but I gleaned from the conversation my parents later had in their bedroom, which was next to mine, that Leiser Dawid considered my father's situation to be very serious. He was convinced that if the UB didn't drop the case, my father had no chance of winning it despite his cleverness and the good lawyers representing him. The polite way in which the UB agent had spoken to my father didn't mean anything. This was just a tactic to dull his senses.

The next day I asked Leiser for his opinion. He told me that Fonye Ganev had various ways of robbing people and hadn't been punished for it yet.

"Why not?" I asked.

"Because everyone who has something to say about it belongs to the same club," he answered.

For the time being, everything seemed the same as before. I went to my high school, and Lusia went to her primary school. Stasia ran after Lusia every morning with a sandwich, then went to church to pray for all of us. Our dog, Lord, always followed her to church. But the atmosphere at home had changed. We were all filled with an instinctive anticipation of a big change in our life of some kind. We felt anxious. Perhaps this was because my father came home from the factory every day in an increasingly agitated state. He stopped telling us what was happening at Agrochemia. We could see he was very worried. At dinner one evening, he told us the troubles at the factory were increasing, and he was starting to lose hope he would be able to resume the production of superphosphate.

THE DISTRICT PUBLIC SECURITY OFFICE IN OŚWIĘCIM:
The owner of Agrochemia returned to Oświęcim in 1945 after its liberation by the Soviet army. At that time, he found himself in a very critical financial situation. After some time, Schönker, with the help of two employees, reactivated the factory's production of artificial fertilizer, hiring from five to sixty workers. These workers place an extraordinary amount of trust in Schönker, because he treats them very well, willingly provides them with workers' benefits, buys shoes for their children, and sends ill employees to sanatoriums.... Due to a supposed shortage of raw materials, Agrochemia has switched to production of horn tiles and is not currently manufacturing artificial fertilizers.

Despite Schönker having received permission to establish a Polish Workers' Party association at his factory, representatives of the Polish Workers' Party failed to form a cell there in 1945 and 1947. Agrochemia's workers are not members of any party except a labor union....

On March 1 of this year, a wedding was held in Schönker's villa between the Israeli consul, Dr. Karmel, and a Mexican citizen.

March–May 1949

Two weeks later, we were visited again by the same UB agent. I don't know what he talked about with my father because, like the previous time, they went into my father's office and closed the door. However, I noticed a look of resignation on my father's face after the man left. My father told us the man hadn't been as polite as before—he had made it clear to my father he had no choice in the matter. Agrochemia was going to be nationalized with or without my father's consent. If my father decided to involve his lawyers in the matter, they would accomplish nothing and would only make the situation worse, for the UB was no longer going to handle my father with kid gloves. If my father looked at what was happening with private companies, even smaller ones than Agrochemia, he would have a better understanding of the situation in which he found himself.

My father consulted with his lawyers in Kraków and Warsaw. They strongly advised him not to take any legal action against the UB. He would surely lose the case, and such a move could put him in a very dangerous position.

I became very scared because I remembered a conversation with my friend Staszek Hutny. He had told me that people sometimes disappeared, and nobody knew what had happened to them. I was afraid something like this could happen to my father.

The stranger visited us again a week later. My father asked him for more time, and the stranger agreed. This was followed by uneasy days in which my father was constantly thinking about the situation and asking my mother and Leiser

Dawid for advice. My father traveled to Kraków and Warsaw, looking for new solutions, but his efforts were all in vain. People in Oświęcim had already been saying for a while that Agrochemia was having difficulties of some kind. The factory's problems were accumulating very rapidly. My father came home from work every day in an increasingly anxious state. The tax office played a large role in this, for it started presenting my father with surtaxes for previous years. My father tried to create the impression that Agrochemia would resume production soon. Our situation in Oświęcim was becoming more and more hopeless.

Finally, after another visit from the UB agent during which there were clear threats, my father came to the conclusion that he had no choice and if he didn't want to be arrested, he must agree to emigrate to Israel. Leiser Dawid thought the UB had hatched a diabolical plan, for it would look as if the Schönker family had emigrated of their own volition. None of the residents of Oświęcim would be aware of the great harm that had been done to us.

My father knew he had to agree to emigrate. However, he wanted to do it in the way he had already planned—namely, to take other Jewish people with him from Bielsko and establish Kfar Bierut in Israel. I don't know who was helping him with this plan in Bielsko, but apparently the idea of creating a Polish *kibbutz* in Israel had been enthusiastically welcomed there by several dozen Jewish people. My father perceived something in this project that would cause—as he explained—his "emigration from Poland to make some kind of sense."

We talked about emigration a lot at that time and slowly got used to the idea. It wasn't easy for me. We had a beautiful house in Oświęcim, and I was attending a high school that I liked very much. I had dreamed of this throughout all those years of wartime suffering. I asked myself, Will I really have to abandon all this? Oświęcim was my hometown. It had helped me regain mental and spiritual balance after the terrible years of the Holocaust. The hardest thing for me to come to terms with was the thought that I would be separated from my friends, especially Romek Maksymowicz.

I felt guilty, however, that I had left the Ichud camp and had betrayed my Jewish friends. Nobody reproached me for this, but it was something that weighed heavily on my conscience. My father said that if we lived in Israel, in the worst scenario he would return to his painting career. He would certainly get more satisfaction from painting than from fighting day after day for a factory that the authorities wanted to take away from him. I had full confidence in my father that he would manage well in Israel, too.

The difficulty stemmed from the fact that the procedure for Jews emigrating from Poland was very long and complicated at that time. Moreover, it usually ended with a refusal to issue a passport. The UB's regional office in Kraków, however, was insisting on us leaving Poland as soon as possible. Knowing that my father was in very close contact with the Israeli legation in Warsaw and that after returning from Germany in 1945, he had declared at Oświęcim's town hall that he was a foreign citizen, the UB pressured my father to apply for Israeli passports for us. They would enable us to leave Poland quickly and without the necessity of renouncing our Polish citizenship, which was something my father strongly opposed.

My father considered the offer to be a very good one, and the next day he went to Warsaw. Dr. Karmel, the vice-consul, told him he needed to obtain the consent of Barzilay, the consul, but he was sure the consul would want to help him and that the matter would have a positive outcome. The consul listened to my father's request and said he couldn't issue my father a passport because he wasn't an Israeli citizen. However, he could issue him a travel document called a *laissez-passer* with which my father would be allowed to leave Poland. The UB in Kraków agreed to let us travel on an Israeli *laissez-passer*. For them the only thing that mattered was to get rid of us as quickly as possible.

After my father presented our *laissez-passer* documents, the UB ordered him to submit a deposition containing a precise summary of his life. They said he should provide as many details as possible, so that it would be clear why he was the only one in our family with foreign citizenship. Shortly afterward they would give us exit visas allowing us to leave Poland. My father appeared at the district authority office in Biała Krakowska on March 8, 1949, and submitted an invented deposition—after all, he had never really been a citizen of a foreign country, and the UB was very well aware of this.

We decided not to tell anyone about our situation until we received our visas. We knew our departure would cause a sensation and might influence the decisions of other Jewish people who weren't sure at that time whether to apply for passports. We assumed we would have to wait just a few days to receive our visas, but time passed, and we didn't receive any notifications to travel to Bielsko to pick them up.

Soon it was time for Leiser Dawid to leave. We all had tears in our eyes as we said goodbye. I had grown very attached to him. Leiser Dawid first traveled to Belgium to visit his sister; then he went to the United States. The Liebermans had already left for Israel. Aunt Genia asked my mother to try to get a passport for her because she wished to die in Israel. She received one a short time later and left Poland with our close friend Paul Gliksman, a tailor from Oświęcim, and his wife.

I felt our beautiful home falling apart. Days passed, and we continued to wait. A UB agent with whom my father was in contact via telephone assured him that his visa was being arranged, and everything was going to be fine. And so, we waited. My father still went to the factory every day, but it was clear to us that our life in Oświęcim was coming to an end.

Beno Mansfeld, a distant relative of ours and close friend, lived in Katowice. He was an extremely wise and cheerful person. We were very close to him and his wife, Bronia, and their young daughter, Irka.

One day, Beno Mansfeld visited us and told us about an idea he had: an acquaintance of his, Netty Ringer, was about to leave Katowice for Israel. She had permission to take all her possessions with her. Even though she didn't have many possessions, she couldn't afford to transport them to Israel. Beno suggested that she take some of our belongings with her, and in return my father would pay for her things to be shipped. It would be worthwhile for us because, even though there were no restrictions on the number of things people could take with them, it would probably be difficult for us to take all our belongings with us when we left. My father agreed—of course we wanted to take as many of our belongings to Israel as possible.

After settling everything with Netty Ringer, my father hired a shipping company from Katowice called Hartwig to take some of our possessions from our villa to Katowice and send them to Israel after all the formalities had been arranged.

All the objects were inspected by customs officers and, after receiving the required permission, they were to be sent to Gdynia and then, from there, to Israel by ship. The matter dragged on because some of our possessions had to be presented to a museum curator for inspection before permission could be given to transport them out of Poland. Several objects didn't receive permission and were returned to us. After settling the formalities, Hartwig scheduled a day when our belongings would be packed and sent to Gdynia.

The day before the scheduled shipment day, several men appeared at our house, including Jan Falewski—the public prosecutor from the Special Commission Against Fraud and Economic Sabotage in Kraków. He informed my father that he was going to conduct a search of our home. He refused to tell my father the reason. My father wanted to contact his lawyer, but the men didn't let him go to the telephone.

They didn't make a mess or cause any damage, but they searched our entire house very thoroughly. They locked the doors and didn't let anyone leave. They interrogated Stasia and Stefan, and from these interrogations it was possible to infer that they were looking for something that could incriminate my father. They asked Stasia if there was any gold in our house. She told them there was, indeed, and showed them her gold-capped teeth. One of the men asked her if she had noticed a machine of some kind in our house. Stasia nodded and led them to the cellar to show them the huge furnace for central heating. They asked me if I had seen any American dollars in our house. They also searched Stefan's rooms and asked him what kind of relationship he had with my father. They clearly didn't know about the shipment of our belongings, since they didn't ask any questions about it.

The search lasted several hours. Even though they didn't find anything and nothing was confiscated, Falewski told my father he was under arrest. My father asked what the charge was, and Falewski responded that he would eventually find out. They took my father to the civic militia station in Oświęcim's main square.

Then they went to our factory and interrogated the workers. They were asked if they had ever noticed anything illegal. They weren't asked about anything specific, just whether they had ever seen or heard anything that aroused their suspicion. They searched the factory's offices and then sealed them up; they told the astonished workers that a special team would come from Kraków the following day to examine all the accounting records and other documentation. It would take several days; then the offices would be reopened for work. All of this seemed very strange to us. It looked as if they first arrested my father, then afterward started looking for something he could be accused of. We had no idea what it was all about—after all, my father had already agreed to give up Agrochemia.

THE DISTRICT PUBLIC SECURITY OFFICE IN BIAŁA KRAKOWSKA TO THE REGIONAL PUBLIC SECURITY OFFICE IN KRAKÓW:
On 14 May 1949 at 7:00 p.m. Leon Schönker was apprehended by representatives of the Special Commission in Kraków... As it was stated, Leon Schönker was arrested for trading in foreign currencies. The above information was provided by the commanding officer of the Civic Militia station in Oświęcim and confirmed by confidential sources.
19 May 1949

THE SPECIAL COMMISSION IN KRAKÓW TO THE MINISTRY OF PUBLIC SECURITY IN WARSAW:
I report that Leon Schönker, owner of a chemical factory in Oświęcim, was... arrested... on suspicion of financial fraud.
3 June 1949

The news of my father's arrest spread through Oświęcim with lightning speed. Our telephone rang constantly. Lusia cried all the time, and Stasia kept repeating, while wringing her hands, "Oh my God! Oh my God!"

My mother and I decided to go to Kraków to see my father's cousin, Maciej Jakubowicz (known as Moniek). My father's other cousin, Moniek's brother—Dawid Jakubowicz, a lawyer by profession—also lived in Kraków. They were our closest relatives, and our friends. Moniek was a rich entrepreneur; he owned a wine factory called Krajowin. They were both very clever and resourceful men, and Moniek had many good connections. We went to Kraków to ask them for advice about my father's situation.

When we told them about my father's arrest, they were both extremely worried and promised to help us as much as they could. They said we first needed to find a good lawyer who specialized in criminal cases. They decided the best lawyer for my father would be Przybylski—a Jewish man who was very well respected.

During our meeting with Przybylski, he told us that first of all we needed to find out what the charges were against my father. He assumed that in two or three days he would be able to tell us something about it, and then we could think about the next steps to take.

We returned to Oświęcim in the evening. Stasia was waiting for us impatiently. She told us my father was locked up at the station in the main square. The militiamen had told Stasia to bring some food to my father. She had gone there with a pot of hot food and a plate. My father told her he needed to see me and my mother. One of the militiamen agreed to us visiting my father in the evening, as long as we kept it a secret. We took some more food with us and went to the jail. Our dog, Lord, leaped through the open gate and ran after us. The militiaman let us into the jail, and then we heard Lord barking at the door. The militiaman was clearly nervous.

"Open the door for him—everyone in Oświęcim knows the Schönker family's dog. If anyone finds out I let you in here, I'm finished."

I opened the door, and Lord leaped into the corridor. The officer led us into the jail cell where my father was sitting. I could tell my father was trying not to show any signs of distress. He stroked Lord and assured us that everything would soon be cleared up and the Special Commission's suspicions would turn out to be groundless. The best proof of this was the fact that they had been unable to find anything in our house and hadn't confiscated anything, and also that he had been left in Oświęcim rather than taken to Kraków. We returned home still in a state of unease but with our spirits slightly raised. We were convinced that in a day or two everything would be cleared up, and my father would come home.

Meanwhile, the Special Commission in Kraków was working on my father's case. On July 23, it sent a report to the Ministry of Public Security in Warsaw, which stated that my father had been arrested for charging extortionate amounts of money in the sale of horn meal fertilizer, with profits reaching tens of millions of złoty, and with exporting, or attempting to export, works of art worth 100 million złoty. In addition to these charges, he was also suspected of having been involved in the trading of foreign currencies and gold in the years 1947–1948.

The report also stated that Agrochemia had committed tax fraud amounting to roughly 60 million złoty. Experts from the Treasury Inspectorate and the Regional Fiscal Protection Inspectorate stated that the money gained through tax fraud amounted to at least 80 million złoty. In turn, the Special Commission estimated the sum at 120 million złoty in a document dated August 14, 1949. In the end, they claimed that there had been tax fraud of over 397 million złoty!

We decided to go to Kraków. Przybylski informed us that he had been unable to find out what my father's charges were. He too felt that they had arrested him first and then started looking for something with which to incriminate him. The whole case seemed strange to him because wherever he went to make inquiries about my father, people refused to speak about him.

The only thing he had managed to find out was that the UB's regional office in Kraków was involved in my father's case. This is how cases were handled if the suspect had foreign contacts of some kind. He promised us he would look into this case, but nobody had access to the UB, and it wasn't legally possible to obtain information about what was happening there.

We went to see Moniek again so we could tell him about our visit to the lawyer. We were just about to say goodbye to him when his telephone rang. It was Stasia calling from Oświęcim. She was very upset and told my mother we shouldn't come home because Falewski, the public prosecutor, had been there with his men, and they were looking for us. They had shouted at Stasia and treated her brutally, trying to force her to tell them where we were. She had insisted she didn't know anything. Falewski had been very dissatisfied and left our house in a rage. My mother had enough presence of mind to ask Stasia not to call her again—we would get in touch with her when we needed to. There's no doubt that by calling us at that time, Stasia saved us from being arrested.

We stayed with Moniek for two days and spent the whole time wondering where we could hide. It was clear to us that we had to leave Kraków. My mother got in touch with a close friend of ours from Oświęcim, Regina Kupperman, and asked her to visit us in Kraków. Her husband, Szlomek, worked for Agrochemia as an accountant and knew what was happening. Regina came right away and told us that a bill from the Hartwig transport company confirming receipt of 100,000 złoty had been found in the accounting records. Apparently, this had intrigued Falewski, who contacted the Hartwig company and found out about the shipment of our belongings, which he had immediately halted. This didn't explain why my father had been arrested, but now the Special Commission had something they could use to start a criminal case against my father.

A short time later, Regina asked her sister and brother-in-law—Bronka and Szymon Kahane, who lived in a small town near Wałbrzych—to let us live with them for a while, to which they agreed. They were taking quite a risk because we couldn't be registered at their address; at that time there was a law stating that everyone needed to be officially registered at the address where they lived. Szymon Kahane was a very talented chemist. He worked as a teacher at a high school in Wałbrzych, but every so often he took part in national projects that aimed to discover new chemical processes. At that time he was leaving Wałbrzych for a few weeks to some holiday resort, where a specially selected group of experts were trying to make new discoveries for the Polish People's Republic. Bronka, his wife, was from Oświęcim and had an adult daughter named Rina from her first marriage. Bronka had a respiratory illness, and so she frequently spent time at a sanatorium, and the house often stood empty.

Lusia and Stasia couldn't stay in Oświęcim, either. They stayed with Haber and his wife, Rózia, in Piotrolesie, near Dzierżoniów in the region known as the Recovered Territories. Haber was a distant relative of ours and a close friend. He ran a representative office for a private cotton mill and sold fabrics. We decided not to contact Stasia while she was staying with the Habers because we were afraid someone might eavesdrop on us. We were sure we would be arrested if Falewski found us. We arranged with Regina Kupperman that she would inform us from time to time about how Lusia and Stasia were doing. She also took special precautions and called the Habers from Kraków or Katowice. I don't know what would have happened to us if we hadn't received so much help from friends.

The Kahanes' villa was small but very comfortable. This arrangement suited Szymon Kahane because my mother cooked, cleaned, and ran the household while his wife was at the sanatorium. We felt as if we were on vacation in his house, but we were very worried about my father. We received news only sporadically from the lawyer, who was powerless while the UB was dealing with my father.

Weeks passed but there was no progress in my father's case. Przybylski reassured us that this wasn't unusual. My father had been doing business with foreign contractors, had allowed the Salesian priests to use his car and chauffeur, was in contact with Israeli diplomats, had bought a car from the British consul, and had hosted various foreigners in his home after the opening of the Auschwitz Museum—all of this could seem suspicious to the UB. We were absolutely certain, however, that no political charges had been made against my father.

Our beautiful home had fallen apart. My father was in prison, Lusia and Stasia were with the Habers in Piotrolesie, and we were hiding near Wałbrzych so we wouldn't be arrested. We hoped, but weren't certain, that the investigation by the UB would end soon.

First my father was taken to the Special Commission in Kraków, where Falewski, the public prosecutor, informed him that the investigation would last a very long time because a large amount of material had been collected. They could shorten the investigation if my father pleaded guilty. The court would take his confession into account and give him a lighter sentence. But my father told him that all the charges were groundless.

There were more interrogations throughout the following days. Falewski constantly urged my father to confess, but my father continued to deny all the charges. Finally, seeing that Falewski was increasing pressure on him and his language was becoming more insulting, my father agreed to confess his guilt but only if Falewski added an annotation stating that it was a forced confession and confirmed this with his signature. Falewski replied that my father would change his mind eventually because Saint Michael's Prison in Kraków had a very positive effect on criminals, and everyone always ended up admitting their guilt—if not after a few months, then certainly after a few years. And if they didn't confess after a few years, then the prison became their permanent home.

My father didn't believe Falewski and didn't think the Special Commission had absolute power over him. He was much more afraid of the UB, which—he assumed—was in charge of everything. His statements at the UB's district office in Biała Krakowska and at the civic militia's headquarters were supposed to have enabled him to emigrate quickly. But instead of being allowed to leave Poland, he had been thrown in prison. The matter now seemed very serious to my father.

It's true my father had declared he was a British citizen in 1945, right after our return to Oświęcim, but this hadn't been binding in any way; he had never signed anything connected with it and had never been questioned by anyone about it. Everyone had forgotten about it, including my father. However, the UB had taken advantage of this and insisted that my father apply for an Israeli passport, which would accelerate our emigration considerably. My father thought it wouldn't make any difference since he would be leaving the country soon, so he signed a false declaration. Now, analyzing the situation, he realized the UB had set a trap for him from which it was impossible to extricate himself. He was certain the UB would soon accuse him of falsifying his identity.

My father wondered how he should respond to this accusation. Should he tell the truth—that the UB had artificially constructed all of this? Should he tell the UB that it was to blame, since it had created the situation? It had become obvious that the best outcome for the UB would be if my father received a long-term prison sentence.

One morning he woke up and felt that something had changed within him. He had a clear idea of how he should proceed. And he remembered having had a sensation during the night of someone standing next to him, whispering, "You need to continue wading through the mud, but in a golden robe." Everything now seemed clear to him—he must under no circumstances admit to having given false statements. On the contrary, he needed to uphold these statements and go even further—he needed to expand them and add fantastical details. Then his testimony would be so intriguing that the interest of those who were going to read it would be focused on the astonishing details rather than whether or not he was a British citizen. He gathered his courage. He had a plan and was ready to fight.

On June 14, 1949, my father was taken to the headquarters of the Special Commission to be interrogated. An extraordinary coincidence occurred during the trip. My father was transported in an open vehicle with several other men who had been arrested. A French journalist was standing in the main square and took a photograph of him. The journalist's attention was most likely caught by my father's long, flowing beard. The next day the photo appeared in a prominent newspaper in Paris and included my father's name. My father was well known in Kraków, and the photographer had clearly found out who he was. It caused a huge sensation at the UB.

This remarkable incident helped a great deal, because it showed that my father was truly a well-known person. The fate of such people couldn't be determined by small clerks but rather by the upper echelons of the UB. In such a situation, it would be difficult to make my father quietly disappear, which is what might have seemed the best solution to the bureaucrats of the UB's regional office in Kraków.

On June 15, 1949, my father was taken to the UB's regional office on Plac Inwalidów, and he was interrogated on the first or second day of his imprisonment there. They asked him mainly about the emigration of Jews to Israel and various people in the Jewish world. Everything my father said was true, except for his property abroad.

OFFICIAL RECORD OF AN INTERROGATION AT THE REGIONAL PUBLIC SECURITY OFFICE IN KRAKÓW:

I was the one who initiated the creation of a colony called "Bierut." Seeing the Polish attitude toward Jews in the years 1945–46 and witnessing the pogrom in Kielce, and then seeing the efforts made by members of the Polish government to normalize relations within the country, I became convinced that the president of Poland, citizen Bierut, is no less deserving than Masaryk to have a colony named after him, so I decided to establish one.

I visited citizen Barzilay at the end of 1948 with this aim ... and I submitted a memorandum to him concerning this matter.

I developed the general statute of this colony on my own. The most important point of the statute was that every emigrant had to donate half his wealth to the colony, in order to finance the Korczak House for orphaned children whose parents perished in concentration camps.

Kraków, 15 June 1949

My father was placed in a solitary cell in which there was an iron bed, a small table, and a chair. There was a pile of blank sheets of paper and a pen on the table. He was ordered to write down a precise account of his life. My father was surprised because he had just testified and the record included his entire life story.

The officer smiled and said, "Schönker, there's no reason to be surprised. During your stay with us, you're going to recall a great many things about yourself."

My father had no choice, so he started writing. A few hours later, the sheets of paper he had covered with writing were taken away from him, and he was ordered to write a precise description of his life from the moment the war ended until the present moment. In the evening, the papers were once again taken from him, and he was told to write down the names of foreigners he had been in contact with after the war and to describe what they looked like. A guard came every half hour to make sure my father hadn't fallen asleep. Finally, in the middle of the night, my father was allowed to sleep for a few hours, but the bare light bulb hanging in the cell was not switched off.

The next morning, he was given two slices of dry bread and some artificial coffee. Then a new pile of blank paper was placed on his table, and he was ordered again to write down a detailed description of his life. There were no interrogations or questions; he just had to write his autobiography. The situation was made worse by the fact that they had taken away his pipe, which he was very attached to. Sometimes it seemed to me that my father couldn't live without it. It's enough to say that while we were in the Bergen-Belsen camp, he smoked sawdust from his mattress.

After seven days of writing his autobiography, my father's head was throbbing, and his hand could no longer hold the pen. He was completely exhausted; he no longer even felt hungry. They finally let him sleep.

They interrogated him a few days later. My father was brought into a room and told to sit in front of a desk. A middle-aged officer entered and sat down on the other side. He scrutinized my father with a restless gaze, then leaned back in his chair, pulled a cigarette case from his pocket, and opened it.

"Would you like a cigarette?" he asked.

"I don't smoke cigarettes, but please give me back my pipe and tobacco pouch," my father responded.

"It'll depend on you—that is, on whether we reach an agreement or not," answered the officer in a quiet, seemingly obliging voice. He even smiled while he spoke.

"What is this all about?" my father asked, trying to hide his anxiety.

"There are many inaccuracies in your autobiography. Gaps, I would say. You wrote down for us only what was convenient for you. But we're interested in your full biography, without any omissions." The officer's voice was still quiet and almost friendly.

"What did I omit?"

"You omitted many things. For example, the contact you had with various foreigners who attended the party at your house after the opening of the Auschwitz museum."

"But I wrote about that," my father said.

"You wrote about it, but very vaguely and without mentioning specific people," the officer continued in a friendly tone.

"I no longer remember all the people who were at my house that day," my father explained.

"Well, in that case we'll remind you." After the officer said this, he stood up and opened a door leading to another room. He made a gesture to invite someone in.

Another officer entered the room. My father felt he knew the man from somewhere but couldn't remember where. He was just about to ask where he knew him from when he realized who the man was. He was unable to contain his immense astonishment. It was the friendly American who had been at the party in our house and had never left his side. My father had assumed at the time that the man was one of the members of the delegation of American Jews who had come to Poland for the opening of the museum at the Auschwitz concentration camp.

My father's amazement seemed to be giving both officers great pleasure. Finally, the officer sitting behind the desk said, "We're aware, with absolute certainty, that one of the members of the American delegation was a spy and had been given the assignment of conveying a report to another spy—and that other spy was you, Schönker."

This time his voice was severe and threatening. My father distinctly felt that he was dealing with a very dangerous man.

Only now did the real interrogation begin. They ordered my father to tell them whom he was working for, what his mission was, and whom he had contact with. They wanted to know about the assignments he had undertaken so far and the assignments he was going to undertake. They claimed to have irrefutable proof of my father's guilt. They knew, however, that he wasn't the only spy.

"You'll tell us everything about your work as a spy, and we'll guarantee you immunity and emigration to Israel. You can even call your lawyer so he can be present at the signing of the agreement between us."

My father couldn't endure any more of this and declared, "I have nothing to say, and even if I did, I wouldn't tell you."

"Why not?"

"Because then you'd arrest me again, along with my lawyer. I've already signed one deal with you, and I can see now what has come of it," my father responded.

The officer sitting near him declared in a commanding tone of voice, "You, Schönker, quite simply have no choice but to tell us everything and confess to what you've done. This is a very generous offer from us. Accept it now, because we won't be offering it again."

"There's already a lawyer involved in your case. We can summon him right now and sign an agreement," the other added.

"I don't trust your lawyers. I'm innocent, and your accusations are groundless. Please let me contact my lawyer."

The officer stood up from behind the desk, leaned over my father, and said derisively, "Don't act like such a wise guy, Schönker. We've crushed much tougher wise guys than you. I'll ask you now, and I'm not going to ask you again: Do you accept our offer or not?"

My father shrugged and said, "I'd gladly accept your offer, but I have nothing to say about the topics that interest you."

The officer pressed a button, and the huge man who had been guarding my father that morning entered the room.

"Take him out!" the officer commanded, and he gave the guard a cell number.

After the interrogation, my father was once again placed in a solitary cell, but in a different wing of the prison. There was no toilet in this cell—just a tin bucket. My father was given some food that was nearly inedible. He overcame his disgust and ate a bowl of what was meant to be soup but resembled dishwater. At least there was a potato floating in it, which my father chewed very slowly—a habit he had learned in Bergen-Belsen. The bare light bulb wasn't switched off, but my father was so tired he collapsed on the bed and immediately fell asleep.

No physical violence was used against my father. He was only interrogated day and night, sometimes for several days in a row, with breaks now and then.

Then he was left alone for a few days. They tried to force him to confess that he was collaborating with some sort of espionage organization that had headquarters outside of Poland. My father's denial had no effect on the men who were interrogating him.

My father went on a hunger strike—he didn't eat anything for several days. He grew very weak. Two guards and a paramedic entered his cell. One was holding a bowl of cream of wheat, and the other had special pliers to force open his mouth.

"Open your mouth!" ordered the paramedic, and he approached my father with the pliers.

"The pliers are unnecessary; I'll eat on my own," my father said, and he started eating.

"So you're no longer starving yourself," said the paramedic with evident satisfaction.

"Nothing of the sort," my father replied. "I'm still continuing my hunger strike."

The paramedic was surprised and said, as he went out, "You can be sure, Schönker, that we'll know how to deal with you here."

The procedure was repeated for the next two days. My father liked cream of wheat very much, and he told us it was the first tasty meal he'd had in prison. He felt that this cream of wheat was giving him a lot of strength.

Unfortunately, the next day he was put into a narrow hole in another cell. An iron plate in the concrete floor was slid to the side, and my father was forced into the hole. It was so tiny my father couldn't sit or stand. He had to remain on his hands and knees. To make matters worse, the floor turned out to be covered in urine and feces. After the iron plate was put back in place, a weak light bulb was switched on. The purpose of this light was clearly so that a prisoner trapped in the hole could have a better idea of where he was.

After a short time in the hole, my father fainted. He was pulled out and allowed to rest for a few hours; then the interrogations resumed. This time the investigator told him that if he didn't make a confession, the hole was going to serve as his home much more often. After some consideration, my father declared he was ready to submit a full confession.

The investigator was clearly pleased to hear this and even smiled at my father.

"You've finally come to your senses. You could have spared yourself all this trouble and enjoyed a comfortable cell and good food," he said. Then he asked my father whom he worked for.

"For the Intelligence Service," my father replied, without batting an eye.

The investigator stood up and opened the door leading to the next room. "Tell Ania to come here," he told someone. My father noticed that the investigator's voice was trembling with excitement. A stenographer entered the room, holding a thick notebook and pen.

"Tell us again, Schönker, whom you worked for."

"I worked for the Intelligence Service in London," my father said, and the stenographer quickly jotted down his answer.

"What was your assignment?"

"To steal documents from Marshal Rola-Żymierski's desk."

"How were you recruited?"

"During my stay in London, right after the war, two men entered my hotel room, introduced themselves as employees of the Intelligence Service, and asked me to go somewhere with them. They took me to their headquarters, and I was recruited there as a collaborator. They promised me a large sum of money, so I agreed."

"When did they give you the assignment to steal documents from Marshal Rola-Żymierski's desk?"

"When Bevin went to Moscow, I received an encrypted dispatch via radio telling me to board the train he was traveling in.[8] After boarding the train, I was given an envelope containing my orders."

"Who was working with you?"

"I worked alone, nobody helped me."

The investigator began to perspire; he wiped his forehead with a handkerchief and left the room. After a while the guard led my father to an elegant office. An officer was sitting behind a desk with an amused look on his face. He stood up and—amazingly!—held out his hand to my father in greeting. Then he invited my father to sit down. My father's pipe and tobacco pouch were lying on the desk with a box of matches next to them.

"Smoke your pipe, Schönker. Smoking is permitted in this room," he said.

My father didn't need to be told twice. The officer leaned back in his chair and remarked, rather casually, "Schönker, you have a very vivid imagination. Well, I suppose every artist needs to have one; otherwise he wouldn't be an artist."

Then he looked straight into my father's eyes and asked, "How is it possible that you were recruited in London after the war? You've never left Poland—at least, you didn't leave Poland after the war."

My father puffed on his pipe and answered, "And how is it possible that I'm a spy?"

The officer seemed to find this amusing, though it wasn't clear why.

"Schönker, you can be congratulated on your good sense of humor. I can see you haven't lost it, even in this place." Then he added, "It's the MI5 that's responsible for English espionage, not the Intelligence Service."

"Thank you for educating me," my father answered.

The officer stood up from behind the desk, shook my father's hand and said, "We don't have any further questions for you."

On October 21, 1949, my father was taken to the Montelupich Prison in Kraków and handed over to the Special Commission.

We felt greatly relieved when we heard this news, even overjoyed. We were now prepared to fight for my father's freedom. We felt that his release from prison would depend, to a great extent, on our efforts. I had never seen my mother so full of energy; she had all kinds of ideas about whom we could turn to for help and was constantly making plans.

Meanwhile, I tried to keep myself occupied so I wouldn't become depressed. I missed school and my friend Romek. I tried to cheer myself up by spending several hours every day at the public library in Wałbrzych, which, including the time I spent going there and back, took up an entire day.

We waited impatiently for news from the lawyer. Przybylski finally sent us a message that my father had two charges against him: one concerned an unspecified transaction made by Agrochemia, and the other was his attempt to ship our belongings out of Poland. If I remember correctly, there was also an accusation of not having registered our works of art. I didn't understand what this was all about, because the paintings we had received permission to ship were copies, not originals, and the paintings there had been doubts about were returned to us. There was no way to accuse my father of smuggling works of art, since everything had been examined by a museum curator.

A few days later we received another message. No progress was being made in my father's case because they were now interrogating him about someone named Müller. Przybylski couldn't find out anything more and asked us if this name meant anything to us. Unfortunately, we had no idea who Müller was. Przybylski had been able to find out, however, that the Agrochemia transaction that Falewski, the prosecutor, had deemed a criminal offense was the purchase of bones, which were used, after being ground up, as a raw material in the production of bone-meal fertilizers. Falewski told Przybylski he would gain access to the indictment after it had been submitted to the court. But this would happen only after the investigation into the case concerning Müller had been concluded, for nobody was presently allowed to visit my father.

Right after arriving at the Montelupich Prison, my father had been placed—at Falewski's request—in a cell for serious criminals who had been given death sentences or life imprisonment. One of the prisoners in the cell seemed familiar to my father, but he couldn't recall how he knew him or whether he just looked like someone he knew. My father was given a spot next to a very dangerous criminal. Everyone else was afraid of this man and stayed away from him because he was mentally disturbed.

That day a prisoner entered the cell, and everyone bombarded him with questions.

"And so?"

"Well? What did you get?"

He waited a while to increase the suspense, and finally, with a broad smile, announced, "Fatherly!"

The inmates were extremely overjoyed. Everyone started dancing and kissing the newcomer. Even the mentally disturbed man next to my father stood up and slapped him on the shoulder so hard he nearly knocked him down.

My father asked someone to explain what it meant. It turned out this prisoner had received his sentence that day. Everyone had expected him to receive a death sentence—execution by hanging—but he had only been given a "fatherly" sentence.

"What's a 'fatherly' sentence?" my father asked.

"What, don't you know? How did you end up here?"

"Well, so how many years is it?"

"Five years. Lenient, like a father. You should be happy if you get such a sentence. It's the greatest dream of every man in this cell."

"What about you?" my father asked.

"A death sentence. Now I'm waiting for an appeal." After a moment of reflection, he added, "I really hope there'll be an appeal. My lawyer keeps reassuring me, but it's impossible to know anything in this system."

"What are you in prison for?" asked my father.

The man snorted and answered, "Political reasons. Almost everyone is here for political reasons. Aren't you?" he asked.

"Actually, I don't know why I'm here," my father replied.

"In that case, you're one of us. None of us knows why we're here."

After dinner, which consisted of watery soup and a slice of bread, everyone lay down to sleep. My father was afraid of closing his eyes and tried with all his strength not to fall asleep, but in the end his exhaustion overcame him. He didn't know how long he had been sleeping when he was awoken by a rustling sound coming from his dangerous neighbor. He froze in terror. Then he felt this terrible man covering him with the blanket that had slipped off him. His heart was pounding, but he pretended to be asleep. This event convinced him that good intentions can exist even in the worst kinds of people.

While thinking it over, he remembered how he knew the man who had seemed familiar to him. He was amazed by his discovery. In this skinny, haggard man dressed in a ragged prison uniform, he recognized SS-Unterscharführer Franz Josef Müller, commander of the Bochnia ghetto where we had stayed in 1943. In the morning my father approached Müller and asked if he recognized him. Müller was visibly frightened. My father reminded him of who he was, and Müller admitted that he recognized him.

That day my father said while being interrogated that he knew Müller from the Bochnia ghetto. Later that same day, he was taken to a different cell, and from then on the interrogations concerned Müller's case. My father stated everything he knew about Müller and described the living conditions in the ghetto. He had the impression that this was a very important case because several times someone came from the Ministry of Public Security in Warsaw.

After a while, the interrogations concerning Müller were concluded, and my father's case moved forward. My father's indictment was soon prepared. It was based on testimony from my father's representative in Bielsko who—as I recall—was responsible for purchasing bones.

Falewski did everything he could for the trial to take place at the courthouse in Kraków, but to no avail. The case was heard by the court in Oświęcim. The residents of Oświęcim were extremely interested in the trial, and the courtroom was crowded. We didn't dare show up at the trial since we were afraid of being arrested.

After reading out the charges and my father's declaration of innocence, Agrochemia's representative from Bielsko was summoned. He was meant to be the prosecution's main witness.

"What was your connection to Agrochemia?" the judge asked.

"There wasn't any connection, I'm an independent entrepreneur," the witness answered.

"Well, all right, but please tell us—what kind of activities were you involved in that concerned Agrochemia?" asked the judge.

"I don't know Agrochemia. I only know Mr. Schönker. I purchase slaughterhouse scraps for him."

"Please explain what that is."

The witness looked surprised, and answered, "What? You don't know, sir, what slaughterhouse scraps are?"

"Please explain," the judge insisted.

The witness threw up his hands and declared emphatically, "Slaughterhouse scraps are slaughterhouse scraps. There's no other explanation."

"And what did Mr. Schönker do with these—as you call them—'slaughterhouse scraps'?" asked the judge.

The witness shrugged and said, "How should I know? Maybe he ate them, but people say he made fertilizers from them."

The judge gave the witness a surprised look. Then my father told Przybylski to ask the witness if he was suffering from meningitis.

Without a moment's hesitation, Przybylski stood up and asked if he could ask the witness a question. The judge gave him permission, and Przybylski, turning to the witness, asked, "Do you suffer from meningitis?"

"Oh, yes, the illness often afflicts me, you know, but at the moment I'm feeling better." The witness seemed pleased by the question.

"Please explain to us what meningitis is," the judge said, clearly amused.

"It's an illness of the brain, but in my family it's hereditary. My mother always told me . . ."

The judge interrupted him: "That's enough—no further explanation is necessary. The witness can leave the stand."

Next there were two witnesses from the defense—one was from the accounting department, and the other was responsible for the production of superphosphate. Their testimony disproved the entire indictment. Falewski was angry, but he didn't give up and questioned my father. My father answered all the questions, but not how the prosecutor expected.

At a certain point, Falewski could no longer bear it and, shaking his finger threateningly at my father, shouted at him, "If you don't answer my questions the way you should, you're going to grow a beard in prison this long!" And he held his hand at the level of his belt.

My father answered, "And you'll grow a tongue this long."[9] And he pointed to his knees.

Everyone in the courtroom snickered, and the judge lowered his head and covered his mouth. It was clear he was trying very hard not to laugh.

After the courtroom had calmed down, the judge ended the trial and postponed the delivery of the verdict. Three days later the court pronounced my father innocent.

We were immediately notified of the verdict. We celebrated by having a wonderful supper cooked by my mother, and Szymon Kahane drank several glasses of wine with me in my father's honor, which was something remarkable since he never drank alcohol.

My father was taken back to the prison in Kraków. In response to his lawyer's insistence that the investigation needed to end soon, the Special Commission replied that the case wasn't yet concluded. Weeks and months passed, and the investigation continued. Przybylski said the whole case seemed very strange to him because the charges against my father weren't serious enough to require such a long investigation. But there was nothing we could do about it, and we had no choice but to wait as patiently as possible.

My father gradually got used to life in prison. He even found a companion who agreed to protect him so his fellow inmates wouldn't cause him any harm. My father paid him for his services with half a food package.

We had some money because my mother sold one of her diamonds in Kraków. She still had three or four left. Przybylski told us that all of my father's private accounts in various banks had been blocked. We never saw any of this money again. It was everything my father had earned from Agrochemia.

One afternoon I went to the park. I sat on a bench and watched some boys my age—strong, tanned, and athletic—playing volleyball. I observed them with longing and regret. Why was I so far removed from their freedom and happiness?

A boy left the playing field, approached me, and asked if I wanted to take his place in the game. I didn't need to be asked twice. I played very well and was surprised at my own athletic ability. I felt as if someone were giving me support and strength.

I played with these boys for the next couple of days, but the playing field soon became empty. I realized that school had begun. I was overwhelmed by longing for my school and my friends. Fate had forced me to live in hiding once again. I missed Oświęcim and the overall atmosphere of the town. I remembered how afraid I'd been of resuming a normal life when I returned to Oświęcim after the war. I had been like a hunted animal, ready to flee at any moment. It had taken me quite a while to overcome that fear. I hadn't overcome it entirely, for a certain anxiety still lingered in me. In Oświęcim it had nearly disappeared; my friends and the residents of the town had unknowingly helped me overcome it with their kind behavior toward me. But I still felt that my life was abnormal, and I so desperately wanted to live like other people, without any fear. Now that wild, animalistic fear had returned to me.

That day I didn't go to the library because I was overcome by a strange inertia, and instead I decided to spend time outdoors. I sat on a bench and watched children playing. Would I someday have children of my own, and maybe even grandchildren? I really wanted to. Life was worth living so that one day I could have a happy family. It seemed to me, however, that to achieve this it would be necessary to live a normal life, and I was very far removed from that.

I went home, and right on the threshold my mother handed me an envelope. It was a letter addressed to Szymon Kahane from Rina Kahane, in Wrocław. She wrote in the letter that one of her old friends from her university studies, who lived in the same town where we were hiding, told her that some strangers were living in her house. Nobody knew who the strangers were or what they were doing there.

We felt the floor give way beneath us. We had no choice but to find somewhere else to live. Regina Kupperman helped us once again. We packed our humble belongings in one suitcase and said goodbye to Szymon Kahane, thanking him profusely for hosting us for so long.

All of this reminded me of our escapes during the war. My fear was even greater now. We were heading into the unknown again. I expressed this to my mother. She told me not to be afraid because even if they found us, in the very worst case they wouldn't send us to gas chambers. This reassured me.

Regina had a friend named Lola who lived in a small apartment in Wałbrzych with her husband. She was a very pretty young woman, and her husband was much older than her. Apparently, he had once been a famous soccer player. I no longer remember exactly, but I think they had a son.

We got along very well with Lola and her husband. It wasn't as comfortable for us there as it had been at Szymon Kahane's home, but we were very grateful that they had agreed to us staying with them. We were unregistered tenants, which was risky for them because if it was discovered, they would be interrogated by the UB and maybe even sent to prison. Lola told her neighbor she was renting a room to us because she needed some money. Our hostess was a very close friend of Regina Kupperman's, and I think she was doing this for her, mostly; but she undoubtedly wanted to help us, too. We tried to disturb them as little as possible. I still went to the library every day to study. My mother barely left the house.

I had long discussions with Lola's husband. He was particularly interested in the question of antisemitism. He didn't believe the current system was nurturing a new kind of person who would view Jews as fellow citizens of equal standing, for communism didn't have much support among Polish people. He said that everything imposed on people by force must eventually fail. I responded by saying that so many Jewish people now occupied high positions in the government that it was unthinkable that antisemitism could appear again, at least in an official sense. But he answered that there was no way to be certain of this.

The government's disposition toward Jews could change at any moment—all it would take is for the government to try to distract people's attention from its own failings by finding a scapegoat. I asked him if he intended to leave for Israel because of this. He looked at Lola and replied that they were considering this possibility. He said this calmly and confidently, as if it were something very obvious.

It was difficult for me to believe what he said because the new regime had so many slogans about human equality regardless of origin or skin color. We didn't know what was happening in Russia at that time and had no idea that Comrade Stalin himself, the "sun of nations," was a veiled antisemite. We had no idea yet how much falsity and hypocrisy was hidden behind the communists' slogans. Perhaps I was simply unable to believe it because I was desperate to finally live a normal life.

We were constantly waiting for news from Kraków, but nothing ever came. All Przybylski knew was that the investigation by the Special Commission wasn't over yet. He said there was nothing unusual about it, but it seemed to him that the case was being unnaturally prolonged. Maciej Jakubowicz thought this might be their way of forcing a confession.

Time flew by, and we started to lose hope that the case would ever end. But at least my mother and I were together and were able to comfort each other. The first message we received from my father was hidden in the seam of a shirt he sent us to be washed. It was a small, thin piece of paper with only a few words written on it, saying that he was doing fine and asking us to send him his warm, tall, shiny boots.

He told us later that these boots saved him in the prison. Not only did they keep him warm but they inspired great respect among his fellow prisoners. Everyone asked him where he had gotten them. Wanting to make their lives a bit more interesting, my father told them he had been an officer of the Polish army in London during the war and had been sent to follow a German division in order to organize partisan warfare. Every evening he told his cellmates incredible stories about his experiences as a partisan. Everyone listened very intently, with growing respect for my father. This was important because the prisoner who had been protecting my father had left the cell.

One day someone contacted us by phone and told us to visit Przybylski immediately because he had some very important information for us. We took the first train to Kraków. Przybylski told us that a very strange thing had happened. My father's case was no longer being investigated by the Special Commission and had been transferred to Warsaw. My father was now somewhere in Warsaw but Przybylski didn't know where. He didn't understand why this had happened.

Przybylski had managed to look through my father's file briefly before it was sent to Warsaw. None of the things mentioned in it were serious enough to be dealt with by the Ministry of Security. It looked as if something must have happened or new information had been found. Przybylski advised us to find a lawyer in Warsaw who would be able to take care of my father's case. Przybylski was willing to defend my father if a new trial began.

Our situation was becoming more complicated. My mother was very anxious. She kept taking out a handkerchief and wiping her eyes.

We decided to go to Warsaw to look for a lawyer. We stayed with Dr. Karmel, who welcomed us very warmly but asked us not to talk about our case in his apartment. Dr. Karmel lived in a beautiful home; his furniture reminded me of our house in Oświęcim. I missed it very much. Now it was empty and abandoned. Even our two dogs, Lord and Baca, were living somewhere else—before Stasia left for Piotrolesie she had given them to someone for, as she said, "safekeeping."

The day after we arrived in Warsaw, we met with Maciej Jakubowicz's friend Ludwik Petszaft, who was going to help us find a lawyer. He was a thin, short, very lively man, about fifty years old. It was clear to us that he understood our situation and was trying to show us some kindness. He told us he had also suffered a great deal during the war, though he had been in Russia the whole time, and so he understood our predicament.

Petszaft gave us the names of some of the best lawyers in Warsaw who had experience with such cases. We chose a lawyer named Ryńca and made an appointment with him that very day. He was relatively young and very friendly. He listened to our story and told us that we first needed to find out where my father was and why his case had been transferred from Kraków to Warsaw.

We agreed to visit Ryńca again two days later. Unfortunately, when he greeted us the second time, he seemed perplexed and told us he hadn't been able to find out which prison my father was in. He asked us to come back in a week. He reassured us by saying that this sort of thing often happened when a prisoner was transferred from one prison to another. Unfortunately, a week later he still didn't know where my father was. He told us the easiest method would be to try to give my father a package. If the package was accepted, it would mean my father was in that prison. If not, we would have to try to give the package to him at another prison. Packages were accepted only once a week, so it might take us several weeks to find my father this way.

We came to the conclusion that it would be best if we moved to Warsaw because then it would be easier for us to follow my father's case, and perhaps an opportunity to help him might even arise. Finding a suitable place to live without registration and without attracting any attention to ourselves wasn't an easy task in a city where there were secret police at every step. We were still afraid of being arrested.

Our devoted friend Regina Kupperman helped us again. She found somewhere for us to live—with Petszaft's cousin, Bronisław Rosenberg, in Świder, near Warsaw. Rosenberg owned two wooden villas there. He told Petszaft he was willing to let us live in one villa for free because he had heard about my father and wanted to help us. And so, we packed our meager belongings and said goodbye to Lola and her husband. My mother thanked them with endless embraces, kisses, and heartfelt wishes.

Świder was a summer resort town on the Warsaw–Otwock railway line. The Rosenberg villas were situated close to each other in a sparse forest not far from the train station. Rosenberg and his family lived in one of them, and the other was empty. They rented it out during the summer. They welcomed us very warmly. My mother said that a good force of some kind was clearly watching over us, since we were constantly encountering kind people who wanted to help us.

Rosenberg, a man in his fifties, had a very serious demeanor; I don't remember ever seeing him smile. He always looked at me with a penetrating gaze as if he were trying to perceive my entire personality in one short glimpse. We had the impression that he was a very kind person who wanted to help us. His wife, Nadia, was also very pleasant and kind. She was about twenty years younger than her husband. They were both lawyers but didn't work professionally; apparently Rosenberg owned many buildings in Warsaw and lived off this income. They stayed at home all the time, taking care of their children—they had a very lovely three-year-old daughter and infant twins. As far as I remember, Nadia was still breast-feeding the twins, but Rosenberg cared for them most of the time. He watched them all day long and often informed us anxiously that one of the twins had a cough, or the other had a stomachache. He was utterly absorbed by his children.

Right after we arrived in Świder, we went to buy some food and clothes for my father. We prepared a package that weighed about five kilos and began our efforts to convey it to my father. We went to the prison in Mokotów, then the prison on Gęsia Street, and then another one. We waited in a line for a long time, and when we finally reached a small window where packages were accepted, our package was refused because my father's name wasn't on the list of prisoners.

After visiting all the prisons in Warsaw, we went to see Ryńca again. After thinking about it, he told us there was one more prison in Warsaw—a very small one for special prisoners. It was located in the main headquarters of the civic militia on Karowa Street. Ryńca told us packages weren't accepted there, as far as he knew, but we could try. He advised me to go there alone, to protect my mother. There was no point exposing both of us to danger.

The next day I went to the civic militia's headquarters with the package. My heart was pounding, but I wasn't scared. I wanted to fulfill my mission at any cost.

I approached the guard and asked if I could give him a package for my father. He looked at me, clearly astonished. It seemed like this was the first time such a thing had happened.

"Your name?" he asked.

"Henryk Schönker," I replied, trying to stay calm.

"Wait a moment," he said, and went through the gate.

There was a telephone on a table. I felt all my courage leave me.

"If it isn't possible, then never mind," I said. I started to leave, but he stopped me.

"I told you to wait." This time his voice was harsher.

I understood that I had no choice and had to wait, but my anxiety was increasing. The guard lifted the telephone receiver and spoke with someone. Then another militia officer appeared and told me to follow him.

I had no choice—I followed him, carrying the five-kilo package. We stopped in front of a door with a nameplate that read "Investigator Łamacz." Łamacz was clearly his surname.[10] The militia officer opened the door and told me to enter. A young officer was sitting behind a desk. He gestured to a chair in front of the desk, and I sat down with the package on my lap. Now my heart was hammering inside me, and I wondered what I had gotten myself into.

The officer stared at me for a moment, but I didn't see any malice in his eyes. I felt him assessing me. He clearly wanted to know whom he was dealing with.

At last, he asked, "And so, what's your name?" His voice was calm and reassuring. Had he noticed I was scared?

"Henryk Schönker," I replied, trying to sound calm.

"Please show me your ID."

I handed it to him. He looked at it and gave it back to me.

"Your father's name?" Now he was looking straight into my eyes.

"Leon Schönker."

"How do you know he's here?"

"I don't know."

"So why did you come here?"

"I heard he's in Warsaw, so I'm trying to give him a package in various prisons."

"Where do you live? Tell me your address!" I saw him pick up a pen to write it down.

Thankfully I was prepared for this question.

"I live with the Israeli consul, Dr. Karmel," I said, and I gave him the address.

He looked at me, surprised. "What, he's a friend of yours?"

"He's my father's friend."

"Do your mother and sister live with him, too?"

"No."

"Where are they?"

"I don't know. My mother disappeared. I think she has been arrested, too. And my sister is being looked after by someone in Oświęcim." I tried to make my answer sound believable.

The officer put down the pen and looked at me for a while as if he were wondering what to do with me. Fear overwhelmed me, but I tried not to show it. Finally, he said, as if reproaching me, "What kind of son are you? Your father's been in prison for over a year, and you're only starting to be interested in him now?"

I spread my hands in embarrassment and said nothing.

"Listen, we don't accept packages here. But since you're already here, we'll make an exception this one time and accept the package. Put it by the door."

"Thank you," I said. I stood up and set the package down. I felt as if a huge weight had been lifted from my heart. The officer seemed to notice this, because he smiled and asked me gently, "You don't have any other questions?"

"I do. What's happening to my father?" I asked in a nearly pleading tone of voice.

The officer turned to the militiaman standing by the door and said, "Tell young Schönker what his father is doing."

The militiaman shrugged and said, "Well, he's in the can."

I looked questioningly at the officer, who explained, with a slight smile, "He's joking. We have proper toilets here." Then he signaled to the militiaman, who opened the door for me.

I said politely, "Goodbye." I thought to myself, "Protect me, Lord."

I was lucky. It might have gone differently with my mother, but it was clear they didn't need me. I was proud of myself for successfully delivering the package.

The trip back to Świder took several hours. I was afraid of being followed, so I did my best to lose anyone who might be tailing me—I slipped through wicket gates, jumped on a tram at the last minute, got off at the next stop, entered a café, and went out through the back exit. I did everything I had seen in detective movies. A few hours later, when I was certain nobody was following me, I went to the station and got on a train. To be on the safe side, I got off in Otwock instead of Świder.

My mother was waiting for me very anxiously. When she saw me, she was overjoyed—she started jumping in the air like a little girl and clapping her hands.

We went to see Ryńca, the lawyer, that same day, in the late afternoon. He told us it would be easier for him to find out about my father's case now that he knew where he was.

Weeks passed without any changes. We visited Ryńca regularly, but he was unable to obtain any concrete information about my father. He told us the situation seemed very strange to him because my father had already been locked up for quite a long time in this special prison on Karowa Street. As for the case itself, he couldn't find out anything, which was unusual. All he knew was that my father was healthy. For us, even this scrap of information was very valuable.

One day my mother made a phone call to Piotrolesie and found out that Lusia had been bitten by a rabid dog and was now being given fifty injections in her stomach, but she felt fine because the injections were just below the skin and not very painful. My mother wrote a letter to Regina Kupperman asking her to travel to Piotrolesie right after the final injection and bring Lusia to us. She agreed to do this, and once again we were all together. Stasia returned to our house in Oświęcim. The town had turned our house into a nursery. Stasia moved into the apartment my father had prepared for Mr. and Mrs. Lieberman and started working in the nursery.

Our life in Świder soon gained an air of normalcy. I went to Warsaw every day and spent several hours in libraries, especially the National Library. I did this to make it look like I was going to work. Rosenberg asked me to do this because he wasn't sure he could trust his neighbors.

We started seeking contact with new people who could help us. We wanted to find out, at any cost, what was happening in my father's case. Ryńca was powerless. One day my mother was struck by the idea of making use of her friendship with Ela, the wife of my father's cousin, Aron Hollender. Her sister Rachela was General Edward Ochab's wife. After many attempts to make contact, we finally managed to communicate with her thanks to help from her friend Marysia Hofman, who was the daughter of one of my father's friends from Oświęcim, Mr. Wulkan.

Marysia told us right away that we had to keep everything we were going to hear from her a secret, or else we could expose various people, including her, to unpleasant situations.

She had found out from Rachela that my father had two minor accusations against him: that he had attempted to send some of his possessions to Israel but had declared them as belonging to someone else (the woman who was emigrating), and that Agrochemia had committed some kind of fraud. But the main issue in my father's case was something else—that we wanted to leave Poland for Israel not on Polish passports but on travel documents we had obtained from the Israeli legation. The UB in Kraków had agreed to this but without consulting with the Ministry of Security in Warsaw. This had caused a huge scandal because it was impossible for Polish Jews to leave Poland on Israeli documents rather than Polish passports. In addition to this, my father had been added to a blacklist of people who were forbidden from receiving Polish passports. Apparently, he knew some state secrets that made it impossible for him to leave, and this was why he was locked up in solitary confinement in the prison of the civic militia's headquarters in Warsaw.

THE MINISTRY OF PUBLIC SECURITY TO THE COMMANDER OF THE REGIONAL PUBLIC SECURITY OFFICE IN KRAKÓW:
According to data we have obtained, citizen Leon Schönker, co-owner of a factory called Agrochemia that produces artificial fertilizers and other chemical substances, lives in Oświęcim at 36 Jagiellońska Street. Citizen Schönker pretends to be a Palestinian citizen and is using this to attempt to obtain a Palestinian passport in order to move his factory out of Poland.

Consequently, we request you to fully interrogate citizen Schönker and investigate the following circumstances at the county governor's office in Oświęcim:

1. Can the Palestinian citizenship of Leon Schönker and his family be verified?
2. Has Leon Schönker renounced his Polish citizenship? If so, when?
3. Did Leon Schönker register himself at the county governor's office as a Palestinian citizen? If so, when?

The collected information must be sent immediately to Division IV, Dep. 1 of the Ministry of Public Security. This case is very urgent.
31 January 1949

After hearing about this, my mother asked Marysia to do everything possible to speed up the case. Marysia promised to help us. She gave us as much reassurance as possible and told us a time would finally come when we could lead normal lives.

When we returned to Świder, we started wondering about the state secrets my father supposedly knew about. We came to the conclusion that this most likely concerned the offer to supply weapons to Israel. Poland's government was certainly planning to make a similar offer to one of the Arab countries and didn't want it to be known that Israel had rejected its earlier offer. We also wondered if my father was holding any secrets from us. This was highly unlikely, however, because my father had never kept anything secret from us before, especially from my mother.

We visited Marysia nearly every week. She comforted us but was unable to tell us anything else. She was only able to assure us that Rachela Ochab was doing everything she could to help my father. The matter was so delicate, however, that we couldn't demand any details from her.

My father's lawyer started losing patience. He no longer reassured us like before—he was clearly feeling dejected because of his powerlessness. One day he told us that if he were in our place, he would try to leave Poland, even illegally. My father's case was very unclear. He tried to convince us that my mother would be arrested sooner or later, and perhaps I would, too. Right then we had an opportunity to leave Poland—a high-ranking French bureaucratic official could take us with him to Paris. When I objected that we didn't have any valid travel documents, Ryńca said this man had a way of arranging the trip for us. He told us the man's name was Rubineau, and he was staying at the Bristol Hotel. My mother refused outright, saying it was out of the question because we couldn't leave my father here alone. I couldn't imagine fleeing to Paris without my father, either.

A few days later, I bought a newspaper, and what I saw on the front page took my breath away. There was a headline stating that security agents had arrested a French spy—a representative of France's ministry of transport who had been operating in Poland. His name was Rubineau. He had been arrested at the airport while boarding an airplane.

My mother and I were stunned. We ruled out one thing immediately—namely, that Ryńca had been involved in a scheme to arrest us along with the spy. Ryńca was always so kind and empathetic toward us that it was impossible to suspect him of any malicious intentions. It seemed to be merely a coincidence. Ryńca also seemed shocked by the news, and during our next visit he asked us never to tell anyone about what he had suggested to us.

One day Marysia invited us to talk with her again. She greeted us with a broad smile. She began by telling us not to be frightened by what she was going to tell us, for it was essentially good news.

My father's trial would take place soon in Warsaw. He was going to be charged with attempting to smuggle works of art out of Poland and committing some kind of fraud connected to the factory. These weren't serious charges since the works of art were copies, and moreover they had been presented to customs officials, as the law required. As for the factory, these were trivial matters, probably concerning taxes. A heavy sentence wasn't expected, therefore, and perhaps my father would even be acquitted.

My mother responded by saying, in her usual way, "From your lips to God's ears."

We said goodbye to Marysia, convinced that the time would come soon when my father's case would finally be resolved. Ryńca sent us a message that my father's case was on the right track, and the trial would soon take place. He hadn't received a copy of the indictment, however, and didn't know what my father's charges would be.

A date was set for the trial. The lawyers—Przybylski and Neuman, who also had a legal office in Kraków—gained access to my father's indictment and studied it, as far as I can recall, for about a week and a half. Przybylski was living in Warsaw at that time. My mother told me we would have to sell another diamond because our money was running out.

One day after leaving the library, I bought a newspaper and was shocked to see a huge headline on the front page stating that an attempt to smuggle precious works of art that were of very high value to Polish culture had been thwarted. The attempt had been made by a rich industrialist from Oświęcim, Leon Schönker. Thanks to the vigilance of the Special Commission in Kraków and other security agencies, this smuggling attempt had been thwarted at the last minute, and Leon Schönker had been arrested and was currently imprisoned in Warsaw. His trial would begin soon.

I bought another newspaper, and there, on the front page, was an even larger headline stating that Schönker would be put on trial in Warsaw for an unsuccessful smuggling attempt. The article explained that this case was an excellent example of how attempts to steal Poland's art were ultimately doomed to fail, and those who dared undertake such crimes would be held responsible for their actions and severely punished. The article also contained praise for the security agents who were vigilantly guarding the nation's property.

I bought a third newspaper, and it was more of the same. I was frightened because these articles were creating a nasty smear campaign against my father. My mother was also terrified. It looked like the whole case had become inflated like a balloon, losing all sense of proportion. Our lawyers reassured us that newspaper articles didn't mean anything and told us not to worry too much yet. Newspaper articles didn't have any influence on court verdicts.

I asked Przybylski if he thought my father's trial would be objective. He replied that it wasn't a political trial, and there was no reason to believe there would be political pressure on the court. He added, "But nothing can be predicted in advance."

We were very excited and full of apprehension. Lusia asked my mother if she thought we would ever see our father again. It was a tragic question. We all felt very upset.

―∞―

Next came a period of anxious waiting. We didn't feel comfortable anywhere. My mother paced around our living room all day long, and Lusia sat in a corner and tried to calm my mother down. I stopped going to the library.

Every day the newspapers contained articles about the trial and how it was about to begin. My father became famous throughout Poland. His lawyers felt that they would have a lot to say in his defense and that they had very strong arguments. They didn't understand why the investigation had taken so long. Judging from my father's files, no new information had been gathered about him for a very long time, and the collected material was very poor in terms of quality and quantity. Why hadn't the trial taken place much earlier, then? Why had my father's case been transferred to Warsaw and taken from the Special Commission in Kraków? Why had my father been held in the civic militia's prison for several months? We mulled over these questions with our hosts, who were lawyers, but they couldn't think of any explanation. It was hard to tell whether the newspaper articles were part of a deliberate smear campaign against my father or simply a result of journalists trying to create a sensational story.

The trial finally began on September 14, 1950. We didn't go to the courthouse because we were still afraid of appearing in public. The lawyers weren't sure, either, if it was safe for us to show up. In Rosenberg's opinion, it would be risky because the prosecutor could apply for a new date for the trial under the pretext of needing to investigate us, as well. So my father's trial began without our presence. During this difficult time in our lives, we were very lucky not to be alone. Good-hearted people were always with us, helping and comforting us.

We met with the lawyers on the evening of the first day of the trial. They told us the judge was Edward Osmólski, and the prosecutor's surname was Menes—he was Jewish. The lawyers weren't happy about this because Jewish prosecutors, in their opinion, were usually overzealous when arraigning other Jews in court. They didn't think it was a very dangerous case, but there was no way of knowing what the judge's stance would be. It seemed like the trial would most likely end the next day. The judge had promised them that their defense statements wouldn't be interrupted or have a time limit. Overall, they could tell that Judge Osmólski was trying to conduct the trial objectively, which was a good sign.

We returned to Świder with mixed feelings. Ludwik Petszaft was waiting for us there; he had been at the trial. In his opinion, there had been a positive, lighthearted atmosphere in the courtroom. Judge Osmólski hadn't been aggressive, and Menes hadn't used any severe language. Petszaft had found out that Osmólski had a reputation of being a very objective judge. Of course, there could be pressure from various sides, but the very fact that this judge had been appointed instead of a harsher judge proved that there wasn't any political pressure coming from above—and if there was, it was very slight.

He continued, saying that the lawyers had been wonderful and had defended my father very well. They had even ridiculed certain points in the indictment. Even Menes had smiled at one point, which caused general amusement in the courtroom. Petszaft reassured us very much, Nadia cooked a delicious supper, and our spirits were greatly lifted. Lusia, who was sitting with us at the table, suddenly started singing: "Poland has not perished yet, as long as we still live."[11]

We stared at her in astonishment. Nadia smiled and said, "She's right."

We agreed with the lawyers that on the second day of the trial we would wait for them in the Warsaw lawyer's apartment. We arrived there at four o'clock in the afternoon. The lawyers finally appeared. We stood up, in a tense state of anticipation. We looked at their faces. They were smiling. I felt as if a great weight had been lifted from my heart. Evidently my mother was feeling the same way, for she exclaimed, nearly shouting, "Is it over?"

"The trial is over. Your husband received a two-year prison sentence," replied Przybylski.

The room fell silent. Then Przybylski said that my father was very lucky, for it could have turned out much worse. Seventeen months would be deducted from his prison sentence due to the time he had already served. This meant he would be released in seven months.

Then Przybylski started laughing and said that my father had been allowed to make a statement before the court announced its verdict. He stood up from the defendant's bench, straightened himself, and said slowly, emphasizing each word in a dignified manner: "I must state that the trial was conducted just like in the best English court." Then he sat down again.

Przybylski said Menes had stiffened, and his eyes had nearly popped out of his head. Judge Osmólski had held a handkerchief to his mouth, clearly to stop himself from laughing. My father's behavior showed he hadn't been psychologically damaged by his time in prison. Hearing this, we smiled slightly. We had been afraid his punishment would be much worse.

Back at home, the Rosenbergs and Petszaft were very happy to hear about my father's sentence. I didn't understand it, since my father was still in prison.

Everyone was of the opinion, however, that after the smear campaign in the newspapers, his sentence could have been much worse. Rosenberg said that an acquittal would have been out of the question after such a long investigation. The Special Commission, other government agencies, and the communist party were incapable of admitting they had been wrong.

Soon I was allowed to visit my father. My mother was still afraid to appear, so I went alone to the prison on Gęsia Street—known as Gęsiówka—where he had been taken. I could see that my father was in good form. He was walking at a normal pace and holding himself up straight. At first it was difficult for me to recognize him, however, because his beard nearly reached his waist. At first, we just looked at each other in silence. I could see he was very moved; tears were flowing down my cheeks, too.

Then he asked me, *"Vifl shteyt der loksh?"* (How much is the American dollar worth?)

The question surprised me and made me laugh. I asked my father whether he didn't have more serious problems to be concerned with, and why this information was necessary for him. My father replied that his cellmates had asked him to find out. Only later did I realize he'd been trying to lighten the mood with this question, after seeing how overwhelmed I'd been by emotion. I have to admit he succeeded.

We had a quick exchange of questions and answers. We both wanted to find out as much as possible about each other. My father felt quite well, just a bit weak at times. He was being treated well in prison and wasn't subjected to severe interrogations. The one exception had been in the UB's prison in Kraków, but it hadn't been unbearable. I described what was happening with us and told him we were living near Warsaw. But I halted in midsentence because my father put his finger to his lips, signaling for me to be quiet. He was evidently afraid of people eavesdropping on us. My father told me to give my mother a kiss for him and to tell her he loved her very much. He managed to add that he'd been very pleased with the lawyers at the trial.

"Finished!" a guard shouted, and my father was led away.

At home I gave a precise report from the visit and kissed my mother on each cheek, saying, "This is from Dad." It made her very happy, and she blushed like a young girl.

Gęsiówka was the twelfth prison my father had been in. He told us that his fellow prisoners were a good group of people, and everyone helped each other.

On his first day at Gęsiówka, someone asked him, "How many years did you get?"

"How do you know I've already received my sentence?"

"This is a cell for prisoners serving their sentences."

"I got two years," my father replied. Everyone stared at him in disbelief. He was afraid the other prisoners would treat him dismissively, so he added, "That's only from the first charge. The second one is still being investigated."

"What kind of sentence will you get for the second one?" someone asked.

"Twenty years ... if it goes well," my father answered.

This apparently impressed them, because they approached my father one by one and patted him on the shoulder in consolation.

"And those boots, where'd you get 'em?" asked an inmate, pointing at his tall, shiny boots.

"Ah, it's a long story; I'll tell you in the evening," my father replied, preparing his bedding on a bunk bed.

On the first evening, my father began a story about how the British Secret Service dropped him from a plane with a parachute, and he joined Tito's partisans. Everyone listened in suspense. Right at the most exciting moment, my father stopped and said, "To be continued tomorrow." And he covered himself with his blanket.

This happened every night. My father became the star of the cell. "It would be boring here without you," one of the prisoners told him, and another, evidently wanting to make my father happy, declared, in all seriousness, "You were made to be locked up in prison."

My father received compliments of various kinds and—as he later told me—they made him feel very proud of himself.

My father seemed to be doing fine in prison, but we still wondered if there was anything we could do to spare him those seven months. The lawyer told us that he couldn't see any way to get my father out of prison earlier, unless he had a serious health problem. But my father was healthy, so there was nothing we could do.

A few days later, Rosenberg told us that he was in the process of liquidating his estate and selling both villas. He had come to the conclusion that Jews could no longer expect a good future in Poland. But he had another place where we could live until my father was released from prison. It was a room in a residential building next to a factory in the Praga district of Warsaw. Petszaft was already living there with his family. He had also applied for a passport and had managed to sell his apartment in Saska Kępa. Petszaft couldn't imagine a future for himself in Poland, either. This was how most Jewish people felt who weren't members of the communist party. Even some who were party members also came to this conclusion eventually.

I had long discussions with Petszaft, mainly about how we could get my father out of prison. We decided the only solution was to gain access to a doctor at Gęsiówka who would be willing to state that my father was seriously ill, obviously by falsifying test results and medical records. On this basis, a lawyer could apply for my father's early release. But this seemed impossible to us. Even if we somehow found a way to contact a doctor, which seemed highly unlikely, nobody would want to risk their lives by committing such a crime. But Petszaft promised us he would keep thinking about it.

I believed that if my father had already endured seventeen months in prison, he could endure seven more. I told my mother this, but she rebuked me: "My heart breaks every single day just at the thought of your father being locked up there."

One day Petszaft visited us and said he had managed, through a friend of his, to contact a prison doctor who worked at Gęsiówka. A few days later he informed us that he had worked out a plan with the doctor to free my father. We needed to convince my father to report to the prison doctor. This time my mother went to visit him, and she told him to go to the doctor because she was worried about his health. At first my father refused, but my mother insisted, and finally he agreed. She was afraid to give secret signals to my father because a guard was standing close by and watching them the whole time.

Two weeks later, we were granted permission to visit him again. This time I went. My father was in a completely altered state—he was staggering and looked as if he had aged twenty years. He informed me with great sorrow that he had two open cavities in his lungs and had been put in solitary confinement. It was clear he was very frightened about his health. I told him not to worry and that we would do everything we could to save him. I reassured him by telling him that very effective medicine was available nowadays and there was no need to despair. I started to tell him what the current exchange rate was for dollars, but he just waved his hand dismissively.

Our conversation was short because the guard took my father away very soon.

"Dad, don't worry!" I shouted as he walked away.

Before my father disappeared from view, he managed to say, "*A lange krenk is a zikhere toyt.*" This was a Jewish proverb that meant "a long illness is certain death."

The whole story developed very quickly. My father's lung x-rays had been swapped with those of a prisoner who had died of tuberculosis. My father's lawyers applied for my father to be released early, and the prison committee decided there was no point in keeping my father in prison any longer.

My father was released from Gęsiówka in January 1951. We waited for him in front of the prison. When he came out, he looked very depressed, and the first thing he asked us was which sanatorium we had decided to send him to. My mother tried to explain to my father what had happened, but she was so excited and overcome with emotion that she couldn't find the right words.

Seeing this, I told my father matter-of-factly, "Dad, you're not dying; all of this is a sham." Then we got in a taxi. My father stared at us, bewildered.

My mother finally came to her senses once we were in the car and repeated to my father with a broad smile, "Don't worry; you're not dying."

We took my father home, and then we told him what had happened. At first he listened in disbelief; then he burst out laughing so hard that—as my mother said—"the walls nearly shook."

A person quickly gets used to good things. We soon got used to being together again. We were very happy. My father thanked everyone who had helped us during those difficult times. I observed my father closely because it seemed to me that he had changed slightly.

My father seemed to notice me observing him, for he said, several days after his return, "You know, there were people there whom I miss now."

"What kind of people?" I asked.

"Honest, decent, intelligent, gentle, distinguished . . . People who shouldn't be locked up in prison."

For the next few days, my father was busy sending messages to the families of about a dozen prisoners who had asked him to do so. Przybylski went to Oświęcim and made a request at the town council for our villa to be vacated so we could live there. The civic militia, which had taken over the villa, immediately moved to another building. We were all surprised by this. We had expected a court battle or at least a very long wait.

Oświęcim had changed a lot during those seventeen months. One could say that the political situation was taking a toll on the lives of all the residents. People were struggling more to survive. The town seemed to be in economic decline. Earnings were very low, and supplies, even of basic products, were becoming scarcer. The communist party had taken over all spheres of life and was making decisions about everything. Its members were being given the best jobs and political positions, and this process was rapidly gaining momentum.

The party attempted to compensate for the general poverty by organizing public entertainment in which vodka played a main role—it was meant to change people's perception of all the shortages and the new system's broken promises. People called it a "dictatorship of the proletariat." At that time, someone told me that this name perfectly corresponded to reality because there was a dictatorship we had to deal with every day, and the proletariat was growing larger and poorer.

People who didn't belong to the communist party became more distrustful, and every stranger was viewed as a potential secret agent of the UB. Even members of the communist party were very cautious in their conversations with other people, at least when they were sober. One day my father took me aside and told me not to make any political jokes to anyone. I really liked to talk about politics, but I realized that now I needed to keep my mouth shut.

Right after we returned to Oświęcim, we were visited by someone from the UB in Oświęcim who demanded "appropriate behavior" from us. My mother asked him what that meant. He replied that we shouldn't flaunt our return and parade around the town ostentatiously. He told my father he should maintain humility in everything he did and . . . and . . . unable to find the right word, he finished by saying, "And hold your tongue."

My father nodded and said he understood. "We'll be emigrating soon, anyway," he added.

"That still remains to be seen," said the agent. Then he said goodbye politely and left.

"It still remains to be seen? What did he mean by that?" my mother asked my father.

"You know, as Leiser Dawid said: 'You can't know anything for sure with these people.'"

I started wondering what I should do. All my friends were already in university. My best friend, Romek Maksymowicz, was studying journalism in Kraków, and Zdzisiek Mróz was studying economics. Wiesiek Kała was wandering somewhere in the Recovered Territories. He had his own band and was playing concerts in a health spa in Lądek-Zdrój. Apparently, girls were crazy about him, and he was greatly enjoying the attention. I didn't feel totally alone, however—my friend Kaziu Biedroń often visited me. He was still in Oświęcim because he hadn't been accepted into any university. To this day, I'm still thankful to him for being my friend during that time.

We behaved normally, as if we had never left Oświęcim—just like the UB had ordered. Nobody asked us where we had been for those twenty months. Stasia returned to our house and told us that people were asking her on the street how we were doing but were afraid of having direct contact with us. This was painful to hear. Stefan Blachura visited us one evening and also told us that people were afraid to visit us. Stefan was now working at Agrochemia and said that the workers often talked about my father. My father was no longer allowed to go there. Only one poor woman who lived in a village near Oświęcim came to visit us on our first day back home and brought us a plucked chicken. She was the mother of Czesław Jurczyk, one of my classmates at the Konarski High School, who later became a priest and my dear friend.

One day an agent from the UB in Oświęcim visited us again. He told my father to report to the UB in Kraków the following day.

Frightened, my mother shouted, "Are you going to arrest my husband again?"

"Don't worry," replied the agent. "Your husband will be fine."

All day and nearly all night, my parents wondered whether we should flee again. At last my father decided he didn't want us to live in hiding anymore; he had no choice but to report to the UB. After all, if they wanted to arrest him, they would have done it right away.

The next day my father prayed and then went to Kraków. In the afternoon he called my mother to tell her everything was fine, but he wouldn't be home until evening because he wanted to visit Maciej and ask him for advice.

We waited anxiously for my father. He got home late in the evening, very tired. He told us we had nothing to fear—his summons to the UB had only concerned extending the validity of our identification documents. We needed to go to Bielsko-Biała to get residence visas.[12] If we didn't do this, we would be arrested. The matter of our emigration from Poland would be settled later. My father had also been told to keep all of this a secret; otherwise he would be arrested.

My parents and I went to Bielsko-Biała. At the militia headquarters we received, as foreigners, a one-month residence visa that was valid until May 1, 1951. We were told we would be notified when we could pick up our exit visas. We were sure that within the next month we would leave Poland. But one month passed, and nobody contacted us. Our residence visa was extended. This procedure was repeated several times, and there was no mention of being granted permission to emigrate. Apparently they didn't want to get rid of us. They made us believe we would be granted exit visas at any moment, but secretly they were beginning a vast surveillance project concerning my father. The UB had already tried to recruit Stefan (the caretaker of our villa), Rydzoń (our chauffeur), and even Stasia (our housekeeper) to spy on us, but to no avail. My father started to realize he was still facing imminent danger and feared his situation could change at any moment.

INTELLIGENCE REPORT FROM SECRET COLLABORATOR: CODE NAME "FAITHFUL":

During the time when citizen Schönker, former owner of a fertilizer factory in Oświęcim (Agrochemia), was in prison, I heard . . . that citizen Błasiak from Grójec, employed at the border as a guard or customs official, intercepted a sack of gold being transported by Schönker's henchmen to Switzerland, and that Schönker and his brother-in-law Hilary Minc own factories in Switzerland and Palestine under false names and invest the money there that they earn in Poland.[13]

I've wondered many times, and have discussed with others, how Schönker has become so wealthy that he can give money to so many people (and their wards), including: athletes of the "Soła" sports club, the Salesian priests and their pupils (who have gone on many trips in the mountains, around the country, etc.). . . . I also heard during this time that the Salesian priests receive a great deal of financial support from Schönker and are on very friendly terms with him, despite the fact that he isn't a Catholic. It was often said in those days that Schönker is a good fellow who never refuses to help anyone who comes to him in need (a common trait among capitalists), but I no longer remember what kind of help he has given, or to whom.

Oświęcim, 17 December 1952

Very few of my friends and acquaintances remained in Oświęcim—all had left for university. I missed them terribly. I had lost two years of my life. I decided to study intensively because even if we were going to leave Poland, it would be better for me to have a high school diploma. With the help of some of my high school teachers, I passed the high school exams in Wałbrzych extramurally.

A short time later, I ran into an acquaintance of mine on the street—Wiesiek Susuł. He told me he had graduated from the Fine Arts High School in Katowice and was going to take the entrance exam for architecture studies at the Academy of Mining and Metallurgy in Kraków. He encouraged me to take the exam, too. This reminded me of how my cousin Arie had taught me about architecture from a book in the Bergen-Belsen camp. The lessons Arie gave me stimulated my imagination and helped me forget how hungry I was. This chance encounter with Wiesiek seemed like a sign for me from Arie, from the afterlife. Common sense told me that it wasn't worth it—I was supposed to emigrate from Poland soon, after all. But the thought of Arie didn't leave me in peace, and I decided to follow Wiesiek's advice, especially since the exam, and the studies themselves, were free of charge.

I scored well on the math exam. I went home from Kraków feeling very satisfied with myself and already beginning to feel like an architecture student. The architecture program in Kraków was very prestigious. Even just the velvet student cap with its thin, colorful band aroused admiration among the girls of Oświęcim. I imagined myself strolling around the main square, proud of the fact that after everything I had experienced, I was making progress in my life—I was studying and living a normal life like my friends. I felt as if there were an angelic force watching over me and giving me support.

I no longer remember what kind of exams I took, but I did well on all of them. There was only one exam left—the most important one, for drawing. I feared this exam the least, however, because I thought I could draw quite well. I didn't prepare for the exam at all, even though I could have done so easily with my father's help.

The day of the drawing exam finally came. We had to draw, if I remember correctly, a plaster replica of the bust of Moses by Michelangelo in the tomb of Pope Julius II. We were given several hours for it. I finished my drawing after only one hour because I felt that it was finished. When Wiesiek, who was taking the exam with me, saw me sitting there idly, he got up to go to the bathroom. As he passed me he glanced at my drawing and then whispered to me, quietly but urgently, "Keep drawing; it's not finished yet." But I didn't know what in my drawing wasn't good enough. I liked my drawing a lot—it was original and not entirely distinct. The sculpture looked as if it were emerging from the afterlife.

When the exam was over, I approached the assistant watching over us and asked him to look at my drawing and tell me what he thought of it.

He glanced at it and then asked me, "Are you a painter?"

"Something like that," I answered, and I felt pride swelling inside me.

"Well, all right," he said with a smile. "But you don't know how to draw."

I was devastated. I could sense that I had failed the exam. Wiesiek and I returned to Oświęcim together. Wiesiek felt happy, though he didn't yet know for sure if he would be accepted. I was despondent. When I got home, I told my father about the exam. He said no matter how it turned out, I needed to have faith that everything was heading in the right direction.

A few days later, I went to Kraków again to get my exam results. A list of students who had been accepted for architecture studies was hanging in the hallway. Wiesiek Susuł had been accepted, but my name wasn't on the list. It wasn't on the other list, either, which contained the names of students who had failed the entrance exams. Below these lists, however, there was a notice stating that if someone's name was missing from both lists, it was necessary to report to the dean's office. There I found out that I had been admitted into the Department of Mechanical Engineering at the Engineering Academy in Częstochowa.

The day before the beginning of the academic year, I went to Częstochowa to familiarize myself with the town and find a room to rent, which turned out to be more difficult than I'd expected. At last I decided to rent a tiny room with a door that led into a courtyard. The landlady assured me I wouldn't find anything better because Częstochowa was already full of students. I felt I had no choice, so I agreed to rent the room. The landlady seemed very pleased; I was less so. When we said goodbye after our first meeting, she said, "You know, I've never had anything against Jews."

I looked at her in amazement and asked, "How do you know I'm Jewish?"

"I can recognize a Jew from far off," she replied.

This amused me, so I asked her, "Do Jews perhaps have horns on their heads that only some people are able to see?"

She grinned and, putting away the money I'd given her, said, "No, but it's obvious they're different from us."

I was dismayed by what she'd said. Not noticing my reaction, she nodded as if wishing to emphasize her positive opinion of Jews and declared, in a friendly tone of voice, "But there are some decent people among them, too."

That was enough for me. I decided to find another room for myself after the first month.

It was a wonderful feeling to enter a lecture hall for the very first time. The thought crossed my mind that none of the other students had any idea how miraculous it was that I was able to be there, among them, after everything I'd experienced during the war and throughout the past year and a half. During that hopeless period of suffering, I had dreamed so many times of being able to live a normal life.

My first days as a university student were happy, but also difficult. I had to get used to learning in a group, to discipline, and to my new classmates. I wasn't sure how my classmates were going to treat me. Everyone knew I was Jewish because I made no effort to hide it. My surname, alone, revealed that I was Jewish. I realized I was oversensitive and could be hurt very easily, so I tried my best not to draw hasty conclusions from people's behavior toward me.

I quickly made a new friend named Wojciech Jagielski who was from Kraków and had also been directed to these studies. He was tall with smooth, brown hair—the kind of hair I could only dream of having. He had a very charming smile.

A few days after my arrival in Częstochowa, my father visited me in my room. He looked around, snorted, and began reproaching me for renting such a foul, musty hovel. He left, then came back two hours later and said he had rented a decent room for me in an apartment owned by a very nice woman. He had gone to the Jewish community council office and asked them to help him find a room for me. Regardless of the fact that I'd already paid for one month's rent in advance, he told me to pack my belongings, and we took a taxi to the new place.

The room was truly lovely and spacious. The landlady, Zosia, was a kind and intelligent old lady. She welcomed us very warmly and served us tea and cookies. Her aristocratic bearing inspired respect; she was evidently from the upper class. Her entire apartment was very elegant and well maintained. Her Biedermeier-style antique furniture and cupboards full of beautiful porcelain reminded me of my grandfather's villa and the period of time when we had lived there before my father was arrested.

Zosia was a widow, and her niece lived with her. I no longer remember what the niece did, but I clearly remember what she looked like. She was my age and often shook her head to get her long, blond hair out of her eyes. She had large blue eyes that were always twinkling with mirth and a heart-shaped mouth. Her presence greatly increased the value of my new home for me.

I had one problem, however—I didn't feel well when I was alone in my room. Nights were particularly difficult for me. Some mornings I felt like I hadn't shut my eyes all night long. I was tormented by unpleasant visions and hallucinations and felt plagued by anxiety . . .

A few days later, I suggested to Wojciech Jagielski that he move in with me. After seeing my room, he agreed immediately, especially since he wouldn't have to pay anything. From then on, I slept very well at night.

Only now was I able to devote myself entirely to my studies. Of all my subjects, I liked math, mechanics, and geometry the most. I was also very good at technical drawing. An assistant told me that I had attracted the professor's attention and had a chance of becoming an assistant the following year. This made me very proud, even though I knew I might not finish that academic year because we were going to emigrate to Israel. My parents were still constantly talking about it.

We had applied for exit visas in Bielsko-Biała and were waiting to hear if they would be approved. We had already packed all our luggage and were practically sitting on our suitcases, ready to go—but after a while we unpacked them because there was no news about our visas. My parents began to lose hope that we would receive permission to leave Poland anytime soon. My father said that since he was on the blacklist, there might not be much hope for us. I was an optimist and believed we would eventually receive permission. For what was Poland gaining, after all, from my father sitting at home all day reading books, painting landscapes, and playing chess, while I was studying for free?

For the time being, we had enough money to live on because my mother had sold another diamond. As far as I remember, before my father's arrest she'd still had a raincoat with two jewels sewn into the seam. It was gone now, however, because after my father had been arrested and we had fled Oświęcim to go into hiding, various people had broken into our house and taken almost everything we'd left in it. My father had a small sum of money outside of Poland that he'd earned through a business he'd been involved in but that had stalled after his arrest. With this money we imported packages of cocoa and chocolate, which our neighbor, Mr. Smrek—a very calm, cheerful, helpful man—sold while traveling around.

Something very surprising happened during one of the national holidays—I can't recall if it was the May 1 or July 22 holiday. At the university we were informed that a huge rally was going to take place, featuring speeches by important people. Each of us received a piece of paper printed with slogans we were supposed to shout. We had to appear at the rally together with our class so the organizers could make sure everyone was present, for attendance at the rally was obligatory.

Someone was giving a speech at the podium. They kept pausing for several seconds at a time, and during these pauses one of the students in the crowd would shout out, "Long live the Soviet Union, a bastion of peace in the world!"

And everyone echoed, "Long live the Soviet Union!"

"Long live Comrade Stalin, the greatest friend of the Polish nation!"

"Long live Stalin!"

"Long live Comrade Bolesław Bierut!"

"Long live Comrade Bolesław Bierut!"

Apparently, I wasn't shouting loudly enough, because someone nudged me and hissed, "Louder! Louder!"

I tried to shout as loudly as I could, and my voice was even getting hoarse.

Someone shouted, "Long live Comrade Stalin, teacher of all the nations of the world!"

"Long live Comrade Stalin!"

"Crap on Comrade Stalin!" a baritone voice resounded from somewhere not far from me.

There was a slight commotion in the crowd. People rushed over to the spot where the voice had been heard, but they couldn't find the culprit.

Meanwhile, a second speaker approached the podium. It was my friend from high school, Zdzisiek Mróz! He spoke bombastically for a long time, and I couldn't get over my surprise.

"What's that guy jabbering about?" someone in the crowd asked scornfully. Others were laughing. I realized my old friend had chosen to pursue a career as a communist bureaucrat.

At the end of the week, I went home, as always, full of anticipation that there might be some news and that soon we would receive permission to leave Poland. We felt as if we were in limbo. The uncertainty was tormenting us. Nothing depended on us any longer—it would be enough if they didn't extend our residence visas, and then we would have to leave. In any case, the UB had achieved its aim. Now they could kick us out of Poland anytime they wished.

Right after I got home, I asked my father, even though he was in the middle of a game of chess, "And so? Is there any news about our visas?"

My father shook his head and, glancing at his chess partner, said, "There's nothing new. Let me play chess in peace."

My father painted very little now. He said there was no point for him to do anything since we'd be leaving soon. He spent every afternoon playing chess with Mr. Smrek.

The dictatorship of the proletariat was transforming very quickly into a communist system. Although there was still talk of the Polish People's Republic, in private conversations people mocked the system and made jokes about it. There were many nice slogans being proclaimed, but life was getting harder and—as some people said—more dangerous.

I scored even higher on my final exams at the end of the academic year than I'd expected. Many students didn't manage to pass their first year, and so there were vacancies in all the faculties of the Academy of Mining and Metallurgy. So I decided to move to Kraków. I was prepared for bureaucratic difficulties, but the transition went far more smoothly than I expected.

At that time, the intellectual, cosmopolitan, and liberal city of Kraków was viewed by the communist authorities as a bastion of enemies of the regime. Thus, in 1949 they started building Nowa Huta. It was intended to be the first city in Poland built strictly according to socialist principles. It marked the absolute end of capitalist exploitation. The communist authorities expected everyone to give as much as possible to the state, and in return they would receive everything according to their needs.

My second year of studies began excellently. After spending my summer vacation doing a mandatory internship at a state-run agricultural farm for one month, and then enjoying a month-long holiday with friends in Krynica Górska, I moved into a comfortable room with windows overlooking the Planty. I enjoyed sitting by the window and looking at the trees. Wiesiek Susuł was my roommate. Our presence made Zosia, the landlady, very happy because the housing bureau was beginning to take interest in her apartment.

However, despite renting a room to me, the housing bureau forced Zosia to accommodate one more person in her apartment. It was a sullen, middle-aged spinster named Janka. Her presence had one positive aspect—she played bridge. Two or three times a week, we spent the evening playing bridge instead of studying. Both Janka and Zosia were weak players, but Zosia played very charmingly. While trying to decide which card to choose, she would touch each of them in turn while humming her favorite song: "Oh, that Don Juan, Don Juan, seducer of other men's wives." Despite being sixty years old, she hadn't lost her youthful spirit.

I met with Romek Maksymowicz, but not very often because he was always busy studying or spending time with his girlfriend, Krzysia, who was also studying in Kraków. Once in a while my father would give me some pocket money, and then I would invite Romek or Wiesiek to have dinner with me at Wierzynek—a restaurant that was considered a relic of capitalism. After dinner we would drink cognac and then leave the restaurant in a very good mood. We were very busy with our studies but still found time to go to the cinema or out dancing.

My family didn't receive any news concerning our emigration. It didn't bother me because I was getting used to student life. I still had two more years of studies ahead of me. I didn't delude myself into believing I would finish my studies because my father was sure we would have to leave Poland very quickly as soon as we received our exit visas. And so we waited. This period of waiting grew longer and longer.

Sometimes I thought that perhaps they had forgotten about us. But my father reminded me of what Leiser Dawid had told us—that Fonye Ganev never forgets about anyone. It was true—when my father was summoned to the UB in Oświęcim for a long interrogation, it became clear that he was still under constant surveillance. It seemed as if the UB agents were suspicious about something in my father's testimony, but my father had managed to fool them so much that they were becoming completely confused. They were trying to observe every step he took and his contact with other people.

The housing bureau was still interested in Zosia's apartment. Wishing to avoid being forced to accommodate strangers in her home, she rented a room to a young couple. He was a driver who worked outside of Kraków and was away from home for several days every week, and his wife—as far as I can recall—didn't have a job. She caught Wiesiek's eye and didn't reject his advances, nor mine. We were playing with fire because if her husband, a tough brute of a man, had found out about it, he would have killed us. At our young age we were excited by adventure and dangerous situations.

In those days, I had the impression that everyone around me was living lives full of hypocrisy and moral decay. The world seemed unstable to me. This affected me deeply, and I became defiant of generally accepted principles. Repressed dissatisfaction with life found a vent in the everyday behavior of many people from all levels of society.

There's one incident from those times that particularly stands out in my memory. One day I went into the bathroom at my university. I locked the door of a cubicle and saw, written on the inside of the door: "Take a crap, Pole, take a crap, because in your country it's the only thing you're still free to do."

After I left the bathroom stall, two men approached me and led me to a room.

"Where's your ink?" one of them asked me.

"I don't have any ink with me," I replied. Then I asked them who they were. They didn't look like students.

The older one answered me impatiently, "Don't ask questions; just take off your clothes."

I had no choice. I got undressed.

"Your underpants, too!"

I hesitated for a moment, then followed their orders. They examined my clothing thoroughly and, not finding what they were looking for, ordered me to put my clothes back on and keep my mouth shut about what had happened.

Evidently the communist party had begun to wage a battle against bathrooms.

Romek Maksymowicz married Krzysia in the winter. Their wedding took place in a church, and the wedding party was held in Romek's house—a lovely villa in Zasole.

The young couple looked beautiful. They were kissed so many times I feared they wouldn't be able to endure this onslaught of affection. Romek's mother had put a lot of effort into everything and prepared an abundance of delicious food. Everyone at the party was very lively and made toasts to the new couple every few minutes. In this merry atmosphere, all the guests were laughing and taking turns telling jokes. In those days, people usually held their tongues around other people, but when they were among people they trusted, they gave vent to their rancor. Sometimes I saw people interrupting themselves in midsentence while talking to friends if someone they didn't know walked into the room. At the wedding, I was a bit tipsy and got swept up by the light atmosphere and the loose way in which everyone seemed to be talking.

My turn came to tell a joke. Everyone was looking at me as if trying to give me courage. Frankly speaking, I lost control of myself slightly, but I was convinced I was among good friends. I told a joke about Jakub Berman.[14] Everyone laughed heartily. Some came up to me afterward and slapped me on the back in appreciation. I saw looks of approval on their faces. I felt great.

I got home late that night. The next morning, my father burst into my room.

"Can't you let me sleep a bit longer?" I asked groggily.

"I have to tell you something very important," my father said in a solemn voice. He sat down on my bed, and I opened one eye.

"All right, so tell me," I mumbled, rubbing my eyes.

My father pulled my blanket off me and commanded, "Get dressed; we're going to the garden."

I understood that something serious had happened. I came to my senses immediately. I got dressed and we went out to the garden. My father was afraid someone had wiretapped our house, so when he had something important to say, he only spoke in the garden or somewhere else outside.

In the garden, my father told me that the husband of a friend of ours who worked for the UB had just stopped by our house and told my father that someone had submitted a report denouncing me. Apparently, I had told a joke the previous evening at Romek Maksymowicz's wedding that was slanderous to the Polish People's Republic and a high-ranking party official. His wife had intercepted and burned the denunciation. If it had gone further, I would have been arrested immediately and given a prison sentence of several years. This woman urgently requested me not to tell any political jokes; she had managed to save me this time by sheer luck.

My father spoke to me calmly, but at the end he asked me harshly, "Do you want to make us all miserable?"

Beno Mansfeld, whom I respected deeply, had the following Yiddish saying: *"Redn bagrobt"* (Idle chatter buries a person). He was right.

At the end of 1952, there were show trials in Prague for General Secretary Rudolf Slánský and thirteen other high-ranking members of the Communist Party of Czechoslovakia. Almost all of them were Jewish. They were accused of treason and spying on behalf of Israel. Slánský and ten of the other accused men were sentenced to death. The executions were carried out. On December 6, 1952, the Czechoslovakian government declared Ariel Kubowy—an Israeli diplomat who worked in both Czechoslovakia and Poland and was associated with Mordechai Oren, one of the men sentenced to death in the show trial—a persona non grata. Two days later the government of the Polish People's Republic made the same declaration.

The trial of Slánský and his associates had a huge effect on the free world. Relations between Israel and the entire communist bloc dramatically deteriorated. Jews living in Poland became frightened. They began to worry that there would be a wave of repressions and discrimination against them. Jewish government officials, even those in high positions, became very uneasy. It looked as if dark clouds were gathering over Polish Jews.

Under these conditions, my father once again started trying to organize the emigration of Jews from Poland. He went to the UB's regional office in Kraków to discuss the matter.

MEMO FROM AN INTERVIEW AT THE REGIONAL PUBLIC SECURITY OFFICE IN KRAKÓW:
On 15 December 1952, Leon Schönker, a resident of Oświęcim, reported to our office to discuss the following matter:
In connection with the trial in Prague and the dismissal of Kubowy, a representative of the state of Israel in both Czechoslovakia and Poland, Jewish people, and particularly Israelis, find themselves in an unpleasant situation and feel unwelcome in Poland....
Schönker would like to remain in Poland as a special envoy and plenipotentiary of the Israeli government with the aim of finding a common platform for remedying political damage caused by the former envoy, Kubowy. As a condition, Schönker requests that the Polish government entrust him with the task of repatriating Jewish citizens to the state of Israel, otherwise his mission will be unsuccessful.
When asked why he supported repatriation of Poland's Jews, he answered: "They're citizens of the state of Israel and will be welcome in that country, whereas in Poland, since they're Jews, they're rather unnecessary."
Then he added that Jews in Poland have been making significant contributions to the People's Democracy, but after the trial in Prague there's a general despondency and uncertainty among them. There's a resurgence of the mood that prevailed among Jewish people during the German occupation and for these reasons it would be better for Jewish people to be repatriated from the Polish state.
Kraków, 15 December 1952

I don't know if my father knew what kind of danger he was exposing himself to. If the Polish government agreed to the mass emigration of Jews from Poland, it would mean that it didn't consider them valued citizens and was willing to rid the country of them. The Jews were Polish citizens and were supposed to be building the Polish People's Republic along with all other Polish citizens, not thinking of emigration to a capitalist country. Leaving the country would be a betrayal of its ideology—after all, it wasn't possible to be happy in a country where there was capitalistic exploitation.

A short time later, I went home and discovered some sensational news waiting for me there. My father had been summoned to the civic militia headquarters in Bielsko-Biała with our travel documents. We were sure the long-awaited moment had finally come, and we would be given exit visas permitting us to leave Poland.

I felt bewildered. The thought of abandoning my studies and friends saddened me. But my father returned from the civic militia headquarters with distressing news. The expiry dates of our documents were checked, and my father was told that this time we would be able to receive extensions of our residence visas allowing us to live in Poland only on Israeli passports, not on *laissez-passer* documents, as they had been so far. When my father asked what was happening with our exit visas, he was told that for the time being there was only information concerning our residence visas. If we didn't present passports to them, we would be viewed as living in Poland illegally and consequently arrested. On Israeli passports, our residence visas would be extended until we received exit visas.

My father went to Warsaw where, after many entreaties, the Israeli consul agreed to inquire at the Ministry of Foreign Affairs in Jerusalem about how he should proceed—whether to issue us Israeli passports despite the fact that we weren't really Israeli citizens, or not issue them to us and thus expose us to the risk of being arrested. If we didn't receive Israeli passports, it would be clear evidence that we had never been Palestinian citizens and that my father had falsified his identity and was attempting to obtain exit visas for our whole family through fraudulent means. The consequences of such a course of events would be catastrophic for our family. Fortunately, the consulate decided to issue us passports.

I continued to be painfully aware of how abnormal my life was. I often talked with my father about this. He was sure we would eventually get exit visas. But he told me I should concentrate on my studies for the time being, and not think about the uncertainties in my life. I shouldn't worry about whether my studies would be interrupted, because if I didn't manage to finish them in Kraków, I'd be able to finish them abroad. He gave me a great deal of comfort and told me that I'd certainly do well in Israel, too. He told me that when he was a young man, he had gone to Amsterdam to study at the Academy of Fine Arts without knowing any Dutch, and he had done well there.

I started wondering if there was anything I could do to make us stay in Poland. Why did we have to leave, anyway? I believed my father could find a way to continue to live in Poland. I would be a qualified engineer and would certainly be able to find a good job, like all the other graduates. My father was a very talented man and had many friends. I had no doubt he'd be able to arrange things well for himself.

I expressed all of these thoughts to my father, and he burst out laughing.

"The abnormality of our lives was created by this new political system, so there'll be no way for us to escape from it in Poland. I don't want to live and strive for normalcy in a country where the government can take away everything a person owns and then throw him in prison. Besides, we still have no idea what the future holds for Jews in Poland."

Then he changed the topic: "Do you remember what Leiser Dawid said about Fonye Ganev?"

"I remember," I said.

"Leiser Dawid was a very wise person with a lot of experience. He didn't want his fate to be determined by the whims of Fonye Ganev. Our family should have left Poland with him."

"Why didn't we go, then? At that time, we could have applied for a Polish passport and emigrated, like he did. Why didn't we do it? We might have managed to leave before they put you on the blacklist."

My father thought about this briefly; then he replied, "I didn't consider it because life was going well for us. The factory was very prosperous, and everyone in Oświęcim respected me, including the authorities. I didn't realize that everything could turn out like this. I was also aware of how difficult it is to start a new life in a foreign country."

"Do you regret it?" I asked.

"Of course I regret it," he answered. "Now nothing depends on us—we're completely powerless. If they want us to stay in Poland, we'll stay; if they want to kick us out of Poland, they'll kick us out."

THE MINISTRY OF PUBLIC SECURITY TO THE REGIONAL PUBLIC SECURITY OFFICE IN KRAKÓW:

In the case conducted by your office (code name: "Capitalist") concerning Henryk Schönker, a citizen of Israel, no concrete purpose has been provided for the investigation.[15] Furthermore, appropriate methods for becoming closely acquainted with the target are lacking, and as a result there has been no progress in the investigation.... The above must be achieved by providing detailed responses to the following questions and problems:

1. An analysis must be conducted of the sources from which information has so far been obtained about Schönker, in order to ascertain the veracity of this information as well as the possibility of expanding it. Namely:
    a. What was the source of the information that before the war, in England, Schönker was detained and interrogated by SIS [the Secret Intelligence Service]? This information must be verified and expanded, if possible.

b. What was the source of the information concerning the negotiations between Schönker and the German authorities during the occupation about the emigration of Jews from Poland? Who took part in these negotiations? More information must be collected about these people.
c. Identify the people who knew Schönker during the German occupation while he was in hiding and imprisoned in the Bergen-Belsen camp.
d. Identify the people who have maintained contact with Schönker due to shared business affairs (revenue) and gather more information about them.
e. Try to determine the precise purpose of Schönker's philanthropic acts, who benefited from them, and to what extent these people became dependent on Schönker.
f. Collect all possible information concerning property owned by Schönker in Poland, when and how he acquired it, the nature of his legal entitlement to the property, the total value of the property, the revenue earned from the property and in what form, rent, lease, etc.
g. Find out if Schönker has settled all formalities related to the income he has earned, such as: taxes, stamp duty, etc. ...
h. Carefully examine the relations between Schönker and the bureaucratic clerks directly dealing with his financial matters, debts, stamp duty payments, taxes, etc. (whether or not there has been a possibility of bribery).
i. Determine how often Schönker leaves his place of residence, where he goes and for what purpose (use surveillance methods).
j. Use surveillance to determine with whom Schönker corresponds.
k. Make use of the fact that Schönker is interested in painting and collecting antiques and works of art through the skillful placement of undercover agents.

After obtaining precise information concerning the above matters, a detailed report should be sent to Section VI Department I of the Ministry of Public Security.

Warsaw, 8 November 1954

My father was clearly depressed, and my mother had fallen into a state of inertia. Perhaps her sister Lida's letters from Israel were affecting her. In every letter she described how difficult things were there. Aunt Lida thought we shouldn't go to Israel but rather somewhere else. In one of her letters she wrote, for example, that in Israel chickens are bred in huge incubators and given hormones, which were causing men to grow breasts. I asked my father what he thought of this. He answered, with a smile, that it wasn't the worst thing that could happen to a man. He thought it was better to live in one's own country with large breasts than in a foreign country without breasts. I had to admit he was right.

In the spring of 1955, I was occupied with my diploma project—I had to construct the front truck of a locomotive. After submitting my project, I was given a date for my final exam and assigned a job in a car factory in Strzemieszyce. I was feeling optimistic.

When I got home, I could tell right away that my parents were very excited about something. It turned out that my father had been ordered to report with our passports to the civic militia's headquarters in Bielsko-Biała to get our exit visas. Our long wait had finally come to an end! But what about my studies?

I went to Bielsko-Biała with my father because I hoped I would be able to request a later date for our departure. I was afraid we would have to leave before my final exam. But the date had been set in advance. I thought I might be able to take the exam early, but in the end I decided not to request this because the mere fact that I was leaving Poland could be enough for me to receive a failing grade. Party members were everywhere.

Our exit visas were stamped into our passports. We had to leave Poland by July 1. I was lucky—I managed to take the exam, and on June 20, 1955, I received a degree from the Kraków Polytechnic Institute and was now a qualified mechanical engineer.[16]

We set our date of departure for June 30—the day before the expiry date of our exit visas. We decided to go to Vienna. We left both of our villas at the disposal of Oświęcim's town council—one became a preschool and the other a nursery. We packed only a few suitcases.

Before we left, I said goodbye to many friends and acquaintances. I also bade farewell to the town itself. I walked down the streets, thinking about how I was never going to return. I crossed paths with various people who bade farewell to me very warmly. We were all deeply moved.

On our way to the train station, windows in the houses on our street opened, and people waved goodbye to us. We all had tears in our eyes.

People were waiting for us at the train station. Among them there were many who didn't know us personally. Stefan Blachura also came to see us off. There was a large crowd on the platform. It was evident that the people of our town hadn't forgotten about us. We boarded the train and, still waving through the window, said goodbye to everyone.

I loved this town.

After leaving Poland in 1955, the Schönker family settled in Vienna. Leon attempted to start up an artificial fertilizer factory there but didn't succeed, so he took up painting again. In 1961 Henryk went to Israel, found employment in an airplane factory, and brought his parents and sister to Israel one year later. Henryk and his wife, Helena, had three daughters and ten grandchildren. Henryk retired in 1987. He started painting in 1979, and all of his works have one main theme—the Holocaust. He died in Tel Aviv in January 2019.

NOTES

1. The house at 36 Jagiellońska Street where Chaim Schenker, the author's great-grandfather, had lived. Before the war, the residents of Oświęcim had called this house the "Schenkerówka"—in accordance with the family name at that time, which was later changed (to Schönker) by the author's grandfather, Józef.
2. Until 1947, the territory of Palestine was part of the British mandate.
3. The first Israeli diplomatic mission was sent to Poland on September 29, 1948, slightly more than four months after the proclamation of independence by the State of Israel. The legation was raised to the status of embassy in 1962.
4. Translator's note: The Polish birthday song.
5. Tomáš Masaryk (1850–1937) was a philosopher, politician, and the first president of Czechoslovakia (1918–1935). Kfar Masaryk was founded in 1938.
6. Actually Israel.
7. Translator's note: The Public Security Office (Urząd Bezpieczeństwa Publicznego—UB for short) was the secret police service, the Polish equivalent of the KGB.
8. Ernest Bevin (1881–1951) was a British politician who was involved in the Cold War, on the American side.
9. Translator's note: "To have a long tongue" is a Polish expression equivalent in meaning to the English expression "to have a big mouth."
10. Translator's note: This is a Polish word that means a person who breaks or crushes things.
11. Translator's note: This is the first line of the Polish national anthem.
12. The town of Bielsko-Biała was established on January 1, 1951, with the joining of Bielsko and Biała Krakowska.
13. Minc is the maiden name of Henryk Schönker's mother. She was not related to the communist activist Hilary Minc; the fact that they had the same surname is purely coincidental.
14. Translator's note: A high-ranking communist-era Polish politician.
15. Actually Leon.
16. Henryk Schönker started studying at the polytechnic faculty of the Academy of Mining and Metallurgy, which became the Polytechnic Institute in 1954.

APPENDIX

AN ACCOUNT OF THE ATTEMPT at the beginning of World War II to rescue Jewish people living under German occupation in the town of Oświęcim (renamed Auschwitz by the Germans) was first published in 1977 by Leon Schönker in *Sefer Oshpitsin: Oświęcim-Auschwitz Memorial Book*—a book containing the memoirs of Jewish people from Oświęcim.[1] However, the events described by Leon became much more well known in 2005 with the publication of a memoir written by Leon's son, Henryk, titled *Dotknięcie anioła (The Touch of an Angel)*. The description of the emigration attempt was the most intriguing element of this remarkable memoir and simultaneously raised the most controversy among historians. There were doubts concerning the two most significant aspects of the story: the existence of the emigration office in Oświęcim, and the visit of a delegation of Jewish council leaders from the Katowice district to Berlin—led by Leon Schönker—and the discussions they had there with many people, including Adolf Eichmann himself, about the planned emigration of Jews.[2] Henryk Schönker's memoir served as the sole proof of the veracity of these events, and he based this section of his memoir on his father's account. No other confirmation of these events could be found at that time.

In the summer of 2008, while doing research in the archives of the American Jewish Joint Distribution Committee in Jerusalem, I came across two astonishing documents.[3] The original versions are in the AJDC's archive in New York, in a collection of documents from the years 1933–1944, while the Jerusalem archive contains only copies on microfilm. When I compared the versions from the Jerusalem and New York archives, I noticed that the microfilm was incomplete—the last page was missing from one of the documents. The documents were English translations (most likely from German) of original letters sent to the AJDC headquarters on January 30, 1940.

The author of the first letter is Leon Schönker, the chairman of the Jewish council in Oświęcim and leader of the delegation of representatives of Jewish councils from the Katowice district. The letter is addressed to Kurt Lischka.[4] The document contains a detailed plan for mass emigration of Jews from the territories occupied by the Third Reich. The second letter was sent to the AJDC office in Amsterdam by the Jewish council in Oświęcim. Both the nature of the document and the information it contains provide evidence of the above-mentioned emigration plan. If the plan had been carried out, the lives of over sixty thousand Polish Jews would have been saved in the initial phase alone.

The documents I found in 2008 seemed at the time to be the sole existing proof confirming the unsuccessful attempt to organize a mass emigration of Polish Jews from the Katowice district. A short time later, Dr. Aleksandra Namysło drew my attention to a book by Saul Friedländer published in New York in 2007, in which the author mentions the activities of the emigration office in Oświęcim.[5] However, only one of the documents I found in the AJDC's archives (the second letter here) is quoted in the book, which shows that the issue was not deeply explored. It should be mentioned that the second document I found (the first letter here) has been generally unknown until now and is of fundamental importance for the understanding of these events. It confirms, first, the visit of the delegation to Berlin and, second, the plan for the mass emigration of Jews from the Katowice district.

Below I present these two highly significant documents along with critical commentary. They confirm the events described in *The Touch of an Angel* while adding a number of previously unknown details.[6]

—*Artur Szyndler, PhD, Auschwitz Jewish Center, Oświęcim (Poland)*

DOCUMENT NO. 1[7]

Leo Schönker
Chairman of the Aeltestenrat der Juden Auschwitz,
at present Berlin W 15, Meinekestr. 16,
Pension Chilcott
To the Secret Police
att. Mr. Lischka (Member of the Government-board)
Berlin

Dear Sirs,
As leader of the delegation of district–Aeltestenraete, who came to Berlin to enable the direct emigration of the Jews of the occupied territory of Silecia, I herewith enclose a confirmation issued by the commander of the

troups who occupied our districts (VI/Dinafü/dated October 23, 1939)[8] stating that I am appointed as such. Our visit to Berlin has been approved by the Secret Police at Bielitz, in order to enable us to contact the competent authorities in Berlin. I herewith request an audience with the competent authority to discuss the problem.

1. To enable the concentration of all Jews who will probably have to leave Silecia we propose an orderly provisional resettlement at Auschwitz (occupied territory) which place counts already 8,000 Jews and which after through examniation could absorb 18–20,000 Jews. Hospitals, old aged homes and other social institutions have formerly been established at that place. The concentration of all Jews from Silecia in Auschwitz requires a support of about RM 200,000. The Reichsvereinigung der Juden in Deutschland together with the Berlin Jewish community shall be permitted to give us this amount.[9]
2. With regard to the resettlement of the Jews an exact control of decrease and increase is necessary to enable a quick emigration.
3. The emigration will be financed by in America living Jews whose relatives are still living in the occupied territory. The money will have to be deposited with a bank in Amsterdam in behalf of relatives living in the occupied territory.[10]
4. Besides, a second emigration casse shall be established in Auschwitz to which emigration charges in our currency are to be paid, and which also will receive the equivalent of blocked Reichsmark and Złoty accounts which have been sold in foreign countries and which so have been released. In return for the release of blocked accounts the German Reichsbank will participate in the foreign currency which we will receive for a certain percentage still to be determined. The equivalent of foreign currency deposited at Amsterdam will be paid to the relatives living in the occupied territory, at a rate which depends on whether the amount originates from blocked Mark accounts or Złoty accounts, for support by the emigration cassa at Auschwitz.
5. The payment of boat tickets, transport charges etc. will be made by the bank at Amsterdam. With the great number of our Jewish Landmannschaften in America and with the support of the American Joint Distribution Committee whose Amsterdam representative should have to come here to discuss the whole problem, the immediate organization of this plan would be possible, and both the balance of foreign currency of the German Reichsbank as well as the balance of foreign currency at Amsterdam would increase rapidly. The Polish Jews in the occupied territory represent immense possibilities. The Polish

Government used to collect large amounts in foreign currency here. No other organization than we from the occupied Polish territory approach our relatives in America without creating suspicion. It is therefore necessary to establish a central representation of the Jews living in the occupied territory, based on the same norms as those of the Reichsvereinigung der Juden in Deutschland.

6. The emigration can take place by making use of the Palestine certificates which as a result of the war could not be used, and would go via Trieste, for which purpose a personal discussion with Dr. Scheps, leader of the Jewish Agency in Geneva, is necessary. Further there is a possibility via Sulina/Danube. Besides there are other emigration possibilities to oversea countries.

7. If it is already possible to give an explanation of the territory to be reserved only for Jews, concerning extension and its legal status, we request to grant this audience so that we may be able to explain the whole situation on our return.

Berlin, November 30, 1939

DOCUMENT NO. 2[11]

Aeltestenrat der Juden
in Auschwitz
January 4, 1940
A.J.D.C.,
Amsterdam

Dear Sirs,

As you might probably know, a central emigration bureau has been established at Auschwitz for the whole district of Kattowitz based on an approval of the competent authorities. To this emigration office belongs also a department emigration to overseas countries and a Palestine office.

At the end of November a delegation was sent by us to Berlin to contact the Reichsvertretung der Juden in Deutschland. The Reichsvereinigung has informed you about our negotiations and has reported the urgency of the matter.[12]

As you will know, the Reichsvertretung is not competent for us, and according to a decree of the Berlin authorities it is not allowed to concern itself with our matters.

To the district of Kattowitz belong the following places in which Jews are living:[13]

Kattowitz, which counts to-day still about 400 Jews
Kosnigshuette, Tarnowitz, Myslowitz, together 400 Jews
Teschen, Skotschau, Oderberg,[14] Weichsel 1, 000 Jews
Bielitz 500 Jews
Kenty 300 Jews
Wadowitz, Andrychau, Zator 1,200 Jews
Auschwitz 8,000 Jews
Chrzanow 10,000 Jews
Jaworzno 1,500 Jews
Trzebina 2,000 Jews

Besides, the places Sossnowitz, Bendzin and Dabrowa with together about 35,000 Jews belong also to this district.[15]

As a result of the urgent requests, our central emigration office is compelled to advise also the following places: Lodsch, Krakau, Tomaschow, which do not belong to the district.

In order to release people from various camps emigration possibilities have to be provided.

From Teschen, as you will know, a transport went to Slovakia to the Hachsharah camps.[16] A considerable number of unused Palestine certificates and several holders of affidavits for America have to be disposed of.[17]

We wrote to Mr. Scheps to Geneva. We received promises still no concrete help.

It is high time that the emigration problem will be solved finally.

We have proposed to the German government the establishment of a foreign currency cassa in Amsterdam according to the enclosed copy. According to this plan support of people by their American relatives will also be possible. At the same time valuta balances could be formed for emigration. Up to that time the AJDC will have to advance certain amounts, afterwards the own valuta sources will supply the necessary funds. In this plan the concentration of the Jews from Silecia in Auschwitz (about 2,000 people) is partly realized.[18] Further concentration has been postponed for the time being, except ill and old aged people, who on the 15th of this month will be brought to old aged homes and hospitals. We have also to solve the problem to cover the expenses for these many homes and hospitals.[19] Out of our own means this is absolutely impossible. The Reichsvereinigung cannot or will not give us a support. We heard that it is impossible for a member of your Committee to come here, but you must grant us help very urgently either through the Reichsvereinigung or by any other way, for emigration possibilities by realizing a plan with your support—unfortunately we must state, that the Reichsvereinigung has only words for us and no concrete help—as well as by remitting us at least an amount of RM 250,000 German marks to support our old aged homes, soupkitchens and hospitals in Auschwitz.

Besides the immediate extension of the number of Hachsharah places in Slovakia and assignment of emigration contingents for our places is very necessary.

We are very sorry that we have to make you the reproach that you have left us without any help whereas it would have been very easy to establish any kind of help through the intermediary of our Landmannschaften in America. Hoping to hear from you very soon, we remain,

Aeltestenrat der Juden in Auschwitz[20]

NOTES

1. Leon (Eliezer) Schönker, "Shoah," in *Sefer Oshpitsin: Oświęcim–Auschwitz Memorial Book*, eds. A. Burstin, M. S. Geshuri, C. Wolnerman (Jerusalem: Oshpitsin Society, 1977), 161–181.

2. The creation of the Katowice (German: Kattowitz) district was decreed by Hitler on October 8, 1939, synonymous with the annexation of this territory by the German Reich, as part of the province of Silesia, becoming part of Upper Silesia in 1941. It encompassed the districts of the former Silesian Voivodeship (with the changes that took place after the incorporation of the Zaolzie region in 1938), three districts belonging to the Reich before 1939 (Bytom, Zabrze, Gliwice), and the "Eastern Strip" (*Oststreifen*)—the later districts of Będzin, Sosnowiec, Olkusk, Chrzanów, and Żywiec, as well as the expanded Bielsko district. See R. Kaczmarek, "Antyżydowska polityka władz niemieckich w rejencji katowickiej" [Anti-Jewish policies of the German authorities in the Katowice district] in *Zagłada Żydów Zagłębiowskich* [The annihilation of the Jews in Zagłębie], ed. A. Namysło (Będzin: Instytut Pamięci Narodowej, Komisja Ścigania Zbrodni przeciwko Narodowi Polskiemu, Oddział w Katowicach, 2004), 13–14.

3. The American Jewish Joint Distribution Committee (AJDC) is a Jewish charity organization founded in the United States in 1914. During the Holocaust, it was very active in aid efforts for Jewish people in ghettoes and labor camps. It organized aid for Jewish refugees, displaced people, and emigrants. The AJDC was officially active in occupied Poland until 1941.

4. Kurt Lischka (1906–1987) served as head of Department B4 of the gestapo from 1938 onward and was in charge of Jewish affairs. He was later appointed head of the Reich Central Office for Jewish Emigration (*Reichszentrale für jüdische Auswanderung*). In November 1939, he was replaced in this post by Adolf Eichmann. Leon Schönker, when addressing his letter to Lischka, may not have known that Eichmann was responsible for emigration at that time.

5. S. Friedländer, *The Years of Extermination: Nazi Germany and the Jews, 1939–1945* (New York: Harper Perennial, 2007). In this book, the author makes

reference to a collection of documents: *Archives of the Holocaust: An International Collection of Selected Documents*, Vol. 10: *American Jewish Joint Distribution Committee*, Part 2, eds. F. D. Bogin, S. Milton, et al. (New York: Garland, 1995).

6. There is a detailed discussion of this topic in my article published in *Studia Judaica* in 2009. It also contains five important source documents. See A. Szyndler, "Leon Schönker i jego plan emigracji Żydów z rejencji katowickiej z końca 1939 roku" [Leon Schönker and his emigration plan for Jews from the Katowice district at the end of 1939], *Studia Judaica*, nos. 1–2 (23–24) (2009): 237–274.

7. American Jewish Joint Distribution Committee Archives, New York (abbreviated as AJDCNY), AR 33–44, Countries and Regions: Poland, Concentration Camps, 1939–1945, file 825. Translation of a letter from Leo Schönker to the Secret Police, att. Mr. Lischka, November 30, 1939. The original translation contained in the AJDC's archive is printed here verbatim. Both of Leo Schönker's letters are cited in: A. Szyndler, "It Is High Time That the Emigration Problem Will Be Solved Finally: Leon Schönker and His Plan for Jewish Emigration from the Katowice District," *Yad Vashem Studies*, vol. 39:1 (2011): 71–115.

8. In German military nomenclature, the abbreviation *Dinafü* stood for *Divisions Nachschubführer*—a position within the structure of the Wehrmacht that can be loosely translated as "divisional supplies commander" or "divisional quartermaster."

9. The Reich Association of Jews in Germany (*Reichsvereinigung der Juden in Deutschland*) was a central organization for German Jews that was involved in all aspects of life within the Jewish community. It also served as the Jewish community's official representation to the German authorities. It functioned under this name from the year 1939 onward; previously, it had been called the Reich Representation of German Jews (*Reichsvertretung der Deutschen Juden*) from 1933, and the Reich Representation of Jews in Germany (*Reichsvertretung der Juden in Deutschland*) from 1935. Leo Baeck (1873–1956), a rabbi, philosopher, and longtime leader of the Jewish community in Germany, served as chairman of the association until 1943, when he was deported to the Theresienstadt concentration camp.

10. At the beginning of World War II, HICEM (formally known as HIAS-ICA-EMIGDIRECT, founded in 1927) handled the emigration of Jews from Europe. HICEM was formed through the merger of three organizations: the Hebrew Immigrant Aid Society (HIAS), the Jewish Colonization Association (JCA), and Emigdirect (based in Berlin). At that time, emigration assistance was given in the following way: HICEM in Paris received money from American relatives and other sources to finance the emigration of Jews from Central Europe. The funds they received covered the costs of tickets and other needs. In exchange, the emigrants helped finance their communities in Berlin, Vienna and Prague (in German marks). There was a similar arrangement in London, and money was transferred through the International Trade and Investment Agency. After France was invaded by the Germans in June 1940, the AJDC sent emigration

support funds to Amsterdam, and then opened a special office at its headquarters (the Transmigration Office). Additionally, American relatives and other people sent money directly to Amsterdam or to HIAS and the National Refugee Service in New York. By June 1941, a total of $3.77 million had been received from relatives to help twenty-nine thousand potential emigrants. This sum was doubled by the end of the year, but at that time the AJDC stopped accepting deposits because the possibilities of escaping from Europe had decreased as a result of the United States joining the war in December 1941. The Transmigration Office was terminated, and the funds that hadn't been spent were returned to the donors. See Y. Bauer, *American Jewry and the Holocaust: The American Joint Distribution Committee, 1939–1945* (Detroit: Wayne State University Press, 1981), 38–39.

11. AJDCNY, AR 33–44, file 825, Translation of a letter from the *Ältestenrat der Juden* in Auschwitz to AJDC Amsterdam, January 4, 1940. The original translation contained in the AJDC's archive is printed here verbatim.

12. Perhaps this was what Ringelblum was referring to when he described a meeting during which there was a discussion of the resettlement of "Jews from Warsaw and three occupied provinces to a sanctuary," as well as the resettlement of "150,000 Jews from Sosnowiec, Będzin, Katowice, Cieszyn (1,200 people), and Zawiercie. The project was initiated because the AJDC, which was helping Jews from surrounding towns, had offered to take charge of the resettlement." E. Ringelblum, *Kronika getta warszawskiego, wrzesień 1939–styczeń 1943* [Chronicle of the Warsaw Ghetto, September 1939–January 1943] (Warsaw: Czytelnik, 1988), 81–82 (January 17, 18, 20, 1940).

13. When the Katowice district was created in October 1939, there were 123,202 Jewish people living in this area. In mid-May 1940, there were 90,323 Jewish people living in Eastern Upper Silesia, which was the eastern part of the Katowice district (cf. A. Konieczny, "Rola Organizacji Schmelt w eksploatacji żydowskiej siły roboczej na Śląsku" [The role of the Schmelt organization in the exploitation of the Jewish labor force in Silesia], in *Zagłada Żydów Zagłębiowskich* [The annihilation of the Jews in Zagłębie], ed. A. Namysło (Będzin: Instytut Pamięci Narodowej, Komisja Ścigania Zbrodni przeciwko Narodowi Polskiemu, Oddział w Katowicach, 2004), 32).

14. A town situated in Cieszyn Silesia (present-day Bohumin, Czech Republic). In 1938 it was occupied by the Polish army along with the rest of Zaolzie (which had belonged to Czechoslovakia since 1920). During World War II, it became part of the Katowice district.

15. At the beginning of the war, these were the three largest Jewish communities in the Katowice district, numbering 47,640 people (Sosnowiec: 20,865; Będzin: 21,625; Dąbrowa Górnicza: 5,150), ibid., 32.

16. There is information showing that there was an attempt to smuggle a group of children through Cieszyn and Romania to Palestine at the end of January 1940. Józef Manheimer and Icek Borenstein from the Jewish council in Oświęcim were in charge of the group. The group was caught, and Manheimer and Borenstein

were detained for two days in Mosti. They returned to Oświęcim after Moniek Merin intervened, which is confirmed by reports from the schupo in Oświęcim and the gestapo in Bielsko written in early February 1940. See S. Steinbacher, *"Musterstadt" Auschwitz. Germanisierungspolitik und Judenmord in Ostoberschlesien* (München: De Gruyter, 2000), 166, note 44.

17. People in possession of certificates, which were first introduced in 1920, were allowed to emigrate legally to Palestine. According to the "White Paper"— issued in May 1939 by the British, who were the mandate rulers of the territory at that time—a limit of 75,000 Jewish emigrants had been set for the next five years. During World War II, 62,000 certificates were issued. Most were issued between May and September 1939 (7,850), April and September 1940 (9,050), April and June 1943 (12,500), and in October 1944 (10,300). Between October 1939 and March 1940 (i.e., in the period that was very crucial for history), Palestinian certificates were blocked. A similar situation occurred between October 1940 and March 1941; cf. M. R. Marrus, *Holocaust, Historiografia* [The Holocaust: Historiography] (Warsaw: Wiedza Powszechna, 1993), 242; D. Ofer, *Escaping the Holocaust: Illegal Immigration to the Land of Israel, 1939–1944* (Oxford: Oxford University Press, 1990), 320 (Appendix B: Distribution of Immigration Permits During the War).

18. A report from the Jewish council in Oświęcim from January 9, 1940, concerning social welfare (*Ältestenrat der Juden in Auschwitz, Bericht über unsere Wohlfart, 9.01.1940*) makes reference to the resettlement of about two thousand Jews from Silesia to Oświęcim. This resettlement significantly worsened the living conditions of the entire Jewish population of the town (cf. Archive of the Emanuel Ringelblum Jewish Historical Institute, Joint 210/532).

19. The above-mentioned report states that in Oświęcim there were three Jewish care homes for senior citizens with seventy-two residents, as well as a hospital with about thirty patients. Twenty-eight more elderly people were going to come to Oświęcim from Bielsko, Katowice, Królewska Huta, Cieszyn, Mysłowice, and Dziedzice, of which thirty invalids would be sent immediately to the hospital, filling it completely (cf. ibid).

20. At the beginning of February, Moniek Merin moved the emigration office from Oświęcim to Sosnowiec and reopened it on February 4, 1940. He notified the AJDC office in Amsterdam about this. His task was to organize and oversee the large-scale emigration of Jews from the former Polish territories (areas incorporated into the Reich as well as the *Generalgouvernement*). The emigration office functioned as part of the Emigration Department of the Central Office in Sosnowiec (*Zentrale Emigrationsabteilung*), which existed from February 1 to the end of April 1940. In Sosnowiec, the Central Emigration Office and the Palestine Office, with a branch in Kraków, were still operating in March 1940. At the end of March, the Office for the Emigration of Polish Jews, which operated in Bratislava under the auspices of HICEM and was led by Dr. M. Bohrer, attempted to join the aid effort for Polish Jews. Slovakia thus became the only transit country to

Palestine for emigrants from the former Polish territories and other countries. The office in Slovakia was presumably in constant contact with Merin. The documents that are currently available show that the issue of emigration, including the liquidation of the office, officially ended in Sosnowiec simultaneously with the dissolution of the aforementioned Emigration Department at the end of April 1940 (cf. A. Szyndler, "Leon Schönker i jego plan emigracji Żydów z rejencji katowickiej z końca 1939 roku" [Leon Schönker and his emigration plan for Jews from the Katowice district at the end of 1939], *Studia Judaica*, nos. 1–2 (23–24) (2009): 251–253).

INDEX OF NAMES

Page numbers in *italics* refer to illustrations.

Ajzenman, 229–231, 236–240, 242–243, 248n5
Aleks, 42–43, 50, 85, 297
Alter, Abraham Mordechai, 41–42, 58n20
Antos, Hanna, xii
Armer, Nina, 88–91, 94, 127, 145, *176*, *178*, 284, 287

Baeck, Leo, 30–33, 44, 56n10, 385n9
Barzilay, Israel, 313, 328, 336
Baścik, Adolf, 319
Ben-Gurion, David, 313
Berman, Jakub, 371
Bernstein, 48
Bevin, Ernest, 340
Biberstein, Marek, 41, 58n20
Biedroń, Kazimierz, 362
Bierut, Bolesław, 307, 314, 322, 327, 335–336, 368
Birnbaum, 62–65, 67–68, 74, 80, 204, 320
Blachura, Stefan, 305, 314, 317, 329–330, 362–363, 377
Bluzhover, Rebbe. *See* Spira, Elimelech Tzvi
Brill, Olaf, xi

Chopin, Frédéric, 18

Dreier, Hans, 38–39, 46, 48, 57n13
Dyczkowska (teacher), 23

Ehrenpreis, Markus (Mordechai), 32, 57n14
Eichmann, Adolf, 31–34, 44, 56n10, 57n12, 379, 384n4
Essle, Stefan, xi

Falewski, Jan, 329–330, 332–334, 341–344
Feniger, 27
Fessel, 94, 96, 132–134, 165
Fiszelberg, Poldek, 261–268, 271–272, 291
Fiszler, Edmund, 91, 93
Frenkel, Arie, 150, *175*, 207–208, 210, 212–213, 217–218, 221, 223, 226, 232, 234–235, 237, 240, 244–247, 251–254, 256, 259–261, 268–269, 271–273, 288, 294, 364
Frenkel, Ignaś, 150–156, 158, 160, 207, 231, 287
Frenkel, Zalman, 150, 207
Frank, Hans, 309, 314
Friedländer, Saul, 380

INDEX OF NAMES

Gebirtig, Mordechai, 80, 81n1
Gerer, Rebbe. *See* Alter, Abraham Mordechai
Gesang, Isidor. *See* Gottowt, John
Gitler, Celina, 223
Gitler, Irena, *185*
Gitler-Barski, Józef, *185*, 226–227, 248n5, 249n7
Gliksman, Paul, 328
Gluza, Zbigniew, ix, xii
Goebbels, Joseph, 99
Goslar, Maria, 16–17, 301–302, 304
Goslar, Władysław, 16–18, 301, 304
Göth, Amon Leopold, 215, 215n2
Gottowt, John, xi, 96–100, 103–105, 115–120, 122, 128n1, *180–183*, 288
Grand, Jakub, 249n7
Grażyński, Michał, 6–7
Greif von, 38, 40, 100
Grinbaum, Baruch, 48
Gross, Abraham, 36, 41, 48
Gross, Józef, 48
Grossfeld, Adaś, 97–98, 102, 112–113, 127, 200
Grossfeld, Iziu, 97, 200
Grossfeld, Madzia, 97
Grossfeld, Regina, 10, 16, 199–200, 208, 247, 251–252, 254, 256, 271, 294–297
Grunoff, 134, 151

Haas, Adolf, *185*, 224–228, 231–332, 237–238, 244, 247n2
Haber, Rózia, 333–334
Haberfeld, 26, 296, 312
Harriman, Averell, 9
Hilfstein, Chaim, 30, 56n8
Himmler, Heinrich, 32, 43–44, 58n18, 248n5
Hitler, Adolf, 18, 32, 67, 100, 128n1, 384n2
Hochman, Henryk, 18, 55n1, 65–67, 75, 78–79, 86–87, 97, 105, 201–203, 205–207, 212–213, 215
Hofman, 29–30

Hofman, Maria, 352–355
Hofmokl-Ostrowski, Zygmunt, 7
Hofsteter, Fela, 87–88, 97, 103, 115–116, 127
Hofsteter, Francis, 87–88, 90–91, 93–94, 97, 102–103, 111–112, 114–116, 127, 130, 219, 287
Hofsteter, Liba. *See* Schönker, Liba
Hollender, Aron, *187*, 313, 352
Hollender, Ela (née Silbiger), *187*, 352
Hollender, Fanny. *See* Schönker, Fanny
Hollender, Maniek, *187*
Hollender, Roma, *187*
Höss, Rudolf, 58n18, 249n8, 309–310
Huterer, Itzhak, 41, 48
Hutny, Staszek, 326

Jachcel, Abraham, 35–36, 41, 48
Jagielski, Wojciech, 366–367
Jakubowicz, Dawid, 331
Jakubowicz, Maciej (Moniek), 331–332, 347–348, 363
Jakubowski, Piotr, xii
Jankiel, 85–87, 90–91, 94, 101, 107, 127, 255
Jurczyk, Czesław, 362

Kahane, Bronka, 333
Kahane, Rina, 346
Kahane, Szymon, 333, 344, 346
Kała, Wiesiek, 304, 362
Karmel, Moshe, 314–315, 321, 326, 328, 348, 351
Kernerówna, Henryka, 65
Kleinbühl (Oberleutnant), 19–20, 22–23
Knapik, Stanisława, 22–25, 49, 305, 310–311, 314, 319, 325, 329–334, 348, 352, 362–363
Königsberg, Zyleg, 27
Kramer, Josef, 244, 249n8
Krawczyk, Maria, xii
Kubowy, Ariel, 372–373

INDEX OF NAMES

Kupperman, Regina, *189*, 332–333, 346, 349, 352
Kupperman, Szlomek, 332

Łamacz, 350
Landau, Irena, *185*
Lehrhaupt, Eliahu, 133–135, 139, 234–235
Lewin (rabbi), 238–239, 242
Lieberman, 306, 328, 352
Liedke, Karl, xi–xii
Lindenbaum, 222, 224, 232
Lischka, Kurt, 380, 384n4, 385n7
Łoziński, 320–321

Madoń-Mitzner, Katarzyna, xi–xii
Maksymowicz, Roman, *191–193*, 303–304, 311–312, 327, 341, 362, 370–372
Manheimer, Józef, 26–29, 55n4, 386n16
Mansfeld, Beno, 62–63, 329, 372
Mansfeld, Bronia, 329
Mansfeld, Heniek, 94
Mansfeld, Irka, 329
Mendelsohn, Cudyk. *See* Ajzenman
Menes, 356–357
Merin, Moniek (Mojżesz), 32, 38–39, 43–49, 53–55, 57n13, 58n21, 59n26, 387n16, 387n20
Mikołajczyk, Stanisław, 307–308
Minc, Hilary, 363, 378n13
Morończyk, 317
Mościcki, Ignacy, 7–8
Mróz, Zdzisiek, 304, 362, 368
Müller, Franz Josef, 201, 203–204, 209–211, 214, 215n1, 341–343
Münz, Fryderyka, 2, 149, 153–156, 158, 160, *169*
Münz, Iciu, 150
Münz, Lida, *172*, 201, 208, 221, 224, 228, 236, 247, 252, 256, 260, 273, 285–287, 290–291, 294–295, 376
Münz, Markus (Motele, Mordechai), 2–4, 150
Münz, Mina. *See* Schönker, Mina
Münz, Szymuś, 150

Namysło, Aleksandra, 380
Neuman, 355
Neumann, Abraham, 80, 81n1
Ninka, 145–149, 163, 281

Ochab, Edward, *187*, 352
Ochab, Rachela (née Silbiger), *187*, 352, 354
Oren, Mordechai, 372
Osmólski, Edward, 356–357
Osóbka-Morawski, Edward, 307

Paw, Kazimierz, *191–192*
Petszaft, Ludwik, 348–349, 357, 359–360
Pick, Rudolf, 30, 56n9
Płotnicka, Frumka, 59n25
Pohl, Oswald, *185*
Przybylski, 331–333, 341, 344–345, 347–348, 355, 357, 361

Rahe, Thomas, xi
Raźny, *191–192*, 320
Ringer, Netty, 329
Rodin, Auguste, 55n1, 215
Rola-Żymierski, Michał, 340
Rommelman, 134, 143–144, 151, 164
Rosenberg, Bronisław, 349, 352, 356–359
Rosenberg, Nadia, 349, 357
Rosing, 87
Roter, Józef, 27–28
Róża (family), 223, 228
Rubineau, 354
Rüdiger (officer), 27–29, 37, 46, 48
Rydzoń, Karol, *194*, 309, 311, 314–315, 319–320, 363
Ryńca, 348–350, 352, 354–355

Sack, Joel, xi
Salpeter, Leon, 30, 56n8, 161–162, 165
Sander, Michael, 41
Schenker, Chaim, 84, 94, 96, 127, 201, 208, 211, 215

Schenker, Gizela, 109
Schenker, Leiser Dawid, 305–308, 313–317, 320–321, 324–328, 362, 370, 375
Schenker, Lulek, 84, 87, 215
Schenker, Muszka, 84, 87, 215
Schneerson (Prof.), 314–315
Schnitzer, Shmuel, 26
Schönker, Eber, 5, 312
Schönker, Eliezer. *See* Schönker, Leon
Schönker, Emanuel (Mendek), 2, 12
Schönker, Fanny, 1–2, *168*
Schönker, Feiga. *See* Schönker, Fanny
Schönker, Helena, xii
Schönker, Izaak Aron, 2, 20, *167*
Schönker, Izaczek, 12
Schönker, Józef, 1–10, 16, 19–20, 39, 62, 79–80, 97, 165, *170*, *176*, 199–201, 208, 210–212, 214, 217–221, 225, 233, 235, 237, 244, 247, 251, 253, 269, 295–296, 312, 378n1
Schönker, Leon, ix–x, xii, 1–13, 15–23, 25–52, 55n4, 59n23, 61–63, 65–67, 75–80, 83–84, 86–87, 91–94, 96–101, 104–110, 112, 116, 122–126, 129–133, 135–137, 139, 142–144, 150–155, 158, 161–165, *167*, *171*, *174*, *181*, *183*, *185*, *188*, *193*, *195*–*196*, 199–205, 207–214, 217–221, 223–228, 233, 235, 237–238, 240–241, 245–246, 249n7, 252–256, 259–260, 262, 267–269, 271, 273–275, 281, 285–286, 289, 291–292, 294–297, 299–302, 304–345, 347, 350–363, 365–367, 369–380, 384n1, 384n4, 385n6, 385n7, 388n20
Schönker, Liba, 2, 87, 90–91, 96–97, 104, 115–116, 127, *174*
Schönker, Lonka, 91
Schönker, Lusia, 1, 5, 12, 16, 21, 49–51, 62, 68–69, 83, 92, 100, 105–106, 109, 111, 120, 122, 124–126, 129, 131–132, 134–137, 142, 144, 153–157, 160, 164, *188*–*189*, *193*, *195*, 204, 210, 212–213, 218–220, 235, 246–247, 252, 259–260,

269, 271, 273, 289, 295, 297, 305, 321, 325, 330, 333–334, 351–352, 356–357, 378
Schönker, Mina, 2–4, 9–11, 16, 21, 23–25, 39–40, 49–52, 61–63, 68–69, 74, 83, 85–89, 92–93, 98, 100–101, 106, 108–109, 122–123, 125–126, 129–133, 136–137, 139–140, 142–145, 149–150, 153–156, 158, 160–165, *172*, *188*–*190*, *193*–*195*, 201, 207, 209–210, 213–214, 224, 234–235, 246–247, 251–252, 256, 259, 261, 269, 271, 273, 275, 285–286, 289, 295–297, 299, 305–306, 310–312, 314, 316, 319–321, 323–324, 326, 328, 331–333, 341, 344–358, 360–363, 367, 376
Schönker, Musiu, 5, 11–12, 42, 61, 71, 79, 90, 151
Schönker, Rózia, 12
Schönker, Sarah, 2
Schwartz, Regina. *See* Grossfeld, Regina
Silbiger, Aron, 41
Składkowski, Felicjan Sławoj, 8
Slanský, Rudolf, 372
Smrek, 368–369
Spira, Elimelech Tzvi, 2–4, 10, 13n2
Stahl, Heinrich, 34, 58n17
Stalin, Joseph, 347, 368
Sternhel, Genia, 306, 314, 328
Stieglitz, Ignacy (Itzhak) 322
Storch Gilel (Hillel), 242–243, 248n6
Susuł, Wiesław, 364–365, 369–370
Szarota, Tomasz, xii
Szczerbowska, 296
Szyndler, Artur, x, xii, 380, 385n6, 385n7, 388n20

Teichtal, Akiba, 207
Teichtal, Lida. *See* Münz, Lida
Teichtal, Menek, 201, 207–208, 221, 236, 256, 259–261, 269, 285–287, 289, 294

Teichtal, Tosia, 201, 208, 236, 256, 259–260, 269, 286, 289, 294
Tezner (German pilot), 17–19, 21–22, 38, 40, 100
Tirone, Piotr, 311
Tohn (Dr.), 32

Wachtel (Dr.), 139
Wald, Rafael, 220
Wallenberg, Raoul, 248n6
Weiss, Joseph, 184, 248n5, 249n7
Wesołowska, Hanka, 317–318

Zaremba (priest), 310
Zawadzka, Halina, xi
Zylek, 86, 88, 93, 102, 127

INDEX OF PLACE NAMES

Page numbers in *italics* refer to illustrations.

Amsterdam, 2, 374, 380–383, 386nn10–11, 387n20
Andrychów, 383
Auschwitz, xii, 36, 43, 53–54, 55n4, 58n18, 59n24, 59n26, 100, 165, 228, 232, 242, 244, 249n8, 299, 309–310, 333, 337, 379–383, 389
Austria, 18, 51, 57n12

Baczków, 215
Będzin, 58n21, 59nn24–25, 383, 384n2, 386n12, 386n15
Bełżec, 101, 108, 127, 134, 138, 160, 165, 200
Bereza Kartuska, 8
Bergen-Belsen, xi, *184–185*, 217, 219, 224, 231, 235, 240–241, 244, 246–247, *247*, 248nn5–6, 249nn7–8, 251, 261, 269, 274, 284, 290, 297n1, 301, 311, 336, 338, 364, 376
Berlin, 29–30, 33–36, 40, 43–45, 47, 54, 56n9, 57n12, 57n14, 58n17, 96, 115–117, 128n1, *185*, 240, 248n5, 379–382, 385n10
Biała Krakowska, 322, 328, 330, 334, 378
Bielitz, 381, 383

Bielsko, 27–29, 36, 46–48, 56n6, 309, 322, 327–328, 343, 384n2, 387n16, 387n19
Bielsko-Biała, 363, 367, 373, 377, 378n12
Birkenau, 43, 249n8, 299
Bluzhov, 13
Bobrek, 316
Bochnia, 127, 164–165, 199–202, 207–208, 212, 214–215, 343
Bogucice, 107–108
Bonn, xi, 248n5
Borek Fałęcki, 83
Bremen, xi
Brzesko, 201
Brzezinka 43
Buchenwald, 244
Bulgaria, 57n14
Bydgoszcz, 20

Celle, 232, 247
Chełm, 233
Chełmek, 21
Chorzów, 56n6
Chrzanów, 30, 34, 36, 53, 383, 384n2
Cieszyn, 29, 40, 383, 386n12, 386n16, 387n19

395

Constanta, 26–27
Czechoslovakia, 57n12, 217, 311, 372–373, 378n5, 386n14
Częstochowa, 316, 365–366

Dąbrowa, 48, 383, 386n15
Dakovo, 57n14
Denmark, 128n1
Dobczyce, 105
Dresden, 273, 297n1
Dzierżoniów, 333

England, 31, 40, 312, 375

Finland, 242
Frankfurt am Main, xi, *180*

Galicia, 57n14
Geneva, 58n15, 383
Germany, xi, 26, 30–33, 40, 47, 52, 96, 115, *180*, *185*, 217, 240, 243, 261, 266, 328
Gliwice, 99, 101, 384n2
Góra Kalwaria, 41, 58n20
Greece, 234
Gross-Rosen, 56n8

Hamburg, 218, 232
Hannover, 218, 232, 264–265
Holland, *184*, 234
Hungary, 59n25, 208, 212, 235, 248n6

Israel, ix, 27, 58n22, 313–314, 318–324, 327–329, 335, 338, 347, 352–354, 367, 372–378
Istanbul, 31, 33, 35
Italy, 58n20

Jaworzno, 383
Jerusalem, 5, 35, 81n1, 314, 374, 379

Kamionka, 59n24
Katowice, 6–7, 9–10, 21, 26, 29, 32, 35, 38–39, 44, 46–48, 54, 56n6, 57n13, 228, 261, 266, 311–312, 314, 324–325, 329, 333, 364, 379, 380, 383, 384n2, 385n6, 386nn12–15, 387n19, 388n20
Kazimierz (district in Kraków), 61, 68, 70, 74
Kazimierz Dolny, 12, 15, 304
Kęty, 383
Kfar Bierut, 322, 327
Kfar Masaryk, 322, 378n5
Kfar Truman, 322
Klasno, 84, 87, 95, 105, 120, 127
Kraków, 4–6, 10, 12, 16, 18, 21, 26, 29–30, 39, 41, 49–50, 52, 55n1, 56n8, 58n20, 61–63, 65–67, 69–70, 78–80, 81n1, 83, 87, 89, 91–94, 97, 127, 128n1, 161, 165, *179*, *187*, 201, 204, 208–209, 213–214, 215n2, 294–295, 305, 309, 311, 317, 319–320, 322–324, 326–336, 341, 343, 345, 347–348, 353, 355–356, 358, 362–366, 369–370, 373–375, 377, 383, 387n20
Krynica Górska, *189*, 369
Kudowa-Zdrój, *190*

Lądek-Zdrój, 362
Leningrad, 5
Libiąż, 21
Linz, 18, 40
Lipin, 56n6
Łódź, 46, 383
London, 10, 312, 340, 347, 385n10
Lublin, 15
Lviv. *See* Lwów
Lwów, 7, 18, 55n1, 57n14, 128n1, 145, 148, 163, 218, 316

Mexico, 220, 243
Montreux, 240
Munich, 55n1, 58n15, 128n1

New York, 10, 55n5, 312, 379–380, 385n7, 386n10
Niepołomice, 105, 107
Nisko, 56n6
Nowa Huta, 369

INDEX OF NAMES

Oświęcim, ix–x, 1–5, 7–10, 12–13, 15–23, 25–32, 34–41, 43, 45–50, 52–53, 55n4, 58n18, 59n23, 61–62, 65, 79, 85, 100, 148–151, *176*, *186*, *188*, *192*, *193–195*, 233, 294–296, 299–306, 308–312, 316–317, 322–324, 326–334, 343, 345, 348, 351–353, 355, 361–365, 367, 370, 373, 375, 377, 378n1, 379–380, 384n1, 386n16, 387nn18–20
Otwock, 162, 349, 352

Palestine, x, 26–27, 31, 33, 41, 44–45, 54, 57–59, 207–208, 211, 219, 224, 231–232, 237, 248, 290, 296–297, 318, 322–323, 363, 378n2, 382–383, 386–388
Paris, 2–4, 55n1, 65, 81n1, 335, 354, 385n10
Piotrolesie, 333–334, 348, 352
Płaszów, 58n20, 127, 161–165, 214–215, 215n2
Portugal, 248n6
Poznań, 20
Prague, 372, 373, 385n10
Przemyśl, 28

Romania, 15, 222, 386n16
Russia, 201, 207, 305–307, 313, 316–317, 322, 347–348
Rzeszów, 2–3, 149

Sachsenhausen, 244, 247n2
Sarasota, xi
Silesia, xii, 9, 26, 29, 31, 34, 36–37, 44, 46, 53–54, 56–58, 306, 322, 384n2, 386nn13–14, 387n18
Slovakia, 26, 40, 59n25, 383–384, 387n20
Sofia, 57n14
Sosnowiec, 32, 38–39, 43–46, 48, 53–55, 55n4, 56n6, 57n13, 58n21, 59n24, 59n26, 383, 384n2, 386n12, 386n15, 387n20
Stalowa Wola, 161–162

Stockholm, 32, 57n14, 242, 321
Sudeten, 54
Sulina, 26–27, 31, 33, 382n6
Sweden, xi, 128n1, *182*, 211, 242–243, 248n6
Switzerland, 54, 211, 240, 242, 363
Środula, 44, 53, 59n24
Świder, 349, 351–353, 357
Świętochłowice, 56n6
Szebnie, 215n2

Tarnów, 94, 96–97, 99–101, 125–127, 129–130, 132, 138, 142–143, 147, 149–150, 160–165, 203, 215, 224, 234, 261, 280–281, 288, 383
Taszyce, 55n2
Tehran, 207
Tel Aviv, ix, 378
Theresienstadt, 56n10, 58n17, 232, 254, 256, 297, 385n9
Tomaszów, 383
Tröbitz, 273, 297n1, 301
Trzebinia, 21, 28, 49–50, 214, 383
Tyresö, xi
Tyrol, 2

United States, xi, 32, 40, 80, 100, 219, 297n1, 310, 328, 384n3, 386n10
USSR, 56n6, 275, 313, 320–321, 368

Varna, 26–27, 31, 33
Vienna, 2, 51–52, 55n1, 57n12, 58n15, 128n1, 377–378, 385n10

Wadowice, 383
Wałbrzych, 333–334, 341, 346, 364
Warsaw, xii, 7–9, 46, 58, 59n25, 79, 163, *178–179*, 218, 223, 230–231, 248, 309, 314–315, 320–321, 326–328, 330–331, 343, 347–350, 352–359, 374, 376, 386n12
Węgrzce, 125–126
Wieliczka, 19–20, 55n2, 80, 83–88, 90–94, 96–102, 104–111, 115, 124, 127,

128n1, 136, 145, 149, *176–179*, *181–183*, 200–202, 212, 215, 219, 255, 284, 288
Wrocław, 346

Zagłębie Dąbrowskie, 55n4, 59n25
Zakopane, *193*
Zaleszczyki, 15
Zasole (district in Oświęcim), 36, 42–43, 371
Zator, 383
Zawiercie, 39, 45, 386n12
Zawoja, *173*
Zbąszyń, 31, 56n11

HENRYK SCHÖNKER was born in 1931 in Kraków, Poland. His father, Leon Schönker, was a painter. In 1937, the Schönker family moved back to their hometown of Oświęcim—the Polish town renamed Auschwitz during the German occupation. After the war, Henryk graduated from the Kraków Polytechnic Institute with a degree in mechanical engineering. In 1955, under pressure from the communist authorities, Henryk's family left Poland for Vienna, then immigrated to Israel in 1961. Henryk worked in the Israeli aeronautical industry until his retirement. He lived in Tel Aviv with his wife, Helena, who is also a Holocaust survivor from Radom, Poland. They had three daughters and ten grandchildren. Henryk started painting in 1979, focusing on one theme in his works—the Holocaust. He died in Tel Aviv in January 2019.

SCOTIA GILROY is a literary translator.

www.ingramcontent.com/pod-product-compliance
Lightning Source LLC
Chambersburg PA
CBHW051243300426
44114CB00011B/865